# The Big Book of Teen Reading Lists

# The Big Book of Teen Reading Lists

## 100 Great, Ready-to-Use Book Lists for Educators, Librarians, Parents, and Teens

### Nancy J. Keane

**LIBRARIES**

UNLIMITED

*A Member of the Greenwood Publishing Group*

Westport, Connecticut • London

**Library of Congress Cataloging-in-Publication Data**

Keane, Nancy J.
    The big book of teen reading lists : 100 great, ready-to-use book lists for educators, librarians, parents, and teens / by Nancy J. Keane.
        p. cm.
    Includes bibliographical references and index.
    ISBN 1-59158-333-0 (pbk. : alk. paper)
    1. Teenagers—Books and reading—United States. 2. Young adults' libraries—Book lists. 3. High school libraries—Book lists. 4. Young adult literature—Bibliography. I. Title.
Z1037.K295 2006
028.5'5—dc22          2006017627

British Library Cataloguing in Publication Data is available.

Library of Congress Catalog Card Number: 2006017627
ISBN: 1-59158-333-0

First published in 2006

Libraries Unlimited, 88 Post Road West, Westport, CT 06881
A Member of the Greenwood Publishing Group, Inc.
www.lu.com

Printed in the United States of America

The paper used in this book complies with the
Permanent Paper Standard issued by the National
Information Standards Organization (Z39.48–1984).

10 9 8 7 6 5 4 3 2 1

*Dedicated to my children, Aureta and Alex,*
*and my grandchildren, Aiden and Jordan*

# Contents

Contents

# Introduction

One good read leads to another, and a good book often leaves readers hungry for more. Whether you and your school use common texts, leveled reading, or a literature-based program, you are probably often called upon to extend the reading beyond the current materials. But how do you find those supplemental materials easily? How do you lead young adults to the next book? This guide provides reading lists that support extended reading demands.

Every day librarians work with teens and recommend literature. They may have some books in mind, or maybe not. It is time consuming to search for books that support the specific themes of a lesson. This book provides valuable reading lists to support public and school librarians in their work with teens.

An infinite number of reading lists could be created to assist professionals in their work. The 100 lists in this book have been chosen in consultation with working secondary teachers and public librarians, and through discussions on professional e-mail lists. They are based on some of the most common needs of educators and librarians who work with young adults. The book is divided into sections on **Genre**, **Character**, **Books about Self**, **Setting**, **Common Themes**, and **Audience**. Additional contributors to the book include Pooja Makhijani, Cathy Belben, Cindi Carey, Patti Cook, Eileen Culkin, Beth Gallaway, Joanna Nigrelli, Ed Nizalowski, and Melissa Rabey.

You'll find fiction and nonfiction on these lists. All were in print as of August 2005. Although the emphasis is on books published within the last ten years, older titles are included if they are still in print and are too good to miss. Information included for each title includes the author, title, publisher, date of publication, and number of pages. A brief annotation describes the plot or premise of the book. Nonfiction books are designated by the code (NF) following the bibliographic information. Books are grouped by age level: "**Books for Ages 12–15**" can be used with children of all ages and are not necessarily restricted to use with younger children, and books that have appeal for ages 14 and up are labeled "**Books for older teens**". Again, the latter are not restricted to these ages but are suggested for high school students. Books published for adults but suitable for teens are designated (adult). You are strongly advised to review the materials before using them with young adults. It is important to look beyond recommended interest level when suggesting books to students.

These lists can be used in a variety of ways. They can be photocopied and handed out to teachers as suggested reading; enlarged and posted in the library, put on the library Web site, or published in the library's newsletter; or used to create book displays. There is room at the top of each page to allow for personalization—add your school or library logo, or even some copyright free clip art. Have fun. Be creative. Be resourceful.

However you use the lists, it is hoped that you will find them to be valuable resources and aids for suggesting reading materials.

# Part 1

## Genres

# Narrative Nonfiction for Young Adults

## Books for Ages 12–15

**Appelt, Kathi.** *Down Cut Shin Creek: The Packhorse Librarians of Kentucky.* HarperCollins, c2001. 58pp. (NF)
> Describes the job of the packhorse librarians, who were responsible for taking books to people in rural Kentucky in the 1930s on horseback.

**Bausum, Ann.** *With Courage and Cloth: Winning the Fight for a Woman's Right to Vote.* National Geographic, c2004. 111pp. (NF)
> Chronicles the long history of the fight for women's voting rights in the United States, beginning in 1848, with a focus on the years between 1913 and 1920 when the Nineteenth Amendment was passed, and includes profiles of notable women involved in the struggle.

**Colman, Penny.** *Where the Action Was: Women War Correspondents in World War II.* Crown, c2002. 118pp. (NF)
> Describes the work of women war correspondents who covered all theaters of World War II, from its beginnings in the 1930s to the surrender of Germany and Japan in 1945.

**Cooper, Michael L.** *Dust to Eat: Drought and Depression in the 1930s.* Clarion Books, c2004. 81pp. (NF)
> Presents a photographic chronicle of the 1930s, focusing on the Great Depression and the dust storms that crippled the Great Plains, and looks at the effects of the twin disasters on U.S. society and domestic policy.

**Fleischman, John.** *Phineas Gage: A Gruesome But True Story About Brain Science.* Houghton Mifflin, c2002. 86pp. (NF)
> The true story of Phineas Gage, whose brain had been pierced by an iron rod in 1848, and who survived and became a case study in how the brain functions.

**Freedman, Russell.** *The Life and Death of Crazy Horse.* Holiday House, c1996. 166pp. (NF)
> A biography of the Oglala leader who relentlessly resisted the white man's attempts to take over Indian lands.

**Freedman, Russell.** *The Voice That Challenged a Nation: Marian Anderson and the Struggle for Equal Rights.* Clarion Books, c2004. 114pp. (NF)
> Tells the life story of singer Marian Anderson, describing her famous performance at the Lincoln Memorial in 1939 and explaining how she helped end segregation in the American arts after being refused the right to perform at Washington's Constitution Hall because of the color of her skin.

**Hampton, Wilborn.** *Meltdown: A Race Against Nuclear Disaster at Three Mile Island: A Reporter's Story.* Candlewick Press, c2001. 104pp. (NF)
> An account of the Three Mile Island nuclear disaster by a reporter who was an eyewitness.

**Harris, Robie H.** *It's Perfectly Normal: A Book About Changing Bodies, Growing Up, Sex, and Sexual Health.* Candlewick Press, c2004. 89pp. (NF)
> Provides answers to nearly every conceivable question teens may have about sexuality, from conception and puberty to birth control and AIDS.

# Narrative Nonfiction for Young Adults

**Hoose, Phillip M.** *The Race to Save the Lord God Bird.* Farrar, Straus & Giroux, c2004. 196pp. (NF)
Tells the story of the extinction of the ivory-billed woodpecker in the United States, describing the encounters between this species and humans, and discussing what these encounters have taught us about preserving endangered creatures.

**Kiyosaki, Robert T.** *Rich Dad Poor Dad for Teens: The Secrets About Money—That You Don't Learn in School!* Warner Books, c2004. 132pp. (NF)
A practical guide about money and investing and how to make the right choices that lead to financial freedom, including advice on managing assets and debts.

**Krull, Kathleen.** *The Book of Rock Stars: 24 Musical Icons That Shine Through History.* Hyperion Books for Children, c2003. 44pp. (NF)
An illustrated collection of twenty mini-biographies of such rock music legends as Jimi Hendrix, Janis Joplin, Bruce Springsteen, and Carlos Santana.

**Krull, Kathleen.** *Lives of Extraordinary Women: Rulers, Rebels (and What the Neighbors Thought).* Harcourt, c2000. 95pp. (NF)
Profiles twenty historically significant women, highlighting their great accomplishments and unique quirks; also includes color caricatures.

**Krull, Kathleen.** *Lives of the Artists: Masterpieces, Messes (and What the Neighbors Thought).* Harcourt Brace, c1995. 96pp. (NF)
A collection of short biographical sketches of famous artists emphasizing their unique personalities and the impressions they made on the people who knew them.

**Krull, Kathleen.** *Lives of the Athletes: Thrills, Spills (and What the Neighbors Thought).* Harcourt Brace, c1997. 96pp. (NF)
Presents biographical sketches of twenty famous athletes, emphasizing their unique personalities and the impressions they made on the people who knew them.

**Krull, Kathleen.** *Lives of the Musicians: Good Times, Bad Times (and What the Neighbors Thought).* Harcourt Brace, c1993, 96pp. (NF)
The lives of twenty composers and musicians, ranging from Vivaldi, Mozart, and Bach to Gershwin, Gilbert & Sullivan, and Woody Guthrie, are profiled in this eclectic, humorous, and informative collection.

**Krull, Kathleen.** *Lives of the Presidents: Fame, Shame, and What the Neighbors Thought.* Harcourt Brace, c1998. 96pp. (NF)
Focuses on the lives of presidents as parents, husbands, pet owners, and neighbors while also including humorous anecdotes about hairstyles, attitudes, diets, fears, and sleep patterns.

**Krull, Kathleen.** *Lives of the Writers: Comedies, Tragedies (and What the Neighbors Thought).* Harcourt Brace, c1994. 96pp. (NF)
The lives of twenty writers, ranging from Dickens, the Brontës, and Poe to Twain, Sandburg, and Langston Hughes, are profiled in this eclectic, humorous, and informative collection.

# Narrative Nonfiction for Young Adults

**Murphy, Jim.** *An American Plague: The True and Terrifying Story of the Yellow Fever Epidemic of 1793.* Clarion Books, c2003. 165pp. (NF)
> Provides an account of the yellow fever epidemic that swept through Philadelphia in 1793, discussing the chaos that erupted when people began evacuating in droves, leaving the city without government, goods, or services, and examining efforts by physicians, the Free African Society, and others to cure and care for the sick.

**Murphy, Jim.** *The Great Fire.* Scholastic, c1995. 144pp. (NF)
> Photographs and text, along with personal accounts of actual survivors, tell the story of the great fire of 1871 in Chicago.

**Murphy, Jim.** *Pick & Shovel Poet: The Journeys of Pascal D'Angelo.* Clarion Books, c2000. 162pp. (NF)
> A biography of an Italian peasant who immigrated to America in the early twentieth century and endured poverty and the difficult life of an unskilled laborer, determined to become a published poet.

**Nelson, Marilyn.** *Carver, a Life in Poems.* Front Street, c2001. 103pp. (NF)
> A collection of poems that combine to provide a portrait of the life of nineteenth-century African American botanist and inventor George Washington Carver.

**Nelson, Peter.** *Left for Dead: A Young Man's Search for Justice for the USS* **Indianapolis.** Delacorte Press, c2002. 201pp. (NF)
> Recalls the sinking of the USS *Indianapolis* at the end of World War II, the Navy cover-up and the unfair court martial of the ship's captain, and how a young boy helped the survivors set the record straight fifty-five years later.

**Schroeder, Andreas.** *Scams!: Ten Stories That Explore Some of the Most Outrageous Swindlers and Tricksters of All Time.* Annick Press (distributed in the United States by Firefly Books), c2004. 154pp. (NF)
> A collection of true accounts of some of the most outrageous scams in history.

## Books for Older Teens

**Aronson, Marc.** *Witch-Hunt: Mysteries of the Salem Witch Trials.* Atheneum Books for Young Readers, c2003. 272pp. (NF)
> Presents information for young people on what really happened in Salem, Massachusetts, in 1692 when a group of girls and young women accused certain people in the village of witchcraft, leading to the executions of innocent men and women.

**Estrich, Susan.** *Getting Away with Murder: How Politics Is Destroying the Criminal Justice System.* Harvard University Press, c1998. 161pp. (NF)
> Explores how the U.S. criminal justice system is failing American society by focusing more on political interests and high-profile figures than on protecting the victims of crime, abuse, and violence, and offers practical suggestions for fixing many of the system's flaws.

# Narrative Nonfiction for Young Adults

**Gantos, Jack.** *Hole in My Life.* Farrar, Straus & Giroux, c2002. 199pp. (NF)
> The author relates how, as a young adult, he became a drug user and smuggler, was arrested, did time in prison, and eventually got out and went to college, all the while hoping to become a writer.

**Genge, Ngaire.** *The Forensic Casebook: The Science of Crime Scene Investigation.* Ballantine Books, 2002. 319pp. (NF)
> Contains accounts based on extensive interviews with police personnel and forensic scientists of criminal cases that have been solved using a variety of forensic techniques.

**Junger, Sebastian.** *The Perfect Storm: A True Story of Men Against the Sea.* W. W. Norton, c1997. 227pp. (adult) (NF)
> Uses interviews, memoirs, radio conversations, and technical research to re-create the last days of the crew of the *Andrea Gail,* a fishing boat that was lost in a storm off the coast of Nova Scotia in October 1991.

**Krakauer, Jon.** *Into Thin Air: A Personal Account of the Mount Everest Disaster.* Villard, c1997. 293pp. (adult) (NF)
> The author relates his experience climbing Mount Everest during its deadliest season and examines what it is about the mountain that makes people willingly subject themselves to such risk, hardship, and expense.

**Preston, Richard.** *The Hot Zone.* Anchor Books, c1995. 422pp. (adult) (NF)
> Tells the dramatic story of U.S. Army scientists and soldiers who worked to stop the outbreak of a deadly and extremely contagious virus in 1989.

**Runyon, Brent.** *The Burn Journals.* Knopf (distributed by Random House), c2004. 374pp. (NF)
> Presents the true story of Brent Runyon, who at fourteen years of age set himself on fire and sustained burns over 80 percent of his body, and describes the months of physical and mental rehabilitation that followed as he attempted to pull his life together.

**Silverstein, Ken.** *The Radioactive Boy Scout: The True Story of a Boy and His Backyard Nuclear Reactor.* Random House, c2004. 209pp. (NF)
> Tells the story of David Hahn, the Michigan teenager who built a nuclear breeder reactor in his backyard in 1994, endangering the residents of his Michigan hometown and raising the ire of the federal government.

**Trope, Zoe.** *Please Don't Kill the Freshman: A Memoir.* HarperTempest, c2003. 295pp. (NF)
> A memoir of the then-fifteen-year-old author's high school experiences, in which diary entries reflect her struggles, angst, and rebellion.

**Vizzini, Ned.** *Teen Angst? Naaah—: A Quasi-Autobiography.* Free Spirit Publications, c2000. 232pp. (NF)
> A collection of essays written by the author between fifteen and seventeen years of age, in which he shares impressions of school, sports, cool people, boring people, friends, family, money, music, and obsessions.

# Action Fantasy

## Books for Ages 12–15

**Clement-Davies, David.** *Fire Bringer.* Firebird, 2002. c1999. 498pp.
Rannoch, born with a fawn mark the shape of an oak leaf on his forehead, is destined to lead the deer out of the Lord of the Herd's tyranny, but he must first complete a journey through the Great Land.

**Colfer, Eoin.** *Artemis Fowl.* Hyperion Books for Children, c2001. 277pp. (and sequels)
When a twelve-year-old evil genius tries to restore his family fortune by capturing a fairy and demanding a ransom in gold, the fairies fight back with magic, technology, and a particularly nasty troll.

**Jacques, Brian.** *Redwall.* Philomel Books, c1986. 351pp. (and sequels)
When the peaceful life of ancient Redwall Abbey is shattered by the arrival of the evil rat Cluny and his villainous hordes, Matthias, a young mouse, determines to find the legendary sword of Martin the Warrior, which he is convinced will help Redwall's inhabitants destroy the enemy.

**Lasky, Kathryn.** *Star Split.* Hyperion Paperbacks for Children, c2001. c1999. 203pp.
In 3038, thirteen-year-old Darci uncovers an underground movement to save the human race from genetic enhancement technology.

**Nicholson, William.** *The Wind Singer: An Adventure.* Hyperion Books for Children, c2000. 358pp.
After Kestrel Hath rebels against the stifling rules of Amaranth society and is forced to flee, she, along with her twin brother and a tagalong classmate, follow an ancient map on a quest for the legendary silver voice of the wind singer, in an attempt to heal Amaranth and its people.

**Nix, Garth.** *Lirael: Daughter of the Clayr.* HarperCollins, c2001. 487pp.
When a dangerous necromancer threatens to unleash a long-buried evil, Lirael and Prince Sameth are drawn into a battle to save the Old Kingdom and reveal their true destinies.

**Philbrick, W. Rodman.** *The Last Book in the Universe.* Blue Sky Press, c2000. 223pp.
After an earthquake has destroyed much of the planet, an epileptic teenager nicknamed Spaz begins the heroic fight to bring human intelligence back to the earth of a distant future.

**Pullman, Philip.** *The Amber Spyglass.* Knopf, c2000. 518pp.
Lyra and Will find themselves at the center of a battle between the forces of the Authority and those gathered by Lyra's father, Lord Asriel.

**Pullman, Philip.** *The Golden Compass.* Knopf, c1995. 399pp.
Accompanied by her daemon, Lyra Belacqua sets out to prevent her best friend and other kidnapped children from becoming the subject of gruesome experiments in the Far North.

**Pullman, Philip.** *The Subtle Knife.* Knopf, c1997. 326pp.
As the boundaries between worlds begin to dissolve, Lyra and her daemon help Will Parry in his search for his father and for a powerful, magical knife.

# Action Fantasy

## Books for Older Teens

**Marsden, John.** *Tomorrow, When the War Began.* Houghton Mifflin, c1995. 286pp.
Seven Australian teenagers return from a camping trip in the bush to discover that their country has been invaded and they must hide to stay alive.

**Nix, Garth.** *Shade's Children.* HarperCollins, c1997. 310pp.
In a savage future world, four young fugitives attempt to overthrow the bloodthirsty rule of the Overlords with the help of Shade, their mysterious mentor.

# Adult Fiction Titles for Young Adults

Written for adults, these novels explore challenging themes of interest to mature high school readers.

## Books for Older Teens

Compiled by Cindi Carey, Lacey Timberland Library, Lacey, Washington.

**Bardi, Abby.** *The Book of Fred.* Washington Square Press, c2001. 292pp. (adult)
Raised in an isolated fundamentalist sect, Mary Fred Anderson experiences upheaval in her life when circumstances leave her in a foster home that opens her eyes to an alien world, and a violent act occurs that changes everyone involved.

**Barry, Max.** *Jennifer Government.* Doubleday, c2003. 321pp. (adult)
Hoping for a promotion from his dead-end job in the not-too-distant future, Hack Nike takes an assignment from Nike executives:—gun down teenagers to promote a tough urban image for Nike's new line of shoes. Jennifer Government takes the case to find the killers and expose the Nike conspiracy.

**Basu, Jay.** *The Stars Can Wait.* H. Holt, c2002. 177pp. (adult)
In occupied Poland during World War II, fifteen-year-old Gracian Sofka breaks curfew to pursue his pastime of stargazing, and as unrest grows in the region, he makes a discovery about his older brother's mysterious life.

**Berg, Elizabeth.** *True to Form.* Atria Books, c2002. 214pp. (adult)
Living with her stern, unapproachable father and his new wife after the death of her mother, fourteen-year-old Katie finds herself lonely and forges an alliance with Cynthia, a fellow misfit.

**Bird, Sarah.** *Yokota Officers Club.* Ballantine Books, c2002. 367pp. (adult)
Eighteen-year-old Bernie returns to her family in Okinawa after her first year in college. Thinking that the disappearance ten years ago of their Japanese maid may be the cause of her parent's deteriorating marriage, Bernie decides to search for answers.

**Box, C. J.** *Open Season.* Putnam, c2001. 293pp. (adult)
As Wyoming game warden Joe Pickett races against time to save an endangered species, he finds himself plunged into a deadly mystery that soon threatens his family and the life he loves.

**Brown, Dan.** *The Da Vinci Code.* Doubleday, c2003. 454pp. (adult)
Harvard symbologist Robert Langdon and French cryptologist Sophie Neveu work to solve the murder of an elderly curator of the Louvre, a case that leads to clues hidden in the works of Da Vinci and a centuries-old secret society.

**Cabot, Meg.** *The Boy Next Door.* Avon Books, c2002. 374pp. (adult)
Mel is bored with her life until the elderly woman next door is nearly murdered. She sets out to find out who is responsible by investigating her neighbors, including the handsome but mysterious man who has come to dog sit for his comatose aunt.

From Nancy J. Keane, *The Big Book of Teen Reading Lists: 100 Great, Ready-to-Use Book Lists for Educators, Librarians, Parents, and Children.* Westport, CT: Libraries Unlimited, 2006. Copyright © 2006 by Libraries Unlimited.

# Adult Fiction Titles for Young Adults

**Carter, Stephen.** *The Emperor of Ocean Park.* Knopf, c2002. 657pp. (adult)
Talcott Garland is a successful African American law professor, devoted father, and the husband of a beautiful and ambitious woman, whose desires may threaten the family he holds so dear. When Talcott's father, a disgraced former Supreme Court nominee, is found dead under suspicious circumstances, Talcott wonders if he may have been murdered.

**Coben, Harlan.** *Gone for Good.* Delacorte Press, c2002. 340pp. (adult)
Investigating his girlfriend's mysterious disappearance, Will Klein learns that she is somehow tied to his brother's death, and he becomes increasingly disturbed when he realizes that everyone he loves is harboring dark secrets.

**Egan, Jennifer.** *Look at Me.* Nan A. Talese/Doubleday, c2001. 415pp. (adult)
Stripped of her image and identity after a devastating car accident and the resulting reconstructive surgery, Charlotte Swenson, a jaded model, struggles to rebuild her life in a culture obsessed with surface appearances.

**Fforde, Jasper.** *The Eyre Affair.* Viking Press, c2002. 374pp. (adult)
In a world where one can literally get lost in literature, Thursday Next, a Special Operative in literary detection, tries to stop the world's Third Most Wanted criminal from kidnapping characters, including Jane Eyre, from works of literature.

**Gilstrap, John.** *At All Costs.* Warner Books, c1998. 452pp. (adult)
Jack and Carolyn Donovan stand accused of massacring sixteen people and setting off one of the country's worst environmental catastrophes, but they are innocent. With their young son Travis, they have eluded capture for thirteen years, remaining at the top of the FBI's 10 Most Wanted List. Now they are driven from their last hiding place and are forced to fight back.

**Godfrey, Rebecca.** *Torn Skirt.* Perennial, c2002. 199pp. (adult)
As a teen in the mid-1980s in British Columbia, Sara Shaw has two lives. At home she is the responsible daughter, while at school she hangs out with a group of stoned delinquents. When her father suddenly abandons her, she leaves home for the back alleys of Victoria where she is swept into the world of runaways, pimps, prostitutes, and addicts.

**Haddon, Mark.** *The Curious Incident of the Dog in the Night-Time.* Doubleday, c2002. 226pp. (adult)
Despite his overwhelming fear of interacting with people, Christopher, a mathematically gifted, autistic fifteen-year-old, decides to investigate the murder of a neighbor's dog and uncovers secret information about his mother.

**Hamilton, Jane.** *Disobedience.* Doubleday, c2000. 275pp. (adult)
When seventeen-year-old Henry stumbles into his mother's e-mail account and epistolary evidence of her affair with a Ukrainian violinist, he becomes consumed with this glimpse into her life as a woman, not simply a mother.

**Haruf, Kent.** *Plainsong..* Knopf, c1999. 301pp. (adult)
This is a story of family and romance, tribulation and tenacity, set in an eastern Colorado town, in which a teacher gets several damaged families to interact with and care for one another.

# Adult Fiction Titles for Young Adults

**Hearn, Lian.** *Across the Nightingale Floor.* Riverhead Books, c2002. 287pp. (adult)
This first book in an epic trilogy begins with the legend of a nightingale floor in a black-walled fortress—a floor that sings in alarm at the step of an assassin. It will take true courage and all the skills of an ancient tribe for one orphaned youth to discover the magical destiny that awaits him . . . across the nightingale floor.

**Hegland, Jean.** *Into the Forest.* Dial Press, c2005. 241pp. (adult)
Set in the near future, this story focuses on the relationship between two teenage sisters living alone in their northern California home in the woods, more than thirty miles from the nearest town. Nell and Eva struggle to survive as technology collapses and society begins to decay around them.

**Inclan, Jessica Barksdale.** *Her Daughter's Eyes.* New American Library, c2001. 218pp. (adult)
In an upper-middle-class neighborhood, on a street like Wildwood Drive, things like this are not supposed to happen.. Sixteen-year-old Kate is going to have a baby. She's done everything to prepare for the new child's birth, except to tell anyone other than her younger sister.

**Kidd, Sue Monk.** *The Secret Life of Bees.* Viking Press, c2002. 301pp. (adult)
After her "stand-in mother," a bold black woman named Rosaleen, insults the three biggest racists in town, Lily Owens joins Rosaleen on a journey to Tiburon, South Carolina, where they are taken in by three black, beekeeping sisters.

**King, Laurie.** *Keeping Watch.* Bantam Books, c2003. 383pp. (adult)
Near retirement after years of rescuing children, Alan Carmichael embarks on one last mission—to rescue a teenager from an abusive parent—but after the boy is safely hidden away, Alan begins to doubt his decision to intervene.

**Kingsolver, Barbara.** *The Poisonwood Bible.* HarperFlamingo, c1998. 546pp. (adult)
This dense and intricate family chronicle follows a Baptist missionary family into the Congo, circa 1959, where their faith in Jesus, democracy, and what we call civilization is severely challenged.

**McDonell, Nick.** *Twelve.* Grove Press, c2002. 244pp. (adult)
White Mike, a seventeen-year-old prep school dropout and drug dealer, and his privileged peers spend their time partying with sex, drugs, and escalating violence in the pursuit of ever more exotic and dangerous thrills.

**McLaughlin, Emma.** *The Nanny Diaries.* St. Martin's Press, c2002. 305pp. (adult)
Struggling to graduate from New York University, Nanny takes a position caring for the only son of the wealthy X family. She rapidly learns the insane amount of juggling involved to ensure that a Park Avenue wife who doesn't work, cook, clean, or raise her own child has a smooth day.

**Packer, Ann.** *The Dive from Clausen's Pier*. Knopf, c2002. 369pp. (adult)
When her fiancé is left paralyzed following a tragic accident, Carrie Bell begins to question her familiar world, from her everyday life in Wisconsin to her relationships, as she sets out to rediscover her own identity.

# Adult Fiction Titles for Young Adults

**Pedersen, Laura.** *Beginner's Luck.* Ballantine Books, c2003. 336pp. (adult)
Sixteen-year-old Hallie Palmer is bored with school and alienated from her family. She spends her spare time at the racetrack or crashing the secret, weekly poker game in the church basement. When she drops out of school, loses her savings at the track, runs away from home, and is accused of robbery, it seems things have nowhere to go but up.

**Rosenfeld, Stephanie.** *Massachusetts, California, Timbuktu.* Ballantine Books, c2003. 388pp. (adult)
Justine Hanley, an amazingly resourceful twelve-year-old, battles to make an ordinary life for herself, her depressive mother, and her cranky five-year-old sister.

**Senna, Danzy.** *Caucasia.* Riverhead Books, c1998. 353pp. (adult)
Birdie and Cole are the daughters of a black father and a white mother, intellectuals and activists in the civil rights movement in Boston in the 1970s. The sisters are so close that they have created a private language, yet to the outside world they can't be sisters: while Cole looks black, Birdie appears to be white. For Birdie, Cole is the mirror in which she can see her own blackness.

**Tan, Amy.** *The Bonesetter's Daughter.* Putnam, c2001. 353pp. (adult)
Set in contemporary San Francisco and in a Chinese village where Peking Man is unearthed, this is the story of LuLing Young, who searches for the name of her mother, the daughter of the famous Bonesetter from the Mouth of the Mountain.

**Vijayaraghavan, Vineeta.** *Motherland.* Soho, c2001. 231pp. (adult)
When fifteen-year-old Maya travels from the United States to spend the summer with her grandmother in India, she discovers a family secret that changes the way she sees her mother and, ultimately, herself.

**Vreeland, Susan.** *The Passion of Artemisia.* Viking Press, c2002. 288pp. (adult)
In sixteenth-century Italy, eighteen-year-old painter Artemisia Gentileschi's painting teacher rapes her. When the papal court in which she brings charges against him humiliates her, she leaves Rome for Florence, and ultimately becomes the first woman elected to the Accademia dell' Arte. Based on a true story.

**Willis, Connie.** *To Say Nothing of the Dog.* Bantam Books, c1997. 434pp. (adult)
In this time travel novel, it is 1888, and Ned Henry is shuttling between the 1940s and modern day, researching Coventry Cathedral for a patron who wants to rebuild it. When the time continuum is disrupted, Ned must scramble to set things right.

# Adult Nonfiction Titles for Young Adults

Written for adults, these books portray complex issues, events, and life stories of interest to mature high school readers. Compiled by Cindi Carey. Lacey Timberland Library, Lacey, Washington.

**Alexander, Caroline.** *The* **Endurance***: Shackleton's Legendary Antarctic Expedition.* Knopf, c1998. 211pp. (adult) (NF)

> In August 1914, the renowned explorer Ernest Shackleton and a crew of twenty-seven set sail for the South Atlantic in pursuit of the last unclaimed prize in the history of exploration: the first crossing on foot of the Antarctic continent.

**Armstrong, Lance.** *It's Not About the Bike: My Journey Back to Life.* Putnam, c2000. 275pp. (adult) (NF)

> A number 1 *New York Times* best seller from the cancer survivor who became a five-time Tour de France champion.

**Bissinger, H. G.** *Friday Night Lights: A Town, a Team, and a Dream.* Da Capo Press, c2000. 371pp. (adult) (NF)

> Bissinger chronicles a season in the life of the Permian Panthers of Odessa—the winningest high school football team in Texas history—and shows how single-minded devotion to the team shapes the community and inspires—and sometimes shatters—the teenagers who wear the Panthers uniform.

**Bradley, James.** *Flags of Our Fathers.* Bantam Books, c2000. 376pp. (adult) (NF)

> James Bradley retraces the lives of his father and the men of his Company, following their path to Iwo Jima, the heroic battle for the Pacific's most crucial island—an island riddled with Japanese tunnels and 22,000 fanatic defenders who would fight to the last man.

**Bryson, Bill.** *A Walk in the Woods: Rediscovering America on the Appalachian Trail.* Broadway Books, c1998. 276pp. (adult) (NF)

> Back in America after twenty years in Britain, Bill Bryson decided to reacquaint himself with his native country by walking the 2,100-mile Appalachian Trail, which stretches from Georgia to Maine. An adventure, a comedy, and a celebration.

**Capuzzo, Michael.** *Close to Shore: A True Story of Terror in an Age of Innocence.* Broadway Books, c2001. 317pp. (adult) (NF)

> Combining historical detail and a pulse-pounding narrative, Capuzzo re-creates the summer of 1916, when a rogue great white shark attacked swimmers along the New Jersey shore, triggering mass hysteria and launching the most extensive shark hunt in history.

**Codell, Esme Raji.** *Educating Esme: Diary of a Teacher's First Year.* Algonquin Books of Chapel Hill, c1999. 204pp. (adult) (NF)

> This is the uncensored diary of an unconventional teacher, in which Codell records her frustrations, achievements, and struggles to maintain her individuality in the face of bureaucracy, and she reveals what it takes to be a "genuine" teacher.

**Colton, Larry.** *Counting Coup.* Warner Books, c2000. 420pp. (adult) (NF)

> Profiles a Montana high school girls' basketball team—made up of Crow Indian and white girls from a rural town—that carries on its shoulders the dreams and hopes of a Native American tribe during their winning season.

# Adult Nonfiction Titles for Young Adults

**Conroy, Pat.** *My Losing Season.* Nan A. Talese, c2002. 402pp. (adult) (NF)
> Moving between the action of the Citadel's 1967 basketball season and flashbacks into his childhood, Conroy relates his love of basketball and how crucial the role of athlete is to young men who are struggling to find their own identity and their place in the world.

**Dominick, Andie.** *Needles.* Scribner, c1998. 220pp. (adult) (NF)
> In an intensely moving story of sisterhood, illness, and loss, this memoir tells of a girl whose older sister dies from complications of diabetes.

**Dragonwagon, Crescent.** *Passionate Vegetarian.* Workman, c2002. 1110pp. (adult) (NF)
> An assortment of more than 1,000 vegetarian recipes that includes a variety of both American and international specialties along with helpful tips and techniques of meatless cooking and advice on ingredients.

**Ehrenreich, Barbara.** *Nickel and Dimed: On (Not) Getting by in America.* Metropolitan Books, c2001. 221pp. (adult) (NF)
> Reveals low-wage America in all its tenacity, anxiety, and surprising generosity—a land of Big Boxes, fast food, and a thousand desperate strategies for survival.

**Fuller, Alexandra.** *Don't Let's Go to the Dogs Tonight: An African Childhood.* Random House, c2001. 301pp. (adult) (NF)
> The author describes her childhood in Africa during the Rhodesian civil war, 1971–1979, relating her life on farms in southern Rhodesia, Milawi, and Zambia with an alcoholic mother and frequently absent father.

**Gottlieb, Lori.** *Stick Figure: A Diary of My Former Self.* Simon & Schuster, c2000. 222pp. (adult) (NF)
> When Lori Gottlieb was eleven years old, she did something girls that age often do: She started a diary. And like far too many other eleven-year-old girls, she also began starving herself.

**Greenlaw, Linda.** *The Hungry Ocean: A Swordboat Captain's Journey.* Hyperion, c1999. 265pp. (adult) (NF)
> One of few women involved in the commercial fishing industry, Linda Greenlaw works the waters east of the Grand Banks of Newfoundland. She tells the story of a thirty-day swordfishing voyage aboard one of the best-outfitted boats on the East Coast, complete with danger, humor, and colorful characters.

**Hart, Elva Trevino.** *Barefoot Heart: Stories of a Migrant Child.* Bilingual Press, c1999. 236pp. (adult) (NF)
> An autobiographical account of the life of a child growing up in a family of migrant farm workers, eventually leaving that world to earn a master's degree in computer science/engineering.

**Krakauer, Jon.** *Into Thin Air.* Anchor Books, c1998. 378pp. (adult) (NF)
> An account of the deadliest season in the history of Everest. Taking the reader step-by-step from Katmandu to the mountain's deadly pinnacle, Krakauer provides a picture of the people and events he witnessed.

# Adult Nonfiction Titles for Young Adults

**Maraniss, David.** *They Marched into Sunlight: War and Peace, Vietnam and America, October 1967.* Simon & Schuster, c2003. 572pp. (adult) (NF)
> Here is the story of Vietnam and the sixties told through the events of a few tumultuous days in October 1967.

**McCullough, David.** *John Adams.* Simon & Schuster, c2001. 751pp. (adult) (NF)
> Chronicles the life of America's second president, including his youth, his career as a Massachusetts farmer and lawyer, his marriage to Abigail, his rivalry with Thomas Jefferson, and his influence on the birth of the United States.

**Nuland, Sherwin B.** *Leonardo da Vinci.* Viking Press, c2000. 170pp. (adult) (NF)
> A distinguished chronicler of the human body and spirit interprets a Renaissance genius. Part of the Penguin Lives biography series.

**Owen, David.** *Hidden Secrets: Complete History of Espionage and the Technology Used to Support It.* Firefly Books, c2002. 224pp. (adult) (NF)
> A compelling look at the real world of the spy. With case studies and hundreds of photographs, this is an intriguing look at surveillance techniques, spy technology, and the spies themselves.

**Patchett, Ann.** *Truth and Beauty: A Friendship.* HarperCollins, c2004. 257pp. (adult) (NF)
> Ann Patchett and Lucy Grealy, two successful writers, met in college in 1981 and began a friendship that would define both of their lives as much as their work did. Through love, fame, drugs, and despair, this book shows what it means to be part of two lives that are intertwined.

**Peterson, Kathy.** *Sew Simple Squares: More Than 25 Fearless Sewing Projects for Your Home.* Watson-Guptill, c2003. 112pp. (adult) (NF)
> Here is a book filled with ideas for cushion covers, tablemats, curtains, and many other decorating projects. Clear steps, fabric suggestions, and full-color photographs are included.

**Philbrick, Nathaniel.** *In the Heart of the Sea: The Tragedy of the Whaleship* Essex. Viking Press, c2000. 302pp. (adult) (NF)
> After an eighty-ton sperm whale splintered the *Essex* in 1820, her crew tried to reach South America in three small boats.

**Santiago, Esmeralda.** *Almost a Woman.* Vintage, c1999. 314pp. (adult) (NF)
> In her new memoir, the acclaimed author of *When I Was Puerto Rican* continues the chronicle of her emergence from the barrios of Brooklyn to the theaters of Manhattan.

**Schlosser, Eric.** *Fast Food Nation: The Dark Side of the All-American Meal.* Houghton Mifflin, c2001. 356pp. (adult) (NF)
> Schlosser unearths changes the fast food industry has wrought in food production, popular culture, and even real estate.

**Sides, Hampton.** *Ghost Soldiers: The Forgotten Epic Story of World War II's Most Dramatic Mission.* Anchor Books, c2002. 344pp. (adult) (NF)
> On January 28, 1945, 121 hand-selected U.S. soldiers slipped behind enemy lines in the Philippines. Their mission: March thirty rugged miles to rescue 513 POWs, among them the last survivors of the infamous Bataan Death March.

# Adult Nonfiction Titles for Young Adults

**Shields, Carol.** *Jane Austen.* Viking Press, c2001. 185pp. (adult) (NF)
A Pulitzer Prize–winning novelist celebrates the life of one of the most renowned and beloved female novelists of all time. Part of the <u>Penguin Lives biography series</u>.

**Stanton, Doug.** *In Harm's Way: The Sinking of the USS* **Indianapolis** *and the Extraordinary Story of Its Survivors.* Bantam Books, c2001. 333pp. (adult) (NF)
A Japanese submarine sank a WWII cruiser a few days before the war ended; the Navy took four days to respond.

**Steinberg, Jacques.** *The Gatekeepers: Inside the Admissions Process of a Premier College*. Viking Press, c2002. 292pp. (adult) (NF)
Follows an admissions officer and his eight counterparts through the daunting task of recruiting students nationwide, reading through each of their applications, and meeting to finalize the incoming class. He also recounts the personal experiences of a half dozen high school seniors of various ethnic and economic backgrounds as they struggle through the selection process.

**Tademy, Lalita.** *Veiled Courage: Inside the Afghan Women's Resistance.* Broadway Books, c2002. 293pp. (adult) (NF)
Tademy reveals the bravery and spirit of the women of the Revolutionary Association of the Women of Afghanistan (RAWA), whose daring, clandestine activities defied the forces of the Taliban and earned the world's fierce admiration.

**Ung, Loung,** *First They Killed My Father: A Daughter of Cambodia Remembers*. HarperCollins, c2000. 240pp. (adult) (NF)
From a childhood survivor of Cambodia's brutal Pol Pot regime comes an unforgettable narrative of war crimes and desperate actions, the unnerving strength of a small girl and her family, and the triumph of their spirit.

# Based on a True Story

## Books for Ages 12–15

**Avi.** *Nothing But the Truth: A Documentary Novel.* Orchard Books, c2003. c1991, 177pp.
A ninth-grader's suspension for singing "The Star-Spangled Banner" during homeroom becomes a national news story, and leads to him and his teacher both leaving the school.

**Beatty, Patricia.** *Jayhawker.* Beech Tree Books, c1995. 214pp.
In the early years of the Civil War, teenage Kansas farm boy Lije Tulley becomes a Jayhawker, an abolitionist raider freeing slaves from the neighboring state of Missouri, and then goes undercover there as a spy.

**Brink, Carol Ryrie.** *Caddie Woodlawn.* Simon & Schuster Books for Young Readers, c1973, 275pp.
The adventures of an eleven-year-old tomboy growing up on the Wisconsin frontier in the mid-nineteenth century.

**Bruchac, Joseph.** *The Winter People.* Dial Press, c2002. 168pp.
Fourteen-year-old Saxso, a member of the Abenaki tribe in Canada, embarks on a dangerous rescue mission when his mother and two younger sisters are taken hostage during an attack by the British on their unprotected village in 1759.

**Curtis, Christopher Paul.** *The Watsons Go To Birmingham—1963: A Novel.* Delacorte Press, c1995. 210pp.
The ordinary interactions and everyday routines of the Watsons, an African American family living in Flint, Michigan, are drastically changed after they go to visit Grandma in Alabama in the summer of 1963.

**Eckert, Allan W.** *Incident at Hawk's Hill.* Little, Brown, c1971. 207pp.
A shy, lonely six-year-old wanders into the Canadian prairie and spends a summer under the protection of a badger.

**Houston, Gloria.** *Bright Freedom's Song: A Story of the Underground Railroad.* Silver Whistle, c1998. 145pp.
In the years before the Civil War, Bright discovers that her parents are providing a safe house for the Underground Railroad and helps to save a runaway slave named Marcus.

**Konigsburg, E. L.** *Silent to the Bone.* Atheneum Books for Young Readers, c2000. 261pp.
Thirteen-year-old Branwell loses his power of speech after being wrongly accused of gravely injuring his baby half-sister, and only his friend Connor is able to reach him and uncover the truth about what happened.

**Lyons, Mary E.** *Dear Ellen Bee: A Civil War Scrapbook of Two Union Spies.* Atheneum Books for Young Readers, c2000. 161pp.
A scrapbook kept by a young black girl details her experiences and those of the older white woman, "Miss Bet," who had freed her and her family, sent her north from Richmond to get an education, and then worked to bring an end to slavery. Based on the life of Elizabeth Van Lew.

# Based on a True Story

**Lyons, Mary E.** *Letters from a Slave Girl: The Story of Harriet Jacobs.* Aladdin Paperbacks, c1996. 175pp.

A fictionalized version of the life of Harriet Jacobs, told in the form of letters that she might have written during her slavery in North Carolina and as she prepared for escape to the North in 1842.

**Lyons, Mary E.** *The Poison Place: A Novel.* Atheneum Books for Young Readers, c1997. 165pp.

A former slave named Moses reminisces about his famous owner, Charles Willson Peale, and the intrigue surrounding Peale's son's suspicious death.

**Meyer, Carolyn.** *Drummers of Jericho.* Gulliver/Harcourt Brace, c1995. 308pp.

A fourteen-year-old Jewish girl goes to live with her father and stepmother in a small town and soon finds herself the center of a civil rights battle when she objects to the high school band marching in the formation of a cross.

**Meyer, Carolyn.** *Where the Broken Heart Still Beats: The Story of Cynthia Ann Parker.* Harcourt Brace, c1992, 197pp.

Having been taken as a child and raised by Comanche Indians, thirty-four-year-old Cynthia Ann Parker is forcibly returned to her white relatives, where she longs for her Indian life and her only friend is her twelve-year-old cousin, Lucy.

**Miklowitz, Gloria D.** *Masada: The Last Fortress.* Eerdmans Books for Young Readers, c1998. 188pp.

As the Roman army marches inexorably across the Judean desert toward the fortress of Masada, Simon and his family and friends prepare, along with the rest of the Jewish Zealots, to fight and never surrender.

**Roth, Arthur J.** *The Iceberg Hermit.* Scholastic, c1974, 219pp.

Shipwrecked in 1757 on an iceberg in the Arctic seas with only an orphaned polar cub for companionship, seventeen-year-old Allan begins a seemingly hopeless struggle for survival.

**Ryan, Pam Muñoz.** *Esperanza Rising.* Scholastic, c2000. 262pp.

Esperanza and her mother are forced to leave their life of wealth and privilege in Mexico to go work in the labor camps of Southern California, where they must adapt to the harsh circumstances facing Mexican farm workers on the eve of the Great Depression.

**Strasser, Todd.** *Give a Boy a Gun.* Simon Pulse, 2002, c2000. 208pp.

Events leading up to a night of terror at a high school dance are told from the points of view of various people involved.

**Wisler, G. Clifton.** *Red Cap.* Puffin Books, 1994. c1991, 160pp.

A young Yankee drummer boy displays great courage when he is captured and sent to Andersonville Prison.

**Wulffson, Don L.** *Soldier X.* Viking Press, c2001. 226pp.

In 1943, sixteen-year-old Erik experiences the horrors of war when he is drafted into the German army and sent to fight on the Russian front.

# Based on a True Story

## Books for Older Teens

Based on a list compiled by Ed Nizalowski, SMS, Newark Valley High School, Newark Valley, New York.

**Atkins, Catherine. *When Jeff Comes Home.*** Puffin, c2001. c1999. 231pp.
   Sixteen-year-old Jeff, returning home after having been kidnapped and held prisoner for three years, must face his family, friends, and school and the widespread assumption that he engaged in sexual activity with his kidnapper.

**Paulsen, Gary. *The Beet Fields: Memories of a Sixteenth Summer.*** Dell Laurel-Leaf, 2002, c2000. 160pp.
   In the summer of 1955, a sixteen-year-old boy runs away from his troubled home and learns about people, friendship, love, and lust while working as a migrant farmer and a carny.

**Paulsen, Gary. *Soldier's Heart: Being the Story of the Enlistment and Due Service of the Boy Charley Goddard in the First Minnesota Volunteers: A Novel of the Civil War.*** Delacorte Press, c1998. 106pp.
   Eager to enlist, fifteen-year-old Charley has a change of heart after experiencing both the physical horrors and mental anguish of Civil War combat.

**Rees, Celia. *Witch Child.*** Candlewick Press, 2001, c2000. 261pp.
   In 1659, fourteen-year-old Mary Newbury keeps a journal of her voyage from England to the New World and her experiences living as a witch in a community of Puritans near Salem, Massachusetts.

**Salisbury, Graham. *Eyes of the Emperor.*** Wendy Lamb Books, c2005. 229pp.
   Following orders from the U.S. Army, several young Japanese American men train K-9 units to hunt Asians during World War II.

**Shusterman, Neal. *What Daddy Did: A Novel.*** HarperCollins, c1993. 230pp.
   A twelve-year-old living with his grandparents learns his father is to be released from prison after killing his mother and feels apprehensive about renewing their relationship. Based on true events.

From Nancy J. Keane, *The Big Book of Teen Reading Lists: 100 Great, Ready-to-Use Book Lists for Educators, Librarians, Parents, and Children.* Westport, CT: Libraries Unlimited, 2006. Copyright © 2006 by Libraries Unlimited.

# Clean Romance

## Books for Ages 12–15

**Austen, Jane.** *Pride and Prejudice*. The Modern Library, c1995. 281pp.
In early nineteenth-century England, a spirited young woman copes with the courtship of a snobbish gentleman as well as the romantic entanglements of her four sisters.

**Bauer, Joan.** *Hope Was Here.* Putnam, c2000. 186pp.
When sixteen-year-old Hope and the aunt who has raised her move from Brooklyn to Mulhoney, Wisconsin, to work as waitress and cook in the Welcome Stairways diner, they become involved with the diner owner's political campaign to oust the town's corrupt mayor.

**Bauer, Joan.** *Squashed*. Putnam, 2001, c1992. 194pp.
As sixteen-year-old Ellie pursues her two goals—growing the biggest pumpkin in Iowa and losing twenty pounds herself—she strengthens her relationship with her father and meets a young man with interests similar to her own.

**Cabot, Meg.** *Nicola and the Viscount*. Avon Books, 2005, c2002. 254pp.
During London's social season, Nicola Sparks falls in love with a viscount, but one of his enemies tries to undermine her opinion of his character.

**Cabot, Meg.** *Victoria and the Rogue*. Avon Books, 2005, c2003. 241pp.
On board a ship to London to meet her fiancé, Lord Malfrey, the ship's captain falls in love with Victoria and interferes with her engagement.

**Cleary, Beverly.** *Fifteen*. Avon, 1996, c1956. 203pp.
Jane is fifteen and dreaming of a new boyfriend. When she meets Stan, he seems to be the answer to her dreams.

**Cleary, Beverly.** *Jean and Johnny*. Avon Books, c1959 (1996 printing). 219pp.
Fifteen-year-old Jean tries very hard to make a good impression on Johnny, who seems to be everything she wants in a boyfriend.

**Cleary, Beverly.** *The Luckiest Girl*. Avon, 1996, c1958. 268pp.
A sixteen-year-old girl gains confidence and perspective in her life by leaving her family in Oregon to live with friends in California for a year.

**Cleary, Beverly.** *Sister of the Bride*. Avon, 1996, c1963. 268pp.
Barbara helps her eighteen-year-old sister plan her wedding.

**Cooney, Caroline B.** *Both Sides of Time.* Bantam Doubleday Dell Books for Young Readers, 1997, c1995. 210pp.
The summer after senior year, Annie, wishing she could have lived a hundred years ago in a more romantic time, finds herself in the 1890s, and it is indeed romantic—and very painful.

**Cooney, Caroline B.** *The Girl Who Invented Romance.* Delacorte Press, 2005, c1988. 182pp.
While waiting for her first big romance and observing the sometimes rocky love affairs of her parents and brother, sixteen-year-old Kelly develops a board game called Romance.

# Clean Romance

**Daly, Maureen.** *Seventeenth Summer.* Simon Pulse, 2002, c1942. 291pp.
   The summer after high school graduation, seventeen-year-old Angie finds herself in love for the first time.

**Danziger, Paula.** *Remember Me to Harold Square.* Penguin Putnam Books for Young Readers, c1999. 139pp.
   When Frank spends the summer with Kendra and her family in their New York City apartment, a friendship develops as the two teenagers set off on a scavenger hunt exploring the city's museums, restaurants, and other landmarks.

**Dessen, Sarah.** *This Lullaby: A Novel.* Viking Press, c2002. 345pp.
   Remy, a master at getting rid of boyfriends before any emotional attachments form, finds herself strangely unwilling to free herself from Dexter, a messy, disorganized, impulsive musician whom she suspects she has come to love.

**Eberhardt, Thom.** *Rat Boys: A Dating Experiment.* Hyperion, c2001. 154pp.
   Fourteen-year-olds Marci and Summer use a magic ring to turn two rats into cute boys so that they can have dates for the Spring Fling.

**Heath, Lorraine.** *Amelia and the Outlaw.* Avon Books, c2003. 245pp.
   In Texas in 1881, nineteen-year-old former bank robber Jesse Lawton arrives at Judge Harper's ranch to work off the remainder of his sentence and promptly falls in love with the judge's daughter.

**Heath, Lorraine.** *Samantha and the Cowboy.* Avon Books, c2002. 250pp.
   Fresh from the Civil War, soldier Matthew Hart wants only to return to his simple life as a cowboy, but matters become complicated when he discovers that Sam, the new boy on the cattle drive, is really Samantha—and she's beautiful.

**Kerr, M. E.** *I Stay Near You: 1 Story in 3.* Harcourt Brace, 1997, c1985. 203pp.
   Three generations suffer the consequences of an ill-fated romance between a young girl from the wrong side of the tracks and the son of the richest family in a small upstate New York town.

**Lubar, David.** *Dunk.* Clarion Books, c2002. 249pp.
   Chad, hoping to work out his frustrations and his anger by taking a summer job as a dunk tank Bozo on the boardwalk at the New Jersey shore, comes to a better understanding of himself and the uses of humor as he undergoes training in the fine art of insults.

**McDaniel, Lurlene.** *One Last Wish.* Bantam Books, c1998. 136pp.
   Presents three tales of teenagers facing death.

**Plummer, Louise.** *The Unlikely Romance of Kate Bjorkman.* Laurel-Leaf, 1997, c1995. 183pp.
   Seventeen-year-old Kate hopes for romance when her older brother's friend Richard comes to stay at their house during Christmas vacation.

# Clean Romance

**Rinaldi, Ann. *The Coffin Quilt: The Feud Between the Hatfields and the McCoys.*** Harcourt Brace, c1999. 228pp.

> In the 1880s, young Fanny McCoy witnesses the growth of a terrible and violent feud between her Kentucky family and the West Virginia Hatfields, complicated by her older sister Roseanna's romance with a Hatfield.

**Spinelli, Jerry. *Stargirl.*** Knopf (distributed by Random House), c2000. 186pp.

> Stargirl, a teen who animates quiet Mica High with her colorful personality, suddenly finds herself shunned for her refusal to conform.

**Van Draanen, Wendelin. *Flipped.*** Knopf (distributed by Random House), c2001. 212pp.

> In alternating chapters, two teenagers describe how their feelings about themselves, each other, and their families have changed over the years.

**Woodson, Jacqueline. *If You Come Softly.*** Putnam, c1998. 181pp.

> After meeting at their private school in New York, fifteen-year-old Jeremiah, who is black and whose parents are separated, and Ellie, who is white and whose mother has twice abandoned her, fall in love and then try to cope with people's reactions.

# E-mails and Blogs and IMs, Oh My!

## Books for Ages 12–15

**Danziger, Paula.** *Snail Mail No More.* Scholastic Signature, c2000. 307pp.

Now that they live in different cities, thirteen-year-olds Tara and Elizabeth use e-mail to "talk" about everything that is occurring in their lives and to try to maintain their closeness as they face big changes.

**Ehrenhaft, Daniel.** *Tell It to Naomi.* Delacorte Press, c2004. 200pp.

In a harebrained scheme, concocted by his neurotic older sister, to forge a romantic relationship with the girl of his dreams, fifteen-year-old Dave Rosen pretends to be a female advice columnist for his school newspaper.

**Goldschmidt, Judy.** *The Secret Blog of Raisin Rodriguez: A Novel.* Razorbill, c2005. 202pp.

In a weblog she sends to her best friends back in Berkeley, seventh-grader Raisin Rodriguez chronicles her successes and her more frequent humiliating failures as she attempts to make friends at her new Philadelphia school.

**Hooper, Mary.** *Amy.* Bloomsbury (distributed by Holtzbrinck), 2004, c2002. 170pp.

Feeling lonely after being dumped by her two best friends, Amy hopes for a romance with Zed, whom she met in an Internet chat room, but the day they spend together in his seaside village near London is not what she expected.

**Moriarty, Jaclyn.** *The Year of Secret Assignments.* Arthur A. Levine Books, c2004. 340pp.

Three female students from Ashbury High write to three male students from rival Brookfield High as part of a pen pal program, leading to romance, humiliation, revenge plots, and war between the schools.

**Myracle, Lauren.** *Ttyl.* Amulet Books, c2004. 209pp.

Chronicles, in "instant message" format, the day-to-day experiences, feelings, and plans of three friends—Zoe, Maddie, and Angela—as they begin tenth grade.

**Rosen, Michael J.** *Chaser Sic: A Novel in E-Mails.* Candlewick Press, c2002. 152pp.

When his parents decide to move to an old house in the country, Chase uses e-mails to his friends back in Columbus, Ohio, and to his sister in college to help him deal with cicadas, deer hunters, and other changes in his life.

**Sones, Sonya.** *One of Those Hideous Books Where the Mother Dies.* Simon & Schuster Books for Young Readers, c2004. 268pp.

Fifteen-year-old Ruby Milliken leaves her best friend, her boyfriend, her aunt, and her mother's grave in Boston and reluctantly flies to Los Angeles to live with her father, a famous movie star who divorced her mother before Ruby was born.

**Vega, Denise.** *Click Here: (To Find Out How I Survived Seventh Grade): A Novel.* Little, Brown, c2005. 211pp.

Seventh-grader Erin Swift writes about her friends and classmates in her private blog. When it accidentally gets posted on the school intranet site, she learns some important lessons about friendship.

# E-mails and Blogs and IMs, Oh My!

## Books for Older Teens

**Cabot, Meg.** *Boy Meets Girl.* Avon Trade, c2004. 387pp.
Kate Mackenzie thinks life can't get any worse, until her tyrannical boss makes her fire the most popular employee in the department, leading to a lawsuit for wrongful termination, and a close encounter with a Manhattan lawyer who embodies everything Kate detests.

**Clair Day, Robynn.** *Confessions of a Boyfriend Stealer: a Blog.* Delacorte Press, c2005. 228pp.
Genesis Bell's blog tells the true story of the unbelievable events that caused the breakup of her friendship with her two best friends.

**Hafer, Todd.** *In The Chat Room with God.* River Oak, c2002. 248pp.
Five teens meet in an Internet chat room for some laughs, but when a mysterious visitor claiming to be God enters the chat, they find their lives, faith, and beliefs tested.

**Maxwell, Katie.** *The Year My Life Went Down the Loo.* Dorchester Publishing, c2003. 221pp.
A novel in e-mail form, in which sixteen-year-old Emily Williams, an American living in England, struggles to adapt to the unfamiliar culture and squash the voices in her head urging her to jump on the first available flight home to Seattle.

**Petersen, P. J.** *Rob&sara.com.* Delacorte Press, c2004. 210pp.
Rob, who lives at a school for troubled teenagers, and Sara, the sixteen-year-old daughter of an army colonel, meet in a poetry chat-room and develop a close relationship via e-mail.

**Stine, Catherine.** *Refugees.* Delacorte Press, c2005. 277pp.
Following the September 11, 2001, terrorist attacks, Dawn, a sixteen-year-old runaway from San Francisco, connects by phone and e-mail with Johar, a gentle, fifteen-year-old Afghani who assists Dawn's foster mother, a doctor, at a Red Cross refugee camp in Peshawar.

**Teller, Astro.** *Exegesis.* Vintage Contemporaries, c1997. 223pp.
A near-future novel presented in the form of e-mail messages between graduate student Alice Lu and EDGAR, an artificial intelligence project she created to browse and summarize information from the World Wide Web, which somehow became conscious and then came to the attention of the government when it started digesting top secret military files.

**Wittlinger, Ellen.** *Heart on My Sleeve.* Simon & Schuster Books for Young Readers, c2004. 219pp.
From the end of high school to the beginning of college, Chloe and Julian deal with major changes in their families and friendships and explore their feelings for each other through e-mails, letters, and a visit.

# Fairy Tale Variations

## Books for Ages 12–15

**Haddix, Margaret Peterson.** *Just Ella*. Simon & Schuster Books for Young Readers, c1999. 185pp.
In this continuation of the Cinderella story, fifteen-year-old Ella finds that accepting Prince Charming's proposal ensnares her in a suffocating tangle of palace rules and royal etiquette, so she plots to escape.

**Kindl, Patrice.** *Goose Chase.* Houghton Mifflin, c2001. 214pp.
Rather than marry a cruel king or a seemingly dim-witted prince, an enchanted goose girl endures imprisonment, capture by several ogresses, and other dangers, before learning exactly who she is.

**Levine, Gail Carson.** *Cinderellis and the Glass Hill*. HarperCollins, c2000. 104pp.
In this humorous retelling of a Perrault tale, a lonely young farm lad uses his unusual inventive ability to pass a nearly impossible test and win the hand of the neighboring princess.

**Levine, Gail Carson.** *Ella Enchanted*. HarperCollins, c1997. 232pp.
In this novel based on the story of Cinderella, Ella struggles against the childhood curse that forces her to obey any order given to her.

**Levine, Gail Carson.** *Princess Sonora and the Long Sleep.* HarperCollins, c1999. 107pp.
In this retelling of the fairy tale "Sleeping Beauty," Princess Sonora, who is ten times smarter than anyone else, vows to choose for herself the best time to be pricked by the spindle.

**Maguire, Gregory.** *Leaping Beauty: And Other Animal Fairy Tales.* HarperCollins, c2004. 197pp.
Retells eight beloved fairy tales, giving them animal protagonists; includes such stories as "Cinder-Elephant," "Hamster and Gerbil," and "Leaping Beauty."

**McKinley, Robin.** *Rose Daughter.* Ace Books, 1998, c1997. 292pp.
A novelized retelling of "Beauty and the Beast" in which Beauty grows to love the Beast at whose castle she is compelled to stay and is forced to follow her heart to make the best choice for their futures.

**McKinley, Robin.** *Spindle's End.* Putnam, c2000. 422pp.
The infant princess Briar Rose is cursed on her name day by Pernicia, an evil fairy, and then whisked away by a young fairy to be raised in a remote part of a magical country, unaware of her real identity and hidden from Pernicia's vengeful powers.

**Napoli, Donna Jo.** *Beast*. Atheneum Books for Young Readers, c2000. 260pp.
Elaborates on "Beauty and the Beast," told from the point of view of the beast and set in Persia.

**Napoli, Donna Jo.** *Bound*. Atheneum Books for Young Readers, c2004. 186pp.
In a novel based on Chinese Cinderella tales, fourteen-year-old stepchild Xing-Xing endures a life of neglect and servitude, as her stepmother cruelly mutilates her own child's feet so that she alone might marry well.

**Napoli, Donna Jo.** *Spinners*. Puffin Books, 2001, c1999. 197pp.
Elaborates on the events recounted in "Rumpelstiltskin," in which a strange little man helps a miller's daughter spin straw into gold for the king on the condition that she will give him her first-born child.

# Fairy Tale Variations

**Napoli, Donna Jo.** *Zel*. Puffin Books, 1998, c1996. 227pp.
Adapted from "Rapunzel," the story is told in alternating chapters from the point of view of Zel, her mother, and the prince, as Zel falls in love with a young prince, and her mother tries everything she can to prevent Zel from leaving her.

**Schmidt, Gary D.** *Straw into Gold*. Clarion Books, c2001. 172pp.
Pursued by greedy villains, two boys on a quest to save innocent lives meet the banished queen whose son was stolen by Rumpelstiltskin eleven years earlier, and she provides much more than the answer they seek.

**Vande Velde, Vivian.** *The Rumpelstiltskin Problem.* Houghton Mifflin, c2000. 116pp.
A collection of variations on the familiar story of a boastful miller and the daughter he claims can spin straw into gold.

**Vande Velde, Vivian.** *Tales from the Brothers Grimm and the Sisters Weird*. Harcourt Brace, c1995. 128pp.
Presents thirteen twisted versions of such familiar fairy tales as "Red Riding Hood," "Jack and the Beanstalk," "Hansel and Gretel," and "The Three Billy Goats Gruff."

## Books for Older Teens

**Card, Orson Scott.** *Enchantment*. Del Rey/Ballantine, 2000, c1999. 419pp.
American graduate student Ivan Smetski, haunted by the vision of a sleeping princess he believes he saw as a ten-year-old boy while exploring the Carpathian forest, returns to his native land to investigate and, with one kiss, is drawn into a world that vanished a thousand years earlier.

**Maguire, Gregory.** *Confessions of an Ugly Stepsister*. ReganBooks, c1999. 368pp.
Retells the story of Cinderella from her stepsister's point of view.

**Maguire, Gregory.** *Mirror Mirror.* Regan Books, c2003. 280pp. (adult)
Presents a retelling of "Snow White," set in early sixteenth-century Italy, in which the life of innocent young Bianca de Nevada is disrupted when her beloved father is sent on an errand by Cesare Borgia, leaving her in the care of Borgia's sister Lucrezia, a decadent woman who orders the child killed.

**Napoli, Donna Jo.** *Breath*. Atheneum Books for Young Readers, c2003. 260pp.
Elaborates on "The Pied Piper," told from the point of view of a boy who is too ill to keep up when a piper spirits away the healthy children of a plague-ridden town after being cheated out of full payment for ridding Hameln of rats.

**Yolen, Jane.** *Briar Rose*. Starscape, 2002, c1992. 241pp.
In this retelling of "Sleeping Beauty," a young woman learns that her grandmother had a secret past tied to the Holocaust.

# Fairy Tale Variations Arranged by Individual Tales

## Donkeyskin

**McKinley, Robin.** *Deerskin.* Ace, c1994. 309pp. (ages 12–15)
A beautiful princess flees from her father's wrath and unlocks a door onto a world of magic, where she finds the key to her own survival.

## The Goose Girl

**Hale, Shannon.** *The Goose Girl.* Bloomsbury (distributed by Holtzbrinck), c2003. 383pp. (ages 12–15)
Princess Anidori, on her way to marry a prince she has never met, is betrayed by her guards and her lady-in-waiting and must become a goose girl to survive, until she can reveal her true identity and reclaim the crown that is rightfully hers.

## East of the Sun and West of the Moon

**Pattou, Edith.** *East.* Harcourt, c2003. 498pp. (ages 12–15)
A young woman journeys to a distant castle on the back of a great white bear who is the victim of a cruel enchantment.

## Hansel and Gretel

**Napoli, Donna Jo.** *The Magic Circle.* Puffin Books, c1995. 118pp. (ages 12–15)
After learning sorcery to become a healer, a good-hearted woman is turned into a witch by evil spirits. She fights their power until her encounter with Hansel and Gretel years later.

## Jack and the Beanstalk

**Napoli, Donna Jo.** *Crazy Jack.* Delacorte Press, c1999. 134pp. (ages 12–15)
In this version of the traditional tale of the young boy who climbs a beanstalk, Jack searches for his father, falls in love with Flora, and learns the value of real treasure.

## Little Red Riding Hood

**Cross, Gillian.** *Wolf.* Holiday House, c1991. 140pp. (ages 12–15)
Cassy is forced to stay with her mother in a squatter's settlement of artists, where she joins the group in producing an educational program about wolves and inadvertently learns that her missing father is a notorious terrorist.

## The Pied Piper

**Napoli, Donna Jo.** *Breath.* Atheneum Books for Young Readers, c2003. 260pp. (ages 12–15)
Elaborates on "The Pied Piper," told from the point of view of a boy who is too ill to keep up when a piper spirits away the healthy children of a plague-ridden town after being cheated out of full payment for ridding Hameln of rats.

# Fairy Tale Variations Arranged by Individual Tales

## Rapunzel

**Napoli, Donna Jo.** *Zel.* Puffin Books, c1998. 227pp. (ages 12–15)
Based on "Rapunzel," the story is told in alternating chapters from the point of view of Zel, her mother, and the prince, and delves into the psychological motivations of the characters.

## Rumplestiltskin

**Napoli, Donna Jo.** *Spinners.* Puffin Books, c2001. 197pp. (ages 12–15)
American graduate student Ivan Smetski, haunted by the vision of a sleeping princess he believes he saw as a ten-year-old boy while exploring the Carpathian forest, returns to his native land to investigate and, with one kiss, is drawn into a world that vanished a thousand years earlier.

**Schmidt, Gary D.** *Straw into Gold.* Clarion Books, c2001. 172pp. (ages 12–15)
Pursued by greedy villains, two boys on a quest to save innocent lives meet the banished queen whose son was stolen by Rumpelstiltskin eleven years earlier, and she provides much more than the answer they seek.

**Vande Velde, Vivian.** *The Rumpelstiltskin Problem.* Houghton Mifflin, c2000. 116pp. (ages 12–15)
A collection of variations on the familiar story of a boastful miller and the daughter he claims can spin straw into gold.

## Sleeping Beauty

**Geras, Adele.** *Watching the Roses.* Harcourt Brace Jovanovich, c1992. 152pp. (older teens)
After being raped at her eighteenth birthday party, an English girl, whose life resembles a modern version of "Sleeping Beauty," withdraws into silent thoughts of her unusual family and the events that led to her trauma.

**Yolen, Jane.** *Briar Rose.* Starscape, c2002. 241pp. (ages 12–15)
In this retelling of "Sleeping Beauty," a young woman learns that her grandmother had a secret past tied to the Holocaust.

# Fractured Fairy Tales

## Books for All Ages

**Ada, Alma Flor.** *Dear Peter Rabbit*. Atheneum Books for Young Readers, c1994. 32pp.
Presents letters between such fairy tale characters as Goldilocks, Baby Bear, Peter Rabbit, and the Three Pigs.

**Ada, Alma Flor.** *With Love, Little Red Hen.* Atheneum Books for Young Readers, c2001. 34pp.
A series of letters describe the actions of Goldilocks, Peter Rabbit, the Three Pigs, the Little Red Hen, and other storybook characters when Little Red Hen and her chicks become the target of the unsavory Wolf and his cousin, Fer O'Cious.

**Ada, Alma Flor.** *Yours Truly, Goldilocks.* Atheneum Books for Young Readers, c1998. 32pp.
Presents the correspondence of Goldilocks, the Three Pigs, Baby Bear, Peter Rabbit, and Little Red Riding Hood as they plan to attend a housewarming party for the pigs and avoid the evil wolves in the forest.

**Calmenson, Stephanie.** *The Principal's New Clothes.* Scholastic, c1989. 40pp.
In this version of the Andersen tale, the vain principal of P.S. 88 is persuaded by two tailors that they will make him an amazing, one-of-a-kind suit that will be visible only to intelligent people who are good at their jobs.

**Cole, Babette.** *Prince Cinders*. Putnam, 1997, c1987, 32pp.
A fairy grants a small, skinny prince a change in appearance and the chance to go to the Palace Disco.

**Edwards, Pamela Duncan.** *Dinorella: A Prehistoric Fairy Tale.* Hyperion Books for Children, c1997. 32pp.
In this story, loosely based on that of Cinderella but featuring dinosaurs, the Duke falls in love with Dinorella when she rescues him from the dreaded deinonychus at the Dinosaur Dance.

**Ernst, Lisa Campbell.** *Goldilocks Returns.* Simon & Schuster Books for Young Readers, c2000. 34pp.
Thirty years after Goldilocks first met the three bears, she returns to fix up their cottage and soothe her guilty conscience.

**Goode, Diane.** *Dinosaur's New Clothes*. Scholastic, c1999. 33pp.
In this retelling of the familiar story about two rascals who sell a vain emperor an invisible suit of clothes, the characters are presented as dinosaurs.

**Granowsky, Alvin.** *That Awful Cinderella.* Steck-Vaughn, c1993. 25pp.
Contains the classic fairy tale of Cinderella, entitled "Cinderella—A Classic Tale," along with a retelling, entitled "That Awful Cinderella," which is written from the point of view of Cinderella's stepsister.

**Granowsky, Alvin.** *The Unfairest of Them All.* Steck-Vaughn, c1999. 25pp.
Presents the classic story of Snow White, a young woman whose beauty drives her stepmother to attempt to kill her; includes an additional tale in which the stepmother gets to tell her side of the story.

**Harris, Jim.** *The Three Little Dinosaurs.* Pelican, c1999. 30pp.
In this variation on the "The Three Little Pigs," three young dinosaurs set out on their own, only to be hassled by a Tyrannosaurus rex who gets a big surprise at the end.

# Fractured Fairy Tales

**Jackson, Ellen B.** *Cinder Edna*. Lothrop, Lee & Shepard, c1994. 32pp.
Cinderella and Cinder Edna, who live next door to each other, each with a cruel stepmother and step-sisters, have different approaches to life. Although both end up with the princes of their dreams, one is a great deal happier than the other.

**Johnston, Tony.** *The Cowboy and the Black-Eyed Pea.* Putnam & Grosset, c1996. 32pp.
In this adaptation of "The Princess and the Pea," the wealthy daughter of a Texas rancher devises a plan to find a real cowboy among her many suitors.

**Ketteman, Helen.** *Bubba the Cowboy Prince: A Fractured Texas Tale.* Scholastic, c1997. 32pp.
Loosely based on "Cinderella," this story is set in Texas. The fairy godmother is a cow, and the hero, named Bubba, is the stepson of a wicked rancher.

**Lasky, Kathryn.** *The Emperor's Old Clothes.* Harcourt, 2002, c1999. 32pp.
A continuation of "The Emperor's New Clothes" in which a simple farmer finds the emperor's old clothes on his way home from the market and decides to put them on.

**Meddaugh, Susan.** *Cinderella's Rat.* Houghton Mifflin, c1997. 32pp.
One of the rats that was turned into a coachman by Cinderella's fairy godmother tells his story.

**Minters, Frances.** *Cinder-Elly.* Puffin Books, 1997, c1994. 32pp.
In this rap version of the traditional fairy tale, the overworked younger sister gets to go to a basketball game and meets a star player, Prince Charming.

**Osborne, Mary Pope.** *Kate and the Beanstalk.* Atheneum Books for Young Readers, c2000. 35pp.
In this version of the classic tale, a girl climbs to the top of a giant beanstalk, where she uses her quick wits to outsmart a giant and make her and her mother's fortune.

**Palatini, Margie.** *Piggie Pie!* Clarion Books, c1995. 32pp.
Gritch the witch flies to Old MacDonald's farm for some pigs to make a piggie pie, but when she arrives she can't find a single porker.

**Palatini, Margie.** *Zoom Broom.* Hyperion Paperbacks for Children, c2000. 32pp.
When her broom breaks down, Gritch the Witch visits a foxy salesman in search of a new Zoom Broom, but ends up with something unexpected.

**Perlman, Janet.** *Cinderella Penguin, or, the Little Glass Flipper.* Puffin Books, 1995, c1992. 32pp.
A retelling of the classic Cinderella story, with penguins as the characters.

**Pratchett, Terry.** *The Amazing Maurice and His Educated Rodents.* HarperCollins, c2001. 241pp.
A talking cat, intelligent rats, and a strange boy cooperate in a Pied Piper scam until they try to con the wrong town and are confronted by a deadly evil rat king.

**Pullman, Philip.** *I Was a Rat!* Knopf (distributed by Random House), 2000. c1999. 164pp.
A little boy turns life in London upside down when he appears at the house of a lonely old couple and insists he was a rat.

# Fractured Fairy Tales

**Scieszka, Jon.** *The Frog Prince, Continued.* Viking Press, c1991. 32pp.

After the frog turns into a prince, he and the Princess do not live happily ever after, and the Prince decides to look for a witch to help him remedy the situation.

**Scieszka, Jon.** *The Stinky Cheese Man and Other Fairly Stupid Tales.* Viking Press, 1992. 51pp.

Madcap revisions of familiar fairy tales.

**Stanley, Diane.** *Rumpelstiltskin's Daughter.* Morrow Junior Books, c1997. 32pp.

Rumpelstiltskin's daughter may not be able to spin straw into gold, but she is more than a match for a monarch whose greed has blighted an entire kingdom.

**Trivizas, Eugenios.** *The Three Little Wolves and the Big Bad Pig.* Margaret K. McElderry Books, c1993. 32pp.

An altered retelling of the traditional tale about the conflict between pig and wolf—with a surprise ending.

**Vande Velde, Vivian.** *The Rumpelstiltskin Problem.* Houghton Mifflin, c2000. 116pp.

A collection of variations on the familiar story of a boastful miller and the daughter he claims can spin straw into gold.

**Vande Velde, Vivian.** *Tales from the Brothers Grimm and the Sisters Weird.* Harcourt Brace, c1995. 128pp.

Presents thirteen twisted versions of such familiar fairy tales as "Red Riding Hood," "Jack and the Beanstalk," "Hansel and Gretel," and "The Three Billy Goats Gruff."

From Nancy J. Keane, *The Big Book of Teen Reading Lists: 100 Great, Ready-to-Use Book Lists for Educators, Librarians, Parents, and Children.* Westport, CT: Libraries Unlimited, 2006. Copyright © 2006 by Libraries Unlimited.

# Hip Hop Literature

## Books for Ages 12–15

**Greenfield, Eloise.** *Nathaniel Talking.* Black Butterfly Children's Books, c1988, 32pp.
Poems by Nathaniel, a spirited nine-year-old poet who raps and rhymes about what it's like to be nine, his education, and his family life. Includes instructions for children on how to create a twelve-bar blues poem.

**Igus, Toyomi.** *I See the Rhythm.* Children's Book Press (distributed by Publishers Group West), c1998. 32pp. (NF)
Chronicles and captures poetically the history, mood, and movement of African American music.

**Myers, Walter Dean.** *Harlem: A Poem.* Scholastic Press, c1997. 32pp.
A poem celebrating the people, sights, and sounds of Harlem.

## Books for Older Teens

**Anglesey, Zoe, ed.** *Listen Up!: Spoken Word Poetry.* One World, 1999. 197pp.
A collection of spoken word poetry by young authors.

**George, Nelson.** *Hip Hop America.* Penguin, 2005, c1998. 238pp. (adult)
Examines the growth of hip hop during the last three decades of the twentieth century, discussing its impact on American society and looking at how advertisers, magazines, fashion companies, MTV, and others are using hip hop as a way to reach not only African American youth, but all young people.

**Ptah, Heru.** *A Hip-Hop Story.* MTV Books/Pocket Books, 2003, c2002. 404pp. (NF)
Rappers Flawless and Hannibal are reaching for the same dream: to be the best hip-hop artist in their generation, but along they way, the must battle industry honchos, crazy fans, and each other.

**Tramble, Nichelle D.** *The Dying Ground: A Hip-Hop Noir Novel.* Vallard Books, c2001. 322pp. (adult)
As Maceo Redfield tries to learn the truth behind his childhood friend's death, he finds himself drawn deeper into Oakland's drug underworld.

**Vibe Magazine, eds.** *Hip-Hop Divas.* Three Rivers Press, c2001. 211pp. (adult) (NF)
A collection of essays and photographs profiling the most influential female hip-hop artists.

From Nancy J. Keane, *The Big Book of Teen Reading Lists: 100 Great, Ready-to-Use Book Lists for Educators, Librarians, Parents, and Children.* Westport, CT: Libraries Unlimited, 2006. Copyright © 2006 by Libraries Unlimited.

# Horror

## Books for Ages 12–15

**Atwater-Rhodes, Amelia.** *Demon in My View.* Delacorte Press, c2000 176pp.

Seventeen-year-old Jessica Allodola discovers that the vampire world of her fiction is real when she develops relationships with an alluring vampire named Aubrey and the teenage witch who is trying to save Jessica from his clutches.

**Bruchac, Joseph.** *Skeleton Man.* HarperCollins, c2001. 114pp.

After her parents disappear and she is turned over to the care of a strange "great-uncle," Molly must rely on her dreams about an old Mohawk story for her safety, and maybe even for her life.

**Duncan, Lois.** *Don't Look Behind You.* Bantam Doubleday Dell Books for Young Readers, 1990, c1989. 179pp.

Seventeen-year-old April finds her comfortable life changed forever when death threats to her father, a witness in a federal case, force her family to go into hiding under assumed names and flee from a hired killer.

**Duncan, Lois.** *Down a Dark Hall.* Bantam Doubleday Dell Books for Young Readers, 1990, c1974. 181pp.

Suspicious and uneasy about the atmosphere at her new boarding school, fourteen-year-old Kit slowly realizes why she and the other three students at the school were selected to attend.

**Duncan, Lois.** *Stranger with My Face.* Bantam Doubleday Dell Books for Young Readers, 1990, c1981. 235pp.

A seventeen-year-old senses she is being spied on and probably impersonated, but when she discovers what actually is occurring, it is even more unbelievable.

**Duncan, Lois.** *Summer of Fear.* Bantam Doubleday Dell Books for Young Readers, 1990, c1976. 219pp.

Soon after the arrival of cousin Julia, insidious occurrences convince Rachel Julia is a witch, who must be stopped before her monstrous plan can be effected.

**Gaiman, Neil.** *Coraline.* HarperCollins, c2002. 162pp.

Looking for excitement, Coraline ventures through a mysterious door into a world that is similar to, yet disturbingly different from, her own, where she must challenge a gruesome entity to save herself, her parents, and the souls of three others.

**Hahn, Mary Downing.** *Look for Me by Moonlight.* Clarion Books, c1995. 198pp.

While staying at the remote and reputedly haunted Maine inn run by her father and pregnant step-mother, sixteen-year-old Cynda feels increasingly isolated from her father's new family and finds solace in the attentions of a charming but mysterious guest.

**Hahn, Mary Downing.** *Wait Till Helen Comes: A Ghost Story.* Clarion, c1986. 184pp.

Molly and Michael dislike their spooky new stepsister Heather but realize that they must try to save her when she seems ready to follow a ghost child to her doom.

**Halam, Ann.** *Dr. Franklin's Island.* Dell Laurel-Leaf, 2003, c2002. 245pp.

When their plane crashes over the Pacific Ocean, three science students are left stranded on a tropical island and then imprisoned by a doctor who is performing horrifying experiments on humans involving the transfer of animal genes.

**Klause, Annette Curtis.** *The Silver Kiss.* Dell, 1992, c1990. 198pp.

A mysterious teenage boy harboring a dark secret helps Zoe come to terms with her mother's terminal illness.

From Nancy J. Keane, *The Big Book of Teen Reading Lists: 100 Great, Ready-to-Use Book Lists for Educators, Librarians, Parents, and Children.* Westport, CT: Libraries Unlimited, 2006. Copyright © 2006 by Libraries Unlimited.

# Horror

**Naylor, Phyllis Reynolds.** *Jade Green: A Ghost Story.* Atheneum, c1999. 168pp.

While living with her uncle in a house haunted by the ghost of a young woman, recently orphaned Judith Sparrow wonders if her one small transgression causes mysterious happenings.

**Shan, Darren.** *Cirque du Freak.* Little, Brown, c2001. 266pp.

Two boys who are best friends visit an illegal freak show, where an encounter with a vampire and a deadly spider forces them to make life-changing choices.

**Vande Velde, Vivian.** *Companions of the Night.* Harcourt Brace, c1995. 212pp.

When sixteen-year-old Kerry Nowicki helps a young man escape from a group of men who claim he is a vampire, she finds herself faced with some bizarre and dangerous choices.

**Zindel, Paul.** *The Doom Stone.* Hyperion Paperbacks for Children, 2004, c1995. 173pp.

Jackson and his new friend Alma investigate the mysterious attacks upon a young man and Jackson's Aunt Sarah at Stonehenge in England.

**Zindel, Paul.** *Night of the Bat.* Hyperion, c2001. 129pp.

Teenage Jake joins his father on an expedition to study bats in the Brazilian rain forest and finds the project menaced by a giant brain-eating bat.

**Zindel, Paul.** *Raptor.* Hyperion Paperbacks for Children, 1999, c1998. 170pp.

Zack and his Native American friend Uta embark on a dangerous investigation when they find a dinosaur egg that hatches into a baby raptor, and set out to explore the mine shafts and tunnels of Silver Mountain in search of the raptor herd.

**Zindel, Paul.** *Rats.* Hyperion Paperbacks, 2000, c1999. 204pp.

When mutant rats threaten to take over Staten Island, which has become a huge landfill, fourteen-year-old Sarah and her younger brother Mike try to figure out how to stop them.

## Books for Older Teens

**Anderson, M. T.** *Thirsty.* Candlewick Press, 2003, c1997. 249pp.

From the moment he knows that he is destined to be a vampire, Chris thirsts for the blood of people around him while also struggling to remain human.

**Atwater-Rhodes, Amelia.** *In the Forests of the Night.* Dell Laurel-Leaf, 2000, c1999. 147pp.

Risika, a teenage vampire, wanders back in time to the year 1684 when, as a human, she died and was transformed against her will.

**King, Stephen.** *Christine.* Signet, c1983. 503pp.

Arnie Cunningham, a bookish and bullied high school senior, becomes obsessed with a 1958 Plymouth he is restoring, named Christine.

**Matheson, Richard.** *I Am Legend.* ORB, c1997. 317pp.

Presents the complete novel, *I Am Legend,* about Robert Neville, the last living man on an Earth in which every other man, woman, and child has become a vampire; includes ten additional short horror stories.

**Preston, Douglas J.** *The Relic.* Forge, c1996. 468pp.

When visitors are killed at the New York Museum of Natural History before the opening of the Superstition exhibition, graduate student Margo Green discovers a link between the killings, a tragic archaeological trip to the Amazon Basin, and a figurine from the exhibit.

# Humor

## Books for Ages 12–15

**Allen, M. E.** *Gotta Get Some Bish Bash Bosh.* Katherine Tegen Books, c2005. 198pp.

After being dumped by his girlfriend, a fourteen-year-old English boy attempts to change his image.

**Allison, Jennifer.** *Gilda Joyce, Psychic Investigator.* Sleuth/Dutton, c2005. 321pp.

During the summer before ninth grade, intrepid Gilda Joyce invites herself to the San Francisco mansion of distant cousin Lester Splinter and his thirteen-year-old daughter, where she uses her purported psychic abilities and detective skills to solve the mystery of the mansion's boarded-up tower.

**Anderson, M. T.** *Whales on Stilts.* Harcourt, c2005. 188pp.

Racing against the clock, shy middle-school student Lily and her best friends, Katie and Jasper, must foil the plot of her father's conniving boss to conquer the world using an army of whales.

**Avi.** *Never Mind!: A Twin Novel.* HarperCollins, c2004. 200pp.

Twelve-year-old New York City twins Meg and Edward have nothing in common, so they are just as shocked as everyone else when Meg's hopes for popularity and Edward's mischievous schemes coincidentally collide in a hilarious showdown.

**Birdseye, Tom.** *Attack of the Mutant Underwear.* Holiday House, c2003. 199pp.

Fifth-grader Cody Carson keeps a journal of his hopes for a fresh start in a town where nobody knows about his humiliating mistakes of the past, but before school even begins, so does his embarrassment.

**Cabot, Meg.** *All-American Girl.* HarperCollins, c2002. 247pp.

Sophomore Samantha Madison stops a presidential assassination attempt, is appointed teen ambassador to the United Nations, and catches the eye of the very cute First Son.

**Cabot, Meg.** *The Princess Diaries.* HarperCollins, c2000. 238pp.

Fourteen-year-old Mia, who is trying to lead a normal life as a teenage girl in New York City, is shocked to learn that her father is the Prince of Genovia, a small European principality, and that she is a princess and the heir to the throne.

**Dodd, Quentin.** *Beatnik Rutabagas from Beyond the Stars.* Farrar, Straus & Giroux, c2001. 215pp.

Whisked away on spaceships to serve as generals of opposing armies, best friends and sci-fi movie fans Walter Nutria and Yselle Meridian soon convince the aliens they must work together against the real menaces, Space Mice from Galaxy Four and their leader, The Boss.

**Eberhardt, Thom.** *Rat Boys: A Dating Experiment.* Hyperion, c2001. 154pp.

Fourteen-year-olds Marci and Summer use a magic ring to turn two rats into cute boys so that they can have dates for the Spring Fling.

**Gantos, Jack.** *Jack on the Tracks: Four Seasons of Fifth Grade.* Farrar, Straus & Giroux, c1999. 182pp.

Moving with his unbearable sister to Miami, Florida, Jack tries to break some of his bad habits but finds himself irresistibly drawn to things disgusting, gross, and weird.

# Humor

**Goldschmidt, Judy.** *The Secret Blog of Raisin Rodriguez: A Novel.* Razorbill, c2005. 202pp.

In a weblog she sends to her best friends back in Berkeley, seventh-grader Raisin Rodriguez chronicles her successes and her more frequent humiliating failures as she attempts to make friends at her new school in Philadelphia.

**LaRochelle, David.** *Absolutely, Positively Not.* Arthur A. Levine Books, c2005. 219pp.

Chronicles a teenage boy's humorous attempts to fit in at his Minnesota high school by becoming a macho, girl-loving, "Playboy" pinup-displaying heterosexual.

**Limb, Sue.** *Girl, 15, Charming But Insane.* Delacorte Press, c2004. 214pp.

Fifteen-year-old Jess, living with her mum, separated from her father in Cornwall, and with a best friend who seems to do everything perfectly, finds her own assets through humor.

**Mlynowski, Sarah.** *Bras & Broomsticks.* Delacorte Press, c2005. 311pp.

Living in New York City with her mother and her younger sister, Miri, fourteen-year-old Rachel tries to persuade Miri, who has recently become a witch, to help her become popular at school and to try to stop their divorced father's wedding.

**Naylor, Phyllis Reynolds.** *Bernie Magruder & The Bats in the Belfry.* Atheneum Books for Young Readers, c2003. 130pp.

Many residents of Middleburg, Indiana, are already going crazy from the ever-ringing church bells and now, after a bat is spotted in the hotel run by Bernie's family, they worry that the dangerous Indiana Aztec bat has finally arrived.

**O'Connell, Tyne.** *Pulling Princes.* Bloomsbury Publishing (distributed by Holtzbrinck), c2004. 224pp.

Calypso Kelly, a California teenager attending an upscale boarding school in England, sets out to become popular by claiming that her mother's gay assistant is her boyfriend and finds herself in a royal mess when she gets a chance at a real relationship with a prince.

**Peck, Richard.** *Fair Weather.* Puffin Books, 2003, c2001. 146pp.

Thirteen-year-old Rosie and members of her family travel from their Illinois farm to Chicago in 1893 to visit Aunt Euterpe and attend the World's Columbian Exposition, which, along with an encounter with Buffalo Bill and Lillian Russell, turns out to be a life-changing experience for everyone.

**Peck, Richard.** *The Teacher's Funeral: A Comedy in Three Parts.* Dial Books, c2004. 190pp.

In rural Indiana in 1904, fifteen-year-old Russell's dreams of quitting school and joining a wheat-threshing crew are disrupted when his older sister takes over the teaching at his one-room schoolhouse after mean old Myrt Arbuckle "hauls off and dies."

**Rennison, Louise.** *Angus, Thongs and Full-Frontal Snogging: Confessions of Georgia Nicolson.* HarperCollins, c2000. 247pp.

Presents the humorous journal of a year in the life of a fourteen-year-old British girl who tries to reduce the size of her nose, stop her mad cat from terrorizing the neighborhood animals, and win the love of handsome hunk Robbie.

# Humor

---

**Singer, Marilyn.** *The Circus Lunicus*. H. Holt, c2000. 168pp.

Solly's stepmother forbids him to go the Circus Lunicus, but gives him an inflatable lizard that turns into his fairy godmother and teaches him how to turn into a space lizard as well.

**Snicket, Lemony.** *The Bad Beginning.* HarperCollins, c1999. 162pp. (and sequels)

After the sudden death of their parents, the three Baudelaire children—Violet, fourteen, Klans, twelve, and baby Sunny—must depend on each other and their wits when it turns out that the distant relative who is appointed their guardian is determined to use any means necessary to get their fortune.

**Weeks, Sarah.** *Guy Time.* HarperTrophy, 2001, c2000. 165pp.

A humorous account of thirteen-year-old Guy's dealing with the separation, and possible divorce, of his eccentric parents and with his own newfound interest in girls.

**Whytock, Cherry.** *My Scrumptious Scottish Dumplings: The Life of Angelica Cookson Potts.* Simon & Schuster Books for Young Readers, c2004. 169pp.

The further adventures of fourteen-year-old Angel Cookson Potts, food-loving cooking enthusiast and worried weight watcher, as she enlists her friends to help her Scottish father, prove that London's famous department store, Harrods, is unknowingly selling inferior haggis. Includes recipes.

**Yourgrau, Barry.** *Nastybook.* HarperCollins, c2005. 183pp.

Forty-three stories feature such characters as guardian angels who run away from their charges, witches who use the Internet to stalk their victims, and pandas who work as assassins.

## Books for Older Teens

**Anderson, M. T.** *Burger Wuss*. Candlewick, 2001, c1999. 192pp.

Hoping to lose his loser image, Anthony plans revenge on a bully, which results in a war between two competing fast food restaurants, Burger Queen and O'Dermott's.

**Bradley, Alex.** *24 Girls in 7 Days.* Dutton Books, c2005. 265pp.

Unlucky in love, teenager Jack Grammar cannot get a date for the prom until his friends play a practical joke and place a personal ad in the school online newspaper on his behalf. Now Jack has twenty-four dates and just seven days until the prom to figure out what to do.

**Brian, Kate.** *Lucky T*. Simon & Schuster Books for Young Readers, c2005. 291pp.

Carrie Fitzgerald has always been the luckiest girl in school, but what no one realizes is that she is also the most superstitious, attributing all her good luck to a T-shirt, so when Carrie's mom accidentally donates her lucky shirt to charity, Carrie's luck starts to run out, forcing her to travel halfway around the world to get it back.

**Juby, Susan.** *Alice Macleod, Realist at Last.* HarperTempest, c2005. 312pp.

After her boyfriend goes to Scotland, her mother is jailed for environmental activism, and her depressed father cannot get a job, sixteen-year-old Alice uses her screenwriting aspirations to help her get through a challenging period in her life.

# Hybrid Literature, Parallel Novels: A Different Perspective

The following entries pair up a contemporary book with a related classic.
Compiled by Eileen Culkin, Librarian, Inter-Lakes Jr. Sr. High School, Meredith, New Hampshire.

***I, Tituba, Black Witch of Salem* by Maryse Conde.** Ballantine Books, c1994.
Fictional account of the true story of the West Indian slave, Tituba, who was accused of witchcraft in Salem, Massachusetts in 1692.

For ***The Crucible* by Arthur Miller.** Penguin Books, c2003.
A vengeful teenager in Salem in 1692 accuses her former lover and his wife of witchcraft. Includes an introduction.

***Jane Fairfax* by Joan Aiken.** St. Martin's Press, c1991.
Sequel to *Emma* by Jane Austen.

For ***Emma* by Jane Austen.** Penguin Books, c2003.
Emma, a self-assured young lady in Regency England, is determined to arrange her life and the lives of those around her in a pattern dictated by her romantic fancy.

***Mansfield Revisited* by Joan Aiken.** Doubleday, c1985.
Sequel to *Mansfield Park* by Jane Austen.

For ***Mansfield Park* by Jane Austen.** Penguin Books, c2003.
Fanny Price, a teenage girl of low social rank brought up on her wealthy relatives' country estate, feels the sharp sting of rejection when her cousin Edmund, the only person who treats her as an equal, is won over by a flirtatious, exciting—and unprincipled—girl from London.

***Mr. Darcy's Daughters* by Elizabeth Aston.** Touchstone, c2003.
A sequel to Jane Austen's *Pride and Prejudice.* Imagines the adventures of Elizabeth and Darcy's five daughters alone in London twenty years after the close of Jane Austen's novel.

For ***Pride and Prejudice* by Jane Austen.** Penguin Books, c2003.
The fervent attempts of a gentlewoman to find husbands for her five daughters, which lead to the questionable pairing of the prejudiced Elizabeth with the proud Mr. Darcy.

***Wide Saragasso Sea* by Jean Rhys.** Buccaneer, c1966.
Story of a young woman in the Caribbean whose family's past will be used against her by her cold-hearted and prideful husband, Rochester.

For ***Jane Eyre* by Charlotte Brontë.** Knopf, c1991.
When a penniless governess falls in love with the brooding master of Thornfield, she is unaware of the tragic events that will follow.

***Mists of Avalon* by Marion Zimmer Bradley.** Ballantine Books, c2000.
A re-creation of the Arthurian legend following the clash between Christianity and paganism that led to the demise of Camelot.

From Nancy J. Keane, *The Big Book of Teen Reading Lists: 100 Great, Ready-to-Use Book Lists for Educators, Librarians, Parents, and Children.* Westport, CT: Libraries Unlimited, 2006. Copyright © 2006 by Libraries Unlimited.

# Hybrid Literature, Parallel Novels: A Different Perspective

For *Morte d'Arthur* by **Sir Thomas Malory.** Modern Library, c1994.
The standard account of King Arthur and his knights, the story of the dream of the Round Table, knightly honor, and a just earthly government, all lost through human frailty.

*Othello: A Novel* by **Julius Lester.** Scholastic, c1995.
A prose retelling of Shakespeare's play in which a jealous general is duped into thinking that his wife has been unfaithful, with tragic consequences.

For *Othello* by **William Shakespeare.** Oxford University Press, c2002.
About the damage caused by deceit and jealousy.

*Julie and Romeo: A Novel* by **Jeanne Ray.** Harmony Books, c2000.
Romeo Cacciamani and Julie Roseman, rival florists whose families have hated each other for generations, become attracted to one another after meeting at a small business seminar and embark on an exploration of their newly found love despite the interference of Julie's ex-husband, Romeo's mother, and a cast of grown children.

For *Romeo and Juliet* by **William Shakespeare.** Modern Library, c2001.
In medieval Verona, two teens from opposite sides of feuding families fall in love and secretly marry, which sets in motion tragic events.

*Romiette and Julio* by **Sharon Draper.** Atheneum Books, c1999.
Romiette, an African American girl, and Julio, a Hispanic boy, discover that they attend the same high school after falling in love on the Internet, but are harassed by a gang whose members object to their interracial dating.

For *Romeo and Juliet* by **William Shakespeare.** Modern Library, c2001.
In medieval Verona, two teens from opposite sides of feuding families fall in love and secretly marry, which sets in motion tragic events.

*Gertrude and Claudius* by **John Updike.** Knopf, c2000.
A fictional re-creation of the lives of Claudius and Gertrude, King and Queen of Denmark, in the years before the action of Shakespeare's *Hamlet* begins.

For *Hamlet* by **William Shakespeare.** Yale University Press, c2003.
Hamlet, the Prince of Denmark, struggles with the decision of whether or not to avenge his father's murder.

*Dating Hamlet: Ophelia's Story* by **Lisa Fielder.** H. Holt, c2002.
In a story based on the Shakespeare play, Ophelia describes her relationship with Hamlet, learns the truth about her own father, and recounts the complicated events following the murder of Hamlet's father.

For *Hamlet* by **William Shakespeare.** Yale University Press, c2003.
Hamlet, the Prince of Denmark, struggles with the decision of whether or not to avenge his father's murder.

# Hybrid Literature, Parallel Novels: A Different Perspective

*Blue Avenger Cracks the Code* by **Norma Howe.** H. Holt, c2000.
　　In his new identity as Blue Avenger, sixteen-year-old David visits Venice, Italy, and continues to pursue various crusades, including trying to solve the mystery of who really wrote Shakespeare's works.

　　For *The Merchant of Venice* by **William Shakespeare.** Cambridge University Press, c2002.
　　　　Dark comedy about young lovers and a Jewish money lender who demands a pound of flesh in payment for a debt.

*Third Witch* by **Rebecca Reisert.** Washington Square Press, c2001.
　　Gilly has spent her life hiding in the shadows of Birnam Woods, hoping to avoid persecution from the witch hunters who want to kill her and the two wise-women who took her in when she was a baby, but Gilly longs to learn the truth about the past that haunts her and the disturbing memories that she can't escape.

　　For *Macbeth* by **William Shakespeare.** Cambridge University Press, c1997.
　　　　A drama about a man who kills the King of Scotland in order to claim the throne for himself.

*Zeena* by **Elizabeth Cooke.** St. Martin's Press, c1996.
　　Retelling of Edith Wharton's *Ethan Frome,* focusing on the story of Zenobia Frome, depicting her as a young girl, then as a young woman who knows a brief moment of happiness before it is snatched from her by a tragic accident.

　　For *Ethan Frome* by **Edith Wharton.** Cambridge University Press, c1999.
　　　　The story of Ethan Frome, a New England farmer who is married to a hypochondriac, but in love with his wife's lively cousin, Mattie.

*Wicked* by **Gregory Maguire.** ReganBooks, c1995.
　　Elphaba, born with emerald green skin, comes of age in the land of Oz, rooming with debutante Glinda at the university, and following a path in life that earns her the label Wicked.

　　For *The Wizard of Oz* by **L. Frank Baum.** H. Holt, c2000.
　　　　After being transported by a cyclone to the land of Oz, Dorothy and her dog are befriended by a scarecrow, a tin man, and a cowardly lion, who accompany her to the Emerald City to look for a wizard who can help Dorothy return home to Kansas.

*Confessions of an Ugly Stepsister* by **Gregory Maguire.** ReganBooks, c1999.
　　Retells the story of Cinderella from one of her stepsisters' point of view.

　　For *Cinderella* by **Charles Perrault.** Atheneum Books, c1954.
　　　　In her haste to flee the palace before the fairy godmother's magic loses effect, Cinderella leaves behind a glass slipper.

*Ahab's Wife* by **Sena Jeter Naslund.** Morrow, c1999.
　　Una Spenser tells the story of her life and discusses her loving marriage to Captain Ahab before the white whale took his leg and drove him to madness.

　　For *Moby Dick* by **Herman Melville.** Knopf, c1991.
　　　　Captain Ahab's determination to find and kill the great white whale becomes an obsession driving him to disaster.

# Hybrid Literature, Parallel Novels: A Different Perspective

***Eaters of the Dead* by Michael Crichton.** Ballantine Books, c1992.
Ibn Fadlan sets out in A.D. 922 as an ambassador from Baghdad to the King of Saqaliba, but before he arrives, he meets Viking chieftain Buliwyf and joins him on a mission to Scandinavia, where they must battle the monsters threatening the land.

For ***Grendel* by John Gardner.** Vintage Books, c1989.
Grendel, the monster, tells his side of the Beowulf story and compares his values with the chief values of human beings.

***Grendel* by John Gardner.** Vintage Books, c1989.
Grendel, the monster, tells his side of the Beowulf story, and compares his values with the chief values of human beings.

For ***Beowulf.*** Penguin Books, c1995.
Tells the story of the hero Beowulf, slayer of the monster Grendel.

***Rebecca* by Daphne du Maurier.** Doubleday, c1938.
For months after her death, the memory of Rebecca de Winter continues to dominate everyone at her former home, Manderley, one of the most famous English country houses.

For ***The Fall of the House of Usher* by Edgar Allan Poe.** Signet, c1998.
After a long journey, Philip arrives at the Usher mansion seeking his loved one, Madeline, only to find that she has become afflicted with a mysterious illness.

***Troy* by Adele Geras.** Harcourt, c2001.
The last weeks of the Trojan War find the women sick of tending the wounded, men tired of fighting, and bored gods and goddesses trying to find ways to stir things up.

For ***The Illiad* by Homer.** Farrar, Straus & Giroux, 2004.
Epic of the Trojan War and the struggle between Achilles and Hector that saved the Greeks and destroyed the Trojans.

***Ender's Game* by Orson Scott Card.** Starscape, c2002.
Ender, who is the product of genetic experimentation, may be the military genius Earth needs in its war against an alien enemy.

Also ***Ender's Shadow* by Orson Scott Card.** Tom Doherty, c1999.
Bean must overcome his past and prove to the recruiters at the Battle School that he can help save the planet from an alien invasion.

***Mary Reilly* by Valerie Martin.** Vintage Books, c2001.
Mary, employed by Dr. Jekyll, finds herself the keeper of her master's house, the guardian of his sanity, and the only one in possession of the dark knowledge that might save his life.

For ***Dr. Jekyll and Mr. Hyde* by Robert Louis Stevenson.** Signet Classic, c2003.
A respected London doctor invents a formula that turns him into an evil and ugly person who stalks the streets at night killing people, and by the time his friends discover his secret, it is too late.

From Nancy J. Keane, *The Big Book of Teen Reading Lists: 100 Great, Ready-to-Use Book Lists for Educators, Librarians, Parents, and Children.* Westport, CT: Libraries Unlimited, 2006. Copyright © 2006 by Libraries Unlimited.

# Hybrid Literature, Parallel Novels: A Different Perspective

*The Young Man and the Sea* **by Rodman Philbrick.** Blue Sky Press, c2004.
   After his mother's death, twelve-year-old Skiff Beaman decides that it is up to him to earn money to take care of himself and his father, so he undertakes a dangerous trip alone on the ocean off the coast of Maine to try to catch a huge bluefin tuna.

   For *The Old Man and the Sea* **by Ernest Hemmingway.** Scribner, c1996.
      An old fisherman battles the sea and sharks to bring home the giant marlin he caught.

*The Wind Done Gone* **by Alice Randall.** Houghton Mifflin, c2001.
   A parody of *Gone with the Wind,* retelling the Civil War story from the perspective of Cynara, the daughter born from the union of the master of Tara and the slave, Mammy.

   For *Gone with the Wind* **by Margaret Mitchell.** Scribner, c1964.
      After the Civil War sweeps away the genteel life to which she has been accustomed, Scarlett O'Hara sets out to salvage her plantation home.

*The Garden* **by Elsie V. Aidinoff.** HarperTempest, c2004.
   Retells the tale of the Garden of Eden from Eve's point of view, as Serpent teaches her everything from her own name to why she should eat the forbidden fruit, and then leaves her with Adam and the knowledge that her choice has made mankind free.

   For the Old Testament.

*In the Shadow of the Ark* **by Anne Provoost.** A. A. Levine, c2004.
   Re Jana, a young healer and masseuse, believes that Noah's son Ham, the married object of her affection, will save her and her family if his father's terrifying predictions about a great flood sent from God come true.

   For the Old Testament.

*Dark Sons* **by Nikki Grimes.** Hyperion Books, c2005.
   Alternating poems compare and contrast the conflicted feelings of Ishmael, son of the biblical patriarch Abraham, and Sam, a teenager in New York City, as they try to come to terms with being abandoned by their fathers and with the love they feel for their younger stepbrothers.

   For the Old Testament.

*My Jim* **by Nancy Rawles.** Crown, c2005.
   Ex-slave Sadie Watson reveals to her granddaughter her experiences while in bondage and the love she had for her husband, Jim, who escaped down the Mississippi with Huck Finn when he learned he was to be sold.

   For *Huckleberry Finn* **by Mark Twain.** Modern Library, c1993.
      Huck, in flight from his murderous father, and Jim, in flight from slavery, pilot their raft down the Mississippi River in search of freedom.

# Jazz

## Books for Ages 12–15

**Collier, James Lincoln.** *The Jazz Kid.* H. Holt, c1994. 216pp.
 Playing the coronet is the first thing that twelve-year-old Paulie Horvath has taken seriously, but his obsession with becoming a jazz musician leads him into conflict with his parents and into the tough underworld of Chicago in the 1920s.

**Curtis, Christopher Paul.** *Bud, Not Buddy.* Delacorte Press, c1999. 245pp.
 Ten-year-old Bud, a motherless boy living in Flint, Michigan, during the Great Depression, escapes a bad foster home and sets out in search of the man he believes to be his father—the renowned bandleader, H. E. Calloway of Grand Rapids.

**Delaney, Mark.** *Growler's Horn.* Peachtree, c2000. 232pp.
 The theft of Jake's clarinet leads him and his friends to investigate other mysterious occurrences, including the theft of millions and the disappearance of an up-and-coming jazz musician.

**Levine, Gail Carson.** *Dave at Night.* HarperTrophy, 2001, c1999. 281pp.
 When orphaned Dave is sent to the Hebrew Home for Boys, where he is treated cruelly, he sneaks out at night and is welcomed into the music- and culture-filled world of the Harlem Renaissance.

**Mack, Tracy.** *Birdland*. Scholastic Press, c2003. 198pp.
 Thirteen-year-old Jed spends Christmas break working on a school project filming a documentary about his East Village, New York City, neighborhood, where he is continually reminded of his older brother, Zeke, a promising poet who died the summer before.

**Townley, Rod.** *Sky: A Novel in Three Sets and an Encore.* Atheneum Books for Young Readers, c2004. 265pp.
 In New York City in 1959, fifteen-year-old Alec Schuyler, at odds with his widowed father over his love of music, finds a mentor and friend in a blind, black jazz musician.

## Books for Older Teens

**Fleming, Charles.** *After Havana.* St. Martin's Minotaur, c2004. 340pp.
 White jazz musician Peter Sloan, nursing his wounded heart in Havana in 1958, feels renewed hope when his lost love, Anita, arrives in town, even though she is accompanied by her new paramour, real estate magnate Nick Calloway, but things start to go bad when Anita is kidnapped by revolutionaries and Sloan, Calloway, and security guard Luis go after her.

**Fulmer, David.** *Chasing the Devil's Tail.* Poisoned Pen Press, c2001. 320pp.
 Creole detective Valentin St. Cyr encounters an extraordinary cast of characters when he sets out to discover why prostitutes are being murdered in Storyville, New Orleans in 1907, at the same time that the jazz age is born.

**Fulmer, David.** *Jass*. Harcourt, c2005. 334pp.
 In 1909 New Orleans, Creole detective Valentin St. Cyr investigates the murders of four musicians and uncovers a link to a woman with a shadowy past and an ulterior motive.

# Jazz

**Hill, Laban Carrick.** *Harlem Stomp!: A Cultural History of the Harlem Renaissance.* Little, Brown, c2003. 151pp. (NF)

Offers a cultural history of the Harlem Renaissance, discussing how it sparked a period of intellectual, artistic, literary, and political blossoming for many African Americans.

**Holmes, Rupert.** *Swing: A Mystery.* Random House, c2005. 372pp.

Jazz saxophonist and arranger Ray Sherwood is haunted by personal tragedy, but when a talented student asks him to help orchestrate a new composition, Ray finds himself drawn to the coed. Their involvement soon causes more problems for Ray and threatens everything he has accomplished. Includes an audio CD-ROM.

**Islas, Arturo.** *La Mollie and the King of Tears: A Novel.* University of New Mexico Press, c1996. 199pp.

Jazz musician Louie Mendoza, speaking from his hospital bed, recounts the events of his harrowing day as he waits to learn the fate of his lover, La Mollie.

**Mackey, Nathaniel.** *Atet, A.D.* City Lights Books, c2001. 184pp.

The third in the From a Broken Bottle Traces of Perfume Still Emanate series, presented in the form of letters written over the course of seven months by N, one of the founding members of a band originally known as the Mystic Horn Society, in which he relates the adventures of the group.

**Mallon, Thomas.** *Bandbox.* Pantheon Books, c2004. 305pp.

Joe Harris, editor of the hugely successful Jazz Age magazine *Bandbox,* becomes engaged in a cutthroat competition to keep himself and his magazine on top when his most ambitious protégé starts up a rival publication, challenging Harris for stories on the stock market, Hollywood, the mob, and other sensational news of the era.

**Moody, Bill.** *Looking for Chet Baker: An Evan Horne Mystery.* Walker, c2002. 253pp.

Pianist Evan Horne, on tour in Europe, is distracted from his music when his friend Ace Buffington disappears while investigating the death of jazz trumpeter Chet Baker, who died on the sidewalk alongside the Prins Hendrik Hotel in Amsterdam.

**Wall, Alan.** *China.* Thomas Dunne Books, 2004, c2003. 378pp.

Aging china company heir Digby Walton considers his life and legacy, accepting the blame for his failed marriage and soured relationship with his son, Theo, a jazz musician, while his companion Daisy, a former actress, struggles to understand her own son, who is involved in an international anarchist movement.

# Keeping 'Em on Their Toes

## Books for Ages 12–15

**Abelove, Joan.** *Go and Come Back.* Puffin Books, 2000, c1998. 176pp.
Alicia, a young tribeswoman living in a village in the Amazonian jungle of Peru, tells about the two American women anthropologists who arrive to study her people's way of life.

**Bauer, Joan.** *Thwonk.* Putnam, 2001, c1995. 215pp.
A cupid doll comes to life and offers romantic assistance to A.J., a teenage photographer suffering from unrequited love.

**Cormier, Robert.** *The Rag and Bone Shop: A Novel.* Delacorte Press, c2001. 154pp.
Trent, an ace interrogator from Vermont, works to procure a confession from an introverted twelve-year-old accused of murdering his seven-year-old friend in Monument, Massachusetts.

**Dickinson, Peter.** *Eva.* Bantam Doubleday Dell Books for Young Readers, 1990, c1988. 219pp.
After a terrible accident, a young girl wakes up to discover that she has been given the body of a chimpanzee.

**Flinn, Alex.** *Fade to Black.* HarperTempest, c2005. 184pp.
An HIV-positive high school student hospitalized after being attacked; the bigot accused of the crime; and the only witness, a classmate with Down Syndrome, reveal how the assault has changed their lives as they tell about its aftermath.

**Plum-Ucci, Carol.** *The Body of Christopher Creed.* Harcourt, c2000. 248pp.
Torey Adams, a high school junior with a seemingly perfect life, struggles with doubts and questions surrounding the mysterious disappearance of the class outcast.

**Sleator, William.** *The Last Universe.* Amulet Books, c2005. 215pp.
When her desperately ill older brother insists that she take him into their mysterious backyard garden, designed by their quantum physicist great uncle, fourteen-year-old Susan discovers that things are not always what they seem.

## Books for Older Teens

**Flinn, Alexandra.** *Breathing Underwater.* HarperCollins, c2001. 263pp.
Sent to counseling for hitting his girlfriend, Caitlin, and ordered to keep a journal, sixteen-year-old Nick recounts his relationship with Caitlin, examines his controlling behavior and anger, and describes living with his abusive father.

**Giles, Gail.** *Shattering Glass.* Roaring Brook Press, c2002. 215pp.
Rob, the charismatic leader of the senior class, provokes unexpected violence when he turns the school nerd into Prince Charming.

**Lester, Julius.** *When Dad Killed Mom.* Harcourt, c2001. 183pp.
After their college psychologist father kills their artist mother, young Jenna and Jeremy struggle with the secret each of them keeps.

# Keeping 'Em on Their Toes

**Myers, Walter Dean.** *Monster*. HarperCollins, c1999. 281pp.

    While on trial as an accomplice to a murder, sixteen-year-old Steve Harmon records his experiences in prison and in the courtroom in the form of a film script as he tries to come to terms with the course his life has taken.

**Werlin, Nancy.** *The Killer's Cousin*. Dell Laurel-Leaf, 2000, c1998. 229pp.

    After being acquitted of murder, seventeen-year-old David goes to stay with relatives in Cambridge, Massachusetts, where he finds himself forced to face his past as he learns more about his strange young cousin, Lily.

**Werlin, Nancy.** *Locked Inside*. Dell Laurel-Leaf, 2001, c2000. 259pp.

    After she is kidnapped from the exclusive boarding school she attends, heiress Marnie Skyedottir must rethink her idealized relationship with her mother, her own sense of who she is, and her relationships with others.

# Novels in Verse

## Books for Ages 12–15

**Carvell, Marlene.** *Who Will Tell My Brother?* Hyperion Paperbacks for Children, 2004, c2002. 150pp.
During his lonely crusade to remove offensive mascots from his high school, a Native American teenager learns more about his heritage, his ancestors, and his place in the world.

**Creech, Sharon.** *Love That Dog.* Joanna Cotler Books, c2001. 86pp.
A young student, who comes to love poetry through a personal understanding of what different famous poems mean to him, surprises himself by writing his own inspired poem.

**Fields, Terri.** *After the Death of Anna Gonzales.* H. Holt, c2002. 100pp.
Poems written in the voices of forty-seven people, including students, teachers, and other school staff, record the aftermath of a high school student's suicide and the preoccupations of teen life.

**Frost, Helen.** *Spinning Through the Universe: A Novel in Poems from Room 214.* Farrar, Straus & Giroux, c2004. 93pp.
A collection of poems written in the voices of Mrs. Williams of room 214, her students, and a custodian about their interactions with each other, their families, and the world around them. Includes notes on the poetic forms represented.

**Glenn, Mel.** *Foreign Exchange: A Mystery in Poems.* Morrow Junior Books, c1999. 159pp.
A series of poems reflect the thoughts of various people—town residents young and old, teachers, and some students visiting from the city—caught up in the events surrounding the murder of a beautiful high school student who had recently moved to the small lakeside community of Hudson Landing.

**Glenn, Mel.** *Jump Ball: A Basketball Season in Poems.* Lodestar Books, c1997. 151pp.
Tells the story of a high school basketball team's season through a series of poems reflecting the feelings of students, their families, teachers, and coaches.

**Grimes, Nikki.** *Bronx Masquerade.* Dial Books, c2002. 167pp.
While studying the Harlem Renaissance, students at a Bronx high school read aloud poems they've written, revealing their innermost thoughts and fears to their formerly clueless classmates.

**Hesse, Karen.** *Aleutian Sparrow.* Margaret K. McElderry Books, c2003. 156pp.
An Aleutian Islander recounts her suffering during World War II in American internment camps designed to "protect" the population from the invading Japanese.

**Hesse, Karen.** *Out of the Dust.* Scholastic Press, c1997. 227pp.
In a series of poems, fifteen-year-old Billie Jo relates the hardships of living on her family's wheat farm in Oklahoma during the dust bowl years of the Great Depression.

**Hesse, Karen.** *Witness.* Scholastic Press, c2001. 161pp.
A series of poems express the views of various people in a small Vermont town, including a young black girl and a young Jewish girl, during the early 1920s when the Ku Klux Klan is trying to infiltrate the town.

**Johnson, Lindsay Lee.** *Soul Moon Soup.* Front Street, c2002. 134pp.
After her father leaves and Phoebe and her mother are struggling to survive in the city, Phoebe finally goes to the country to live with her grandmother, where she learns family secrets and hopes her mother will return for her.

# Novels in Verse

**Koertge, Ronald.** *Shakespeare Bats Cleanup.* Candlewick Press, c2003. 116pp.
> When a fourteen-year-old baseball player catches mononucleosis, he discovers that keeping a journal and experimenting with poetry not only helps fill the time, it also helps him deal with life, love, and loss.

**Rylant, Cynthia.** *God Went to Beauty School.* HarperTempest, c2003. 56pp.
> A novel in poems that reveal God's discovery of the wonders and pains in the world He has created.

**Sones, Sonya.** *One of Those Hideous Books Where the Mother Dies.* Simon & Schuster Books for Young Readers, c2004. 268pp.
> Fifteen-year-old Ruby Milliken leaves her best friend, her boyfriend, her aunt, and her mother's grave in Boston and reluctantly flies to Los Angeles to live with her father, a famous movie star who divorced her mother before Ruby was born.

**Sones, Sonya.** *Stop Pretending: What Happened When My Big Sister Went Crazy.* HarperTempest, 2001, c1999. 149pp.
> A younger sister has a difficult time adjusting to life after her older sister has a mental breakdown.

**Sones, Sonya.** *What My Mother Doesn't Know.* Simon & Schuster Books for Young Readers, c2001. 259pp.
> Sophie describes her relationships with a series of boys as she searches for Mr. Right.

**Testa, Maria.** *Becoming Joe DiMaggio.* Candlewick Press, c2002. 51pp.
> Joseph Paul grows up following the career of baseball great Joe DiMaggio and learning the rules of the game from his grandfather, dreaming of becoming a famous baseball player himself and somehow healing his grandfather's broken heart.

**Testa, Maria.** *Something About America.* Candlewick Press, c2005. 84pp.
> A collection of poems that relate a fictional story, inspired by actual events, in which a young girl struggles with the difficulty of growing up in America as an immigrant from Kosova, Yugoslavia.

**Turner, Ann.** *Learning to Swim: A Memoir.* Scholastic, c2000. 115pp.
> A series of poems convey the feelings of a young girl whose sense of joy and security at the family's summer house is shattered when an older boy who lives nearby sexually abuses her.

**Wayland, April Halprin.** *Girl Coming in for a Landing: A Novel in Poems.* Knopf (distributed by Random House), c2002. 134pp.
> A collection of over 100 poems recounting the ups and downs of one adolescent girl's school year.

**Wolff, Virginia Euwer.** *Make Lemonade.* H. Holt, c1993. 200pp. (and sequels)
> Fourteen-year-old LaVaughn, trying to earn money for college, takes a job caring for the two children of Jolly, a single teenage mom, and must find the courage to make the right decision for all of them after Jolly is fired from her job.

**Woodson, Jacqueline.** *Locomotion.* Putnam, c2003. 100pp.
> Inspired by his teacher, eleven-year-old Lonnie begins to write about his life in a series of poems in which he discusses his feelings about his friends, his foster mom, his little sister Lili, and the death of his parents.

# Novels in Verse

## Books for Older Teens

**Corrigan, Eireann.** *You Remind Me of You: A Poetry Memoir.* Push/Scholastic, c2002. 123pp.
A collection of poems in which the author details her struggle with eating disorders and her changed outlook on life after the suicide attempt of her boyfriend.

**Frost, Helen.** *Keesha's House.* Farrar, Straus & Giroux, c2003. 116pp.
Seven teens facing such problems as pregnancy, closeted homosexuality, and abuse each describe in poetic forms what caused them to leave home and where they found home again.

**Glenn, Mel.** *Split Image: A Story in Poems.* HarperCollins, c2000. 159pp.
A series of poems reflect the thoughts and feelings of various people—students, the librarian, parents, the principal, and others—about the seemingly perfect Laura Li and her life inside and out of Tower High School.

**Hahn, Mary Downing.** *The Wind Blows Backward.* Clarion Books, c1993. 263pp.
Although they share a love of poetry and problems with their parents, a shy high school senior's attraction to a popular classmate is tempered by her fear of his moody, self-destructive side.

**Hemphill, Stephanie.** *Things Left Unsaid: A Novel in Poems.* Hyperion, c2005. 261pp.
After a lifetime of conforming to the image of what her parents and high school friends want her to be, Sarah must come to terms with her own identity when her destructive best friend tries to commit suicide. Told in the form of free-verse poems.

**Herrera, Juan Felipe.** *Crashboomlove: A Novel in Verse.* University of New Mexico Press, c1999. 155pp.
After his father leaves home, sixteen-year-old Cesar Garcia lives with his mother and struggles through the painful experiences of growing up as a Mexican American high school student.

**Herrick, Steven.** *A Place Like This.* Simon Pulse, c2004. 137pp.
A verse novel set in Australia in which two young lovers postpone college to embark on a road trip and find themselves working at an apple orchard, where they become immersed in the life of the owner's teenage daughter, who is pregnant as the result of rape.

**Herrick, Steven.** *The Simple Gift.* Simon Pulse, 2004, c2000. 188pp.
Sixteen-year-old Billy runs away from his alcoholic, abusive father and takes up residence in an abandoned freight car, where he meets Old Bill, a fellow hobo, and together they form a friendship based on small kindnesses that change their lives.

**High, Linda Oatman.** *Sister Slam and the Poetic Motormouth Roadtrip.* Bloomsbury (distributed by Holtzbrinck), c2004. 256pp.
In this novel told in slam verse, after graduating from high school best friends and aspiring poets Laura and Twig embark on a road trip from Pennsylvania to New York City, to compete at slam poetry events.

**Johnson, Angela.** *The First Part Last.* Simon & Schuster Books for Young Readers, c2003. 131pp.
Bobby's carefree teenage life changes forever when he becomes a father and must care for his adored baby daughter.

# Novels in Verse

**Koertge, Ronald.** *The Brimstone Journals.* Candlewick Press, c2001. 113pp.
In a series of short, interconnected poems, students at a high school nicknamed Brimstone reveal the violence existing and growing in their lives.

**Rosenberg, Liz.** *17: A Novel in Prose Poems.* Cricket Books, c2002. 142pp.
Seventeen-year-old Stephanie journeys from fall to spring and from childhood to womanhood as she experiences first love and deals with her fear of inheriting her mother's mental illness.

**Wild, Margaret.** *Jinx.* Simon Pulse, 2004, c2002. 215pp.
With the help of her understanding mother and a close friend, Jen eventually outgrows her nickname, Jinx, and deals with the deaths of two boys with whom she had been involved.

**Wild, Margaret.** *One Night.* Knopf (distributed by Random House), 2004, c2003. 236pp.
In this novel written in free verse and narrated by alternating characters, after a "one night stand" results in pregnancy, a teenage girl decides to have her baby and care for it on her own.

# Short and Sweet

## Books for Ages 12–15

**Avi.** *Nothing But the Truth: A Documentary Novel.* Orchard Books, 2003, c1991. 177pp.
A ninth-grader's suspension for singing "The Star-Spangled Banner" during homeroom becomes a national news story; one of the consequences is that he and his teacher both leave the school.

**Blume, Judy.** *Blubber.* Atheneum Books for Young Readers, 2001, c1974. 153pp.
Jill goes along with the rest of the fifth-grade class in tormenting a classmate and then finds out what it's like when she, too, becomes a target.

**Bunting, Eve.** *Blackwater.* Joanna Cotler Books, 2000, c1999. 146pp.
When a boy and girl are drowned in the Blackwater River, thirteen-year-old Brodie must decide whether to confess that he may have caused the accident.

**Cushman, Karen.** *The Midwife's Apprentice.* Clarion Books, c1995. 122pp.
In medieval England, a nameless, homeless girl is taken in by a sharp-tempered midwife, and in spite of obstacles and hardship, eventually gains the three things she most wants: a full belly, a contented heart, and a place in this world.

**Flake, Sharon.** *Money Hungry.* Jump at the Sun/Hyperion Books for Children, c2001. 187pp.
All thirteen-year-old Raspberry can think of is making money so that she and her mother never have to worry about living on the streets again.

**Fleischman, Paul.** *Seek.* Cricket Books, c2001. 167pp.
Rob becomes obsessed with searching the airwaves for his long-gone father, a radio announcer.

**Haddix, Margaret Peterson.** *Among the Hidden.* Simon & Schuster Books for Young Readers, c1998. 153pp.
In a future where the Population Police enforce the law limiting a family to only two children, Luke has lived all his twelve years in isolation and fear on his family's farm, until another "third" convinces him that the government is wrong.

**Hamilton, Virginia.** *Bluish: a Novel.* Blue Sky Press, c1999. 127pp.
Ten-year-old Dreenie feels both intrigued and frightened when she thinks about the girl nicknamed Bluish, whose leukemia is making her pale and causing her to use a wheelchair.

**Hautman, Pete.** *Invisible.* Simon & Schuster Books for Young Readers, c2005. 149pp.
Doug and Andy are unlikely best friends—one a loner obsessed by his model trains, the other a popular student involved in football and theater—who grew up together and share a bond that nothing can sever.

**Johnson, Angela.** *Toning the Sweep.* Scholastic, 1994, c1993. 103pp.
On a visit to her grandmother Ola, who is dying of cancer in her house in the desert, fourteen-year-old Emmie hears many stories about the past and her family history.

**Lester, Julius.** *Day of Tears: A Novel in Dialogue.* Jump at the Sun/Hyperion Books for Children, c2005. 177pp.
Historical fiction written in first-person format that follows Emma, the slave of Pierce Butler, through a series of events in her life as her master hosts the largest slave auction in American history in Savannah, Georgia, in 1859 in order to pay off his mounting gambling debts.

# Short and Sweet

**McDonald, Janet.** *Twists and Turns*. Farrar, Straus & Giroux, c2003. 135pp.

With the help of a couple of successful friends, eighteen- and nineteen-year-old Teesha and Keeba try to capitalize on their talents by opening a hair salon in the run-down Brooklyn housing project where they live.

**Sleator, William.** *Rewind*. Puffin Books, 2001, c1999. 120pp.

Not long after learning that he was adopted, eleven-year-old Peter is hit by a car and then given several chances to alter events that could lead to his death.

## Books for Older Teens

**Anderson, M. T.** *Burger Wuss*. Candlewick Press, 2001, c1999. 192pp.

Hoping to lose his loser image, Anthony plans revenge on a bully, which results in a war between two competing fast food restaurants, Burger Queen and O'Dermott's.

**Cormier, Robert.** *The Rag and Bone Shop: A Novel.* Delacorte Press, c2001. 154pp.

Trent, an ace interrogator from Vermont, works to procure a confession from an introverted twelve-year-old accused of murdering his seven-year-old friend in Monument, Massachusetts.

**Koertge, Ronald.** *Stoner & Spaz*. Candlewick Press, c2002. 169pp.

A troubled youth with cerebral palsy struggles toward self-acceptance with the help of a drug-addicted young woman.

**Myers, Walter Dean.** *The Beast.* Scholastic, c2003. 170pp.

A teenager from Harlem struggles to save his girlfriend from herself when she develops a drug problem while he is away at a Connecticut prep school.

# Tearjerkers

## Books for Ages 12–15

**Abelove, Joan.** *Saying It Out Loud.* Puffin Books, 2001, c1999. 136pp.
With the help of her best friend, sixteen-year-old Mindy sorts through her relationships with her solicitous mother and her detached father as she tries to come to terms with the fact that her mother is dying from a brain tumor.

**Banks, Kate.** *Walk Softly, Rachel.* Farrar, Straus & Giroux, c2003. 149pp.
When fourteen-year-old Rachel reads the journal of her brother, who died when she was seven, she learns secrets that help her understand her parents and herself.

**Bechard, Margaret.** *Hanging on to Max.* Roaring Brook Press, c2002. 142pp.
When his girlfriend decides to give their baby away, seventeen-year-old Sam is determined to keep him and raise him alone.

**Blume, Judy.** *Tiger Eyes.* Bantam Doubleday Dell Books for Young Readers, 1991, c1981. 217pp.
Resettled in New Mexico with her mother and brother, Davey Wexler recovers from the shock of her father's death during a holdup of his 7-Eleven store in Atlantic City.

**Cooney, Caroline B.** *Driver's Ed.* Bantam Doubleday Dell Books for Young Readers, 1996, c1994. 199pp.
Three teenagers' lives are changed forever when they thoughtlessly steal a stop sign from a dangerous intersection and a young mother is killed in an automobile accident there.

**Creech, Sharon.** *Walk Two Moons.* HarperCollins, c1994. 280pp.
After her mother leaves home suddenly, thirteen-year-old Sal and her grandparents take a car trip retracing her mother's route. Along the way, Sal recounts the story of her friend Phoebe, whose mother also left.

**Crist-Evans, Craig.** *Amaryllis*. Candlewick Press, c2003. 184pp.
Jimmy and his older brother Frank share a love of surfing and their problems with a drunken father, until Frank turns eighteen and goes to Vietnam.

**Deans, Sis Boulos.** *Every Day and All the Time.* H. Holt, c2003. 234pp.
Eleven-year-old Emily, still reeling from the car accident that took her older brother's life and badly injured her, uses psychotherapy and ballet dancing to cope with her parents' decision to sell their house—the only place she can still feel and talk to her brother.

**Deaver, Julie Reece.** *Say Goodnight, Gracie.* HarperCollins, 1989, c1988. 214pp.
When a car accident kills her best friend Jimmy, with whom she has shared everything from childhood escapades to entering the professional theater in Chicago, seventeen-year-old Morgan must find her own way to cope with his death.

**Draper, Sharon M.** *Tears of a Tiger*. Atheneum, Maxwell Macmillan International, c1994. 162pp.
The death of high school basketball star Rob Washington in an automobile accident affects the lives of his close friend Andy, who was driving the car, and many others in the school.

**Johnson, Angela.** *The First Part Last.* Simon & Schuster Books for Young Readers, c2003. 131pp.
Sixteen-year-old Bobby finds out that he is going to become a father, and suddenly all the things that seemed important to him before are insignificant, as he and his girlfriend, Nia, try to sort out the situation and decide what to do.

From Nancy J. Keane, *The Big Book of Teen Reading Lists: 100 Great, Ready-to-Use Book Lists for Educators, Librarians, Parents, and Children*. Westport, CT: Libraries Unlimited, 2006. Copyright © 2006 by Libraries Unlimited.

# Tearjerkers

**Kadohata, Cynthia.** *Kira-Kira.* Atheneum Books for Young Readers, c2004. 244pp.
Chronicles the close friendship between two Japanese American sisters growing up in rural Georgia during the late 1950s and early 1960s, and the despair when one sister becomes terminally ill.

**Lewis, Catherine** *Postcards to Father Abraham: A Novel.* Atheneum Books for Young Readers, c2000. 288pp.
When sixteen-year-old Meghan loses her leg to cancer and her brother to the Vietnamese War, she expresses intense anger in postcards that she writes to her idol, Abraham Lincoln.

**Lowry, Lois.** *A Summer to Die.* Houghton Mifflin, c1977. 154pp.
Thirteen-year-old Meg is envious of her sister's beauty and popularity. Her feelings don't make it any easier for her to cope with Molly's strange illness and eventual death.

**McDaniel, Lurlene.** *Garden of Angels.* Dell Laurel-Leaf, 2005, c2003. 272pp.
Fourteen-year-old Darcy's life undergoes a drastic change when her mother is diagnosed with breast cancer in 1974 and is unable to help Darcy deal with the teenage struggles of starting high school, falling in love, and worrying about the Vietnam War.

**Park, Barbara.** *Mick Harte Was Here.* Random House, 1996, c1995. 89pp.
Thirteen-year-old Phoebe recalls the death of her younger brother Mick in a bicycle accident, which might not have been fatal had he been wearing his helmet, and how she and her family reacted to the tragedy. Closes with an appeal to bikers to wear protective bicycle helmets.

**Peck, Richard.** *Remembering the Good Times*. Bantam Doubleday Dell Books for Young Readers, 1986, c1985. 181pp.
Trav, Kate, and Buck make up a trio during their freshman year in high school, but their special friendship may not be enough to save Trav as he pressures himself relentlessly to succeed.

**Pfeffer, Susan Beth.** *The Year Without Michael.* Delacorte Press, 2003, c1987, 164pp.
The remaining members of the Chapman family try to cope with the disappearance of fourteen-year-old Michael.

## Books for Older Teens

**Berg, Elizabeth.** *Never Change.* Washington Square Press, 2002, c2001. 214pp.
Myra Lipinsky, a fifty-one-year-old visiting nurse who never married and has resigned herself to a solitary life with her dog, crosses paths with the man she admired from afar in high school when he becomes one of her patients—one with a terminal illness.

**Berg, Elizabeth.** *Range of Motion.* Berkley Books, c2000. 251pp.
Lainey must draw on a number of sources to keep her faith strong when her husband, Jay, is injured in an accident and lingers in a coma.

**Brooks, Kevin.** *Lucas.* Chicken House/Scholastic, c2003. 423pp.
On an isolated English island, fifteen-year-old Caitlin McCann makes the painful journey from adolescence to adulthood through her experiences with a mysterious boy, whose presence has an unsettling effect on the island's inhabitants.

# Tearjerkers

**Cook, Karin.** *What Girls Learn: A Novel.* Vintage Contemporaries, 1998, c1997. 304pp.

Tilden and her younger sister Elizabeth are uprooted again when their ever optimistic, romantic mother Frances moves them north to live with Nick, the owner of a limousine service., Everything seems to be going just fine until Frances discovers a lump in her breast.

**Crutcher, Chris.** *Whale Talk.* Greenwillow Books, c2001. 220pp.

Intellectually and athletically gifted, TJ, a multiracial, adopted teenager, shuns organized sports and the gung-ho athletes at his high school, until he agrees to form a swimming team and recruits some of the school's less popular students.

**Frank, E. R.** *America: A Novel.* Atheneum Books for Young Readers, c2002. 242pp.

America, a runaway boy who is being treated at Ridgeway, a New York hospital, finds himself opening up to one of the doctors on staff and revealing things about himself that he had always vowed to keep secret.

**Giles, Gail.** *Shattering Glass.* Roaring Brook Press, c2002. 215pp.

Rob, the charismatic leader of the senior class, provokes unexpected violence when he turns the school nerd into Prince Charming.

**Hosseini, Khaled.** *The Kite Runner.* Riverhead Books, c2003. 324pp.

Amir, haunted by his betrayal of Hassan, the son of his father's servant and a childhood friend, returns to Kabul as an adult after he learns Hassan has been killed, in an attempt to redeem himself by rescuing Hassan's son from a life of slavery to a Taliban official.

**Hurwin, Davida.** *A Time for Dancing: A Novel.* Puffin Books, 1997, c1995. 257pp.

Seventeen-year-old best friends Samantha and Juliana tell their stories in alternating chapters after Juliana is diagnosed with cancer.

**Maynard, Joyce.** *The Usual Rules.* St. Martin's Griffin, 2004, c2003. 386pp.

Thirteen-year-old Wendy, grieving over the death of her mother in the collapse of the World Trade Center, is taken to live with her father in California, where she learns important life lessons from a variety of people before returning home to her stepfather and brother, where she feels she truly belongs.

**Orr, Wendy.** *Peeling the Onion.* Holiday House, c1997. 166pp.

Following an automobile accident in which her neck is broken, a teenage karate champion begins a long and painful recovery with the help of her family.

**Peck, Robert Newton.** *A Day No Pigs Would Die.* Knopf (distributed by Random House), c1999. 150pp.

To a thirteen-year-old Vermont farm boy whose father slaughters pigs for a living, maturity comes early as he learns "doing what's got to be done," especially regarding his pet pig who cannot produce a litter.

**Pennebaker, Ruth.** *Both Sides Now.* H. Holt, c2000. 202pp.

Fifteen-year-old Liza tries to deal with the normal everyday crises of life in an Austin, Texas, high school, a process complicated by her mother's fight with breast cancer.

**Sebold, Alice.** *The Lovely Bones: A Novel.* Little, Brown, c2002. 328pp.

Fourteen-year-old Susie Salmon, the victim of a sexual assault and murder, looks on from the afterlife as her family deals with their grief, and waits for her killer to be brought to some type of justice.

From Nancy J. Keane, *The Big Book of Teen Reading Lists: 100 Great, Ready-to-Use Book Lists for Educators, Librarians, Parents, and Children.* Westport, CT: Libraries Unlimited, 2006. Copyright © 2006 by Libraries Unlimited.

# Tearjerkers

**Shreve, Anita.** *The Pilot's Wife: A Novel.* Back Bay Books, 1999, c1998. 293pp. (adult)
Kathryn Lyon's life was peacefully routine, she had a good job and a happy marriage, so when she receives the news that her pilot husband has died in a crash, her world is drastically changed. Even before his body is recovered the media discover that her husband had a secret life, and Kathryn sets out to learn who her husband really was.

**Sparks, Nicholas.** *A Walk to Remember.* Warner Books, 2001, c1999. 240pp.
When a twist of fate made Jamie Sullivan his date at the homecoming dance, Landon Carter never dreamed they would fall in love, but as he comes to realize his true feelings for Jamie, he learns of a terrible secret that will take his love away from him forever.

**Strasser, Todd.** *Can't Get There from Here.* Simon & Schuster Books for Young Readers, c2004. 198pp.
Tired of being hungry, cold, and dirty living on the streets of New York City with a tribe of other homeless teenagers who are dying, one by one, a girl named Maybe ponders her future and longs for someone to care about her.

**Zeises, Lara M.** *Bringing up the Bones.* Delacorte Press, c2002. 213pp.
Bridget Edelstein mourns the loss of her high school boyfriend, who died in a car crash, and rebounds with a new love.

# True Adventure

Compiled by Beth Gallaway Youth Services Consultant/Trainer, Metrowest MA
Regional Library System, Waltham, Massachusetts.

**Armstrong. Jennifer.** *Shipwreck at the Bottom of the World: Shackleton's Incredible Voyage.* Crown, c2000. 134pp. (ages 12–15) (NF)
> Story of the explorer who attempted to visit the poles.

**Ballard, Robert.** *The Discovery of the Titanic.* Warner Books, c1995. 287pp. (ages 12–15) (NF)
> The oceanographe recounts his finding of the sunken ship *Titanic.*

**Bryson, Bill.** *A Walk in the Woods*: *Rediscovering America on the Appalachian Trail.* Broadway Books, c1999. 276pp. (older teens) (NF)
> One man's tale of trying to walk the entire Appalachian Trail.

**Callahan, Steve.** *Adrift: Seventy-Six Days Lost at Sea.* Houghton Mifflin, c2002. 237pp. (ages 12–15) (NF)
> Steven Callahan tells the story of his experiences after his small sloop capsized in the middle of the Atlantic Ocean and he was forced to survive in an inflatable raft for seventy-six days.

**Cordingly, David.** *Under the Black Flag: The Romance and Reality of Life Among the Pirates.* Harcourt, c1997. 296pp. (older teens) (NF)
> Exposes the truths and lies about piracy on the high seas.

**Davidson, Robyn.** *Tracks.* Vintage Books, c1995. 256pp. (older teens) (NF)
> The author chronicles her 1977 trek alone across Australia by camel at the age of twenty-seven, a journey shaped by discoveries about the country's land and indigenous peoples, and one that transformed her into a new person.

**Duncan, Lois.** *Who Killed My Daughter.* Dell, c1994. 354pp. (older teens) (NF)
> The novelist for teens tells the true story of her daughter's unsolved murder.

**Fendler, Donn.** *Lost on a Mountain in Maine.* Beech Tree Books, c1992. 109pp. (ages 12–15) (NF)
> A twelve-year-old describes his nine-day struggle to survive after being separated from his companions in the mountains of Maine in 1939.

**Gammelgaard, Lene.** *Climbing High: A Woman's Account of the Everest Tragedy.* Seal Press, c1999. 211pp. (older teens) (NF)
> Lene Gammelgaard, the first Scandinavian woman to summit Mount Everest, provides a step-by-step account of her weeks of training, her arrival in Nepal, and her climb to the peak of the world's highest mountain on May 10, 1996, and discusses the deadly storm that claimed the lives of eight members of the expedition.

**Graham, Robin Lee.** *The Boy Who Sailed Around the World Alone.* Golden Press, 1973. 140pp. (ages 12–15) (NF)
> Recounts the voyage of a California sixteen-year-old who spent nearly five years sailing around the world alone.

# True Adventure

**Krakauer, Jon.** *Into Thin Air: A Personal Account of the Mount Everest Disaster.* Villard, c1997. 293pp. (older teens) (NF)
> An outdoorsman reporter tackles the highest mountain.

**Kropp, Goran.** *Ultimate High: My Everest Odyssey.* Discovery Books, c1999. 227pp. (older teens) (NF)
> Account of a man who climbed Mt. Everest.

**Jenkins, Peter.** *Walk Across America.* Perennial, c2001. 290pp.(older teens) (NF)
> The author describes his experiences during the two years he spent walking across the United States, from Alfred, New York, to the Gulf of Mexico.

**Junger, Sebastian.** *The Perfect Storm: A True Story of Men Against the Sea.* W. W. Norton, c1997. 227pp. (older teens) (NF)
> Gloucester fishermen battle the elements in one of the worst storms ever.

**Mayes, Frances.** *Under the Tuscan Sun: At Home in Italy.* Chronicle Books, c1996. 280pp. (older teens) (NF)
> A couple purchase a villa and love life in Tuscany—rich with sights, smells, and tastes.

**Paulsen, Gary.** *Woodsong.* Simon & Schuster Books for Young Readers, c1990. 132pp. (ages 12–15) (NF)
> The popular author runs the Iditarod dogsled race across the Alaskan tundra.

**Paulsen, Gary.** *Winterdance: The Fine Madness of Running the Iditarod.* Harcourt, c1994. 256pp. (older teens) (NF)
> The YA novelist participates in the famous Alaskan dogsled race.

**Pfetzer, Mark.** *Within Reach: My Everest Story.* Puffin Books, c2000. 224pp. (ages 12–15) (NF)
> A teen struggles twice to become the youngest person to achieve the summit of Mt. Everest.

**Read, Piers Paul.** *Alive.* Avon Books, c1975. 318pp. (older teens) (NF)
> Story of plane crash victims who committed cannibalism to survive.

**Riddles, Libby.** *Race Across Alaska: First Woman to Win the Iditarod Tells Her Story.* Stackpole Books, c1988. 239pp. (older teens) (NF)
> Story of the Iditarod.

**Severin, Tim.** *The Ulysses Voyage: Sea Search for the Odyssey.* Dutton, c1987. 253pp. (older teens) (NF)
> Retraces Ulysses's logical homeward route using a replica of a Bronze Age galley.

**Sis, Peter.** *Tibet: Through the Red Box.* Farrar, Straus & Giroux, c1998. 57pp. (ages 12–15) (NF)
> Story of a man's travels through Communist China and into Tibet.

**Sobel, Dava.** *Longitude: The True Story of a Lone Genius Who Solved the Greatest Scientific Problem of His Time.* Walker, c1995. 184pp. (ages 12–15) (NF)
> Story of the discovery of longitude and its significance in navigation.

# Wordless

## Books for All Ages

**Aruego, Jose.** *Look What I Can Do.* Aladdin Paperbacks, 1988, c1971. 32pp.
   Two *carabaos* discover that being a copycat can lead to trouble.

**Baker, Jeannie.** *Home.* Greenwillow Books, c2004. 32pp.
   A wordless picture book that observes the changes in a neighborhood, from before a girl is born until she is an adult, as it first decays and then is renewed by the efforts of the residents.

**Baker, Jeannie.** *Window.* Greenwillow Books, c1991. 32pp.
   Chronicles the events and changes in a young boy's life and in his environment, from babyhood to adulthood, through wordless scenes observed from the window of his room.

**Banyai, Istvan.** *Re-zoom.* Puffin Books, 1998, c1995. 64pp.
   A wordless picture book presenting a series of scenes, each one from farther away, showing, for example, a boat that becomes the image on a magazine, which is held in a hand, which belongs to a boy, and so on.

**Banyai, Istvan.** *Zoom.* Viking Press, c1995. 64pp.
   A wordless picture book presenting a series of scenes, each from farther away, showing, for example, a girl playing with toys, which is actually a picture on a magazine cover, which is part of a sign on a bus, and so on.

**Blake, Quentin.** *Clown.* H. Holt, 1998, c1995. 32pp.
   After being discarded, Clown makes his way through town, having a series of adventures as he tries to find a home for himself and his other toy friends.

**Briggs, Raymond.** *The Snowman.* Random House, c1978. 32pp.
   A wordless book using over 175 picture frames to relate the story of the adventure shared by a little boy and the snowman he built in the yard.

**Carle, Eric.** *Do You Want to Be My Friend?* HarperCollins, c1976. 32pp.
   A mouse searches everywhere for a friend.

**Catalanotto, Peter.** *Dylan's Day Out.* Orchard Books, 1993, c1989, 32pp.
   In a story where almost everything is black and white, Dylan, a Dalmatian, escapes from his home and becomes involved in a soccer game between penguins and skunks.

**Collington, Peter.** *A Small Miracle.* Knopf, c1997. 16pp.
   The figures in a nativity scene come to life to help an old woman in need at Christmas.

**Day, Alexandra.** *Carl Goes Shopping.* Farrar, Straus & Giroux, c1989. 32pp.
   While his mistress shops, Carl, a large dog, and the baby in his care explore the department store quite thoroughly and have a wonderful time.

**Day, Alexandra.** *Carl Goes to Daycare.* Farrar, Straus & Giroux, c1993. 32pp.
   Carl the rottweiler takes charge when things take an unexpected turn at the day care center he is visiting.

# Wordless

**Day, Alexandra.** *Carl's Birthday.* Farrar, Straus & Giroux, c1995. 32pp.
Carl, a rottweiler, and Madeline fool her mother once again as they inspect his presents and cake for his surprise birthday party, all while she thinks they are taking a nap.

**Day, Alexandra.** *Good Dog, Carl.* Aladdin Paperbacks, 1997, c1985. 36pp.
Lively and unusual things happen when Carl the dog is left in charge of the baby.

**De Paola, Tomie.** *The Hunter and the Animals: A Wordless Picture Book.* Holiday House, c1981. 32pp.
When the discouraged hunter falls asleep, the forest animals play a trick on him.

**De Paola, Tomie.** *Pancakes for Breakfast.* Harcourt Brace, c1978. 32pp.
A little old lady's attempts to have pancakes for breakfast are hindered by a scarcity of supplies and the participation of her pets.

**Felix, Monique.** *The Boat.* Creative Education, c1993. 28pp.
A mouse trapped inside a book makes a boat out of paper and goes sailing.

**Felix, Monique.** *The Colors.* Creative Education, c1991. 28pp.
A mouse trapped in a book discovers what colors are.

**Felix, Monique.** *The House.* Creative Education, c1991. 30pp.
A little mouse trapped in a book makes a house.

**Felix, Monique.** *The Wind.* Stewart, Tabori & Chang, Creative Education, c1991. 30pp.
A little mouse trapped in a book discovers the wind.

**Hoban, Tana.** *Shadows and Reflections.* Greenwillow Books, c1990. 32pp.
Photographs without text feature shadows and reflections of various objects, animals, and people.

**Hutchins, Pat.** *Changes, Changes.* Aladdin Paperbacks, 1987, c1971. 32pp.
Two wooden dolls rearrange wooden building blocks to form various objects.

**Kalan, Robert.** *Blue Sea.* Mulberry, 1992, c1979. 24pp.
Several fishes of varying size introduce space relationships and size differences.

**Liu, Jae Soo.** *Yellow Umbrella.* Kane/Miller, c2002. 32pp.
Combines a wordless picture book, in which an increasing number of colorful umbrellas appear in the falling rain, with a CD of background music designed to enrich the images.

**Mayer, Mercer.** *A Boy, a Dog, a Frog and a Friend.* Dial Books for Young Readers, c1971. 32pp.
A boy, a dog, and a frog catch a turtle while fishing down by the pond. Soon the three friends become four.

**Mayer, Mercer.** *Frog Goes to Dinner.* Dial Books for Young Readers, c1974. 32pp.
When a boy goes with his parents to a fancy restaurant, Frog cannot resist the temptation to stow away in an empty pocket.

**Mayer, Mercer.** *One Frog Too Many.* Dial Books for Young Readers, 2003?, c1975. 32pp.
A boy's pet frog thinks that the new little frog the boy gets for his birthday is one frog too many.

# Wordless

**McCully, Emily Arnold.** *Four Hungry Kittens.* Dial Books for Young Readers, c2001. 32pp.

In this wordless story, four kittens share adventures while their mother is away hunting food.

**Ormerod, Jan.** *Moonlight.* Frances Lincoln Children's Books (distributed in the United States by Publishers Group West), 2004, c1982. 26pp.

As her parents attempt to help a child fall asleep at bedtime, they themselves become more and more sleepy.

**Ormerod, Jan.** *Sunshine.* Frances Lincoln Children's Books (distributed in the United States by Publishers Group West), 2004, c1981. 26pp.

Awakened by the sun, a little girl proceeds to wake her parents and sees that they all leave the house on time.

**Rohmann, Eric.** *Time Flies.* Crown, c1994. 32pp.

A wordless tale in which a bird flying around the dinosaur exhibit in a natural history museum has an unsettling experience when the dinosaurs seem to come alive and view the bird as a potential meal.

**Sneed, Brad.** *Picture a Letter.* Phyllis Fogelman Books, c2002. 32pp.

A wordless alphabet book in which the illustrations show people, objects, and animals that form the shapes of the individual letters.

**Spier, Peter.** *Noah's Ark.* Doubleday, c1977. 46pp.

Retells in pictures how a pair of every manner of creature climbed on board Noah's ark and thereby survived the Flood.

**Turkle, Brinton.** *Deep in the Forest.* Puffin Books, 1987, c1976. 32pp.

A curious bear explores a cabin in the forest, with disastrous results.

**Vincent, Gabrielle.** *A Day, a Dog.* Front Street, c2000. 64pp.

Pictures tell the story of a dog's day, from the moment he is abandoned on the highway until he finds a friend in a young boy.

**Weitzman, Jacqueline Preiss.** *You Can't Take a Balloon into the Museum of Fine Arts.* Dial Books for Young Readers, c2002. 35pp.

While a brother and sister, along with their grandparents, visit the Museum of Fine Arts, the balloon they were not allowed to bring into the museum floats around Boston, causing a series of mishaps at various tourist sites.

**Wiesner, David.** *Free Fall.* Lothrop, Lee & Shepard, c1988. 32pp.

A young boy dreams of daring adventures in the company of imaginary creatures inspired by the things surrounding his bed.

**Wiesner, David.** *Sector 7.* Clarion Books, c1999. 50pp.

While on a school trip to the Empire State Building, a boy is taken by a friendly cloud to visit Sector 7, where he discovers how clouds are shaped and channeled throughout the country.

**Wilson, April.** *April Wilson's Magpie Magic: A Tale of Colorful Mischief.* Dial Books for Young Readers, c1999. 36pp.

A wordless picture book that depicts a young artist who draws a picture of a magpie, which then comes to life and interacts with a series of colorful drawings.

# Part 2

## Characters

# Adventure with Female Protagonists

## Books for Ages 12–15

**Armstrong, Jennifer.** *The Kindling.* HarperCollins, c2002. 224pp. (and sequels)
In 2007, a small band of children have joined together in a Florida town, trying to survive in a world where it seems that all the adults have been killed off by a catastrophic virus.

**Avi.** *The True Confessions of Charlotte Doyle.* Orchard Books, 2003, c1990. 215pp.
Thirteen-year-old Charlotte Doyle, the only passenger aboard a seedy ship on a transatlantic voyage from England to America in 1832, becomes caught up in a feud between the murderous captain and his mutinous crew.

**Farmer, Nancy.** *A Girl Named Disaster.* Orchard Books, 2003, c1996. 309pp.
While journeying to Zimbabwe, eleven-year-old Nhamo struggles to escape drowning and starvation, and in so doing comes close to the luminous world of the African spirits.

**George, Jean Craighead.** *Julie of the Wolves.* HarperCollins, c1972. 170pp.
While running away from home and an unwanted marriage, a thirteen-year-old Eskimo girl becomes lost on the North Slope of Alaska and is befriended by a wolf pack.

**Kehret, Peg.** *The Secret Journey.* Pocket Books, c1999. 135pp.
In 1834 when a storm at sea destroys the slave ship on which she is a stowaway, twelve-year-old Emma musters all her resourcefulness to survive in the African jungle.

**Meyer, L. A.** *Bloody Jack: Being an Account of the Curious Adventures of Mary "Jacky" Faber, Ship's Boy.* Harcourt, c2002. 278pp. (and sequels)
Reduced to begging and thievery in the streets of London, a thirteen-year-old orphan disguises herself as a boy and connives her way onto a British warship destined for high sea adventure .

**Nelson, O. T.** *The Girl Who Owned a City.* Bantam Doubleday Dell Books for Young Readers, 1977, c1975. 189pp.
When a plague sweeps over the earth, killing everyone except children under twelve, ten-year-old Lisa organizes a group to rebuild a new way of life.

**Thesman, Jean.** *When the Road Ends.* Houghton Mifflin, c1992. 184pp.
Sent to spend the summer in the country, three foster children and a woman recovering from a serious accident are abandoned by their slovenly caretaker and must try to survive on their own.

## Books for Older Teens

**Marsden, John.** *Tomorrow, When the War Began.* Houghton Mifflin, c1995. 286pp.
Seven Australian teenagers return from a camping trip in the bush to discover that their country has been invaded and they must hide to stay alive.

**O'Brien, Robert C.** *Z for Zachariah.* Aladdin Paperbacks, 1987, c1974. 249pp.
After living alone for a year, believing herself to be the only survivor of a nuclear holocaust, sixteen-year-old Ann makes a startling discovery—a scientist named John Loomis has also survived—but this pleasant surprise very quickly turns sinister.

# Adventure with Female Protagonists

**Rees, Celia.** *Pirates!: The True and Remarkable Adventures of Minerva Sharpe and Nancy Kington, Female Pirates.* Bloomsbury (distributed by Holtzbrinck), c2003. 379pp.
   At the dawn of the eighteenth century, Nancy Kington and Minerva Sharpe set sail from Jamaica on a pirate vessel, hoping to escape from an arranged marriage and slavery.

# African American Girls: Positive Image

## Books for Ages 12–15

**Codell, Esmé Raji.** *Sahara Special.* Hyperion Books for Children, c2003. 175pp.
Struggling with school and her feelings since her father left, Sahara gets a fresh start with a new and unique teacher who supports her writing talents and the individuality of each of her classmates.

**Creary, Eve M.** *A Silent Witness in Harlem.* Silver Moon Press, c2002. 91pp.
Felicia's grandmother tells her the story of a twelve-year-old girl named Lily, who witnessed a mysterious kidnapping one night in 1928 in Harlem, New York.

**Draper, Sharon M.** *Romiette and Julio.* Atheneum Books for Young Readers, c1999. 236pp.
Romiette, an African American girl, and Julio, a Hispanic boy, discover that they attend the same high school after falling in love on the Internet, but are harassed by a gang whose members object to their interracial dating.

**Duey, Kathleen.** *Zellie Blake: Lowell, Massachusetts, 1834.* Aladdin Paperbacks, c2002. 133pp.
Zellie faces a difficult decision that could cost her a job when her boss, the owner of a boarding house for the girls employed in the textile mills of Lowell, Massachusetts, asks her to spy on the young workers.

**Flake, Sharon.** *The Skin I'm In.* Jump at the Sun/Hyperion Books for Children, c1998. 171pp.
Thirteen-year-old Maleeka, uncomfortable because her skin is extremely dark, meets a new teacher with a birthmark on her face and makes some discoveries about how to love who she is and what she looks like.

**Fogelin, Adrian.** *Crossing Jordan.* Peachtree, c2000. 140pp.
Twelve-year-old Cass meets her new African American neighbor, Jemmie, and despite their families' prejudices, they build a strong friendship around their mutual talent for running and a pact to read *Jane Eyre*.

**Grimes, Nikki.** *Jazmin's Notebook.* Dial Books, c1998. 102pp.
Jazmin, an African American teenager who lives with her older sister in a small Harlem apartment in the 1960s, finds strength in writing poetry and keeping a record of the events in her sometimes difficult life.

**Hamilton, Virginia.** *Cousins.* Philomel Books, c1990. 125pp.
Concerned that her grandmother may die, Cammy is unprepared for the accidental death of another relative.

**Hamilton, Virginia.** *Arilla Sun Down.* Scholastic, 1995, c1976. 296pp.
A young girl, half African American and half Indian, lives in a small town, where her life revolves around family, school, and friends.

**Hamilton, Virginia.** *Time Pieces: The Book of Times.* Blue Sky Press, c2002. 199pp.
Valena, her family, and their dog live in rural Ohio, where she and her cousin Melinda share experiences that include seeing the aurora borealis, surviving a tornado, and going to an amazing circus.

# African American Girls: Positive Image

**Hamilton, Virginia.** *Zeely.* Macmillan, c1967. 122pp.
Greeder's summer at her uncle's farm is made special because of her friendship with a very tall, composed woman who raises hogs and who closely resembles the magazine photograph of a Watutsi queen.

**Hansen, Joyce.** *One True Friend.* Clarion Books, c2001. 154pp.
Fourteen-year-old orphan Amir, living in Syracuse, exchanges letters with his friend Doris, still living in their old Bronx neighborhood, in which they share their lives and give each other advice on friendship, family, foster care, and making decisions.

**Hesse, Karen.** *Witness.* Scholastic Press, c2001. 161pp.
A series of poems express the views of various people in a small Vermont town, including a young black girl and a young Jewish girl, during the early 1920s when the Ku Klux Klan is trying to infiltrate the town.

**Hewett, Lorri.** *Dancer.* Puffin Books, 2000, c1999. 214pp.
Sixteen-year old Stephanie struggles to perfect her ballet dancing as her classes are complicated by the introduction of a new male dancer.

**Hoffman, Mary.** *Bravo, Grace!* Frances Lincoln Children's Books (distributed in the United States by Publishers Group West), c2005. 112pp.
Grace has mixed feelings when she finds out that her mom and stepdad are going to have a baby and confides those feelings to her grandmother.

**Jenkins, Beverly.** *Belle and the Beau.* Avon Books, c2002. 296pp.
Just before the American Civil War, Belle Palmer escapes from slavery in the South to freedom in the North, where she meets and falls in love with Daniel Best.

**Johnson, Angela.** *Heaven.* Simon & Schuster Books for Young Readers, c1998. 138pp.
Fourteen-year-old Marley's seemingly perfect life in the small town of Heaven is disrupted when she discovers that her father and mother are not her real parents.

**Johnson, Angela.** *Looking for Red.* Simon & Schuster Books for Young Readers, c2002. 116pp.
A thirteen-year-old girl struggles to cope with the loss of her beloved older brother, who disappeared four months earlier off the coast of Cape Cod.

**Johnson, Angela.** *Songs of Faith.* Dell Laurel-Leaf, 2001, c1998. 103pp.
Living in a small town in Ohio in 1975 and desperately missing her divorced father, thirteen-year-old Doreen comes to terms with disturbing changes in her family life.

**Mantell, Paul.** *Fairway Phenom.* Little, Brown, c2003. 132pp.
Malik Edwards, a young African American living in Brooklyn, decides to learn how to play golf in spite of many obstacles in his path, especially the ridicule of his friends.

**McDonald, Janet.** *Twists and Turns.* Farrar, Straus & Giroux, c2003. 135pp.
With the help of a couple of successful friends, eighteen- and nineteen-year-old Teesha and Keeba try to capitalize on their talents by opening a hair salon in the run-down Brooklyn housing project where they live.

From Nancy J. Keane, *The Big Book of Teen Reading Lists: 100 Great, Ready-to-Use Book Lists for Educators, Librarians, Parents, and Children.* Westport, CT: Libraries Unlimited, 2006. Copyright © 2006 by Libraries Unlimited.

# African American Girls: Positive Image

**McGill, Alice.** *Here We Go Round.* Houghton Mifflin, c2002. 119pp.
In 1946, seven-year-old Roberta goes to her grandparents' North Carolina farm during the last month of her mother's pregnancy.

**Mead, Alice.** *Junebug.* Farrar, Straus & Giroux, c1995. 101pp.
An inquisitive young boy who lives with his mother and younger sister in a rough housing project in New Haven, Connecticut, approaches his tenth birthday with a mixture of anticipation and worry.

**Meyer, Carolyn.** *White Lilacs.* Harcourt Brace Jovanovich, c1993. 242pp.
In 1921 in Dillon, Texas, twelve-year-old Rose Lee sees trouble threatening her black community when the whites decide to take the land there for a park and forcibly relocate the black families to an ugly stretch of territory outside the town.

**Myers, Walter Dean.** *Crystal.* HarperTrophy, 2001, c1987. 196pp.
Fifteen-year-old Crystal has difficulty trying to reconcile her personal and school life with the sexy, sophisticated persona her career as a quickly advancing high-fashion model has forced upon her.

**Myers, Walter Dean.** *Darnell Rock Reporting.* Dell, 1996, c1994. 135pp.
Thirteen-year-old Darnell's twin sister and the other members of the Corner Crew have doubts about his work on the school newspaper, but the article he writes about a homeless man changes his attitude about school.

**Myers, Walter Dean.** *The Journal of Biddy Owens: The Negro Leagues.* Scholastic, c2001. 139pp.
Teenager Biddy Owens's 1948 journal about working for the Birmingham Black Barons includes the games and the players, racism the team faces from New Orleans to Chicago, and his family's resistance to his becoming a professional baseball player. Includes a historical note about the evolution of the Negro Leagues.

**Myers, Walter Dean.** *The Mouse Rap.* HarperTrophy, 1992, c1990. 186pp.
During an eventful summer in Harlem, fourteen-year-old Mouse and his friends fall in and out of love and search for a hidden treasure from the days of Al Capone.

**Pfeffer, Susan Beth.** *The Riddle Streak.* H. Holt, 1995, c1993. 57pp.
Since her older brother always wins at ping pong, checkers, and everything else, Amy decides to learn riddles in hope of finding some way she can beat him.

**Robinet, Harriette.** *Walking to the Bus-Rider Blues.* Atheneum Books for Young Readers, c2000. 146pp.
Twelve-year-old Alfa Merryfield, his older sister, and their grandmother struggle for rent money, food, and their dignity as they participate in the Montgomery, Alabama, bus boycott in the summer of 1956.

**Slote, Alfred.** *Finding Buck McHenry.* HarperTrophy, 1993, c1991. 250pp.
Eleven-year-old Jason, believing the school custodian, Mack Henry, to be Buck McHenry, a famous pitcher from the old Negro League, tries to enlist him as a coach for his Little League team by revealing his identity to the world.

**Williams-Garcia, Rita.** *Like Sisters on the Homefront.* Puffin Books, 1997, c1995. 165pp.
Troubled fourteen-year-old Gayle is sent down South to live with her uncle and aunt, where her life begins to change as she experiences the healing power of the family.

# African American Girls: Positive Image

**Wolff, Virginia Euwer.** *Make Lemonade.* H. Holt, c1993. 200pp.
Fourteen-year-old LaVaughn, trying to earn money for college, takes a job caring for the two children of Jolly, a single teenage mom, and must find the courage to make the right decision for all of them after Jolly is fired from her job.

**Woodson, Jacqueline.** *Hush.* Putnam, c2002. 181pp.
Twelve-year-old Toswiah finds her life changed when her family enters the witness protection program.

**Woodson, Jacqueline.** *If You Come Softly.* Putnam, c1998. 181pp.
After meeting at their private school in New York, fifteen-year-old Jeremiah, who is black and whose parents are separated, and Ellie, who is white and whose mother has twice abandoned her, fall in love and then try to cope with peoples' reactions.

**Woodson, Jacqueline.** *Miracle's Boys.* Putnam, c2000. 133pp.
Twelve-year-old Lafayette's close relationship with his older brother Charlie changes after Charlie is released from a detention home and blames Lafayette for the death of their mother.

## Books for Older Teens

**Coleman, Evelyn.** *Born in Sin.* Atheneum Books for Young Readers, c2001. 234pp.
Despite serious obstacles and setbacks, fourteen-year-old Keisha pursues her dream of becoming an Olympic swimmer and medical doctor.

**Placide, Jaira.** *Fresh Girl.* Wendy Lamb Books, c2002. 216pp.
After having been sent, at a very young age, from New York to live with her grandmother in Haiti, fourteen-year-old Mardi rejoins her parents and tries to shape a new life in Brooklyn.

**Sanders, Dori.** *Clover: A Novel.* Algonquin Books of Chapel Hill, c1990. 183pp.
After her father dies within hours of being married to a white woman, a ten-year-old black girl learns with her new mother to overcome grief and to adjust to a new place in their rural African American South Carolina community.

# Author Memoirs

## Books for Ages 12–15

**Ada, Alma Flor.** *Under the Royal Palms: A Childhood in Cuba.* Atheneum Books for Young Readers, c1998. 85pp. (NF)
> The author recalls her life and impressions growing up in Cuba.

**Bagdasarian, Adam.** *First French Kiss and Other Traumas.* Farrar, Straus & Giroux, c2002. 134pp. (NF)
> The author recounts humorous, sad, traumatic, romantic, and confusing episodes from his childhood.

**Bauer, Marion Dane.** *A Writer's Story: From Life to Fiction.* Clarion Books, c1995. 134pp. (NF)
> The author explores the influences that led her to become a writer, including the importance of inspiration.

**Berenstain, Stan.** *Down a Sunny Dirt Road: An Autobiography.* Random House, c2002. 202pp. (NF)
> In alternating chapters, Stan and Jan Berenstain, creators of the Berenstain Bears, tell their own stories, from early childhood until their marriage, then continue the tale together to the present day.

**Byars, Betsy Cromer.** *The Moon and I.* Beech Tree Books, 1996, c1991. 96pp. (NF)
> While describing her humorous adventures with a black snake, Betsy Byars recounts childhood anecdotes and explains how she writes a book.

**Cleary, Beverly.** *A Girl from Yamhill: A Memoir.* Morrow Junior Books, c1988. 279pp. (NF)
> Follows the popular children's author from her childhood years in Oregon through high school and into young adulthood, highlighting her family life and her growing interest in writing.

**Dahl, Roald.** *Boy: Tales of Childhood.* Puffin Books, 1999, c1984. 176pp. (NF)
> Presents humorous anecdotes from the author's childhood, including his summer vacations in Norway and life at an English boarding school.

**Fleischman, Sid.** *The Abracadabra Kid: A Writer's Life.* Greenwillow Books, c1996. 198pp. (NF)
> The autobiography of the Newbery award–winning children's author, who set out from childhood to be a magician.

**Fritz, Jean.** *Homesick: My Own Story.* Putnam, c1982. 163pp.
> The author's fictionalized version, although all the events are true, of her childhood in China in the 1920s.

**Kehret, Peg.** *Five Pages a Day: A Writer's Journey.* Whitman, c2002. 185pp. (NF)
> A biography of the author of numerous books for young people, describing her childhood bout with polio, how she became a writer, family relationships, and the importance of writing in her life.

**Kehret, Peg.** *Small Steps: The Year I Got Polio.* Whitman, c1996. 179pp. (NF)
> The author describes her battle against polio when she was thirteen and her efforts to overcome its debilitating effects.

**King-Smith, Dick.** *Chewing the Cud.* Knopf (distributed by Random House), c2002. 196pp. (NF)
> Dick King-Smith recounts his life from soldier to farmer to salesman to factory worker to teacher to, finally, author.

**Lobel, Anita.** *No Pretty Pictures: A Child of War.* Greenwillow Books, c1998. 193pp. (NF)
> The author, known as an illustrator of children's books, describes her experiences as a Polish Jew during World War II and for years in Sweden afterward.

From Nancy J. Keane, *The Big Book of Teen Reading Lists: 100 Great, Ready-to-Use Book Lists for Educators, Librarians, Parents, and Children.* Westport, CT: Libraries Unlimited, 2006. Copyright © 2006 by Libraries Unlimited.

# Author Memoirs

**Lowry, Lois.** *Looking Back: A Book of Memories.* Houghton Mifflin, c1998. 181pp. (NF)
Using family photographs and quotes from her books, the author provides glimpses into her life.

**Nixon, Joan Lowery.** *The Making of a Writer.* Delacorte Press, c2002. 97pp. (NF)
The author recalls events from her childhood that contributed to her development as a writer.

**Paulsen, Gary.** *Caught by the Sea: My Life on Boats.* Delacorte Press, c2001. 103pp. (NF)
A memoir in which author Gary Paulsen discusses his lifelong love for the sea and shares his adventures exploring the oceans.

**Paulsen, Gary.** *Guts: The True Stories Behind Hatchet and the Brian Books.* Delacorte Press, c2001. 148pp. (NF)
The author relates incidents in his life and how they inspired parts of his books about the character Brian Robeson.

**Paulsen, Gary.** *My Life in Dog Years.* Delacorte Press, c1998. 137pp. (NF)
The author describes how dogs have impacted his life, from childhood through the present day, recounting the stories of his first dog, Snowball, in the Philippines; Dirk, who protected him from bullies; and Cookie, who saved his life.

**Sleator, William.** *Oddballs: Stories.* Puffin Books, 1995, c1993. 134pp. (NF)
A collection of stories based on experiences from the author's youth and peopled with an unusual assortment of family and friends.

**Spinelli, Jerry.** *Knots in My Yo-Yo String: The Autobiography of a Kid.* Knopf (distributed by Random House), c1998. 148pp. (NF)
This Italian American Newbery Medalist presents a humorous account of his childhood and youth in Norristown, Pennsylvania.

**Yep, Laurence.** *The Lost Garden.* Beech Tree Books, c1996. 116pp. (NF)
The author describes how he grew up as a Chinese American in San Francisco and how he came to use his writing to celebrate his family and his ethnic heritage.

## Books for Older Teens

**Crutcher, Chris.** *King of the Mild Frontier: An Ill-Advised Autobiography.* Greenwillow Books, c2003. 260pp. (NF)
Chris Crutcher, author of young adult novels such as *Ironman* and *Whale Talk,* as well as short stories, tells of growing up in Cascade, Idaho, and becoming a writer.

**Gantos, Jack.** *Hole in My Life.* Farrar, Straus & Giroux, c2002. 199pp. (NF)
The author relates how, as a young adult, he became a drug user and smuggler, was arrested, did time in prison, and eventually got out and went to college, all the while hoping to become a writer.

**Paulsen, Gary.** *The Beet Fields: Memories of a Sixteenth Summer.* Dell Laurel-Leaf, 2002, c2000. 160pp. (NF)
In the summer of 1955, the author, then a sixteen-year-old boy ran away from his troubled home and learned about people, friendship, love, and lust while working as a migrant farmer and a carny.

# Biracial Characters

## Books for Ages 12–15

**Adoff, Jaime.** *Names Will Never Hurt Me.* Dutton Children's Books, c2004. 185pp.

Several high school students relate their feelings about school, themselves, and events as they unfold on the fateful one-year anniversary of the killing of a fellow student.

**Curry, Jane Louise.** *The Black Canary.* Margaret K. McElderry Books, c2005. 279pp.

As the child of two musicians, twelve-year-old James has no interest in music, until he discovers a portal to seventeenth-century London in his uncle's basement and finds himself in a situation where his beautiful voice and the fact that he is biracial might serve him well.

**Hamilton, Virginia.** *Bluish: A Novel.* Blue Sky Press, c1999. 127pp.

Ten-year-old Dreenie feels both intrigued and frightened when she thinks about the girl nicknamed Bluish, whose leukemia is making her pale and causing her to use a wheelchair.

**Hamilton, Virginia.** *Plain City.* Scholastic, c1993. 194pp.

Twelve-year-old Buhlaire, a "mixed" child who feels out of place in her community, struggles to unearth her past and her family history as she gradually discovers more and more about her long-missing father.

**Hesse, Karen.** *Aleutian Sparrow.* Margaret K. McElderry Books, c2003. 156pp.

An Aleutian Islander recounts her suffering during World War II in American internment camps designed to "protect" the population from the invading Japanese.

**Meyer, Carolyn.** *Jubilee Journey.* Harcourt Brace, c1997. 271pp.

Emily Rose has always felt comfortable growing up in Connecticut with her African American mother and her French American father, but when they spend some time with her great-grandmother in Texas, Emily Rose learns about her black heritage and uncovers some new and exciting parts of her own identity.

**Namioka, Lensey.** *Half and Half.* Delacorte Press, c2003. 136pp.

At Seattle's annual Folk Fest, twelve-year-old Fiona and her older brother are torn between trying to please their Chinese grandmother and making their Scottish grandparents happy.

**Peck, Richard.** *The River Between Us.* Dial Books, c2003. 164pp.

During the early days of the Civil War, the Pruitt family takes in two mysterious young ladies who have fled New Orleans to come north to Illinois.

**Pullman, Philip.** *The Broken Bridge.* Knopf (distributed by Random House), 1998, c1992. 218pp.

Over the course of a long summer in Wales, sixteen-year-old Ginny, the mixed-race, artist daughter of an English father and a Haitian mother, learns that she has a half-brother from her father's earlier marriage, and that her own mother may still be alive.

**Saksena, Kate.** *Hang on in There, Shelley.* Bloomsbury Children's Books (distributed by Holtzbrinck), c2003. 217pp.

Living in London, fourteen-year-old Shelley writes letters to a pop star describing her life with friends and family, including her divorced alcoholic mother, and her struggles with a school bully.

# Biracial Characters

**Wyeth, Sharon Dennis.** *The World of Daughter Mcguire.* Bantam Doubleday Dell Books for Young Readers, c1994. 167pp.

Eleven-year-old Daughter, called a "zebra" by a boy at school because one of her parents is black and the other is white, wonders exactly who and what she is.

**Yep, Laurence.** *Angelfish.* Putnam, c2001. 216pp.

Robin, a young ballet dancer who is half Chinese and half white, works in a fish store for Mr. Tsow, a brusque Chinese who accuses her of being a half-person and who harbors a bitter secret.

## Books for Older Teens

**Crutcher, Chris.** *Whale Talk.* Greenwillow Books, c2001. 220pp.

Intellectually and athletically gifted, TJ, a multiracial, adopted teenager, shuns organized sports and the gung-ho athletes at his high school, until he agrees to form a swimming team and recruits some of the school's less popular students.

**Frank, E. R.** *America: A Novel.* Atheneum Books for Young Readers, c2002. 242pp.

America, a runaway boy who is being treated at Ridgeway, a New York hospital, finds himself opening up to one of the doctors on staff and revealing things about himself that he had always vowed to keep secret.

**Luntta, Karl.** *Know It by Heart: A Novel.* Curbstone Press, c2003. 336pp.

Teenagers Dub Teed, his sister Susan, and a neighbor, Doug Hammer, befriend Ricky Dubois, the daughter of a mixed marriage, when someone puts a burning cross on her parents' front lawn.

**Wyeth, Sharon Dennis.** *Orphea Proud.* Delacorte Press, c2004. 189pp.

A lyrical story about Orphea Proud, who shares her experiences with an audience in a dramatic performance as she talks about her sexuality, her family, prejudices, and identity.

**Young, Karen Romano.** *Cobwebs.* Greenwillow Books, c2004. 388pp.

Sixteen-year-old Nancy enjoys the colorful ethnic mix of her heritage in several different Brooklyn households, not suspecting how very strange that heritage is.

# Boy Bonding

## Books for Ages 12–15

**Lynch, Chris.** *Extreme Elvin*. HarperTrophy, 2001, c1999. 234pp.
>As he enters high school, fourteen-year-old Elvin continues to deal with his weight problem as he tries to find his place among his peers.

**Paulsen, Gary.** *Harris and Me: A Summer Remembered.* Harcourt Brace, c1993. 157pp.
>Sent to live with relatives on their farm because of his unhappy home life, an eleven-year-old city boy meets his distant cousin, Harris, and is given an introduction to a whole new world.

**Paulsen, Gary.** *How Angel Peterson Got His Name: And Other Outrageous Tales About Extreme Sports.* Wendy Lamb Books, c2003. 111pp.
>Author Gary Paulsen relates tales from his youth in a small town in northwestern Minnesota in the late 1940s and early 1950s, such as skiing behind a souped-up car and imitating daredevil Evel Knievel.

**Paulsen, Gary.** *The Schernoff Discoveries.* Bantam Doubleday Dell Books for Young Readers, 1998, c1997. 103pp.
>Harold and his best friend, both hopeless geeks and societal misfits, try to survive unusual science experiments, the attacks of the football team, and other dangers of junior high school.

**Philbrick, W. R.** *Freak the Mighty*. Scholastic, c1993. 169pp.
>At the beginning of eighth grade, learning disabled Max and his new friend Freak, whose birth defect has affected his body but not his brilliant mind, find that when they combine forces they make a powerful team.

**Powell, Randy.** *Three Clams and an Oyster*. Farrar, Straus & Giroux, c2002. 216pp.
>During their humorous search to find a fourth player for their flag football team, three high school juniors are forced to examine their long friendship, their individual flaws, and their inability to try new experiences.

## Books for Older Teens

**Crutcher, Chris.** *Stotan!* Greenwillow Books, c1986. 183pp.
>A high school coach invites members of his swimming team to a memorable week of rigorous training that tests their moral fiber as well as their physical stamina.

**Crutcher, Chris.** *Whale Talk.* Greenwillow Books, c2001. 220pp.
>Intellectually and athletically gifted, TJ, a multiracial, adopted teenager, shuns organized sports and the gung-ho athletes at his high school, until he agrees to form a swimming team and recruits some of the school's less popular students.

**Galloway, Steven.** *Finnie Walsh*. Raincoast Books, c2000. 165pp.
>Paul Woodward, the son of a mill worker, and Finnie Walsh, the mill owner's son, develop a strong friendship despite their class difference, built primarily on their love of hockey, and their devotion to each other stands even when they find themselves on opposing teams as adults.

# Boy Bonding

**Going, Kelly.** *Fat Kid Rules the World.* Putnam, c2003. 187pp.
Seventeen-year-old Troy, depressed, suicidal, and weighing nearly 300 pounds, gets a new perspective on life when Curt, a semi-homeless teen who is a genius on the guitar, asks Troy to be the drummer in a rock band.

**Green, John.** *Looking for Alaska.* Dutton Books, c2005. 221pp.
Sixteen-year-old Miles's first year at Culver Creek Preparatory School in Alabama includes good friends and great pranks but is defined by the search for answers about life and death after a fatal car crash.

**Levithan, David.** *The Realm of Possibility.* Knopf (distributed by Random House), c2004. 210pp.
A variety of students at the same high school describe their ideas, experiences, and relationships in a series of interconnected, free verse stories.

**Minter, J.** *The Insiders.* Bloomsbury Children's Books (distributed by Holtzbrinck), c2004. 280pp.
In downtown New York City, a sophisticated, stylish high school junior is already having trouble keeping his group of lifelong friends together, when his wild cousin Kelli arrives from St. Louis and stirs things up.

**Saenz, Benjamin Alire.** *Sammy & Juliana in Hollywood.* Cinco Puntos Press, c2004. 291pp.
Sammy Santos and Juliana Rios live amongst the racism, discrimination, and everyday violence during the Vietnam War years of the 1960s in a small town in Southern New Mexico.

# Chick Lit with Minority Characters

## Books for Ages 12–15

**Banerjee, Anjali.** *Maya Running.* Wendy Lamb Books, c2005. 209pp.
Maya, a Canadian of East Indian descent, struggles with her ethnic identity; her infatuation with a classmate; and the presence of her beautiful Bengali cousin, Pinky, who comes for a visit bearing a powerful statue of the god Ganesh, the Hindu elephant boy. (East Indian)

**Davidson, Dana.** *Jason & Kyra.* Jump at the Sun/Hyperion, c2004. 330pp.
Kyra Evans, a smart, less-than-popular high-schooler, begins to fall for Jason Vincent, a popular basketball star. (African American)

**Dhami, Narinder.** *Bindi Babes.* Delacorte Press, 2004, c2003. 184pp.
Three Indian British sisters team up to marry off their traditional, nosy aunt and get her out of the house. (East Indian)

**Dhami, Narinder.** *Bollywood Babes.* Delacorte Press, 2005, c2004. 213pp.
The Indian British Dhillon sisters open their home to a down-on-her-luck former movie star from India and employ her talents to raise money for their school. (East Indian)

**Draper, Sharon M.** *Double Dutch.* Atheneum Books for Young Readers, c2002. 183pp.
Three eighth-grade friends, preparing for the International Double Dutch Championship jump rope competition in their hometown of Cincinnati, Ohio, cope with Randy's missing father, Delia's inability to read, and Yo Yo's encounter with the class bullies. (African American)

**Draper, Sharon M.** *Forged by Fire.* Atheneum Books for Young Readers, c1997. 151pp.
Gerald, a teenager who has spent years protecting his fragile half-sister from their abusive father, must face the prospect of one final confrontation before the problem can be solved. (African American)

**Draper, Sharon M.** *Romiette and Julio.* Atheneum Books for Young Readers, c1999. 236pp.
Romiette, an African American girl, and Julio, a Hispanic boy, discover that they attend the same high school after falling in love on the Internet, but are harassed by a gang whose members object to their interracial dating. (African American)

**Flake, Sharon.** *Begging for Change.* Jump at the Sun/Hyperion Books for Children, c2003. 235pp.
African American teenager Raspberry Hill, off the streets after years of homelessness with her mother, inexplicably steals money from one of her best friends and wonders if she is no different than her recently returned, drug-addicted, thieving father. (African American)

**Flake, Sharon.** *Money Hungry.* Jump at the Sun/Hyperion Books for Children, c2001. 187pp.
All thirteen-year-old Raspberry can think of is making money so that she and her mother never have to worry about living on the streets again. (African American)

**Flake, Sharon.** *Who Am I Without Him?: Short Stories About Girls And the Boys in Their Lives.* Jump at the Sun/Hyperion Books for Children, c2004. 168pp.
Presents ten short stories about teenage girls struggling with issues of self-worth. (African American)

**Hopkins, Cathy.** *Mates, Dates, and Inflatable Bras.* Simon Pulse, 2003, c2001. 164pp. (and sequels)
Fourteen-year-old Lucy finds herself desperately in need of a self-esteem boost when she is completely stumped by a class writing assignment, gets a bad haircut, and decides her physical development is lacking in comparison with her friends'. (Jamaican)

# Chick Lit with Minority Characters

**McDonald, Janet.** *Spellbound*. Farrar, Straus & Giroux, c2001. 138pp.

Raven, a teenage mother and high school dropout living in a housing project, decides, with the help and sometime interference of her best friend Aisha, to study for a spelling bee that could lead to a college preparatory program and four-year scholarship. (African American)

**McDonald, Janet.** *Twists and Turns*. Farrar, Straus & Giroux, c2003.135pp.

With the help of a couple of successful friends, eighteen- and nineteen-year-old Teesha and Keeba try to capitalize on their talents by opening a hair salon in the run-down Brooklyn housing project where they live. (African American)

## Books for Older Teens

**De la Cruz, Melissa.** *Fresh off the Boat*. HarperCollins, c2005. 243pp.

When her family emigrates from the Philippines to San Francisco, California, fourteen-year-old Vicenza Arambullo struggles to fit in at her exclusive, all-girl private school. (Filipino)

**Ewing, Lynne.** *Party Girl*. Knopf (distributed by Random House), 1999, c1998. 110pp.

The death of her best friend Ana in a drive-by shooting causes fifteen-year-old Kata to question her position in the Los Angeles gang life. (Hispanic)

**Johnson, R. M.** *Dating Games: A Novel*. Simon & Schuster, c2003. 310pp. (adult)

The lives of the women in the Rodgers family change forever when thirty-three-year-old mom Livvy announces her plans to move to a smaller apartment and begin nursing school, leaving her teenage twin daughters to fend for themselves. Hennesey goes off to college on a scholarship, while Alize embarks on a dangerous money-making scheme. (African American)

**McDonald, Janet.** *Chill Wind*. Farrar, Straus & Giroux, c2002. 134pp.

Afraid that she will have nowhere to go when her welfare checks are stopped, nineteen-year-old high school dropout Aisha tries to figure out how she can support herself and her two young children in New York City. (African American)

**Monroe, Mary.** *God Still Don't Like Ugly*. Dafina Books/Kensington, c2003. 311pp. (adult)

Annette Goode meets the father who left her and her mother when she was an infant, loses her groom when her uncle announces that she used to be a prostitute, and reconnects with the friend who murdered her rapist. (African American)

**Triana, Gaby.** *Cubanita*. HarperCollins, c2005. 195pp.

Seventeen-year-old Isabel, eager to leave Miami to attend the University of Michigan and escape her overprotective Cuban mother, learns some truths about her family's past and makes important decisions about the type of person she wants to be. (Cuban American)

**Velasquez, Gloria.** *Teen Angel*. Piñata Books, c2003. 154pp. (and sequels)

When fifteen-year-old Celia Chavez becomes pregnant, she receives help from her friends, family, and a psychiatrist who recently had a miscarriage. (Mexican American)

**Williams-Garcia, Rita.** *Like Sisters on the Homefront*. Lodestar Books, c1995. 165pp.

Troubled fourteen-year-old Gayle is sent down South to live with her uncle and aunt, where her life begins to change as she experiences the healing power of the family. (African American)

From Nancy J. Keane, *The Big Book of Teen Reading Lists: 100 Great, Ready-to-Use Book Lists for Educators, Librarians, Parents, and Children*. Westport, CT: Libraries Unlimited, 2006. Copyright © 2006 by Libraries Unlimited.

# Female Quest Stories

## Books for Ages 12–15

**Armstrong, Jennifer.** *Becoming Mary Mehan: Two Novels.* Dell Laurel-Leaf, c2002. 292pp.
Contains the complete text of two novels by Jennifer Armstrong featuring Mary Mehan and her experiences during the Civil War and its aftermath.

**Armstrong, Jennifer.** *The Kindling.* HarperCollins, c2002. 224pp. (and sequels)
In 2007, a small band of children have joined together in a Florida town, trying to survive in a world where it seems that all the adults have been killed off by a catastrophic virus.

**Avi.** *The True Confessions of Charlotte Doyle.* Orchard Books, 2003, c1990. 215pp.
Thirteen-year-old Charlotte Doyle, the only passenger aboard a seedy ship on a transatlantic voyage from England to America in 1832, becomes caught up in a feud between the murderous captain and his mutinous crew.

**Bauer, Joan.** *Rules of the Road.* Putman, c1998. 201pp.
Sixteen-year-old Jenna gets a job driving the elderly owner of a chain of successful shoe stores from Chicago to Texas to confront the son who is trying to force her to retire, and along the way Jenna hones her talents as a saleswoman and finds the strength to face her alcoholic father.

**Cushman, Karen.** *The Ballad of Lucy Whipple.* Clarion Books, c1996. 195pp.
In 1849, twelve-year-old California Morning Whipple, who renames herself Lucy, is distraught when her mother moves the family from Massachusetts to a rough California mining town.

**Cushman, Karen.** *Rodzina.* Clarion Books, c2003. 215pp.
A twelve-year-old Polish American girl is boarded onto an orphan train in Chicago, fearing traveling to the West and a life of slavery.

**Erdrich, Louise.** *The Birchbark House.* Hyperion Books for Children, c1999. 244pp.
Omakayas, a seven-year-old Native American girl of the Ojibwa tribe, lives through the joys of summer and the perils of winter on an island in Lake Superior in 1847.

**George, Jean Craighead,** *Julie of the Wolves.* HarperCollins, c1972. 170pp.
While running away from home and an unwanted marriage, a thirteen-year-old Eskimo girl becomes lost on the North Slope of Alaska and is befriended by a wolf pack.

**Haddix, Margaret Peterson.** *Just Ella.* Simon & Schuster Books for Young Readers, c1999. 185pp.
In this continuation of the Cinderella story, fifteen-year-old Ella finds that accepting Prince Charming's proposal ensnares her in a suffocating tangle of palace rules and royal etiquette, so she plots to escape.

**Haddix, Margaret Peterson.** *Running Out of Time.* Simon & Schuster Books for Young Readers, c1995. 184pp.
When a diphtheria epidemic hits her 1840s village, thirteen-year-old Jessie discovers it is actually a 1995 tourist site under unseen observation by heartless scientists, and it's up to Jessie to escape the village and save the lives of the dying children.

# Female Quest Stories

**Hahn, Mary Downing.** *The Gentleman Outlaw and Me—Eli: A Story of the Old West.* Clarion Books, c1996. 212pp.

> In 1887 twelve-year-old Eliza, disguised as a boy and traveling to Colorado in search of her missing father, falls in with a Gentleman Outlaw and joins him in his illegal schemes.

**Hendry, Frances Mary.** *Quest for a Maid.* Farrar, Straus & Giroux, c1992. 273pp.

> Aware of her sister's deadly efforts to secure the Scottish throne for Robert de Brus, Meg realizes she must protect the young Norwegian princess who has been chosen as rightful heir.

**Hesse, Karen.** *Out of the Dust.* Scholastic Press, c1997. 227pp.

> In a series of poems, fifteen-year-old Billie Jo relates the hardships of living on her family's wheat farm in Oklahoma during the dust bowl years of the Great Depression.

## Books for Older Teens

**Le Guin, Ursula K.** *Tehanu.* Aladdin Paperbacks, 2001, c1990. 281pp.

> Sparrowhawk, the Archmage of Earthsea, returns from the dark land stripped of his magic powers and finds refuge with the aging widow Tenar and a crippled girl child, who carries an unknown destiny.

**Le Guin, Ursula K.** *The Tombs of Atuan.* Atheneum, c1971. 163pp.

> Arha's isolated existence as high priestess in the tombs of Atuan is disrupted by a thief who seeks a special treasure.

**Levine, Gail Carson.** *Ella Enchanted.* HarperCollins, c1997. 232pp.

> In this novel based on the story of Cinderella, Ella struggles against the childhood curse that forces her to obey any order given to her.

**Lowry, Lois.** *Taking Care of Terrific.* Houghton Mifflin, c1983. 168pp.

> Taking her overprotected young charge to the public park to broaden his horizons, fourteen-year-old baby sitter Enid enjoys unexpected friendships with a black saxophonist and a bag lady, until she is charged with kidnapping.

**McGovern, Ann.** *The Secret Soldier: The Story of Deborah Sampson.* Scholastic, c1975. 63pp. (NF)

> A brief biography of the woman who disguised herself as a man and joined the Continental Army during the Revolutionary War.

**McKinley, Robin.** *Beauty: A Retelling of the Story of Beauty & the Beast.* HarperCollins, c1978. 247pp.

> Kind Beauty grows to love the Beast, at whose castle she is compelled to stay, and through her love she releases him from the spell that had turned him from a handsome prince into an ugly beast.

**McKinley, Robin.** *The Hero and the Crown.* Greenwillow Books, c1984, 246pp.

> Aerin, with the guidance of the wizard Luthe and the help of the blue sword, wins the birthright due her as the daughter of the Damarian king and a witchwoman of the mysterious, demon-haunted North.

From Nancy J. Keane, *The Big Book of Teen Reading Lists: 100 Great, Ready-to-Use Book Lists for Educators, Librarians, Parents, and Children.* Westport, CT: Libraries Unlimited, 2006. Copyright © 2006 by Libraries Unlimited.

# Female Quest Stories

**Napoli, Donna Jo.** *Sirena*. Scholastic Signature, 2000, c1998. 210pp.
The gods grant immortality to the mermaid Sirena when she rescues a human man from the sea and they fall in love, but his mortality creates great conflict between love and honor when he is called to defend Greece in the Trojan War.

**Nix, Garth.** *Sabriel*. HarperCollins, c1995. 292pp.
Sabriel, daughter of the necromancer Abhorsen, must journey into the mysterious and magical Old Kingdom to rescue her father from the Land of the Dead.

**Nolan, Han.** *Dancing on the Edge*. Harcourt Brace, c1997. 244pp.
A young girl from a dysfunctional family creates for herself an alternative world, which nearly results in her death but ultimately leads her to reality.

**O'Brien, Robert C.** *Z for Zachariah*. Aladdin Paperbacks, 1987, c1974. 249pp.
After living alone for a year, believing herself to be the only survivor of a nuclear holocaust, sixteen-year-old Ann makes a startling discovery—a scientist named John Loomis has also survived—but this pleasant surprise very quickly turns sinister.

**O'Dell, Scott.** *Island of the Blue Dolphins*. Houghton Mifflin, c1990. 181pp.
Left alone on a beautiful but isolated island off the coast of California, a young Indian girl spends eighteen years not only merely surviving through her enormous courage and self-reliance, but also finding a measure of happiness in her solitary life.

**Paterson, Katherine.** *Lyddie*. Lodestar Books, c1991. 182pp.
Impoverished Vermont farm girl Lyddie Worthen is determined to gain her independence by becoming a factory worker in Lowell, Massachusetts, in the 1840s.

**Pierce, Tamora.** *Alanna: The First Adventure*. Atheneum Books for Young Readers, 2002, c1983. 216pp.
Eleven-year-old Alanna, who aspires to be a knight even though she is a girl, disguises herself as a boy to become a royal page, learning many hard lessons along her path to high adventure.

**Pierce, Tamora.** *First Test*. Random House, c1999. 216pp.
Ten-year-old Keladry of Mindalen, daughter of nobles, serves as a page but must prove herself to the males around her if she is ever to fulfill her dream of becoming a knight.

**Pullman, Philip.** *The Golden Compass*. Knopf, c1995. 399pp.
Accompanied by her daemon, Lyra Belacqua sets out to prevent her best friend and other kidnapped children from becoming the subject of gruesome experiments in the Far North.

**Rylant, Cynthia.** *Missing May*. Orchard Books, c1992. 89pp.
After the death of the beloved aunt who has raised her, twelve-year-old Summer and her uncle Ob leave their West Virginia trailer in search of the strength to go on living.

**Taylor, Mildred D.** *The Gold Cadillac*. Dial Press, c1987. 43pp.
Two black girls living in the North are proud of their family's beautiful new Cadillac until they take it on a visit to the South and encounter racial prejudice for the first time.

# Female Quest Stories

**Tchana, Katrin.** *The Serpent Slayer: And Other Stories of Strong Women.* Little, Brown, c2000. 113pp.
A collection of twenty traditional tales from various parts of the world, each of whose main character is a strong and resourceful woman.

**Voigt, Cynthia.** *Elske.* Atheneum Books for Young Readers, c1999. 245pp.
Thirteen-year-old Elske escapes rape and certain death at the hands of the leaders of her barbaric society and later becomes handmaiden to a rebellious noblewoman whose rightful throne they reclaim together.

**Voigt, Cynthia.** *Homecoming.* Atheneum Books for Young Readers, c1981. 312pp.
Abandoned by their mother, four children begin a search for a home and an identity.

**Wilson, Diane Lee.** *I Rode a Horse of Milk White Jade.* HarperTrophy, c1999. 288pp.
In early fourteenth-century China, Oyuna tells her granddaughter about her girlhood in Mongolia and how love for her horse enabled her to win an important race and bring good luck to her family.

**Wrede, Patricia C.** *Dealing with Dragons.* Harcourt Brace Jovanovich, c1990, 212pp.
Bored with traditional palace life, a princess goes off to live with a group of dragons and soon becomes involved with fighting against some disreputable wizards, who want to steal away the dragons' kingdom.

**Yolen, Jane.** *Not One Damsel in Distress: World Folktales for Strong Girls.* Silver Whistle/Harcourt, c2000. 116pp.
A collection of thirteen traditional tales from various parts of the world, each of whose main character is a fearless, strong, heroic, and resourceful woman.

## Books for Older Teens

**Bradley, Marion Zimmer.** *Lady of Avalon.* Roc, c1997. 460pp.
Three different generations of holy women of Avalon—Caillean, Dierna, and Ana—struggle to guide the fortunes of Roman Britain and their own destinies in the years before the birth of the legendary King Arthur.

**Bradley, Marion Zimmer.** *The Mists of Avalon.* Ballantine, 2000, c1982. 876pp.
A re-creation of the Arthurian legend following the clash between Christianity and paganism that led to the demise of Camelot.

**Jones, Diana Wynne.** *Fire and Hemlock.* HarperTrophy, 2002, c1985. 420pp.
At nineteen, Polly has two sets of sometimes overlapping, sometimes conflicting memories: the real-life ones of school days and her parents' divorce, and the heroic adventure ones that began the day she accidentally gate-crashed a funeral and met the cellist Thomas Lynn.

**Jones, Diana Wynne.** *The Spellcoats.* GreenwillowBooks, c2001. 279pp.
Tanqui discovers she has the only means to conquer the evil Kankredin, who threatens her own people, and the Heathens who have invaded prehistoric Dalemark.

**Yolen, Jane.** *Briar Rose.* Starscape, 2002, c1992. 241pp.
In this retelling of "Sleeping Beauty," a young woman learns that her grandmother had a secret past tied to the Holocaust.

From Nancy J. Keane, *The Big Book of Teen Reading Lists: 100 Great, Ready-to-Use Book Lists for Educators, Librarians, Parents, and Children.* Westport, CT: Libraries Unlimited, 2006. Copyright © 2006 by Libraries Unlimited.

# Freshman Experience

## Books for Ages 12–15

**Cabot, Meg.** *The Princess Diaries.* HarperCollins, c2000. 238pp.
> Fourteen-year-old Mia, who is trying to lead a normal life as a teenage girl in New York City, is shocked to learn that her father is the Prince of Genovia, a small European principality, and that she is a princess and the heir to the throne.

**Cabot, Meg.** *Princess in Pink.* HarperCollins, c2004. 256pp.
> In a series of humorous diary entries, high school freshman (and Genovian Princess) Mia tries to get her reluctant boyfriend to take her to the prom.

**Clarke, Judith.** *Kalpana's Dream.* Front Street, 2005, c2004. 164pp.
> Neema's struggle to complete an essay on the topic "Who Am I" for her freshman English class is complicated by the arrival of Kampala, her Indian great-grandmother, who has come to Australia chasing her dream of flying, and although they do not speak the same language, the two find common ground in skateboarder Gull Oliver.

**Fredericks, Mariah.** *The True Meaning of Cleavage.* Atheneum Books for Young Readers, c2003. 211pp.
> When Jess and Sari, best friends since seventh grade, begin their freshman year of high school, and Sari becomes obsessed with a senior boy, Jess wonders if their friendship will survive.

**Gardner, Graham.** *Inventing Elliot.* Dial Books, 2004, c2003. 181pp.
> Elliot, a victim of bullying, invents a calmer, cooler self when he changes schools in the middle of freshman year, but soon attracts the wrong kind of attention from the Guardians who "maintain order" at the new school.

**Naylor, Phyllis Reynolds.** *Patiently Alice.* Atheneum Books for Young Readers, c2003. 243pp.
> Alice experiences a lot of changes during the summer of her freshmen year when she gets to work as an assistant camp counselor for three weeks, and then returns home to find the orderly world she left behind in turmoil.

**Naylor, Phyllis Reynolds.** *Simply Alice.* Atheneum Books for Young Readers, c2002. 222pp.
> In her freshman year, fourteen-year-old Alice experiences changes and challenges with friends, family, and school activities, which leave her feeling better about herself than ever before.

**Rallison, Janette.** *Life, Love, and the Pursuit of Free Throws.* Walker, c2004. 185pp.
> High school freshmen Josie and Cami try to remain best friends as they compete for basketball awards and boys.

## Books for Older Teens

**Chbosky, Stephen.** *The Perks of Being a Wallflower.* MTV Books/Pocket Books, c1999. 213pp.
> Charlie, a freshman in high school, explores the dilemmas of growing up through a collection of letters he sends to an unknown recipient.

# Freshman Experience

**Farrell, Juliana.** *High School, the Real Deal: From GPAs to Graduation.* HarperTrophy, c2001. 142pp. (NF)
>Provides advice for incoming freshmen on how to handle high school, listing dos and don'ts for the first day and beyond, and discussing academics, extracurricular activities, working, stress, the social scene, and post–high school concerns.

**Frank, Hillary.** *Better Than Running at Night.* Houghton Mifflin, c2002. 263pp.
>Ellie, having endured a lonely high school existence, tries to make a place for herself as a freshman art student at the New England College of Art and Design.

**Garfinkle, Debra.** *Storky: How I Lost My Nickname and Won the Girl.* Putnam, c2005. 184pp.
>Fourteen-year-old high school student Michael "Storky" Pomerantz's journal describes his freshman year, from dealing with his mother's dating his dentist to attempting to win the heart of the girl he loves.

**Lubar, David.** *Sleeping Freshmen Never Lie.* Dutton Children's Books, c2005. 279pp.
>While navigating his first year of high school and awaiting the birth of his new baby brother, Scott loses old friends and gains some unlikely new ones as he hones his skills as a writer.

**Matthews, Andrew.** *A Winter Night's Dream.* Delacorte Press, 2004, c1997. 151pp.
>Casey, a high school freshman, and Stew, a senior, search for love separately, with the help of a favorite teacher, before meeting each other.

**Myracle, Lauren.** *Rhymes with Witches.* Amulet Books, c2005. 209pp.
>High school freshman Jane believes that she would do anything to be popular, until she is selected to be in the school's most exclusive clique and learns that popularity has a very high price.

**Trope, Zoe.** *Please Don't Kill the Freshman: A Memoir.* HarperTempest, c2003. 295pp. (NF)
>A memoir of the then-fifteen-year-old author's high school experience to that point, in which diary entries reflect her struggles, angst, and rebellion.

**Zeises, Lara M.** *Contents Under Pressure.* Delacorte Press, c2004. 244pp.
>Lucy, a fourteen-year-old high school freshman, experiences the happiness and confusion of dating a popular older boy, changing relationships with lifelong friends, and sharing a bedroom with her older brother's pregnant girlfriend.

# Girls in Sports

## Books for Ages 12–15

**Adler, C. S.** *Winning.* Clarion Books, c1999. 156pp.
Vicky is thrilled to be on the eighth-grade tennis team, until she realizes that her new playing partner, Brenda, is ruthless about winning and will even cheat to do so.

*Girls Got Game: Sports Stories & Poems.* H. Holt, c2001. 152pp.
A collection of short stories and poems written by and about young women in sports.

**Levy, Marilyn.** *Run for Your Life.* Putnam & Grosset, 1997, c1996. 217pp.
While living in a housing project in Oakland, California, thirteen-year-old Kisha joins a track team, which helps her discover that she can be a winner.

**Mackel, Kathy.** *MadCat.* HarperCollins, c2005. 185pp.
Fast-pitch softball catcher MadCat Campione's love for the sport is strained when her team competes on a national level and her best pal Jess puts the game before her friends.

**Nitz, Kristin Wolden.** *Defending Irene.* Peachtree, c2004. 185pp.
Thirteen-year-old Irene Benenati, a top soccer player on the girls' team at her Missouri school, plays on a fiercely competitive boy's soccer team during the year her family spends in Italy and experiences culture clashes both on and off the field.

**Rallison, Janette.** *Life, Love, and the Pursuit of Free Throws.* Walker, c2004. 185pp.
High school freshmen Josie and Cami try to remain best friends as they compete for basketball awards and boys.

**Roberts, Kristi.** *My 13th Season.* H. Holt, c2005. 154pp.
Already downhearted due to the loss of her mother and her father's overwhelming grief, thirteen-year-old Fran decides to give up her dream of becoming the first female in professional baseball, after a coach attacks her just for being a girl.

**Rottman, S. L.** *Head Above Water.* Peachtree, c1999. 196pp.
Skye, a high school junior, tries to find the time for both family obligations and personal interests, which include caring for her brother who has Down Syndrome, dating her first boyfriend, and swimming competitively.

**Smith, Charles R.** *Hoop Queens: Poems.* Candlewick Press, c2003. 35pp.
A collection of twelve poems that celebrate contemporary women basketball stars, including Yolanda Griffith, Chamique Holdsclaw, and Natalie Williams.

**Spinelli, Jerry.** *There's a Girl in My Hammerlock.* Aladdin Paperbacks, 1993, c1991. 199pp.
Thirteen-year-old Maisie joins her school's formerly all-male wrestling team and tries to last through the season, despite opposition from other students, her best friend, and her own teammates.

**Wells, Rosemary.** *When No One Was Looking.* Puffin Books, 2000, c1980. 189pp.
A tragic chain of events threatens a fourteen-year-old girl's promising tennis career.

# Girls in Sports

**Wolff, Virginia Euwer.** *Bat 6: A Novel*. Scholastic Signature, 1999, c1998. 230pp.
In small town, post–World War II Oregon, twenty-one sixthgrade girls recount the story of an annual softball game, during which one girl's bigotry comes to the surface.

## Books for Older Teens

**Lamott, Anne.** *Crooked Little Heart.* Anchor Books, c1998. 326pp.
Thirteen-year-old tennis champion Rosie Ferguson, her mother Elizabeth, and her stepfather, James, all struggle with their own heartbreak along the road to becoming a united family.

**Ripslinger, Jon.** *How I Fell in Love & Learned to Shoot Free Throws.* Roaring Brook Press, c2003. 170pp.
Seventeen-year-old Danny Henderson, an indifferent basketball player, has his eye on Angel McPherson, star of the girls' team in their Iowa high school.

# Gay, Lesbian, Bisexual, Transsexual, and Questioning

## Books for Ages 12–15

Compiled by Joanna Nigrelli, Wired for Youth Librarian, Austin Public Library.

**Hartinger, Brent.** *Geography Club*. HarperTempest, c2003. 226pp.
A group of gay and lesbian teenagers find mutual support when they form the Geography Club at their high school.

**Howe, James.** *The Misfits.* Atheneum Books for Young Readers, c2001. 274pp.
Four middle-schoolers band together against those who ridicule them for being different and decide to run in the upcoming student council elections.

**Kerr, M. E.** *Deliver Us from Evie.* HarperTrophy, 1995, c1994. 177pp.
Sixteen-year-old Parr Burrman and his family face some difficult times when word spreads through their rural Missouri town that his older sister is a lesbian, and she leaves the family farm to live with the daughter of the town's banker.

**Koertge, Ronald.** *The Arizona Kid.* Candlewick Press, c2005. 283pp.
Sixteen-year-old Billy comes to terms with his own values when he is sent to live with his gay uncle in Tucson and is introduced to the world of rodeos, where he falls in love with an outspoken race-horse rider named Cara.

**Matthews, Andrew.** *The Flip Side: A Novel.* Delacorte Press, c2003. 147pp.
Robert, a British fifteen-year-old, is confused when he plays the part of Rosalind while studying Shakespeare in school and discovers parts of his personality that he did not know existed.

**Myracle, Lauren.** *Kissing Kate.* Dutton Books, c2003. 198pp.
Sixteen-year-old Lissa's relationship with her best friend changes after they kiss at a party and Lissa does not know what to do, until she gets help from an unexpected new friend.

## Books for Older Teens

*Am I Blue?: Coming Out from the Silence.* HarperTrophy, c1994. 273pp.
A collection of short stories about homosexuality by such authors as Bruce Coville, M. E. Kerr, William Sleator, and Jane Yolen.

**Boock, Paula.** *Dare Truth or Promise.* Houghton Mifflin, c1999. 170pp.
Louie Angelo, a Woodhaugh High prefect who plans to be a lawyer, falls in love with a girl who lives in a pub and just wants to get through her exams so she can become a chef.

**Garden, Nancy.** *Annie on My Mind.* Farrar, Straus & Giroux, 1992, c1982. 233pp.
Liza puts aside her feelings for Annie after a disaster at school, but eventually she allows love to triumph over the ignorance of people.

# Gay, Lesbian, Bisexual, Transsexual, and Questioning

**Griffith, Nicola.** *Slow River.* Ballantine Books, c1996. 343pp.
A near-future novel in which eighteen-year-old Lore van de Oest, stripped of her identity chip by the kidnappers who stole her from her wealthy family, struggles for control of her life after she is rescued by Spanner, a data pirate who offers Lore a world of possibilities.

**Levithan, David.** *Boy Meets Boy.* Knopf (distributed by Random House), c2003. 185pp.
Paul's simple high-school life is confused by his desire for another boy, who seems unattainable until Paul's friends help him find the courage to pursue him.

**Moore, Terry.** *Strangers in Paradise. 1: Pocket Book Collection.* Abstract Studio, c2004. 344pp.
Katchoo, a talented artist in love with her best friend Francine, finds her life becoming complicated when she meets David, a young man determined to win her heart. The gentle love triangle is threatened when Katchoo's dangerous past catches up with her. Presented in graphic novel form.

**Mowry, Jess.** *Babylon Boyz.* Simon & Schuster Books for Young Readers, c1997. 188pp.
Inner-city teenagers find a suitcase full of cocaine and must decide whether to sell it and take the opportunities the money would provide or to destroy it to keep the drug from poisoning their community.

***Not the Only One: Lesbian and Gay Fiction for Teens*** Alyson Books, c2004. 302pp.
A collection of short stories portraying gay and lesbian teenagers at different moments in their lives.

**Peters, Julie Anne.** *Keeping You a Secret: A Novel.* Little, Brown, c2003. 250pp.
As she begins a very tough last semester of high school, Holland finds herself puzzled about her future and intrigued by a transfer student who wants to start a Lesbigay club at school.

**Peters, Julie Anne.** *Luna: A Novel.* Little, Brown, c2004. 248pp.
Fifteen-year-old Regan's life, which has always revolved around keeping her older brother Liam's transsexuality a secret, changes when Liam decides to start the process of "transitioning" by first telling his family and friends that he is a girl who was born in a boy's body.

**Ryan, Sara.** *Empress of the World.* Viking Press, c2001. 213pp.
While attending a summer institute, fifteen-year-old Nic meets a girl named Battle, falls in love with her, and finds the relationship to be difficult and confusing.

**Sanchez, Alex.** *Rainbow Boys.* Simon & Schuster, c2001. 233pp.
Three high school seniors—a jock with a girlfriend and an alcoholic father, a closeted gay, and a flamboyant gay rights advocate—struggle with family issues, gay bashers, first sex, and conflicting feelings about each other.

**Weyr, Garret.** *My Heartbeat.* Houghton Mifflin, c2002. 154pp.
As she tries to understand the closeness between her older brother and his best friend, fourteen-year-old Ellen finds her relationship with each of them changing.

# Gay, Lesbian, Bisexual, Transsexual, and Questioning

**Winick, Judd.** *Green Lantern: Brother's Keeper.* DC Comics, c2003. 124pp.
When not fighting crime as Green Lantern, Kyle Rayner is a freelance artist in New York. When Terry Berg, his homosexual intern and his friend, becomes the victim of a vicious hate crime, Kyle must temper his rage and use the power of the ring wisely as he pursues Terry's attackers.

**Winick, Judd.** *Pedro and Me: Friendship, Loss, and What I Learned.* H. Holt, c2000. 187pp. (NF)
In graphic art format, describes the friendship between two roommates on the MTV show *Real World,* one of whom died of AIDS.

**Wittlinger, Ellen.** *Hard Love.* Simon & Schuster Books for Young Readers, c1999. 224pp.
After starting to publish a zine in which he writes his secret feelings about his lonely life and his parents' divorce, sixteen-year-old John meets an unusual girl and begins to develop a healthier personality.

**Woodson, Jacqueline.** *From the Notebooks of Melanin Sun: A Novel.* Scholastic, c1995. 141pp.
Thirteen-year-old Melanin Sun's comfortable, quiet life is shattered when his mother reveals she has fallen in love with a woman.

**Woodson, Jacqueline.** *The House You Pass on the Way.* Putnam, c2003, c1997. 114pp.
When fourteen-year-old Staggerlee, the daughter of a racially mixed marriage, spends a summer with her cousin Trout, she begins to question her sexuality to Trout and catches a glimpse of her possible future self.

**Yamanaka, Lois-Ann.** *Name Me Nobody.* Hyperion Paperbacks, 2000, c1999. 229pp.
Emi-Lou struggles to come of age in her middle school years in Hawaii.

# Kindness of Strangers

## Books for Ages 12–15

**Cameron, Ann.** *Colibri*. Farrar, Straus & Giroux, c2003. 227pp.
Kidnapped when she was very young by an unscrupulous man who has forced her to lie and beg to get money, a twelve-year-old Mayan girl endures an abusive life, always wishing she could return to the parents she can hardly remember.

**Choldenko, Gennifer.** *Al Capone Does My Shirts*. Putnam, c2004. 225pp.
A twelve-year-old boy named Moose moves to Alcatraz Island in 1935 when guards' families are housed there, and has to contend with his extraordinary new environment in addition to life with his autistic sister.

**Frost, Helen.** *Keesha's House*. Farrar, Straus & Giroux, c2003. 116pp.
Seven teens facing such problems as pregnancy, closeted homosexuality, and abuse each describe in poetic forms what caused them to leave home and where they found home again.

**Funke, Cornelia Caroline.** *The Thief Lord*. Scholastic, c2002. 349pp.
Orphaned brothers Prosper and Bo, having run away from their cruel aunt and uncle, decide to hide out in Venice, where they fall in with the Thief Lord, a thirteen-year-old boy who leads a crime ring of street children.

**Spinelli, Jerry.** *Maniac Magee: A Novel*. Little, Brown, c1990. 184pp.
After his parents die, Jeffrey Lionel Magee's life becomes legendary, as he accomplishes athletic and other feats that awe his contemporaries.

**Spinelli, Jerry.** *Stargirl*. Knopf (distributed by Random House), c2000. 186pp.
Stargirl, a teen who animates quiet Mica High with her colorful personality, suddenly finds herself shunned for her refusal to conform.

**Strasser, Todd.** *Can't Get There from Here*. Simon & Schuster Books for Young Readers, c2004. 198pp.
Tired of being hungry, cold, and dirty living on the streets of New York City with a tribe of other homeless teenagers who are dying, one by one, a girl named Maybe ponders her future and longs for someone to care about her.

**Weeks, Sarah.** *So B. It: A Novel*. Laura Geringer Books, c2004. 245pp.
After spending her life with her mentally retarded mother and agoraphobic neighbor, twelve-year-old Heidi sets out from Reno, Nevada, to New York to find out who she is.

## Books for Older Teens

**Brooks, Martha.** *True Confessions of a Heartless Girl*. Farrar, Straus & Giroux, c2003. 181pp.
A confused seventeen-year-old girl, a single mother and her young son, two elderly women, and a sad and lonely man, with their own individual tragedies to bear, come together in a small Manitoba town and find a way to a better future.

# Kindness of Strangers

**Herrick, Steven.** *The Simple Gift.* Simon Pulse, 2004, c2000. 188pp.

Sixteen-year-old Billy runs away from his alcoholic, abusive father and takes up residence in an abandoned freight car, where he meets Old Bill, a fellow hobo, and together they form a friendship based on small kindnesses that change their lives.

**Hyde, Catherine Ryan.** *Pay It Forward: A Novel.* Pocket Books, 2000, c1999. 311pp.

A young boy who believes in the goodness of human nature sets out to change the world with his seemingly simple plan, but he soon learns that some people are not willing to help him.

**Kluger, Steve.** *Last Days of Summer: A Novel.* Bard, 1999, c1998. 353pp.

Joey Margolis, a young boy whose father has deserted the family, begins writing to baseball player Charlie Banks and forms a relationship with the third baseman that changes both their lives for the better.

**Letts, Billie.** *Where the Heart Is.* Warner Books, 1998, c1995. 376pp.

Novalee Nation, seventeen, pregnant, and living in a Wal-Mart store, discovers friendship, encouragement, direction and love with a group of caring people in Sequoyah, Oklahoma.

**Pearson, Mary** *A Room on Lorelei Street.* H. Holt, 2005. 266pp.

To escape a miserable existence taking care of her alcoholic mother, seventeen-year-old Zoe rents a room from an eccentric woman, but her earnings as a waitress after school are minimal and she must go to extremes to cover expenses.

# Mental Illness

## Books for Ages 12–15

**Fischer, Jackie.** *An Egg on Three Sticks.* Thomas Dunne Books/St. Martin's Griffin, c2004. 309pp.
In the San Francisco Bay Area in the early 1970s, twelve-year-old Abby watches her mother fall apart and must take on the burden of holding her family together.

**Fritz, April Young.** *Waiting to Disappear.* Hyperion Books for Children, c2002. 316pp.
In a small Southern town during the summer of 1960, two years after her older brother's death, thirteen-year-old Buddy tries to cope with the absence of her mother, who has been hospitalized after suffering a nervous breakdown.

**Griffin, Adele.** *Where I Want to Be.* Putnam, c2005. 150pp.
Two teenage sisters, separated by death but still connected, work through their feelings of loss over the closeness they shared as children that was destroyed by one's mental illness, and finally make peace with each other.

**Hautman, Pete.** *Invisible*. Simon & Schuster Books for Young Readers, c2005. 149pp.
Doug and Andy are unlikely best friends—one a loner obsessed by his model trains, the other a popular student involved in football and theater—who grew up together and share a bond that nothing can sever.

**Hermes, Patricia.** *Summer Secrets.* Marshall Cavendish, c2004. 141pp.
Twelve-year-old Missy tries to learn more about her mother's odd behavior as she and her two friends share some secrets during a long, hot summer in Mississippi toward the end of World War II.

**Hesser, Terry Spencer.** *Kissing Doorknobs.* Bantam Doubleday Dell Books for Young Readers, 1999, c1998. 149pp.
Fourteen-year-old Tara describes how her increasingly strange compulsions begin to take over her life and affect her relationships with her family and friends.

**McCord, Patricia.** *Pictures in the Dark.* Bloomsbury (distributed by Holtzbrinck), c2004. 288pp.
Life with their mentally ill mother becomes unbearable for twelve-year-old Sarah and fifteen-year-old Carlie, who are deprived of food and forbidden to use the bathroom.

**Rinaldi, Ann.** *Or Give Me Death: A Novel of Patrick Henry's Family.* Harcourt, c2003. 226pp.
With their father away most of the time advocating independence for the American colonies, the children of Patrick Henry try to raise themselves, manage the family plantation, and care for their mentally ill mother.

**Sones, Sonya.** *Stop Pretending: What Happened When My Big Sister Went Crazy.* HarperTempest, 2001, c1999. 149pp.
A younger sister has a difficult time adjusting to life after her older sister has a mental breakdown.

**Tashjian, Janet.** *Multiple Choice.* H. Holt, c1999. 186pp.
Monica, a fourteen-year-old perfectionist and word game expert, tries to break free from the suffocating rules in her life by creating a game for living called Multiple Choice.

# Mental Illness

**Weeks, Sarah.** *So B. It: A Novel.* Laura Geringer Books, c2004. 245pp.

After spending her life with her mentally retarded mother and agoraphobic neighbor, twelve-year-old Heidi sets out from Reno, Nevada, to New York to find out who she is.

**White, Ruth.** *Memories of Summer.* Farrar, Straus & Giroux, c2000. 135pp.

In 1955, thirteen-year-old Lyric finds her whole life changing when her family moves from the hills of Virginia to a town in Michigan, and her older sister Summer begins descending into mental illness.

**Wilson, Dawn.** *Saint Jude*. Tudor Publishers, c2001. 171pp.

When committed to an upscale group home outside Asheville, North Carolina, eighteen-year-old Taylor Drysdale pretends that her bipolar disorder is under control and that she will leave soon, but relationships with her fellow residents may hold the key to real recovery.

## Books for Older Teens

**Fensham, Elizabeth.** *Helicopter Man.* Bloomsbury (distributed by Holtzbrinck), 2005. 159pp.

Australian youth Peter Sinclair, living on the run with his father, who claims he is being pursued by a secret organization, comes to the realization that his dad is mentally ill and must have treatment if they are ever to have a normal life together.

**Fuqua, Jonathon Scott.** *King of the Pygmies*. Candlewick Press, c2005. 246pp.

After hearing what he believes are other peoples' thoughts, high school sophomore Penn learns that he may have schizophrenia and makes some important decisions about how to live his life.

**Moore, Peter.** *Caught in the Act*. Viking Press, c2005. 260pp.

Everyone believes that sophomore honors student Ethan Lederer is a top-notch scholar and a great guy, but a new student helps Ethan to discover and disclose that he is just acting a role, even as she reveals her own mental instability.

# Physically Handicapped

## Books for Ages 12–15

**Bloor, Edward.** *Tangerine*. Harcourt Brace, c1997. 294pp.

Twelve-year-old Paul, who lives in the shadow of his football hero brother Erik, fights for the right to play soccer despite his near blindness, and slowly begins to remember the incident that damaged his eyesight.

**Farrell, Mame.** *Marrying Malcolm Murgatroyd*. Farrar, Straus & Giroux, 1998, c1995. 121pp.

Hannah Billings hates being teased about marrying Malcolm Murgatroyd, the most unpopular and misunderstood boy in her sixth-grade class, until he reveals his true personality when her brother succumbs to muscular dystrophy.

**Ferris, Jean.** *Of Sound Mind*. Farrar, Straus & Giroux, c2001. 215pp.

Tired of interpreting for his deaf family and resentful of their reliance on him, high school senior Theo finds support and understanding from Ivy, a new student who also has a deaf parent.

**Fleischman, Paul.** *Mind's Eye*. Dell Laurel-Leaf, 2001, c1999. 108pp.

A novel in play form in which sixteen-year-old Courtney, paralyzed in an accident, learns about the power of the mind from an elderly blind woman, who takes Courtney on an imaginary journey to Italy using a 1910 guidebook.

**Hamilton, Virginia.** *Bluish: A Novel*. Blue Sky Press, c1999. 127pp.

Ten-year-old Dreenie feels both intrigued and frightened when she thinks about the girl nicknamed Bluish, whose leukemia is making her pale and causing her to use a wheelchair.

**Hatrick, Gloria.** *Masks*. Orchard Books, c1996. 120pp.

Desperate to help his older brother Will, who has become paralyzed by a rare disease, Pete uses tribal animal masks to communicate with Will, allowing him to escape his useless body and embark on a series of strange and powerful dream journeys.

**Hobbs, Valerie.** *Stefan's Story*. Farrar, Straus & Giroux, c2003. 165pp.

Thirteen-year-old, wheelchair-bound Stefan renews his friendship with Carolina as they work together to save an old-growth forest from destruction by loggers.

**Johnson, Scott.** *Safe At Second*. Puffin Books, 2001, c1999. 245pp.

Paulie Lockwood's best friend, Todd Bannister, is destined for the major leagues, until a line drive to the head causes him to lose an eye and they both must find a new future for themselves.

**Johnston, Julie.** *Hero of Lesser Causes*. Tundra Books of Northern New York, c2003. 222pp.

In 1946 twelve-year-old Keely is devastated when her older brother Patrick is paralyzed by polio, and she starts a campaign to reawaken his waning interest in life.

**Jung, Reinhardt.** *Dreaming in Black & White*. P. Fogelman, 2003, c2000. 112pp.

A boy dreams that he is a student during the period of the Nazi Third Reich in Germany, where he is persecuted for being physically handicapped.

# Physically Handicapped

**Kehret, Peg.** *Earthquake Terror.* Puffin Books, 1998, c1996. 132pp.

When an earthquake hits the isolated island in northern California where his family were camping, twelve-year-old Jonathan Palmer must find a way to keep himself, his partially paralyzed younger sister, and their dog alive until help arrives.

**Kehret, Peg.** *Small Steps: The Year I Got Polio.* Whitman, c1996. 179pp. (NF)

The author describes her battle against polio when she was thirteen and her efforts to overcome its debilitating effects.

**Lowry, Lois.** *Gathering Blue.* Dell Laurel-Leaf, 2002, c2000. 215pp.

Lame and suddenly orphaned, Kira is mysteriously removed from her squalid village to live in the palatial Council Edifice, where she is expected to use her gifts as a weaver to do the bidding of the all-powerful Guardians.

**Martin, Ann M.** *A Corner of the Universe.* Scholastic Press, c2002. 189pp.

The summer that Hattie turns twelve, she meets the childlike uncle she never knew and becomes friends with a girl who works at the carnival that comes to Hattie's small town.

**McKay, Hilary.** *Saffy's Angel.* Margaret K. McElderry Books, c2002. 152pp.

After learning that she was adopted, thirteen-year-old Saffron's relationship with her eccentric, artistic family changes, until they help her go back to Italy, where she was born, to find a special memento of her past.

**Mikaelsen, Ben.** *Petey.* Hyperion Books for Children, c1998. 280pp.

In 1922 Petey, who has cerebral palsy, is misdiagnosed as an idiot and institutionalized; sixty years later, still in the institution, he befriends a boy and shares with him the joy of life.

**Mitchell, Marianne.** *Finding Zola.* Boyds Mills Press, c2005. 144pp.

While trying to discover what happened to her elderly neighbor, who has mysteriously disappeared, thirteen-year-old Crystal confronts her feelings of guilt related to the car accident that killed her father and left her confined to a wheelchair.

**Orr, Wendy.** *Peeling the Onion.* Holiday House, c1997. 166pp.

Following an automobile accident in which her neck is broken, a teenage karate champion begins a long and painful recovery with the help of her family.

**Philbrick, W. R.** *Freak the Mighty.* Scholastic, c1993. 169pp.

At the beginning of eighth grade, learning disabled Max and his new friend Freak, whose birth defect has affected his body but not his brilliant mind, find that when they combine forces they make a powerful team.

**Platt, Chris.** *Willow King: Race the Wind.* Random House, c2002. 248pp.

Fifteen-year-old Katie Durham learns about courage and independence as she befriends a blind girl and fights to become a jockey and ride in the Kentucky Derby despite her own physical handicap.

**Roos, Stephen.** *The Gypsies Never Came.* Simon & Schuster Books for Young Readers, c2001. 116pp.

Sixth-grader Augie Knapp, who has a deformed hand, is convinced by Lydie Rose, the strange new girl in town, that the gypsies are coming for him.

From Nancy J. Keane, *The Big Book of Teen Reading Lists: 100 Great, Ready-to-Use Book Lists for Educators, Librarians, Parents, and Children.* Westport, CT: Libraries Unlimited, 2006. Copyright © 2006 by Libraries Unlimited.

# Physically Handicapped

**Scrimger, Richard.** *From Charlie's Point of View.* Dutton Books, c2005. 278pp.

Best friends Bernadette and Charlie begin seventh grade and help unravel the mysterious case of the Stocking Bandit.

**Sleator, William.** *The Last Universe.* Amulet Books, c2005. 215pp.

When her desperately ill older brother insists that she take him into their mysterious backyard garden, designed by their quantum physicist great uncle, fourteen-year-old Susan discovers that things are not always what they seem.

## Books for Older Teens

**Koertge, Ronald.** *Stoner & Spaz.* Candlewick Press, c2002. 169pp.

A troubled youth with cerebral palsy struggles toward self-acceptance with the help of a drug-addicted young woman.

**Lebert, Benjamin.** *Crazy.* Vintage, 2001, c2000. 177pp.

An English translation of the German novel about Benjamin Lebert, a sixteen-year-old with a disability who has been sent to a remedial boarding school, where he embarks on a discovery of life, friends, love, booze, girls, and sex.

**Martin, Rafe.** *Birdwing.* A. A. Levine Books, c2005. 357pp.

Prince Ardwin, known as Birdwing, the youngest of six brothers turned into swans by their stepmother, is unable to complete the transformation back into human form, so he undertakes a journey to discover whether his feathered arm will be a curse or a blessing to him.

**McBay, Bruce.** *Waiting for Sarah.* Orca Book Publishers, c2003. 170pp.

After teenager Mike Scott loses his family and his legs in a car accident, he withdraws from life, until he meets the mysterious Sarah, a girl who is not what she seems.

**Trueman, Terry.** *Cruise Control.* HarperTempest, c2004. 149pp.

A talented basketball player struggles to deal with the helplessness and anger that come with having a brother rendered completely dysfunctional by severe cerebral palsy and a father who deserted the family.

**Trueman, Terry.** *Stuck in Neutral.* HarperCollins, c2000. 114pp.

Fourteen-year-old Shawn McDaniel, who suffers from severe cerebral palsy and cannot function, relates his perceptions of his life, his family, and his condition, especially as he believes his father is planning to kill him.

**Walters, Eric.** *Rebound.* Stoddart Kids (distributed in the United States by General Distribution Services), 2001, c2000. 262pp.

The friendship of Sean and David helps them to get on the basketball team.

**Whelan, Gloria.** *Forgive the River, Forgive the Sky.* Eerdmans Books for Young Readers, 1999, c1998. 85pp.

After her father dies in the river they both love, twelve-year-old Lily struggles to come to terms with her loss, and in so doing, she helps a paraplegic former pilot accept his condition and move on with his life.

From Nancy J. Keane, *The Big Book of Teen Reading Lists: 100 Great, Ready-to-Use Book Lists for Educators, Librarians, Parents, and Children.* Westport, CT: Libraries Unlimited, 2006. Copyright © 2006 by Libraries Unlimited.

# Politically Active

## Books for Ages 12–15

**Avi.** *Nothing But the Truth: A Documentary Novel.* Orchard Books, 2003, c1991. 177pp.
A ninth-grader's suspension for singing "The Star-Spangled Banner" during homeroom becomes a national news story. One of the consequences is that he and his teacher both leave the school.

**Barron, T. A.** *The Ancient One*. Philomel Books, c1992. 367pp.
While helping her Great Aunt Melanie try to protect an Oregon redwood forest from loggers, thirteen-year-old Kate goes back five centuries through a time tunnel and faces the evil creature Gashra, who is bent on destroying the same forest.

**Bauer, Joan.** *Hope Was Here.* Putnam, c2000. 186pp.
When sixteen-year-old Hope and the aunt who has raised her move from Brooklyn to Mulhoney, Wisconsin, to work as waitress and cook in the Welcome Stairways diner, they become involved with the diner owner's political campaign to oust the town's corrupt mayor.

**Bennett, Cherie.** *A Heart Divided.* Delacorte Press, c2004. 306pp.
When sixteen-year-old Kate, an aspiring playwright, moves from New Jersey to attend high school in the South, she becomes embroiled in a controversy to remove the school's Confederate flag symbol.

**D'Adamo, Francesco.** *Iqbal: A Novel.* Atheneum Books for Young Readers, c2003. 120pp.
A fictionalized account of the Pakistani child who escaped from bondage in a carpet factory and went on to help liberate other children like him, before being gunned down at the age of thirteen.

**Halpin, Mikki.** *It's Your World—If You Don't Like It, Change It: Activism for Teenagers.* Simon Pulse, c2004. 305pp. (NF)
Presents advice for teenagers who desire to cultivate changes within their schools and communities and provides information on racism, animal and human rights, environmental issues, HIV/AIDS, school violence, and tolerance.

**Hentoff, Nat.** *The Day They Came to Arrest the Book: A Novel.* Bantam Doubleday Dell Books for Young Readers, 1983, c1982. 169pp.
Students and faculty at a high school became embroiled in a censorship case about *Huckleberry Finn*.

**Hiaasen, Carl.** *Flush*. Knopf (distributed by Random House), c2005. 263pp.
With their father jailed for sinking a river boat, Noah Underwood and his younger sister, Abbey, must gather evidence that the owner of this floating casino is emptying his bilge tanks into the protected waters around their Florida Keys home.

**Hiaasen, Carl.** *Hoot.* Knopf (distributed by Random House), c2002. 292pp.
Roy, who is new to his small Florida community, becomes involved in another boy's attempt to save a colony of burrowing owls from a proposed construction site.

**Keizer, Garret.** *God of Beer.* HarperTempest, 2003, c2002. 242pp.
To complete a class assignment at his high school in rural Vermont, Kyle and his friends Quake and Diana do a social protest project involving alcohol.

# Politically Active

**Konigsburg, E. L.** *The Outcasts of 19 Schuyler Place.* Atheneum Books for Young Readers, c2004. 296pp.

Upon leaving an oppressive summer camp, twelve-year-old Margaret Rose Kane spearheads a campaign to preserve three unique towers her great-uncles have been building in their back yard for over forty years.

**Tashjian, Janet.** *The Gospel According To Larry.* H. Holt, c2001. 227pp.

Seventeen-year-old Josh, a loner-philosopher who wants to make a difference in the world, tries to maintain his secret identity as the author of a Web site that is receiving national attention.

**Tashjian, Janet.** *Vote for Larry.* H. Holt, c2004. 224pp.

Not yet eighteen years old, Josh, a.k.a. Larry, comes out of hiding and returns to public life, this time to run for president as an advocate for issues of concern to youth and to encourage voter turnout.

**Williams, Laura E.** *Up a Creek.* H. Holt, c2001. 135pp.

Thirteen-year-old Starshine Bott learns how to cope with an unconventional, politically active mother and does a lot of growing up in the process.

## Books for Older Teens

**Gitlin, Todd.** *Letters to a Young Activist.* Basic Books, c2003. 174pp. (NF)

Todd Gitlin offers advice to young activists who want to make a difference in the world, discussing how they can have the most impact on their community and the world in general.

# Royally Good Reads

## Books for Ages 12–15

**Alexander, Lloyd.** *The Iron Ring.* Puffin Books, c1999. 283pp.

Driven by his sense of "dharma," or honor, young King Tamar sets off on a perilous journey, with a significance greater than he can imagine, during which he meets talking animals, villainous and noble kings, demons, and the love of his life.

**Cabot, Meg.** *The Princess Diaries.* HarperCollins, c2000. 238pp. (and sequels)

Fourteen-year-old Mia, who is trying to lead a normal life as a teenage girl in New York City, is shocked to learn that her father is the Prince of Genovia, a small European principality, and that she is a princess and the heir to the throne.

**Haddix, Margaret Peterson.** *Just Ella.* Simon & Schuster Books for Young Readers, c1999. 185pp.

In this continuation of the Cinderella story, fifteen-year-old Ella finds that accepting Prince Charming's proposal ensnares her in a suffocating tangle of palace rules and royal etiquette, so she plots to escape.

**Kindl, Patrice.** *Goose Chase.* Houghton Mifflin, c2001. 214pp.

Rather than marry a cruel king or a seemingly dim-witted prince, an enchanted goose girl endures imprisonment, capture by several ogresses, and other dangers before learning exactly who she is.

**Lasky, Kathryn.** *Elizabeth I, Red Rose of the House of Tudor.* Scholastic, c1999. 237pp.

In a series of diary entries, Princess Elizabeth, the eleven-year-old daughter of King Henry VIII, celebrates holidays and birthdays, relives her mother's execution, revels in her studies, and agonizes over her father's health.

**Lasky, Kathryn.** *Marie Antoinette, Princess of Versailles.* Scholastic, c2000. 236pp.

In 1769 thirteen-year-old Maria Antonia Josepha Johanna, daughter of Empress Maria Theresa, begins a journal chronicling her life at the Austrian court and her preparations for her future role as queen of France.

**McKinley, Robin.** *Spindle's End.* Putnam, c2000. 422pp.

The infant princess Briar Rose is cursed on her name day by Pernicia, an evil fairy, and then whisked away by a young fairy to be raised in a remote part of a magical country, unaware of her real identity and hidden from Pernicia's vengeful powers.

**Meyer, Carolyn.** *Anastasia, the Last Grand Duchess.* Scholastic, c2000. 220pp.

A novel in diary form in which the youngest daughter of Czar Nicholas II describes the privileged life her family led up until the time of World War I and the tragic events that befell them.

**Meyer, Carolyn.** *Doomed Queen Anne.* Harcourt, c2002. 230pp.

In 1520 thirteen-year-old Anne Boleyn, jealous of her older sister's beauty and position at court, declares that she will one day be queen of England, and that her sister will kneel at her feet.

**Meyer, Carolyn.** *Mary, Bloody Mary.* Harcourt, 2001, c1999. 227pp.

Mary Tudor, who would reign briefly as Queen of England during the mid-sixteenth century, tells the story of her troubled childhood as daughter of King Henry VIII.

**Meyer, Carolyn.** *Patience, Princess Catherine.* Harcourt, c2004. 198pp.

In 1501 fifteen-year-old Catharine of Aragon arrives in England to marry Arthur, the eldest son of King Henry VII, but soon finds her expectations of a happy settled life radically changed when Arthur unexpectedly dies and her future becomes the subject of a bitter dispute between the kingdoms of England and Spain.

# Royally Good Reads

**Meyer, Carolyn.** *Isabel: Jewel of Castilla*. Scholastic, c2000. 204pp.
While waiting anxiously for others to choose a husband for her, Isabella, the future Queen of Spain, keeps a diary account of her life as a member of the royal family.

**O'Connell, Tyne.** *Pulling Princes.* Bloomsbury (distributed by Holtzbrinck), c2004. 224pp.
Calypso Kelly, a California teenager attending an upscale boarding school in England, sets out to become popular by claiming that her mother's gay assistant is Calypso's boyfriend and finds herself in a royal mess when she gets a chance at a real relationship with a prince.

**Wyatt, Melissa.** *Raising the Griffin*. Wendy Lamb Books, c2004. 279pp.
When the people of Rovenia vote to restore their monarchy, sixteen-year-old Alex Varenhoff must suddenly leave his native England to become prince of a land he knows only from his grandfather's stories.

**Yolen, Jane.** *Girl in a Cage*. Philomel Books, c2002. 234pp.
As English armies invade Scotland in 1306, eleven-year-old Princess Marjorie, daughter of the newly crowned Scottish king, Robert the Bruce, is captured by England's King Edward (Longshanks) and held in a cage on public display.

**Yolen, Jane.** *Queen's Own Fool: A Novel of Mary Queen of Scots*. Philomel Books, c2000. 390pp.
When twelve-year-old Nicola leaves Troupe Brufort and serves as the fool for Mary, Queen of Scots, she experiences the political and religious upheavals in both France and Scotland.

## Books for Older Teens

**Card, Orson Scott.** *Enchantment*. Del Rey/Ballantine, 2000, c1999. 419pp.
American graduate student Ivan Smetski, haunted by the vision of a sleeping princess he believes he saw as a ten-year-old boy while exploring the Carpathian forest, returns to his native land to investigate and, with one kiss, is drawn into a world that vanished a thousand years earlier.

**Goldman, William.** *The Princess Bride: S. Morgenstern's Classic Tale of True Love and High Adventure: The "Good Parts" Version.* Ballantine Books, c1998. 399pp.
Westley, a farm boy, goes off to seek his fortune shortly after declaring his love for Buttercup, the most beautiful woman in the world, but their relationship is put to the test when his ship is captured by pirates and she is summoned to become the bride of the prince.

**McKinley, Robin.** *Deerskin*. Ace, 1994, c1993. 309pp.
A beautiful princess flees from her father's wrath and unlocks a door into a world of magic, where she finds the key to her own survival.

**Rawn, Melanie.** *Dragon Prince*. DAW Books, c1985. 574pp.
Rohan, newly crowned prince of the Desert, aspires to bring permanent peace to his world of divided princedoms and stop the dragon slaying that is regarded as proof of manhood. He finds a champion in his quests when he falls in love with Sioned, a Sunrunner witch.

# Fantasy Sheroes

## Books for Ages 12–15

**Bell, Hilari.** *The Goblin Wood*. EOS, c2003. 294pp.

A young Hedgewitch, an idealistic knight, and an army of clever goblins fight against the ruling hierarchy that is trying to rid the land of all magical creatures.

**Billingsley, Franny.** *The Folk Keeper.* Atheneum Books for Young Readers, c1999. 162pp.

Orphan Corinna disguises herself as a boy to pose as a Folk Keeper, one who keeps the Evil Folk at bay, and discovers her heritage as a seal maiden when she is taken to live with a wealthy family in their manor by the sea.

**Donoghue, Emma.** *Kissing the Witch: Old Tales in New Skins.* HarperCollins, 1999, c1997. 228pp.

A collection of thirteen interconnected stories that give old fairy tales a new twist.

**Gaiman, Neil.** *Coraline*. HarperCollins, c2002. 162pp.

Looking for excitement, Coraline ventures through a mysterious door into a world that is similar to, yet disturbingly different from, her own, where she must challenge a gruesome entity in order to save herself, her parents, and the souls of three others.

**Goodman, Alison.** *Singing the Dogstar Blues.* Viking Press, 2002, c1998. 261pp.

In a future Australia, the saucy eighteen-year-old daughter of a famous newscaster and a sperm donor teams up with a hermaphrodite from the planet Choria in a time travel adventure that may significantly change both of their lives.

**Hanley, Victoria.** *The Seer and the Sword.* Holiday House, c2000. 341pp.

Princess Torina, who has the ability to see the future, and her friend Landen, who seeks a sword that belongs to his conquered kingdom, are separated when a treacherous murderer gains power, but from exile each works to restore peace and the rightful rulers.

**Hoffman, Mary.** *Stravaganza: City of Stars.* Bloomsbury Children's Books (distributed by Holtzbrinck), c2003. 452pp. (and sequels)

Fifteen-year-old Georgia, who loves horses as much as she hates her bullying stepbrother, buys a figurine of a winged horse and finds it has magical powers that transport her from present-day London to the sixteenth-century world of Talia, where, in the city of Remora, similar to Sienna, Italy, she finds danger and intrigue as well as friendship and a chance to perfect her riding skills.

**McKinley, Robin.** *Beauty: A Retelling of the Story of Beauty & the Beast.* HarperCollins, c1978. 247pp.

Kind Beauty grows to love the Beast, at whose castle she is compelled to stay, and through her love releases him from the spell that had turned him from a handsome prince into an ugly beast.

**McKinley, Robin.** *The Hero and the Crown.* Greenwillow Books, c1984. 246pp.

Aerin, with the guidance of the wizard Luthe and the help of the blue sword, wins the birthright due her as the daughter of the Damarian king and a witchwoman of the mysterious, demon-haunted North.

**McKinley, Robin.** *Spindle's End.* Putnam, c2000. 422pp.

The infant princess Briar Rose is cursed on her name day by Pernicia, an evil fairy, and then whisked away by a young fairy to be raised in a remote part of a magical country, unaware of her real identity and hidden from Pernicia's vengeful powers.

# Fantasy Sheroes

**Pierce, Tamora.** *First Test.* Random House, c1999. 216pp.
Ten-year-old Keladry of Mindalen, daughter of nobles, serves as a page but must prove herself to the males around her if she is ever to fulfill her dream of becoming a knight.

**Smith, Sherwood.** *Wren to the Rescue.* Firebird, 2004, c1990, 216pp.
With the help of a prince and an apprentice wizard, Wren strives to rescue her best friend, a princess named Tess, from the fortress of a wicked king.

**Vande Velde, Vivian.** *Heir Apparent.* Harcourt, c2002. 315pp.
While playing a total immersion virtual reality game of kings and intrigue, fourteen-year-old Giannine learns that demonstrators have damaged the equipment to which she is connected, and she must win the game quickly or be damaged herself.

**Wrede, Patricia C.** *Dealing with Dragons.* Harcourt Brace Jovanovich, c1990. 212pp. (and sequels)
Bored with traditional palace life, a princess goes off to live with a group of dragons and soon becomes involved in fighting against some disreputable wizards, who want to steal away the dragons' kingdom.

## Books for Older Teens

**Black, Holly.** *Tithe: A Modern Faerie Tale.* Simon & Schuster, c2002. 310pp.
Sixteen-year-old Kaye, who has been visited by faeries since childhood, discovers that she herself is a magical faerie creature with a special destiny.

**Bull, Emma.** *War for the Oaks.* Tor, 2004, c1987, 332pp.
The people of modern Minneapolis go about their daily business, unaware that an age-old war between the Seelie and Unseelie Courts is being fought in their midst. Only Eddi can see the battle, and she has been drafted into the war.

**Butler, Octavia E.** *Parable of the Sower.* Warner Books, 2000, c1993. 345pp.
The odyssey of a sensitive young woman in a world that has become almost completely dehumanized. Set in California in the years 2024 through 2027.

**De Lint, Charles.** *Jack of Kinrowan.* Orb, c1995. 412pp.
Presents two tales of faerie magic in "Jack, the Giant Killer," about a faceless gang of bikers in Ottawa who throw Jacky Rowan into the perilous land of Faerie, and "Drink Down the Moon," about Johnny Faw, a young fiddler who has to set the realm of the Faerie free from a horrible creature.

**Flewelling, Lynn.** *Hidden Warrior.* Bantam Books, c2003. 551pp.
Prince Tobin, second heir to the throne of Skala, learns to his surprise that he was given the shape of a boy as an infant in order to protect him from his enemies, and that his true destiny is to claim that throne in his real form, as a woman.

**Gibson, William.** *Virtual Light.* Bantam Books, c1994. 352pp.
Chevette Washington, a bike messenger in early twenty-first-century California, finds herself in danger when the sunglasses she pickpocketed from a drunk turn out to be a high-tech device owned by the deadly and powerful DatAmerica corporation.

# Fantasy Sheroes

**Lackey, Mercedes.** *The Fire Rose.* Baen Books (distributed by Simon & Schuster), c1995. 433pp.
Medieval scholar Rosalind Hawkins, left destitute when her family fortune disappears, accepts a position as governess in a house where there are no children, one servant, and a seemingly invisible employer.

**Pratchett, Terry.** *Monstrous Regiment: A Novel of Discworld.* HarperCollins, c2003. 353pp.
Polly Perks, fearing that the national deity's decree against female ownership of a business is going to cause her to lose the family's inn, disguises herself as a man in order to join the military and find her brother, whom she fears has been killed in Borogravia's latest war.

**Willis, Connie.** *Doomsday Book.* Bantam Books, c1994. 578pp.
Young twenty-first-century historian Kivrin Engle becomes stranded in the fourteenth century after a time-travel expedition goes wrong, and she finds herself cast in the role of an angel of hope during one of history's darkest hours.

# Teen Romance with African American Characters

## Books for Ages 12–15

**Coleman, Evelyn.** *Born in Sin*. Atheneum Books for Young Readers, c2001. 234pp.
Despite serious obstacles and setbacks, fourteen-year-old Keisha pursues her dream of becoming an Olympic swimmer and medical doctor.

**Davidson, Dana.** *Jason & Kyra*. Jump at the Sun/ Hyperion Books for Children, c2005. 330pp.
Kyra Evans, a smart, less-than-popular high-schooler, begins to fall for Jason Vincent, a popular basketball star.

**Flake, Sharon.** *Money Hungry.* Jump at the Sun/Hyperion Books for Children, c2001. 187pp.
All thirteen-year-old Raspberry can think of is making money so that she and her mother never have to worry about living on the streets again.

**Grimes, Nikki.** *Bronx Masquerade.* Dial Books, c2002. 167pp.
While studying the Harlem Renaissance, students at a Bronx high school read aloud poems they've written, revealing their innermost thoughts and fears to their formerly clueless classmates.

**McDonald, Janet.** *Spellbound*. Farrar, Straus & Giroux, c2001. 138pp.
Raven, a teenage mother and high school dropout living in a housing project, decides, with the help and sometime interference of her best friend Aisha, to study for a spelling bee that could lead to a college preparatory program and four-year scholarship.

## Books for Older Teens

**Draper, Sharon M.** *Darkness Before Dawn.* Atheneum Books for Young Readers, c2001. 233pp.
Recovering from the recent suicide of her ex-boyfriend, senior class president Keisha Montgomery finds herself attracted to a dangerous, older man.

**Frost, Helen.** *Keesha's House.* Farrar, Straus & Giroux, c2003. 116pp.
Seven teens facing such problems as pregnancy, closeted homosexuality, and abuse each describe in poetic forms what caused them to leave home and where they found home again.

**Woodson, Jacqueline.** *Behind You.* Putnam, c2004. 118pp.
After fifteen-year-old Jeremiah is mistakenly shot by police, the people who love him struggle to cope with their loss as they recall his life and death, unaware that 'Miah is watching over them.

# Part 3

## Books About Self

# Aftereffects of Violence

## Books for Ages 12–15

**Blume, Judy.** *Tiger Eyes*. Bantam Doubleday Dell Books for Young Readers, 1991, c1981. 217pp.
Resettled in New Mexico with her mother and brother, Davey Wexler recovers from the shock of her father's death during a holdup at his 7-Eleven store in Atlantic City.

**Flinn, Alex.** *Fade to Black*. HarperTempest, c2005. 184pp.
An HIV-positive high school student hospitalized after being attacked; the bigot accused of the crime;, and the only witness, a classmate with Down Syndrome, reveal how the assault has changed their lives as they describe its aftermath.

**Kerr, M. E.** *Slap Your Sides: A Novel*. HarperCollins, c2001. 198pp.
Life in their Pennsylvania hometown changes for Jubal Shoemaker and his family when his older brother witnesses to his Quaker beliefs by becoming a conscientious objector during World War II.

**Mikaelsen, Ben.** *Touching Spirit Bear*. HarperCollins, c2001. 241pp.
After his anger erupts into violence, fifteen year-old Cole, to avoid going to prison, agrees to participate in a sentencing alternative based on the Native American Circle Justice. He is sent to a remote Alaskan Island, where an encounter with a huge Spirit Bear changes his life.

**Peretti, Frank E.** *Hangman's Curse*. T. Nelson, c2001. 281pp.
When several students at Baker High School are stricken by an alleged curse of the school's ghost, Elijah and Elisha Springfield and their parents, undercover investigators, are sent to uncover the truth behind the events.

**Prose, Francine.** *After*. Joanna Cotler Books, c2003. 330pp.
In the aftermath of a shooting at a nearby school, a grief and crisis counselor takes over Central High School and enacts increasingly harsh measures to control students; those who do not comply, disappear.

**Soto, Gary.** *The Afterlife*. Harcourt, 2005, c2003. 161pp.
After he is brutally murdered in the restroom of a club where he had gone to dance, a senior at East Fresno High School lives on as a ghost .

**Strasser, Todd.** *Give a Boy a Gun*. Simon Pulse, 2002, c2000. 208pp.
Events leading up to a night of terror at a high school dance are told from the point of view of various people involved.

## Books for Older Teens

**Anderson, Laurie Halse.** *Speak*. Farrar, Straus & Giroux, c1999. 197pp.
A traumatic event near the end of the summer has a devastating effect on Melinda's freshman year in high school.

**Carbone, Elisa Lynn.** *The Pack*. Viking Press, c2003. 153pp.
Akhil Vyas, a new boy in school, reluctantly decides that  to prevent a violent crime, he must tell Omar and Becky his secret.

# Aftereffects of Violence

**Cole, Brock.** *The Facts Speak for Themselves.* Front Street, c1997. 184pp.

At the request of her social worker, thirteen-year-old Linda gradually reveals how her life with her unstable mother and her younger brother led to her being raped and the murder that she witnessed.

**Coman, Carolyn.** *Many Stones.* Front Street, c2000. 158pp.

After her sister Laura is murdered in South Africa, Berry and her estranged father travel there to participate in the dedication of a memorial in her name.

**Corrigan, Eireann.** *Splintering.* Scholastic, c2004. 184pp.

Relates, in a series of poems from different perspectives, the events and after-effects of an intruder's violent attack on a family.

**Crutcher, Chris.** *Staying Fat for Sarah Byrnes.* Greenwillow Books, c1993. 216pp.

The daily class discussions about the nature of man, the existence of God, abortion, organized religion, suicide and other contemporary issues serve as a backdrop for a high-school senior's attempt to answer a friend's dramatic cry for help.

**Dessen, Sarah.** *Dreamland: A Novel.* Viking Press, c2000. 250pp.

After her older sister runs away, sixteen-year-old Caitlin decides that she needs to make a major change in her own life and begins an abusive relationship with a boy who is mysterious, brilliant, and dangerous.

**Flinn, Alex.** *Breaking Point.* HarperTempest, 2003, c2002. 240pp.

Fifteen-year-old Paul enters an exclusive private school and falls under the spell of a charismatic boy, who may be using him.

**Flinn, Alex.** *Breathing Underwater.* HarperTempest, 2002, c2001. 263pp.

Sent to counseling for hitting his girlfriend, Caitlin, and ordered to keep a journal, sixteen-year-old Nick recounts his relationship with Caitlin, examines his controlling behavior and anger, and describes living with his abusive father.

**Flinn, Alex.** *Nothing to Lose.* HarperTempest, c2004. 277pp.

A year after running away with a traveling carnival to escape his unbearable home life, sixteen-year-old Michael returns to Miami, Florida, to find that his mother is going on trial for the murder of his abusive stepfather.

**Giles, Gail.** *Shattering Glass.* Roaring Brook Press, c2002. 215pp.

Rob, the charismatic leader of the senior class, provokes unexpected violence when he turns the school nerd into Prince Charming.

**Johnson, Kathleen Jeffrie.** *Target.* Roaring Brook Press, c2003. 175pp.

After being brutally raped, Grady finally goes to a new high school, where he meets an outgoing African American and several other students who try to help him deal with the horrible secret that is robbing him of his life.

**Jones, Patrick.** *Things Change.* Walker, 2004. 216pp.

Sixteen-year-old Johanna, one of the best students in her class, develops a passionate attachment for troubled seventeen-year-old Paul and finds her plans for the future changing in unexpected ways.

# Aftereffects of Violence

**Koertge, Ronald.** *The Brimstone Journals.* Candlewick Press, c2001. 113pp.
In a series of short, interconnected poems, students at a high school nicknamed Brimstone reveal the presence of growing violence in their lives.

**Mac, Carrie.** *The Beckoners*. Orca Book Publishers, c2004. 217pp.
Zoe, unhappy to be moving once again, falls in with the Beckoners, a group of bullies at her new school. She soon finds herself trying to get free from the gang, whose actions against their favorite target, a girl they call Dog, are escalating to violence.

**Myers, Walter Dean.** *Monster.* HarperCollins, c1999. 271pp.
While on trial as an accomplice to a murder, sixteen-year-old Steve Harmon records his experiences in prison and in the courtroom, in the form of a film script, as he tries to come to terms with the course his life has taken.

**Myers, Walter Dean.** *Shooter*. HarperTempest, 2005, c2004. 223pp.
Written in the form of interviews, reports, and journal entries, the story of three troubled teenagers ends in a tragic school shooting.

**Plum-Ucci, Carol.** *What Happened to Lani Garver.* Harcourt, c2002. 307pp.
Sixteen-year-old Claire is unable to face her fears about a recurrence of her leukemia, her eating disorder, her need to fit in with the popular crowd on Hackett Island, and her mother's alcoholism, until the enigmatic Lani Garver helps her get control of her life, at the risk of his own.

**Sebold, Alice.** *The Lovely Bones.* Little, Brown, c2002. 328pp.
Fourteen-year-old Susie Salmon, the victim of a sexual assault and murder, looks on from the afterlife as her family deals with their grief, and waits for her killer to be brought to some type of justice.

**Shepard, Jim.** *Project X: A Novel.* Knopf (distributed by Random House), c2004. 163pp.
Eight-grade misfits Edwin Hanratty and his only friend, Flake, feed each other's misery and discontent, until they decide the only solution is violence.

**Shriver, Lionel.** *We Need to Talk About Kevin.* Counterpoint, c2003. 400pp.
Eva Khatchadourian has been living a life plagued by guilt and denial since her son opened fire and killed seven of his classmates two years earlier, and as she tries to come to terms with her son's actions, she examines the parenting choices she made when raising him and wonders where she went wrong.

**Werlin, Nancy.** *Black Mirror: A Novel.* Dial Books, c2001. 249pp.
Convinced her brother's death was murder rather than suicide, sixteen-year-old Frances begins her own investigation into suspicious student activities at her boarding school.

**Werlin, Nancy.** *The Killer's Cousin.* Dell Laurel-Leaf, 2000, c1998. 229pp.
After being acquitted of murder, seventeen-year-old David goes to stay with relatives in Cambridge, Massachusetts, where he finds himself forced to face his past as he learns more about his strange young cousin, Lily.

# Anger

## Fiction

### Books for Ages 12–15

**Crowe, Carole.** *Waiting for Dolphins.* Boyds Mills Press, c2000. 139pp.
In the aftermath of her father's untimely death, fifteen-year-old Molly must deal with grief and her anger toward her mother.

**Ferris, Jean.** *Of Sound Mind.* Farrar, Straus & Giroux, c2001. 215pp.
Tired of interpreting for his deaf family and resentful of their reliance on him, high school senior Theo finds support and understanding from Ivy, a new student who also has a deaf parent.

**Lewis, Catherine.** *Postcards to Father Abraham: A Novel.* Atheneum Books for Young Readers, c2000. 288pp.
When sixteen-year-old Meghan loses her leg to cancer and her brother to the Vietnam War, she expresses intense anger in postcards she writes to her idol, Abraham Lincoln.

**Lynch, Chris.** *Who the Man.* HarperCollins, c2002. 186pp.
Thirteen-year-old Earl Pryor is much too big for his age, and much too powerful for the anger that rages within him when classmates tease him, the girl he likes disappoints him, or his parents' problems get too real.

**Mikaelsen, Ben.** *Touching Spirit Bear.* HarperCollins, c2001. 241pp.
After his anger erupts into violence, fifteen-year-old Cole, to avoid going to prison, agrees to participate in a sentencing alternative based on the Native American Circle Justice. He is sent to a remote Alaskan Island, where an encounter with a huge Spirit Bear changes his life.

**Paterson, Katherine.** *Jacob Have I Loved.* Crowell, c1980. 216pp.
Filled with resentment over the attention showered upon her twin sister and awaiting the day she can leave her town behind, young Louise meets a wise old sea captain and begins learning how to let go of her anger.

**Ritter, John H.** *Over the Wall.* Philomel Books, c2000. 312pp.
Thirteen-year-old Tyler, who has trouble controlling his anger, spends an important summer with his cousins in New York City, playing baseball and sorting out how he feels about violence, war, and in particular the Vietnamese conflict, which took his grandfather's life.

**Strasser, Todd.** *Give a Boy a Gun.* Simon Pulse, 2002, c2000. 208pp.
Events leading up to a night of terror at a high school dance are told from the point of view of various people involved.

**Trueman, Terry.** *Cruise Control.* HarperTempest, c2004. 149pp.
A talented basketball player struggles to deal with the helplessness and anger that come with having a brother rendered completely dysfunctional by severe cerebral palsy and a father who deserted the family.

# Anger

## Books for Older Teens

**Crutcher, Chris.** *Ironman*. HarperTempest, 2004, c1995. 279pp.
>   While training for a triathlon, seventeen-year-old Bo attends an anger management group at school, which leads him to examine his relationship with his father.

**Flinn, Alex.** *Breathing Underwater.* HarperTempest, 2002. c2001. 263pp.
>   Sent to counseling for hitting his girlfriend, Caitlin, and ordered to keep a journal, sixteen-year-old Nick recounts his relationship with Caitlin, examines his controlling behavior and anger, and describes living with his abusive father.

**Lubar, David.** *Dunk*. Clarion Books, c2002. 249pp.
>   Chad, hoping to work out his frustrations and his anger by taking a summer job as a dunk tank Bozo on the boardwalk at the New Jersey shore, comes to a better understanding of himself and the uses of humor as he undergoes training in the fine art of insults.

**Mochizuki, Ken.** *Beacon Hill Boys.* Scholastic Press, c2002. 201pp.
>   In 1972 in Seattle, a teenager in a Japanese American family struggles for his own identity, along with a group of three friends who share his anger and confusion.

## Nonfiction

### Books for Ages 12–15

**Hershorn, Michael.** *Cool It!: Teen Tips to Keep Hot Tempers from Boiling Over.* New Horizon Press, c2003. 195pp. (NF)
>   Gives teenagers strategies for managing anger, showing how to recognize anger antecedents and how to walk away, calm down, control one's thoughts, communicate, negotiate, and stand up for oneself, and explains how to reflect upon behaviors and consequences. Also covers such topics as sibling rivalry, blended families, bullying, catastrophic stress, and making therapy work.

**Licata, Renora.** *Everything You Need To Know About Anger.* Rosen Publishing, c1999. 64pp. (NF)
>   Discusses the causes of anger and its ill effects on people, as well as ways to control it.

**O'Donnell Rawls, Bea.** *Drugs and Anger*. Rosen Publishing, c1994. 64pp. (NF)
>   Examines the connection between drugs and anger, showing what can happen when an angry person uses drugs or alcohol.

**Peacock, Judith.** *Anger Management.* LifeMatters, c2000. 64pp. (NF)
>   Discusses the issues of anger and anger management, providing a definition of the problem, examining its effects on teens, and offering advice to young people on how to deal with their own angry feelings as well as anger in others. Includes addresses and Internet sites for further information and assistance.

# Anger

## Books for Older Teens

**Enright, Robert D.** *Forgiveness Is a Choice: A Step-by-Step Process for Resolving Anger and Restoring Hope.* American Psychological Association, c2001. 299pp. (NF)

Explains how to end anger, depression, and resentment by understanding and undertaking the process of forgiveness, and covers related issues, including helping children forgive and wanting forgiveness from someone else.

**Seaward, Brian Luke.** *Hot Stones & Funny Bones: Teens Helping Teens Cope with Stress & Anger.* Health Communications, c2002. 376pp. (NF)

Provides an inside look at ways in which teens cope with their stress and anger, such as keeping a journal, meditating, or having a good laugh, and includes advice for parents and other teens.

# Beating the Odds

## Books for Ages 12–15

**Davis, Sampson.** *We Beat the Street: How a Friendship Pact Helped Us Succeed.* Dutton Children's Books, c2005. 194pp. (NF)

Shares anecdotes from the childhoods, teen years, and young adult lives of three men from Newark, New Jersey, who made a pledge to each other in high school to stay safe from drugs, gangs, and crime, and work to become doctors—a goal they have achieved.

**Filipovic, Zlata.** *Zlata's Diary: A Child's Life in Sarajevo.* Penguin Books, 1995, c1994. 197pp. (NF)

The diary of a thirteen-year-old girl living in Sarajevo, begun just before her eleventh birthday, when there was still peace in her homeland.

**Hamilton, Bethany.** *Soul Surfer: A True Story of Faith, Family, and Fighting to Get Back on the Board.* Pocket Books/MTV Books, c2004. 213pp. (NF)

Bethany Hamilton shares the story of her lifelong love of surfing, and tells how, after losing her arm in a shark attack at the age of thirteen, she was able to recover and return to competition with the help of her family, friends, and faith.

**Jiang, Ji-li.** *Red Scarf Girl: A Memoir of the Cultural Revolution.* HarperCollins, c1997. 285pp. (NF)

The author tells about the happy life she led in China until she was twelve-years-old, when her family became a target of the Cultural Revolution, and discusses the choice she had to make between denouncing her father and breaking with her family, or refusing to speak against him and losing her future in the Communist Party.

**Jimenez, Francisco.** *Breaking Through.* Houghton Mifflin, c2001. 195pp.

Having come from Mexico to California ten years ago, fourteen-year-old Francisco is still working in the fields but fighting to improve his life and complete his education.

**Lobel, Anita.** *No Pretty Pictures: A Child of War.* Greenwillow Books, c1998. 193pp. (NF)

The author, known as an illustrator of children's books, describes her experiences as a Polish Jew during World War II and for years in Sweden afterward.

**McKernan, Victoria.** *Shackleton's Stowaway.* Knopf (distributed by Random House), c2005. 317pp.

A fictionalized account of the adventures of eighteen-year-old Perce Blackborow, who stowed away with the 1914 Shackleton Antarctic expedition. After their ship, *Endurance,* was crushed by ice, he endured many hardships, including the loss of his toes to frostbite, during the nearly two-year return journey across sea and ice.

## Books for Older Teens

**Cox, Lynne.** *Swimming to Antarctica: Tales of a Long-Distance Swimmer.* Knopf (distributed by Random House), c2004. 323pp. (NF)

Distance swimmer Lynne Cox describes her emotional and spiritual need to swim and the mythical act of swimming itself, also chronicling some of her more memorable swims.

**Crutcher, Chris.** *Staying Fat for Sarah Byrnes.* Greenwillow Books, c1993. 216pp.

Daily class discussions about the nature of man, the existence of God, abortion, organized religion, suicide and other contemporary issues serve as a backdrop for a high-school senior's attempt to answer a friend's dramatic cry for help.

# Beating the Odds

**Crutcher, Chris.** *Whale Talk.* Greenwillow Books, c2001. 220pp.

Intellectually and athletically gifted, TJ, a multiracial, adopted teenager, shuns organized sports and the gung-ho athletes at his high school, until he agrees to form a swimming team and recruits some of the school's less popular students.

**Davis, Sampson.** *The Pact: Three Young Men Make a Promise and Fulfill a Dream.* Riverhead Books, 2003, c2002. 263pp. (NF)

Presents the true story of three African American kids from the inner city of Newark, New Jersey, who made a pact to support each other as they rose from an environment of poverty, crime, and drugs to become successful doctors.

**Flake, Sharon.** *Bang!* Jump at the Sun/Hyperion Books for Children, c2005. 298pp.

A teenage boy must face the harsh realities of inner-city life, a disintegrating family, and destructive temptations as he struggles to find his identity as a young man.

**Frank, E. R.** *America: A Novel.* Atheneum Books for Young Readers, c2002. 242pp.

America, a runaway boy who is being treated at Ridgeway, a New York hospital, finds himself opening up to one of the doctors on staff and revealing things about himself that he had always vowed to keep secret.

**Gantos, Jack.** *Hole In My Life.* Farrar, Straus & Giroux, c2002. 199pp. (NF)

The author relates how, as a young adult, he became a drug user and smuggler, was arrested, did time in prison, and eventually got out and went to college, all the while hoping to become a writer.

**Kaysen, Susanna.** *Girl, Interrupted.* Vintage, 1994, c1993. 168pp. (NF)

The author describes her two-year stay at a psychiatric hospital renowned for its famous clientele and for its progressive methods of treatment.

**Mathabane, Mark.** *Kaffir Boy: The True Story of a Black Youth's Coming of Age in Apartheid South Africa.* Free Press, 1998, c1986. 354pp. (NF)

The author recalls his personal experiences growing up under apartheid in South Africa during the 1970s, the poverty and oppression of living in the ghettos of Alexandra, and those who helped him escape from it.

**Rodriguez, Luis J.** *Always Running: La Vida Loca: Gang Days in L.A.* Simon & Schuster, c1994. 260pp. (NF)

The author recounts growing up in poverty in Los Angeles; his encounters with racism in school and on the streets; and his struggle to overcome prejudice, drugs, and violence.

**Runyon, Brent.** *The Burn Journals.* Knopf (distributed by Random House), c2004. 374pp. (NF)

Presents the true story of Brent Runyon, who at fourteen set himself on fire and sustained burns over 80 percent of his body; describes the months of physical and mental rehabilitation that followed as he attempted to pull his life together.

# Child Abuse: Emotional, Physical, and Sexual Abuse

Compiled by Beth Gallaway Youth Services Consultant/Trainer, Metrowest MA
Regional Library System, Waltham, Massachusetts.

## Fiction

### Books for Ages 12–15

**Anderson, Laurie Halse.** *Speak*. Farrar, Straus & Giroux, c1999. 197pp.
Miranda is so traumatized by an event at a summer party that led to her being shunned socially, she can barely talk.

**Block, Francesca Lia.** *I Was a Teenage Fairy*. Joanna Cotler, c2000. 186pp.
A former teen model reveals how she was exploited.

**Bloor, Edward.** *Tangerine*. Harcourt, c1997. 294pp.
A boy with vision problems has dreams of being a soccer star, when a move to Florida forces him to confront his past.

**Deem, James M.** *The 3 NB's of Julian Drew*. Houghton Mifflin, c1994. 227pp.
Fifteen-year-old Julian keeps a cryptic notebook that reveals physical and emotional abuse at the hands of his stepfather.

**Klass, David.** *You Don't Know Me*. Farrar, Straus & Giroux, c2001. 262pp.
A teen suffers physical and emotional abuse at the hands of his stepfather.

**Konigsburg, E. L.** *Silent to the Bone*. Atheneum Books for Young Readers, c2000. 261pp.
In this book about shaken baby syndrome, a teen who isn't talking is the only one who knows what his nanny did to his infant sister.

### Books for Older Teens

**Alphin, Elaine Marie.** *Counterfeit Son*. Harcourt, c2000. 180pp.
After his father Hank, a serial killer, is finally captured by police, abused son Cameron adopts the identity of one of his father's victims to distance himself from the crimes

**Atkins, Catherine.** *When Jeff Comes Home*. Puffin Books, c2001. 231pp.
Jeff is abducted and abused for several years before his captor guiltily releases him; Jeff's eventual return home is traumatic.

**Chbosky, Stephen.** *The Perks of Being a Wallflower*. MTV Books/Pocket Books, c1999. 213pp.
Sensitive Charlie has a secret . . . .

**Coman, Carolyn.** *Bee and Jacky*. Front Street, c1998. 101pp.
Thirteen-year-old Bee resumes a physical relationship with her seventeen-year old brother, forcing them to confront their past.

# Child Abuse: Emotional, Physical, and Sexual Abuse

**Dessen, Sarah.** *Dreamland*. Speak, c2000. 250pp.
> Can Caitlyn disengage from an abusive relationship?

**Flinn, Alexandra.** *Breathing Underwater*. HarperCollins, c2001. 263pp.
> Sixteen-year-old Nick, in counseling for beating his girlfriend, keeps a journal that reveals his relationships with his girlfriend and his abusive father.

**Mazer, Norma Fox.** *When She Was Good.* Scholastic Signature, 2000, c1997. 228pp.
> Em's manipulative older sister is dead, but her abusive torment lives on.

**Sparks, Beatrice.** *Treacherous Love: The Diary of an Anonymous Teenager.* Avon Books, c2000. 164pp.
> A girl develops a crush on her teacher, and he responds inappropriately by luring her into a relationship.

**Whitcher, Susan.** *The Fool Reversed.* Farrar, Straus & Giroux, c2000. 183pp.
> A young woman develops an inappropriate relationship with a much older man.

## Nonfiction

**Pelzer, David J.** *A Child Called It*. Health Communications, c1995. 184pp. (NF)
> Describes the life of a young boy who suffers abuse, including starvation, beating, verbal abuse, and neglect, at the hands of his mother.

**Tarbox, Katherine.** *A Girl's Life Online (Katie.com).* Plume, c2004. 196pp. (NF)
> Katie (the author) uses poor judgment online, and is lured into a relationship with a pedophile that comes to a head when the two agree to meet.

**Theodore, Wayne.** *Wayne: An Abused Child's Story of Courage, Survival and Hope.* Harbor Press, c2003. 212pp. (NF)
> Local boy Wayne Theodore tells a tale of physical abuse and neglect.

**Turner, Ann.** *Learning to Swim*. Scholastic, c2000. 115pp. (NF)
> A memoir, in poems, of a girl (the author) abused by an older cousin.

From Nancy J. Keane, *The Big Book of Teen Reading Lists: 100 Great, Ready-to-Use Book Lists for Educators, Librarians, Parents, and Children.* Westport, CT: Libraries Unlimited, 2006. Copyright © 2006 by Libraries Unlimited.

# Coming of Age

## Books for Ages 12–15

**Blume, Judy.** *Deenie.* Dell, c1991. 143pp.

A thirteen-year-old girl seemingly destined for a modeling career finds she has a deformation of the spine called scoliosis.

**Blume, Judy.** *Then Again, Maybe I Won't: A Novel.* Bantam Doubleday Dell Books for Young Readers, 1991, c1971, 127pp.

Unable to accept or explain his family's newly acquired wealth, his growing interest in sex, and a friend's shoplifting habit, a thirteen-year-old finds the pains in his stomach getting worse and worse.

**Hunt, Irene.** *Up a Road Slowly.* Berkley Jam Books, 2003, c1966, 183pp.

After her mother's death, Julie goes to live with Aunt Cordelia, a spinster schoolteacher, where she experiences many emotions and changes as she grows from seven to eighteen.

**Rennison, Louise.** *Angus, Thongs and Full-Frontal Snogging: Confessions of Georgia Nicolson.* HarperCollins, c2000. 247pp.

Presents the humorous journal of a year in the life of a fourteen-year-old British girl who tries to reduce the size of her nose, stop her mad cat from terrorizing the neighborhood animals, and win the love of handsome hunk Robbie.

## Books for Older Teens

**Cisneros, Sandra.** *The House on Mango Street.* Knopf (distributed by Random House), c1998. 134pp.

A young girl living in a Hispanic neighborhood in Chicago ponders the advantages and disadvantages of her environment and evaluates her relationships with family and friends.

**Gibbons, Kaye.** *Charms for the Easy Life.* Avon Books, c1993, 290pp.

A story of three generations of women in the Kate family, living in rural North Carolina.

**Kidd, Sue Monk.** *The Secret Life of Bees.* Viking Press, c2002. 301pp. (adult)

Fourteen-year-old Lily and her companion, Rosaleen, an African American woman who has cared for Lily since her mother's death ten years earlier, flee their home after Rosaleen is victimized by racist police officers, finding a safe haven in Tiburon, South Carolina, at the home of three beekeeping sisters, May, June, and August.

**Strout, Elizabeth.** *Amy and Isabelle.* Vintage Contemporaries, 2000, c1998. 303pp.

Isabelle Goodrow, horrified and enraged when she discovers her teenage daughter Amy is involved with a math teacher at the high school, comes to realize that her outrage is mostly the result of the secret she has been keeping for most of Amy's life.

**Thomas, Rob.** *Rats Saw God.* Aladdin Paperbacks, c1996. 202pp.

In hopes of graduating, Steve York agrees to complete a hundred-page writing assignment, which helps him to sort out his relationship with his famous astronaut father and the events that changed him from a promising student into a troubled teen.

# Cutting

## Books for Ages 12–15

**Hoffman, Alice.** *Green Angel.* Scholastic Press, c2003. 116pp.

Haunted by grief and her past after losing her family in a fire, fifteen-year-old Green begins carving tattoos into her body. She retreats into her ruined garden as she struggles to survive emotionally and physically on her own.

**Peters, Julie Anne.** *Define "Normal".* Little, Brown, c2000. 196pp.

When she agrees to meet with Jasmine as a peer counselor at their middle school, Antonia never dreams that this girl with the black lipstick and pierced eyebrow will end up helping her deal with the serious problems she faces at home and become a good friend.

**Wilson, Dawn.** *Saint Jude.* Tudor Publishers, c2001. 171pp.

When committed to an upscale group home outside Asheville, North Carolina, eighteen-year-old Taylor Drysdale pretends that her bipolar disorder is under control and that she will leave soon, but relationships with her fellow residents may hold the key to her real recovery.

## Books for Older Teens

**Collins, Max Allan.** *Skin Game.* Ballantine Books, c2003. 260pp.

Max and Joshua decide to look for the brutal killer of several normal humans, suspecting that the perpetrator may be a transgenic.

**Holmes, Ann.** *Cutting the Pain Away: Understanding Self-Mutilation.* Chelsea House, c1999. 91pp. (NF)

Examines the nature, causes, and treatment of self-mutilation and related disorders, as well as ways of helping someone who inflicts self-injuries.

**Levenkron, Steven.** *Cutting: Understanding and Overcoming Self-Mutilation.* W.W. Norton, c1998. 269pp. (NF)

Explains the psychological disorder of self-mutilation, using case studies and interviews to present a portrait of the self-mutilator, and offering advice on how to overcome the affliction.

**Levenkron, Steven.** *The Luckiest Girl in the World.* Penguin Books, 1998, c1997. 188pp.

Figure-skating star Katie Roskova, unable to express her feelings of panic and anger, develops a habit of cutting herself with scissors and hiding her scars beneath long-sleeve shirts, but as pressure mounts her wounds become more serious, and soon her secret is revealed.

**Marsden, John.** *So Much to Tell You.* Fawcett Books, c1990. 119pp.

Sent to a boarding school by her mother, Marina, a disfigured Australian girl who refuses to speak, reveals her thoughts and feelings in a diary.

**McCormick, Patricia.** *Cut.* Front Street, c2000. 168pp.

While confined to a mental hospital, thirteen-year-old Callie slowly comes to understand some of the reasons behind her self-mutilation and gradually starts to get better.

From Nancy J. Keane, *The Big Book of Teen Reading Lists: 100 Great, Ready-to-Use Book Lists for Educators, Librarians, Parents, and Children.* Westport, CT: Libraries Unlimited, 2006. Copyright © 2006 by Libraries Unlimited.

# Drug Abuse

## Books for Ages 12–15

**Fletcher, Ralph J.** *Uncle Daddy*. H. Holt, c2001. 133pp.
When his long-absent father suddenly reappears, nine-year-old Rivers struggles with conflicting feelings and re-examines his relationship with the great-uncle who had served as his father.

**Harrison, Mette Ivie.** *The Monster in Me.* Holiday House, c2003. 156pp.
In a small town near Salt Lake City, Utah, a caring foster family and her love of running help twelve-year-old Natalie Wills feel that she can be part of normal life, despite having been raised by a drug-addicted mother.

**McCormick, Patricia.** *My Brother's Keeper.* Hyperion Books for Children, c2005. 187pp.
Thirteen-year-old Toby Malone struggles to keep his family together after his father leaves; however, keeping his older brother Jake's drug habit from their mother is getting harder and harder.

**Murray, Jaye.** *Bottled Up.* Speak, 2004, c2003. 220pp.
A high school boy comes to terms with his drug addiction, life with an alcoholic father, and a younger brother who looks up to him.

**Peck, Richard.** *Remembering the Good Times.* Bantam Doubleday Dell Books for Young Readers, 1986, c1985. 181pp.
Trav, Kate, and Buck make up a trio during their freshman year in high school, but their special friendship may not be enough to save Trav as he pressures himself relentlessly to succeed.

## Books for Older Teens

**Brooks, Kevin.** *Candy*. The Chicken House/Scholastic, c2005. 364pp.
Joe, an English boy from the right side of the tracks, is poised to get everything he has ever wanted, but he risks it all when he falls for Candy and is drawn into her seedy, dangerous world.

**Burgess, Melvin.** *Smack*. H. Holt, c1998. 327pp.
After running away from their troubled homes, two English teenagers move in with a group of squatters in the port city of Bristol and try to find ways to support their growing addiction to heroin.

**Butcher, A. J.** *Spy High: Mission Three: The Serpent Scenario.* Little, Brown, 2004, c2003. 218pp.
The members of the Bond team at Deveraux Academy, a special high school that trains students to be secret agents, are on the lookout for the source of a new street drug called Drac, while one student seeks revenge on a gang called the Serpents.

**Douglas, Lola.** *True Confessions of a Hollywood Starlet: A Novel.* Razorbill, c2005. 260pp.
Teen movie star Morgan Carter retreats to a small midwestern town to recuperate anonymously after an overdose and rehabilitation, recording her thoughts in a diary.

**Dunnion, Kristyn.** *Mosh Pit.* Red Deer Press, 2005, c2004. 270pp.
Simone is torn between her loyalty to Cherry and her love for Carol, in a story that finds them on the dark streets and alleys of the city's drug scene.

# Drug Abuse

**Ellis, Bret Easton.** *Less Than Zero.* Vintage Contemporaries, 1998, c1985, 208pp.
Clay comes home from an Eastern college for Christmas vacation and finds himself caught up in a spiral of desperation as he renews old ties.

**Glovach, Linda.** *Beauty Queen.* HarperCollins, c1998. 168pp.
In an attempt to leave behind her unhappy home life, Sam becomes a dancer and a heroin addict.

**Going, Kelly.** *Fat Kid Rules the World.* Putnam, c2003. 187pp.
Seventeen-year-old Troy—depressed, suicidal, and weighing nearly 300 pounds—gets a new perspective on life when Curt, a semi-homeless teen who is a genius on guitar, asks Troy to be the drummer in a rock band.

**Hardrick, Jackie.** *Imani in Never Say Goodbye.* Enlighten, c2003. 264pp.
High school senior Imani has dreams of getting into Howard University on a basketball scholarship; however, a broken wrist and the deception of one of her teammates propels her into a world of bad choices that takes everything she and her boyfriend can muster to overcome.

**Hopkins, Ellen.** *Crank.* Simon Pulse, c2004. 537pp.
Kristina Georgia Snow's life is turned upside down when she visits her absentee father; gets turned on to the drug "crank"; becomes addicted; and is led down a desperate path that threatens her mind, soul, her life.

**James, Brian.** *Pure Sunshine.* Push/Scholastic, c2002. 159pp.
Seventeen-year-old Brendon embarks on a path-changing, two-day high on California acid, or "pure sunshine," during which he begins to break away from his friends, Will and Kevin.

**Koertge, Ronald.** *Stoner & Spaz.* Candlewick Press, c2002. 169pp.
A troubled youth with cerebral palsy struggles toward self-acceptance with the help of a drug-addicted young woman.

**Lawler, Pat.** *What About Me?* Scholastic, c1982, 170pp.
During her junior year, Brett runs for student body president against her boyfriend, Paul, discovers a drug problem when her best friend dates a bad user, and learns about having friends and losing friends.

**Mackall, Dandi Daley.** *Kyra's Story.* Tyndale House, c2003. 277pp.
When seventeen-year-old Kyra of Macon, Iowa, becomes overwhelmed by the stress of senior year in high school, the school play, and early admission to drama school, she begins taking prescription drugs, unaware that her twin brother will suffer the consequences.

**Myers, Walter Dean.** *The Beast.* Scholastic, c2003. 170pp.
A teenager from Harlem struggles to save his girlfriend from herself when she develops a drug problem while he is away at a Connecticut prep school.

**Qualey, Marsha.** *One Night.* Speak, 2003, c2002. 170pp.
Nineteen-year-old Kelly, ex-addict niece of a nationally renowned Minnesota talk show host, has an unexpected adventure with the visiting prince of a war-torn Eastern European country.

# Drug Abuse

**Rapp, Adam.** *Under the Wolf, Under the Dog.* Candlewick Press, c2004. 310pp.
Sixteen-year-old Steve struggles to make sense of his mother's terminal breast cancer and his brother's suicide.

**Schraff, Anne E.** *The Darkest Secret.* Perfection Learning, c1993. 115pp.
Brian tries to find his long-lost uncle Steve and struggles to help his friend Michelle when drugs take over her life.

**Voigt, Cynthia.** *Orfe.* Simon Pulse, 2002, c1992, 151pp.
Enny tells of her relationship with Orfe, an unusually talented musician, and of the love between Orfe and Yuri, a recovering addict.

# Gangs

## Books for Ages 12–15

**Ashley, Bernard.** *Little Soldier.* Scholastic, 2003, c1999. 230pp.
Taken from Africa to a foster home in London after his family is killed by an enemy tribe, Kaninda discovers the meaning of hate and the value of not hating.

**Bertrand, Diane Gonzales.** *Trino's Choice.* Pinata Books/Arte Publico, c1999. 124pp.
Frustrated by his poor financial situation and hoping to impress a smart girl, seventh-grader Trino falls in with a bad crowd led by an older teen with a vicious streak.

**Bonham, Frank.** *Durango Street.* Puffin Books, 1999, c1965. 190pp.
As headman of his teenage gang, Rufus Henry has to deal not only with other gangs, but also with the police-sanctioned sponsor who has involved himself with Rufus and his friends.

**Bunting, Eve.** *Someone Is Hiding on Alcatraz Island.* Berkley Books, 1994, c1984. 136pp.
When he offends the toughest gang in his San Francisco school, Danny tries to elude them by going to Alcatraz, only to find himself and a Park Service employee trapped by the gang in an old prison cell block.

**Conly, Jane Leslie.** *In the Night, on Lanvale Street.* H. Holt, c2005. 250pp.
While helping a stranger solve the murder of a neighbor, thirteen-year-old Charlie and her younger brother are endangered by what they learn about gangs and drugs in the neighborhood.

**Draper, Sharon M.** *Romiette and Julio.* Atheneum Books for Young Readers, c1999. 236pp.
Romiette, an African American girl, and Julio, a Hispanic boy, discover that they attend the same high school after falling in love on the Internet, but are harassed by a gang whose members object to their interracial dating.

**Ewing, Lynne.** *Drive-By.* HarperTrophy, 1998, c1996. 85pp.
While helping to care for his little sister, twelve-year-old Tito struggles to find his way during the aftermath of his brother's death in a gang-related shooting.

**Garland, Sherry.** *Letters from the Mountain.* Harcourt Brace, c1996. 211pp.
A teenage boy, sent for the summer to relatives in the mountains to remove him from gang influences, discovers life's important values through his unlikely friendship with an economically challenged boy.

**Hinton, S. E.** *The Outsiders.* Viking Press, c1967. 188pp.
The struggle of three brothers to stay together after their parents' death and their quest for identity among the conflicting values of their adolescent society.

**Hinton, S. E.** *That Was Then, This Is Now.* Speak, 2003, c1971, 159pp.
Sixteen-year-old Mark and Bryon have been like brothers since childhood, but now, as their involvement with girls, gangs, and drugs increases, their relationship seems to gradually disintegrate.

**Myers, Walter Dean.** *Scorpions.* HarperCollins, c1988. 216pp.
After reluctantly taking on the leadership of a Harlem gang, the Scorpions, Jamal finds that his enemies treat him with respect when he acquires a gun—until a tragedy occurs.

# Gangs

**Rodriguez, Luis J.** *It Doesn't Have to Be This Way: A Barrio Story.* Children's Book Press/Libros Para Niños (distributed by Publishers Group West), c1999. 31pp.

Reluctantly a young boy becomes more and more involved in the activities of a local gang, until a tragic event involving his cousin forces him to make a choice about the course of his life.

## Books for Older Teens

**Hinojosa, Maria.** *Crews.* Harcourt Brace, c1995. 168pp. (NF)

Presents a sampling of interviews with gang members, portraying a sometimes shocking and sometimes heartening picture of the young men and women who live on the edge of poverty and violence.

**Howe, Quincy.** *Broken Chains.* Globe Fearon, c1995. 59pp.

Julio, infatuated with Vanessa, agrees to act as a big brother for her fourteen-year-old brother Hector, who has recently fallen in with a bad crowd, but Julio does not realize his involvement with Hector is going to compromise his relationship with Vanessa.

**Howe, Quincy.** *Looking for Trouble.* Globe Fearon, c1995. 58pp.

When Vasey's friend Hi-C arrives in the city and becomes involved with a gang, Vasey's friends team up to try to teach Hi-C that life on the streets isn't as cool as he thinks it is.

**Myers, Walter Dean.** *Autobiography of My Dead Brother.* HarperTempest, c2005. 212pp.

Jesse pours his heart and soul into his sketchbook to make sense of life in his troubled Harlem neighborhood and the loss of a close friend.

**Myers, Walter Dean.** *Monster.* HarperCollins, c1999. 281pp.

While on trial as an accomplice to murder, sixteen-year-old Steve Harmon records his experiences in prison and in the courtroom, in the form of a film script, as he tries to come to terms with the course his life has taken.

**Rodriguez, Luis J.** *Always Running: La Vida Loca: Gang Days in L.A.* Simon & Schuster, c1994. 260pp. (NF)

The author recounts growing up in poverty in Los Angeles; his encounters with racism in school and on the streets; and his struggle to overcome prejudice, drugs, and violence.

**Ruiz, Mona.** *Two Badges: The Lives of Mona Ruiz.* Arte Publico Press, c1997. 288pp. (NF)

The autobiography of Mona Ruiz, a woman who overcame a difficult childhood in a neighborhood with street gangs and became a police officer serving her community.

**Williams, Stanley.** *Life In Prison.* SeaStar Books, 2001, 1998, 80pp. (NF)

The author, imprisoned on Death Row since 1981, describes life in prison, warning young readers not to make the mistakes he made.

**Worth, Richard.** *Gangs and Crime.* Chelsea House, c2002. 101pp. (NF)

Chronicles the history of American street gangs, describing their changing values, appearance, and behavior as well as the efforts of law enforcement, the criminal justice system, and community leaders to address them.

# Gangs

**Wright, Richard.** *Rite of Passage*. HarperTrophy, 1996, c1994. 151pp.
When fifteen-year-old Johnny Gibbs is told that he is really a foster child, he runs off into the streets of Harlem and meets up with a gang that wants him to participate in a mugging.

**Zephaniah, Benjamin.** *Gangsta Rap.* Bloomsbury (distributed by Holtzbrinck), c2004. 332pp.
When teenage Ray and his two friends, Prem and Tyronne, form a successful rap band in London's East End where they live, they soon find themselves embroiled in increasingly violent gang warfare.

From Nancy J. Keane, *The Big Book of Teen Reading Lists: 100 Great, Ready-to-Use Book Lists for Educators, Librarians, Parents, and Children.* Westport, CT: Libraries Unlimited, 2006. Copyright © 2006 by Libraries Unlimited.

# Life in the Fat Lane:
# Books About Food Issues for Teens

Compiled by Beth Gallaway Youth Services Consultant/Trainer, Metrowest MA Regional Library System, Waltham, Massachusetts.

## Overweight/Obesity

**Bennett, Cherie.** *Life in the Fat Lane.* Bantam Doubleday Dell Books for Young Readers, 1999. 260pp. (ages 12–15)
> A pretty, popular, thin girl discovers what life is like on the other side when she gains weight suddenly.

**Bone, Ian.** *Fat Boy Saves World.* Pocket Pulse, c2001. 228pp. (older teens)
> Teen boarding school reject Susan Bennett returns to her parents' mansion—the scene of many battles observed by her bloated older brother, Neat, who has not said one word in eight years. But when their parents are away, Neat suddenly speaks, saying he wants to save the world. With the help of young street actor Todd, Neat goes on local cable TV and dispenses advice. And when Susan's parents return home, she decides to face them.

**Crutcher, Chris.** *Staying Fat for Sarah Byrnes.* Greenwillow Books, c1993. 216pp. (ages 12–15)
> Daily class discussions about the nature of man, the existence of God, abortion, organized religion, suicide, and other contemporary issues serve as a backdrop for a high school senior's attempt to answer a friend's dramatic cry for help.

**Danziger, Paula.** *The Cat Ate My Gymsuit.* Putnam, c2004. 151pp. (ages 12–15)
> When the unconventional English teacher who helped her conquer many of her feelings of insecurity is fired, a junior high student uses her newfound courage to campaign for the teacher's reinstatement.

**Lipsyte, Robert.** *One Fat Summer.* HarperTrophy, c1991. 232pp. (older teens)
> An overweight, fourteen-year-old boy experiences a turning-point one summer in which he learns to stand up for himself.

**Lynch, Chris.** *Extreme Elvin.* HarperTrophy, c2001. 234pp. (ages 12–15)
> As he enters high school, fourteen-year-old Elvin continues to deal with his weight problem as he tries to find his place among his peers.

## Eating Disorders

**Sparks, Beatrice.** *Kim: Empty Inside,* Avon Books, c2002. 165pp. (older teens)
> Kim's distorted body image leads to binging, purging, crash dieting, and eventually a hospital stay

**Eliot, Eve.** *Insatiable: The Compelling Story of Four Teens, Food and Its Power.* Health Communications, c2001. 284pp. (ages 12–15) (NF)
> A quartet of girls worry about their body image and attempt to use food to gain control over their lives. The interlinked stories deal with self-mutilation, bulimia, and overeating.

# Life in the Fat Lane:
# Books About Food Issues for Teens

**Eliot, Eve.** *Ravenous: The Stirring Tale of Teen Love, Loss and Courage.* Health Communications, c2002. (older teens) (NF)

> Phoebe, the size-sixteen dreamer, finally gets a boyfriend, and readers witness her euphoria and her fear during a particularly fragile time of life.

**Frank, Lucy.** *I Am an Artichoke.* Holiday House, c1995. 187pp. (ages 12–15)

> A preteen girl's babysitter tries to get her charge to admit she has anorexia.

**Hanauer, Cathi.** *My Sister's Bones.* Delacorte Press, c1996. 258pp. (older teens)

> Against a backdrop of malls and emerald-carpet lawns, Cassie Weinstein is slowly killing herself with anorexia. And there seems to be nothing her younger sister Billie can do to stop her.

**Levenkron, Steven.** *The Best Little Girl in the World.* Warner Books, c1997. 253pp. (older teens)

> Teenager Francesca Deitrich feels too fat, giving into the pressures of her ballet teacher and the pencil-thin models in the media, in a revealing story about a "perfect" little girl suffering from the destructive obsession of anorexia nervosa.

**Naylor, Phyllis.** *The Grooming of Alice.* Atheneum Books for Young Readers, c2000. 215pp. (ages 12–15)

> The support of best friends Alice and Pamela helps prevent Elizabeth's descent into an eating disorder.

**Porter, Tracey.** *A Dance of Sisters.* Joanna Cotler Books, c2002. 276pp. (ages 12–15)

> Although almost totally consumed by her intense ballet training and her obsession with her weight, thirteen-year old Delia finds time to worry about her strange and rebellious older sister, Pearl, who has been sent away to a private school.

**Wilson, Jacqueline.** *Girls Under Pressure.* Delacorte Press, c2002. 214pp. (ages 12–15)

> Pretty, plump Ellie feels pressured to be as thin as her two best friends.

## Nonfiction

**Gold, Tracey.** *Room to Grow.* New Millennium Press, c2003. 184pp. (older teens) (NF)

> The actress and child star of *Growing Pains* reveals her struggles with body image and eating disorders and her eventual road to recovery.

**Gottlieb, Lori.** *Stick Figure: A Diary of My Former Self.* Simon & Schuster, c2000. 222pp. (older teens) (NF)

> Memoir about anorexia.

**Hornbacher, Marya.** *Wasted.* HarperPerennial, c1998. 298pp. (older teens) (NF)

> A memoir about anorexia and bulimia.

**Siegler, Jamie Lyn.** *Wise Girl: What I've Learned About Love, Life and Loss.* Pocket Books, c2002. 161pp. (older teens) (NF)

> The actress and star of *The Sopranos* reveals her struggles with body image and eating disorders and her eventual road to recovery.

# Making Choices

## Books for Ages 12–15

**Avi.** *The Good Dog.* Atheneum Books for Young Readers, c2001. 243pp.
McKinley, a malamute, is torn between the domestic world of his human family and the wild world of Lupin, a wolf that is trying to recruit dogs to replenish the dwindling wolf population.

**Avi.** *A Place Called Ugly.* Avon Books, c1995. 134pp.
At the end of the summer, fourteen-year-old Owen refuses to leave the beach house that has been his family's summer home for ten years but is scheduled for demolition.

**Babbitt, Natalie.** *Tuck Everlasting.* Farrar, Straus & Giroux, c1975. 139pp.
The Tuck family is confronted with an agonizing situation when they discover that a ten-year-old girl and a malicious stranger now share their secret about a spring whose water prevents one from ever growing any older.

**Buchanan, Paul.** *Heads I Win, Tails You Lose.* Concordia Publishing, c1999. 126pp.
Eighth grader Willie asks for God's forgiveness when he neglects his friends in order to win a coin collecting contest.

**Bunting, Eve.** *Blackwater.* Joanna Cotler Books, 2000, c1999. 146pp.
When a boy and girl are drowned in the Blackwater River, thirteen-year-old Brodie must decide whether to confess that he may have caused the accident.

**Cheaney, J. B.** *My Friend the Enemy.* Knopf (distributed by Random House), c2005. 266pp.
In Oregon in 1943, eleven-year-old Hazel befriends a fifteen-year-old Japanese American orphan boy she discovers hiding from internment on her neighbor's farm.

**Crutcher, Chris.** *Staying Fat for Sarah Byrnes.* Greenwillow Books, c1993, 216pp.
Daily class discussions about the nature of man, the existence of God, abortion, organized religion, suicide, and other contemporary issues serve as a backdrop for a high school senior's attempt to answer a friend's dramatic cry for help.

**Duncan, Lois.** *I Know What You Did Last Summer.* Bantam Doubleday Dell Books for Young Readers, 1999, c1973, 199pp.
Four teenagers who have desperately tried to conceal their responsibility for a hit-and-run accident are pursued by a mystery figure seeking revenge.

**Hobbs, Will.** *Wild Man Island*. HarperCollins, c2002. 184pp.
After fourteen-year-old Andy slips away from his kayaking group to visit the wilderness site of his archaeologist father's death, a storm strands him on Admiralty Island, Alaska, where he manages to survive, encounters unexpected animal and human inhabitants, and looks for traces of the earliest prehistoric immigrants to America.

**Kehret, Peg.** *Don't Tell Anyone.* Dutton Children's Books, c2000. 137pp.
Twelve-year-old Megan does not realize that feeding a group of feral cats living in a field near her house will involve her as a witness to a traffic accident and in the dangerous plan of an unstable criminal.

# Making Choices

**Mazer, Norma Fox.** *Out of Control*. Avon Books, 1994, c1993. 217pp.
> After joining his two best friends in a spontaneous attack on a girl at their school, sixteen-year-old Rollo finds that his life has changed forever.

**McDaniel, Lurlene.** *Angel of Mercy*. Dell Laurel-Leaf, 2003, c1999. 211pp.
> Eighteen-year-old Heather travels as a volunteer to Africa, where she provides direly needed medical help in Kenya and Uganda and hopes to act as God's hands on Earth.

**McDaniel, Lurlene.** *Saving Jessica*. Bantam Books, c1996. 191pp.
> When Jessica is diagnosed as having kidney failure, her only hope is a kidney transplant, but her boyfriend Jeremy must find the strength to defy his parents in order to be the donor and save Jessica's life.

**McDonald, Joyce.** *Swallowing Stones*. Bantam Doubleday Dell Books for Young Readers, 1999, c1997. 245pp.
> Dual perspectives reveal the aftermath of seventeen-year-old Michael MacKenzie's birthday celebration, during which he discharges an antique Winchester rifle and unknowingly kills the father of high school classmate Jenna Ward.

**Mikaelsen, Ben.** *Stranded*. Hyperion Paperbacks for Children, 1996, c1995. 247pp.
> Twelve-year-old Koby, who has lost a foot in an accident, sees a chance to prove her self-reliance to her parents when she tries to rescue two stranded pilot whales near her home in the Florida Keys.

**Mikaelsen, Ben.** *Touching Spirit Bear*. HarperCollins, c2001. 241pp.
> After his anger erupts into violence, fifteen year-old Cole, to avoid going to prison, agrees to participate in a sentencing alternative based on the Native American Circle Justice. He is sent to a remote Alaskan Island, where an encounter with a huge Spirit Bear changes his life.

**Paterson, Katherine.** *Jacob Have I Loved*. Crowell, c1980. 216pp.
> Filled with resentment about the attention showered upon her twin sister and awaiting the day she can leave her town behind, young Louise meets a wise old sea captain and begins learning how to let go of her anger.

**Paterson, Katherine.** *Jip: His Story*. Puffin Books, 2005, c1996. 180pp.
> While living on a Vermont poor farm during 1855 and 1856, Jip learns his identity and that of his mother and comes to understand how he arrived at this place.

**Paulsen, Gary.** *The Voyage of the Frog*. Bantam Double Dell Books for Young Readers, 1990, c1989. 141pp.
> When David goes out on his sailboat to scatter his recently deceased uncle's ashes to the wind, he is caught in a fierce storm and must survive many days on his own as he works out his feelings about life and his uncle.

**Peck, Robert Newton.** *Horse Thief: A Novel*. HarperTrophy, 2003, c2002. 277pp.
> In 1938, with the help of a lady doctor and an aging, card-cheating, dice-rolling horse thief, a seventeen-year-old orphan steals thirteen horses from Chickalookee, Florida's doomed rodeo, and finds a family in the process.

# Making Choices

**Richter, Conrad.** *The Light in the Forest.* Knopf (distributed in the United States by Random House), 2005, c1953, 162pp.

John Cameron Butler, kidnapped by the Lenne Indians when he was only four years old, is returned to his white family eleven years later and struggles to fit into the unfamiliar culture.

## Books for Older Teens

**Picoult, Jodi.** *My Sister's Keeper: A Novel.* Atria Books, c2004. 423pp. (adult)

Thirteen-year-old Anna, conceived specifically to provide blood and bone marrow for her sister Kate, who was diagnosed with a rare form of leukemia at the age of two, decides to sue her parents for control of her body when her mother wants her to donate a kidney to Kate.

**Steinbeck, John.** *Of Mice and Men.* Penguin Books, 1994, c1937. 105pp.

Sustained by the hope of someday owning a farm of their own, two migrant laborers arrive to work on a ranch in central California.

**Voigt, Cynthia.** *Seventeen Against the Dealer.* Atheneum, c1989. 181pp.

Dicey struggles to make a go of a boatbuilding business while facing family concerns, romantic problems, and the uncertainties of a drifter who offers to help her in her work.

**Woodson, Jacqueline.** *From the Notebooks of Melanin Sun: A Novel.* Scholastic, c1995. 141pp.

Thirteen-year-old Melanin Sun's comfortable, quiet life is shattered when his mother reveals she has fallen in love with a woman.

# Meaning of Life

## Books for Ages 12–15

**Hautman, Pete.** *Godless*. Simon & Schuster Books for Young Readers, c2004. 198pp.

When sixteen-year-old Jason Bock and his friends create their own religion to worship the town's water tower, what started out as a joke begins to take on a power of its own.

**Perkins, Lynne Rae.** *Criss Cross.* Greenwillow Books, c2005. 337pp.

Teenagers in a small town in the 1960s experience new thoughts and feelings, question their identities, connect, and disconnect as they search for the meaning of life and love.

**Tashjian, Janet.** *The Gospel According to Larry.* H. Holt, c2001. 227pp.

Seventeen-year-old Josh, a loner-philosopher who wants to make a difference in the world, tries to maintain his secret identity as the author of a Web site that is receiving national attention.

## Books for Older Teens

**Albom, Mitch.** *Tuesdays with Morrie: An Old Man, a Young Man, and Life's Greatest Lesson.* Doubleday, c1997. 192pp. (adult) (NF)

The author, an alumnus of Brandeis University, tells about his meetings with a former professor suffering from Lou Gehrig's disease and of the lessons he learned about life and death from this college mentor.

**Crutcher, Chris.** *The Sledding Hill.* Greenwillow Books, c2005. 230pp.

Billy, recently deceased, keeps an eye on his best friend, fourteen-year-old Eddie, and helps him stand up to a conservative minister and English teacher who is orchestrating a censorship challenge.

**Gaarder, Jostein.** *Sophie's World: A Novel About the History of Philosophy.* Berkley, c1996. 523pp.

A novel about the history of philosophy, which uses the life of a schoolgirl, Sophie, as a backdrop for a discussion of the meaning of life.

**Golding, William.** *Lord of the Flies*. Berkley, 2003, c1954. 315pp.

After a plane crash strands them on a tropical island while the rest of the world is ravaged by war, a group of British schoolboys attempt to form a civilized society but descend into brutal anarchy.

**Kushner, Harold S.** *When Bad Things Happen to Good People.* Schocken Books, 2001, c1981. 202pp. (NF)

Provides insight into the question of how to deal with human suffering and death.

**Martel, Yann.** *Life of Pi: A Novel.* Harcourt, c2001. 319pp. (adult)

Pi Patel, having spent an idyllic childhood in Pondicherry, India, as the son of a zookeeper, sets off with his family at the age of sixteen to start anew in Canada, but his life takes a marvelous turn when their ship sinks in the Pacific, leaving him adrift on a raft with a 450-pound Bengal tiger for company.

**Trueman, Terry.** *Stuck in Neutral.* HarperCollins, c2000. 114pp.

Fourteen-year-old Shawn McDaniel, who suffers from severe cerebral palsy and cannot function, relates his perceptions of his life, his family, and his condition, especially as he believes his father is planning to kill him.

# Overcoming Poverty

## Books for Ages 12–15

**Anderson, Laurie Halse.** *Fever, 1793.* Simon & Schuster Books for Young Readers, c2000. 251pp.
Sixteen-year-old Matilda Cook, separated from her sick mother, learns about perseverance and self-reliance when she is forced to cope with the horrors of a yellow fever epidemic in Philadelphia in 1793.

**Jimenez, Francisco.** *Breaking Through.* Houghton Mifflin, c2001. 195pp.
Having come from Mexico to California ten years ago, fourteen-year-old Francisco is still working in the fields but fighting to improve his life and complete his education.

**Mawi Asgedom.** *Of Beetles & Angels: A Boy's Remarkable Journey from a Refugee Camp to Harvard.* Little, Brown, c2002. 142pp.
An autobiography that tells the story of how, at the age of three, the author fled civil war in Ethiopia by walking with his mother and brother to a Sudanese refugee camp, and later moved to Chicago, where he earned a full scholarship to Harvard University. Includes recipes and discussion questions.

**Town, Florida.** *With a Silent Companion.* Red Deer Press, 2000, c1999. 176pp.
A historical novel based on the true story of Margaret Anne Bulkley, a young woman born in Ireland in the early 1800s who disguised herself as a man to attend medical school, and continued the ruse throughout her career as a military doctor.

**Wolff, Virginia Euwer.** *Make Lemonade.* H. Holt, c1993. 200pp.
Fourteen-year-old LaVaughn, trying to earn the money for college, takes a job caring for the two children of Jolly, a single teenage mom, and must find the courage to make the right decision for all of them after Jolly is fired.

**Wolff, Virginia Euwer.** *True Believer.* Atheneum Books for Young Readers, c2001. 264pp.
Living in the inner city amid guns and poverty, fifteen-year-old LaVaughn learns from old and new friends, and inspiring mentors, that life is what you make it—an occasion to rise to.

## Books for Older Teens

**Carson, Benjamin S.** *Gifted Hands.* Zondervan, c1990. 232pp. (NF)
Captures this physician's fight to beat the odds, the secret behind his outstanding accomplishments, and what drives him to take risks.

**Coleman, Michael.** *On the Run.* Dutton Children's Books, c2004. 199pp.
When a persistent youth offender is caught yet again, he is sentenced to community service as the partner to a blind runner.

**Davis, Sampson.** *The Pact: Three Young Men Make a Promise and Fulfill a Dream.* Riverhead Books, 2003, c2002. 263pp. (NF)
Presents the true story of three African American kids from the inner city of Newark, New Jersey, who made a pact to support each other as they rose from an environment of poverty, crime, and drugs, and went on to become successful doctors.

# Overcoming Poverty

**Myers, Walter Dean.** *The Beast.* Scholastic, c2003. 170pp.

A teenager from Harlem struggles to save his girlfriend from herself when she develops a drug problem while he is away at a Connecticut prep school.

**Suskind, Ron.** *A Hope in the Unseen: An American Odyssey from the Inner City to the Ivy League.* Broadway Books, 1999, c1998. 373pp. (NF)

Follows gifted African American student Cedric Jennings from his crime-infested high school in Washington, D.C., to his junior year at Brown University, discussing the problems he encountered along the road out of the ghetto.

# Perfectionism

## Books for Ages 12–15

**Anderson, Laurie Halse.** *Catalyst.* Viking Press, c2002. 232pp.
Eighteen-year-old Kate, who sometimes chafes at being a preacher's daughter, finds herself losing control in her senior year as she faces difficult neighbors, the possibility that she may not be accepted by the college of her choice, and an unexpected death.

**Bennett, Cherie.** *Life in the Fat Lane.* Bantam Doubleday Dell Books for Young Readers, 1999, c1998. 260pp.
Sixteen-year-old Lara, winner of beauty pageants and Homecoming Queen, is distressed and bewildered when she starts gaining weight and becomes overweight.

**Dessen, Sarah.** *The Truth About Forever.* Viking Press, c2004. 374pp.
The summer following her father's death, Macy plans to work at the library and wait for her brainy boyfriend to return from camp, but instead she goes to work at a catering business, where she makes new friends and finally faces her grief.

**Kantor, Melissa.** *Confessions of a Not It Girl.* Hyperion, c2004. 247pp.
High schooler Jan Miller, hoping for a senior year romance, just cannot seem to do anything right, especially when compared to her best friend Rebecca, who has just been named a New York "It Girl"; but things start looking up when an old crush moves back to town.

**Mackler, Carolyn.** *The Earth, My Butt, and Other Big Round Things.* Candlewick Press, c2003. 246pp.
Feeling that she does not fit in with the other members of her family, who are all thin, brilliant, and good-looking, fifteen-year-old Virginia tries to deal with her self-image, her first physical relationship, and her disillusionment with some of the people closest to her.

## Books for Older Teens

**Bunting, Josiah.** *All Loves Excelling.* Bridge Works (distributed by National Book Network), c2001. 301pp.
Amanda Bahringer, a bright, impressionable student at a prestigious boarding school, struggles to measure up to everyone's demands, from her mother to her instructors, as she tries to gain the credentials needed for admission to Dartmouth.

**Elliott, Miriam.** *Perfectionism: What's Bad About Being Too Good?* Free Spirit, c1999. 129pp. (NF)
Discusses the dangers of being a perfectionist, with tips for easing up on oneself, gaining control over life, and getting professional help.

**Lee, Marie G.** *Finding My Voice.* HarperTrophy, 2001, c1992. 214pp.
As she tries to enjoy her senior year and choose which college she will attend, Korean American Ellen Sung must deal with the prejudice of some of her classmates and pressure from her parents to get good grades.

**Lee, Marie G.** *Saying Goodbye.* Houghton Mifflin, c1994. 219pp.
Ellen Sung explores her interest in creative writing and in her Korean heritage during her freshman year at Harvard.

**Mackler, Carolyn.** *Vegan Virgin Valentine.* Candlewick Press, c2004. 228pp.
Mara's niece, who is only one year younger, moves in, bringing conflict between the two teenagers because of their opposite personalities.

# Road Trip

## Books for Ages 12–15

**Bauer, Joan.** *Rules of the Road.* Putman, c1998. 201pp.
Sixteen-year-old Jenna gets a job driving the elderly owner of a chain of successful shoe stores from Chicago to Texas to confront the woman's son, who is trying to force her to retire, and along the way Jenna hones her talents as a saleswoman and finds the strength to face her alcoholic father.

**Callan, Annie.** *Taf.* Cricket Books, c2001. 248pp.
Thinking she has killed her half-brother, twelve-year-old Taf flees her abusive home and sets out to find her long-missing father. On her way from Idaho to Pendleton, Oregon, she discovers not only adventure and sorrow, but also a number of people who love her.

**Carlson, Melody.** *Road Trip: A Novel.* Multnomah Publishers, c2003. 292pp.
After signing a contract with a major recording company, Chloe, Allie, and Laura set off on tour as the opening act for the most popular Christian band in the country, but life on the road is not as glamorous as the girls thought it would be, and they soon begin to feel overwhelmed.

**Creech, Sharon.** *Walk Two Moons.* HarperCollins, c1994. 280pp.
After her mother leaves home suddenly, thirteen-year-old Sal and her grandparents take a car trip retracing her mother's route. Along the way, Sal recounts the story of her friend Phoebe, whose mother also left.

**Creech, Sharon.** *The* Wanderer. HarperCollins, c2000. 305pp.
Thirteen-year-old Sophie and her cousin Cody record their transatlantic crossing aboard the *Wanderer,* a forty-five foot sailboat, which, along with uncles and another cousin, is en route to visit their grandfather in England.

**Fritz, April Young.** *Praying at the Sweetwater Motel: A Novel.* Hyperion Books for Children, c2003. 266pp.
Sarah Jane and her mother move into the Sweetwater Motel in Ohio after her mother leaves Sarah's abusive father. Eventually Sarah begins to miss her old life and even her father.

**Lieberg, Carolyn S.** *West with Hopeless.* Dutton Children's Books, c2004. 180pp.
Bound for Reno and their divorced father for the summer, two half-sisters leave from Iowa in an old Ford Escort and learn a great deal on the way about the people they encounter and even more about themselves.

**Young, Karen Romano.** *The Beetle and Me: A Love Story.* HarperTrophy, 2001, c1999. 207pp.
Surrounded by her busy extended family and their many cars, fifteen-year-old Daisy pursues her goal of single-handedly restoring the car of her dreams, the old purple Volkswagen Beetle from her childhood.

## Books for Older Teens

**Brooks, Martha.** *True Confessions of a Heartless Girl.* Farrar, Straus & Giroux, c2003. 181pp.
A confused seventeen-year-old girl, a single mother and her young son, two elderly women, and a sad and lonely man, with their own individual tragedies to bear, come together in a small Manitoba town and find a way to a better future.

# Road Trip

**Cooney, Caroline B.** *Hit the Road.* Delacorte Press, c2006. 192pp.

Sixteen-year-old Brittany acts as chauffeur for her grandmother and three other eighty-plus-year-old women going to what is supposedly their college reunion, on a long drive that involves lies, theft, and kidnappings.

**Fleischman, Paul.** *Whirligig.* H. Holt, c1998. 133pp.

While traveling to each corner of the country to build a whirligig in memory of the girl whose death he caused, sixteen-year-old Brian finds forgiveness and atonement.

**High, Linda Oatman.** *Sister Slam and the Poetic Motormouth Roadtrip.* Bloomsbury (distributed by Holtzbrinck), c2004. 256pp.

In this novel told in slam verse, after graduating from high school, best friends and aspiring poets Laura and Twig embark on a road trip from Pennsylvania to New York City, to compete at slam poetry events.

**Kerouac, Jack.** *On the Road.* Viking Press, c1997. 307pp.

A fortieth-anniversary edition of the novel that defined the beat generation of the 1950s, in which Sal Paradise tells about his travels throughout the North American continent in search of belief and meaning.

**Kingsolver, Barbara.** *The Bean Trees: A Novel.* HarperFlamingo, c1998. 261pp.

Taylor, a poor Kentuckian, makes her way west with an abandoned baby girl and stops in Tucson. There she finds friends and discovers resources in apparently empty places.

**Lowry, Brigid.** *Guitar Highway Rose.* Holiday House, c2003. 196pp.

Two fifteen-year-olds, Rosie and Asher, upset about the various unhappy circumstances of their lives in the Australian city of Perth, decide to run away.

**Paulsen, Gary.** *The Car.* Harcourt Brace, c1994. 180pp.

A teenager takes off on his travels west in a kit car he built himself, and along the way picks up two Vietnam veterans, who take him on an eye-opening journey.

**Rottman, S. L.** *Stetson.* Viking Press, c2002. 222pp.

Seventeen-year-old Stetson meets the sister he never knew he had, and together they try to make sense of their pasts.

**Shaw, Tucker.** *Confessions of a Backup Dancer.* Simon Pulse, c2004. 265pp.

Kelly Kimbal lands a job as a backup dancer for pop diva Darcy Barnes, but is soon fired by Darcy's overbearing mother, until Darcy develops the courage to tell her mother off and bring Kelly back into the show.

**Steinbeck, John.** *Travels with Charley: In Search of America.* Penguin Books, 1986, c1962. 277pp. (NF)

Contains observations about life and descriptions of nature experienced by Steinbeck as he traveled from coast to coast at sixty years of age with his French poodle, Charley.

# Road Trip

**Wittlinger, Ellen.** *Zigzag*. Simon & Schuster Books for Young Readers, c2003. 264pp.
A high-school junior makes a trip with her aunt and two cousins, discovering places she did not know existed and strengths she did not know she had.

**Yansky, Brian.** *My Road Trip To the Pretty Girl Capital of the World.* Cricket Books, c2003. 178pp.
In 1979, when his life in Mansfield, Iowa, seems to fall apart, seventeen-year-old Simon takes his father's car and sets out for Texas, looking for his birth parents and picking up a man claiming to be Elvis, two bums, and an abused young wife along the way.

# Runaways

## Books for Ages 12–15

**Adler, C. S. *The No Place Cat*.** Clarion Books, c2002. 153pp.

Tired of the strict rules and annoying children at her father and stepmother's house, twelve-year-old Tess walks across Tucson to her mother's condo, stopping for the night at a state park, where she is adopted by a very special cat.

**Avi. *Beyond the Western Sea. Book 1, The Escape from Home*.** Avon Books, c1996. 325pp.

Driven from their impoverished Irish village, fifteen-year-old Maura and her younger brother meet their landlord's runaway son in Liverpool while all three wait for a ship to America.

**Butcher, Kristin. *The Runaways*.** Kids Can Press, c1998. 168pp.

Twelve-year-old Nick Battle's life takes an unexpected turn when he runs away from home after learning that his mom and new stepfather are expecting a baby. He becomes friends with Luther, an angry old man who lives on the streets.

**Callan, Annie. *Taf*.** Cricket Books, c2001. 248pp.

Thinking she has killed her half-brother, twelve-year-old Taf flees her abusive home and sets out to find her long-missing father. On her way from Idaho to Pendleton, Oregon, she discovers not only adventure and sorrow but also a number of people who love her.

**Curtis, Christopher Paul. *Bud, Not Buddy*.** Delacorte Press, c1999. 245pp.

Ten-year-old Bud, a motherless boy living in Flint, Michigan, during the Great Depression, escapes a bad foster home and sets out in search of the man he believes to be his father—the renowned bandleader, H. E. Calloway of Grand Rapids.

**Funke, Cornelia Caroline. *The Thief Lord*.** Scholastic, c2002. 349pp.

Orphaned brothers Prosper and Bo, having run away from their cruel aunt and uncle, decide to hide out in Venice, where they fall in with the Thief Lord, a thirteen-year-old boy who leads a crime ring of street children.

**Hobbs, Valerie. *Charlie's Run*.** Farrar, Straus & Giroux, c2000. 165pp.

Hoping to stop his parents' impending separation and keep them from getting a divorce, eleven-year-old Charlie runs away from their house in the California countryside and finds a ride to the coast.

**Hobbs, Will. *The Maze*.** Morrow Junior Books, c1998. 197pp.

Rick, a fourteen-year-old foster child, escapes from a juvenile detention facility near Las Vegas and travels to Canyonlands National Park in Utah, where he meets a bird biologist working on a project to reintroduce condors to the wild.

**Hrdlitschka, Shelley. *Disconnected*.** Orca Book Publishers, c1998. 160pp.

Fourteen-year-old Canadians Tanner and Alex discover they have a mysterious connection when drug dealers kidnap Tanner while he is on a hockey trip, mistaking him for Alex, who met them while running away from an abusive father.

# Runaways

**Johnson, Angela.** *Bird*. Dial Books, c2004. 133pp.
Devastated by the loss of a second father, thirteen-year-old Bird follows her stepfather from Cleveland to Alabama in hopes of convincing him to come home, and along the way helps two boys cope with their difficulties.

**Lawrence, Iain.** *The Convicts*. Delacorte Press, c2005. 198pp.
His efforts to avenge his father's unjust imprisonment force thirteen-year-old Tom Tin into the streets of nineteenth-century London. After he is convicted of murder, Tom is eventually sent to Australia, where he has a surprise reunion.

**Lawrence, Iain.** *Ghost Boy*. Dell Laurel-Leaf, 2002, c2000. 326pp.
Unhappy in a home seemingly devoid of love, a fourteen-year-old albino boy who thinks of himself as Harold the Ghost runs away to join the circus, where he works with the elephants and searches for a sense of who he is. Includes reading group discussion guide.

**Napoli, Donna Jo.** *North*. Greenwillow Books, c2004. 344pp.
Tired of his mother's over-protectiveness and intrigued by the life of African American explorer Matthew Henson, twelve-year-old Alvin travels north and spends a season with a trapper near the Arctic Circle.

**Philbrick, W. R.** *Max the Mighty*. Scholastic, c1998. 166pp.
Fourteen-year-old Max helps a younger girl escape from her abusive stepfather by running away with her to the distant town of Chivalry, Montana, searching for her real father.

**Smith, Sherri L.** *Lucy the Giant*. Delacorte Press, c2002. 217pp.
Fifteen-year-old Lucy, the largest girl in her school, leaves her small Alaska town and her alcoholic father and discovers hardship—and friendship—posing as an adult aboard a commercial fishing boat.

**Tocher, Timothy.** *Chief Sunrise, John McGraw, and Me*. Cricket Books, c2004. 154pp.
In 1919, fifteen-year-old Hank escapes an abusive father and goes looking for a chance to become a baseball player, accompanied by a man who calls himself Chief Sunrise and claims to be a full-blooded Seminole.

**Whelan, Gloria.** *Chu Ju's House*. HarperCollins, c2004. 227pp.
To save her baby sister, fourteen-year-old Chu Ju leaves her rural home in modern China and earns food and shelter by working on a sampan, tending silk worms, and planting rice seedlings, while wondering if she will ever see her family again.

**Willis, Patricia.** *The Barn Burner*. Clarion Books, c2000. 196pp.
In 1933, while running from a bad situation at home and suspected of having set fire to a barn, fourteen-year-old Ross finds haven with a loving family, which helps him make an important decision.

**Wyss, Thelma Hatch.** *Ten Miles from Winnemucca*. HarperTrophy, 2003, c2002. 154pp.
When his mother and her new husband take off on a long honeymoon, and his new stepbrother throws his belongings out the window, sixteen-year-old Martin J. Miller takes off in his Jeep and settles in Red Rock, Idaho, where he finds a job, enrolls in school, and suffers from loneliness.

# Runaways

## Books for Older Teens

**Bell, William.** *Death Wind.* Orca Book, c2002. 92pp.

Allie, failing school and fearing she is pregnant by her ex-boyfriend, decides there is no way she can face her always fighting parents and decides to run away. She gets a different perspective on her life and future when a tornado hits, destroying her home and injuring her mother.

**Collins, Pat Lowery.** *The Fattening Hut.* Houghton Mifflin, c2003. 186pp.

A teenage girl living on a tropical island runs away to escape her tribe's customs of arranged marriages and female genital mutilation.

**Cormier, Robert.** *Tenderness*. Delacorte Press, 2004, c1997. 229pp.

A psychological thriller told from the points of view of a teenage serial killer and the runaway girl who falls in love with him.

**Dessen, Sarah.** *Dreamland*. Speak, 2004, c2000. 250pp.

After her older sister runs away, sixteen-year-old Caitlin decides that she needs to make a major change in her own life and begins an abusive relationship with a boy who is mysterious, brilliant, and dangerous.

**Flinn, Alex.** *Nothing To Lose.* HarperTempest, c2004. 277pp.

A year after running away with a traveling carnival to escape his unbearable home life, sixteen-year-old Michael returns to Miami, Florida, to find that his mother is going on trial for the murder of his abusive stepfather.

**Frank, E. R.** *America: A Novel.* Atheneum Books for Young Readers, c2002. 242pp.

America, a runaway boy who is being treated at Ridgeway, a New York hospital, finds himself opening up to one of the doctors on staff and revealing things about himself that he had always vowed to keep secret.

**Koja, Kathe.** *The Blue Mirror.* Farrar, Straus & Giroux, c2004. 119pp.

Seventeen-year-old loner Maggy Klass, who frequently seeks refuge from her alcoholic mother's apartment by sitting and drawing in a local cafe, becomes involved in a destructive relationship with a charismatic homeless youth named Cole.

**MacCullough, Carolyn.** *Stealing Henry*. Roaring Brook, c2005. 196pp.

Seventeen-year-old Savannah, fed up with her violent stepfather, hits him over the head with a frying pan and takes to the road with her eight-year-old half-brother on a journey that echoes in reverse the one her mother Alice took as a young, unwed mother running away from home.

**Murphy, Rita.** *Looking for Lucy Buick*. Delacorte Press, c2005. 165pp.

Following the death of her favorite adoptive aunt, Lucy goes searching for her biological family, who abandoned her in an old Buick eighteen years before.

**Paulsen, Gary.** *The Beet Fields: Memories of a Sixteenth Summer.* Dell Laurel-Leaf, 2002, c2000. 160pp.

In the summer of 1955, a sixteen-year-old boy runs away from his troubled home and learns about people, friendship, love, and lust while working as a migrant farmer and a carny.

# Runaways

**Stine, Catherine.** *Refugees*. Delacorte Press, c2005. 277pp.
Following the September 11, 2001. terrorist attacks, Dawn, a sixteen-year-old runaway from San Francisco, connects by phone and e-mail with Johar, a gentle, fifteen-year-old Afghani who assists Dawn's foster mother, a doctor, at a Red Cross refugee camp in Peshawar.

**Stone, Phoebe.** *All the Blue Moons at the Wallace Hotel.* Little, Brown, c2000. 198pp.
Though very different, events in their lives have made eleven-year-old Fiona and her younger sister Wallace close, so when Wallace disappears, Fiona risks missing the dance audition she has worked so hard to get.

# Search for Identity

## Books for Ages 12–15

**Avi.** *Crispin: The Cross of Lead.* Hyperion Books for Children, c2002. 262pp.
Falsely accused of theft and murder, an orphaned peasant boy in fourteenth-century England flees his village and meets a larger-than-life juggler who holds a dangerous secret.

**Cushman, Karen.** *The Midwife's Apprentice.* Clarion Books, c1995. 122pp.
In medieval England, a nameless, homeless girl is taken in by a sharp-tempered midwife. In spite of obstacles and hardship, she eventually gains the three things she most wants: a full belly, a contented heart, and a place in this world.

**Durrant, Lynda.** *Echohawk.* Clarion Books, c1996. 181pp.
A twelve-year-old white boy, adopted and raised by Mochicans in the Hudson River Valley during the 1730s, is sent with his younger brother to an English settlement, for schooling.

**Fleischman, Paul.** *Saturnalia.* HarperKeypoint, 1992, c1990. 112pp.
In 1681 in Boston, fourteen-year-old William, a Narraganset Indian captured in a raid six years earlier, leads a productive and contented life as a printer's apprentice but is increasingly anxious to make some connection with his Indian past.

**Fleischman, Paul.** *Seek.* Cricket Books, c2001. 167pp.
Rob becomes obsessed with searching the airwaves for his long-gone father, a radio announcer.

**Haddix, Margaret Peterson.** *Double Identity.* Simon & Schuster Books for Young Readers, c2005. 218pp.
Thirteen-year-old Bethany's parents have always been overprotective, but when they suddenly drop out of sight with no explanation, leaving her with an aunt she never knew existed, Bethany uncovers shocking secrets that make her question everything she thought she knew.

**Hale, Janet Campbell.** *The Owl's Song.* University of New Mexico Press, c1997. 153pp.
Billy White Hawk leaves his Idaho reservation in search of a better life in California, where instead he encounters hatred and hostility that are increasingly difficult to cope with.

**Hamilton, Virginia.** *Plain City.* Scholastic, c1993. 194pp.
Twelve-year-old Buhlaire, a "mixed" child who feels out of place in her community, struggles to unearth her past and her family history as she gradually discovers more and more about her long-missing father.

**Kretzer-Malvehy, Terry.** *Passage to Little Bighorn.* Rising Moon, c1999. 217pp.
Fifteen-year-old Dakota, who has Lakota blood in him, is hurled back through time to meet his ancestor Sitting Bull and witness the massacre at the Battle of Little Bighorn.

**Markle, Sandra.** *The Fledglings.* Boyds Mills Press, c1998. 138pp.
Orphaned after the death of her mother, fourteen-year-old Kate runs away to live with her grandfather, a Cherokee Indian who is trying to stop the poaching of predator birds.

**Meyer, Carolyn.** *Gideon's People.* Harcourt Brace, c1996. 297pp.
Torn between youthful rebellion and their traditional heritages, two boys from very different cultures—one Amish, one Orthodox Jew—discover just how similar they really are.

# Search for Identity

**Namioka, Lensey.** *Half and Half.* Delacorte Press, c2003. 136pp.
>At Seattle's annual Folk Fest, twelve-year-old Fiona and her older brother are torn between trying to please their Chinese grandmother and making their Scottish grandparents happy.

**Paterson, Katherine.** *Come Sing, Jimmy Jo.* Puffin Books, c1995. 197pp.
>When his family becomes a successful country music group and makes him a featured singer, eleven-year-old James has to deal with big changes in all aspects of his life, even his name.

**Paterson, Katherine.** *Jip: His Story.* Puffin, 2005, c1996. 180pp.
>While living on a Vermont poor farm in 1855 and 1856, Jip learns his identity and that of his mother and comes to understand how he arrived at this place.

**Paulsen, Gary.** *The Island.* Bantam Doubleday Dell Books for Young Readers, 1990, c1988. 202pp.
>Fifteen-year-old Wil discovers himself and the wonders of nature when he leaves home to live on an island in northern Wisconsin.

**Richter, Conrad.** *The Light in the Forest.* Knopf (distributed in the United States by Random House), 2005, c1953. 162pp.
>John Cameron Butler, kidnapped by the Lenne Indians when he was only four years old, is returned to his white family eleven years later and struggles to fit into the unfamiliar culture.

**Weeks, Sarah.** *Regular Guy.* HarperTrophy, 2000, c1999. 120pp.
>Because he is so different from his eccentric parents, twelve-year-old Guy is convinced he has been switched at birth with a classmate whose parents seem more normal.

## Books for Older Teens

**Hinton, S. E.** *Tex.* Bantam Doubleday Dell Books for Young Readers, 1989, c1979. 211pp.
>The love between two teenage brothers helps to alleviate the harshness of their usually parentless life as they struggle to grow up.

**Irwin, Hadley.** *Kim/Kimi.* Puffin Books, 1988, c1987. 200pp.
>Despite a warm relationship with her mother, stepfather, and half-brother, sixteen-year-old Kim feels the need to find answers about the Japanese American father she never knew.

**Thomas, Rob.** *Rats Saw God.* Aladdin Paperbacks, c1996. 202pp.
>In hopes of graduating, Steve York agrees to complete a hundred-page writing assignment, which helps him to sort out his relationship with his famous astronaut father and the events that changed him from a promising student into a troubled teen.

**Wolff, Virginia Euwer.** *The Mozart Season.* Scholastic Signature, 2000, c1991, 249pp.
>Allegra spends her twelfth summer practicing a Mozart concerto for a violin competition and finding many significant connections in her world.

**Woodson, Jacqueline.** *From the Notebooks of Melanin Sun: A Novel.* Scholastic, c1995. 141pp.
>Thirteen-year-old Melanin Sun's comfortable, quiet life is shattered when his mother reveals she has fallen in love with a woman.

**Wright, Richard.** *Rite of Passage.* HarperTrophy, 1996, c1994, 151pp.
>When fifteen-year-old Johnny Gibbs is told that he is really a foster child, he runs off into the streets of Harlem and meets up with a gang that wants him to participate in a mugging.

From Nancy J. Keane, *The Big Book of Teen Reading Lists: 100 Great, Ready-to-Use Book Lists for Educators, Librarians, Parents, and Children.* Westport, CT: Libraries Unlimited, 2006. Copyright © 2006 by Libraries Unlimited.

# Self-Mutilation

## Books for Ages 12–15

**Hoffman, Alice.** *Green Angel.* Scholastic Press, c2003. 116pp.
Haunted by grief and her past after losing her family in a fire, fifteen-year-old Green retreats into her ruined garden as she struggles to survive emotionally and physically on her own.

**Holt, Kimberly Willis.** *Keeper of the Night.* H. Holt, c2003. 308pp.
Isabel, a thirteen-year-old girl living on the island of Guam, and her family try to cope with the death of Isabel's mother, who committed suicide.

**Klass, David.** *You Don't Know Me: A Novel.* Farrar, Straus & Giroux, c2001. 262pp.
Fourteen-year-old John creates alternative realities in his mind as he tries to deal with his mother's abusive boyfriend, his crush on a beautiful but shallow classmate, and other problems at school.

**Konigsburg, E. L.** *Silent to the Bone.* Atheneum Books for Young Readers, c2000. 261pp.
Thirteen-year-old Branwell loses the power of speech after being wrongly accused of gravely injuring his baby half-sister, and only his friend Connor is able to reach him and uncover the truth about what happened.

**Mackler, Carolyn.** *The Earth, My Butt, and Other Big Round Things.* Candlewick Press, c2003. 246pp.
Feeling that she does not fit in with the other members of her family, who are all thin, brilliant, and good-looking, fifteen-year-old Virginia tries to deal with her self-image, her first physical relationship, and her disillusionment with some of the people closest to her.

**Marsden, John.** *Checkers.* Dell Laurel-Leaf, 2000, c1996. 122pp.
Speaking from a mental hospital, a teenage girl recounts the tremendous media pressure that preceded the breaking scandal of her father's unethical business dealings.

**McCormick, Patricia.** *Cut.* Front Street, c2000. 168pp.
While confined to a mental hospital, thirteen-year-old Callie slowly comes to understand some of the reasons behind her self-mutilation and gradually starts to get better.

**Peters, Julie Anne.** *Define "Normal".* Little, Brown, c2000. 196 p
When she agrees to meet with Jasmine as a peer counselor at their middle school, Antonia never dreams that this girl with the black lipstick and pierced eyebrow will end up helping her deal with the serious problems she faces at home and become a good friend.

**Weill, Sabrina Solin.** *We're Not Monsters: Teens Speak Out About Teens in Trouble.* HarperCollins, c2002. 234pp. (NF)
Commentaries by teenagers about their fellow teens who commit crimes or violate social norms.

**Wilson, Dawn.** *Saint Jude.* Tudor Publishers, c2001. 171pp.
When committed to an upscale group home outside Asheville, North Carolina, eighteen-year-old Taylor Drysdale pretends that her bipolar disorder is under control and that she will leave soon, but relationships with her fellow residents may hold the key to her real recovery.

# Self-Mutilation

## Books for Older Teens

**Goobie, Beth.** *The Dream Where the Losers Go.* Roussan, c1999. 206pp.

After spending five months in treatment, Skey still doesn't know why she hurt herself, but when she meets another boy her own age who has many of the same problems, she begins to understand her own destructive behavior.

**Kettlewell, Caroline.** *Skin Game.* St. Martin's Griffin, c1999. 178pp.

A memoir in which the author, a former "cutter," discusses the reasons why she began cutting herself as an adolescent, and shares the story of how she was finally able to overcome the affliction.

**Levenkron, Steven.** *The Luckiest Girl in the World.* Penguin Books, 1998, c1997. 188pp.

Figure-skating star Katie Roskova, unable to express her feelings of panic and anger, develops a habit of cutting herself with scissors and hiding her scars beneath long-sleeve shirts, but as pressure mounts her wounds become more serious, and soon her secret is revealed.

**Mackall, Dandi Daley.** *Kyra's Story.* Tyndale House, c2003. 277pp.

When seventeen-year-old Kyra of Macon, Iowa, becomes overwhelmed by the stress of senior year in high school, the school play, and early admission to drama school, she begins taking prescription drugs, unaware that her twin brother will suffer the consequences.

**Marsden, John.** *So Much to Tell You.* Fawcett Books, c1990. 119pp.

Sent to a boarding school by her mother, Marina, a disfigured Australian girl who refuses to speak, reveals her thoughts and feelings in a diary.

**Slade, Arthur G.** *Tribes.* Wendy Lamb Books, c2002. 134pp.

For Percy, the loss of his father and the suicide of his best friend come to a head during the last week before high school graduation.

**Stoehr, Shelley.** *Crosses.* Delacorte, c1991. 153pp.

Unhappy at home, Nancy and her friend Katie adopt punk lifestyles and find relief in cutting themselves, until Nancy is forced to confront her problems.

From Nancy J. Keane, *The Big Book of Teen Reading Lists: 100 Great, Ready-to-Use Book Lists for Educators, Librarians, Parents, and Children.* Westport, CT: Libraries Unlimited, 2006. Copyright © 2006 by Libraries Unlimited.

# Surviving Peer Pressure

## Nonfiction

### Books for Ages 12–15

**Davis, Anthony C.** *"Yo, Little Brother—": Basic Rules of Survival for Young African American Males.* African American Images, c1998. 157pp. (NF)
> Offers straightforward advice for young African American males on how to live safe, successful lives, discussing courtesy, sex, friends, faith, racism, money, driving, and street smarts.

**Mosatche, Harriet S.** *Girls—What's So Bad About Being Good?: How to Have Fun, Survive the Preteen Years, and Remain True to Yourself.* Prima Pub, c2001. 218pp. (NF)
> Presents guidance for preteen girls on such topics as self-image, healthy relationships, peer pressure, bullies, learning, community service, and dreams and goals.

**Mosatche, Harriet S.** *Too Old for This, Too Young for That!: Your Survival Guide for the Middle-School Years.* Free Spirit, c2000. 190pp. (NF)
> Quizzes, stories, surveys, and activities for middle schoolers addressing such issues as physical and emotional changes, connecting with friends and family, setting goals, and handling peer pressure.

**Sommers, Michael A.** *Chillin': A Guy's Guide to Friendship.* Rosen Central, c2000. 48pp. (NF)
> Provides advice on making new friends and negotiating issues such as peer pressure, acceptance, and conformity.

### Books for Older Teens

**Glodoski, Ron.** *How to Be a Successful Criminal: The Real Deal On Crime (Drugs, and Easy Money.* Turn Around Publications, 2005, c1998. 259pp. (NF)
> The author's firsthand account of his experiences as a criminal, street thug, drug dealer, and prison inmate, providing advice for troubled teens on how to avoid the same mistakes and stay out of jail.

**Healy, Kent.** *"Cool Stuff" They Should Teach in School.* Cool Stuff Media, c2005. 303pp. (NF)
> A practical guide written by teens, who provide suggestions on what should be taught in school, such as surviving in the real world, controlling attitude, conquering peer pressure, setting proper goals, and handling money.

**McGraw, Jay.** *Life Strategies for Teens.* Simon & Schuster, c2000. 236pp. (NF)
> A self-help guide for teenagers, including information on peer pressure, popularity, and ambition.

**Palmer, Pat.** *Teen Esteem: A Self-direction Manual for Young Adults.* Impact Publishers, c2000. 97pp. (NF)
> Provides guidance on developing self-esteem and the positive attitude necessary to cope with such adolescent challenges as peer pressure, substance abuse, and sexual expression.

# Part 4

## Setting

# Ancient Civilizations

## Books for Ages 12–15

**Alexander, Lloyd.** *Time Cat: The Remarkable Journeys of Jason and Gareth*. H. Holt, c2003. 211pp.
Jason and his magic cat Gareth travel through time to visit countries all over the world during different periods of history.

**Barrett, Tracy.** *On Etruscan Time*. H. Holt, c2005. 172pp.
While spending the summer on an archaeological dig near Florence, Italy, with his mother, eleven-year-old Hector meets an Etruscan boy who needs help to foil his treacherous uncle's plan to make him a human sacrifice—1,000 years in the past.

**Bunting, Eve.** *I Am the Mummy Heb-Nefert*. Harcourt Brace, c1997. 32pp.
A mummy recalls her past life in ancient Egypt as the beautiful wife of the pharaoh's brother.

**Carter, Dorothy Sharp.** *His Majesty, Queen Hatshepsut*. Lippincott, c1987. 248pp.
A fictionalized account of the life of Hatshepsut, a queen in ancient Egypt who declared herself king and ruled as such for more than twenty years.

**Fletcher, Susan.** *Shadow Spinner*. Aladdin Paperbacks, 1999, c1998. 219pp.
When Marjan, a thirteen-year-old crippled girl, joins the Sultan's harem in ancient Persia, she gathers for Shahrazad the stories that will save the queen's life.

**Lawrence, Caroline.** *The Thieves of Ostia: A Roman Mystery*. Puffin Books, c2004. 152pp.
In Rome in the year A.D.79, a group of children from very different backgrounds work together to discover who beheaded a pet dog and why.

**Lester, Julius.** *Pharaoh's Daughter: A Novel of Ancient Egypt*. Silver Whistle/Harcourt, c2000. 182pp.
A fictionalized account of a biblical story in which an Egyptian princess rescues a Hebrew infant, who becomes a prophet of his people, while his sister finds her true self as a priestess to the Egyptian gods.

**McGraw, Eloise Jarvis.** *The Golden Goblet*. Puffin Books, 1986, c1961. 248pp.
A young Egyptian boy struggles to reveal a hideous crime and reshape his own destiny.

**McGraw, Eloise Jarvis.** *Mara, Daughter of the Nile*. Puffin Books, 1985, c1953. 278pp.
The adventures of an ingenious Egyptian slave girl who undertakes a dangerous assignment as a spy in the royal palace of Thebes, in the days when Queen Hatshepsut ruled.

**Napoli, Donna Jo.** *Song of the Magdalene*. Simon Pulse, 2004, c1996. 240pp.
Relates the story of Miriam, a young girl being raised by her widowed father in ancient Israel, who grows up to be Mary Magdalene.

**Rubalcaba, Jill.** *A Place in the Sun*. Clarion Books, c1997. 86pp.
In ancient Egypt, the gifted young son of a sculptor is taken into slavery when he attempts to save his father's life and is himself almost killed before his exceptional talent leads Pharoah to name him Royal Sculptor.

# Ancient Civilizations

**Rubalcaba, Jill.** *The Wadjet Eye.* Clarion Books, c2000. 156pp.
After his mother dies Damon, a young medical student living in Alexandria, Egypt, in 45 B.C. makes a perilous journey to Spain to locate his father, who is serving in the Roman army led by Julius Caesar.

**Scieszka, Jon.** *Tut, Tut.* Viking Press, c1996. 74pp.
Sam, Joe, and Fred finish their school project on ancient Egypt without using their magical time travel book, but when Joe's sister Anna plays with it and travels to the land of pyramids, they must follow her back in time to bring her back to 1996.

**Service, Pamela F.** *The Reluctant God.* Fawcett Juniper, 1990, c1988. 182pp.
While his brother prepares to mount the throne of Egypt as the next member of the Twelfth Dynasty, the teenage prince Ameni is sealed in a secret tomb in a state of suspended animation, to be revived 4,000 years later.

**Sutcliff, Rosemary** *Black Ships Before Troy.* Laurel-Leaf Books, c2005. 128pp.
Retells the story of the Trojan War, from the quarrel over the golden apple, to the flight of Helen with Paris, to the destruction of Troy.

**Sutcliff, Rosemary.** *The Eagle of the Ninth.* Farrar, Straus & Giroux, c1993. 291pp.
A young centurion ventures among the hostile tribes beyond the Roman Wall to recover the eagle standard of the Ninth, a legion that mysteriously disappeared under his father's command.

**Sutcliff, Rosemary.** *The Wanderings of Odysseus: The Story of the Odyssey.* Frances Lincoln Children's Books (distributed by Publishers Group West), 2005, c1995. 119pp.
A retelling of the adventures of Odysseus on his long voyage home from the Trojan War.

## Books for Older Teens

**Bradshaw, Gillian.** *The Sand-Reckoner.* Forge, c2000. 351pp.
Tells the early life of the ancient Greek mathematician Archimedes.

**Cook, Robin.** *Sphinx.* Signet, 1980, c1979. 313pp. (adult)
When Erica Baron finds a previously undiscovered pharaoh's tomb in Egypt's Valley of the Kings, she becomes involved in intrigue, corruption, and murder.

**Graves, Robert.** *Claudius the God: And His Wife Messalina.* Vintage, 1989, c1935. 533pp.
A historical novel in which Claudius, a self-professed cripple, stammerer, and fool of the royal family, tells why he was persuaded to take the throne—a position he never wanted—and attempts to justify his actions during his thirteen-year reign as emperor of Rome.

**Robinson, Lynda Suzanne.** *Eater of Souls.* Ballantine Books, 1998, c1997. 276pp.
While investigating the death of Queen Nefertiti, Lord Meren must discover whether the killer is one the god called the Devourer or a human in disguise, all while combating court intrigue.

# Civil War

## Books for Ages 12–15

**Alphin, Elaine Marie.** *Ghost Soldier*. H. Holt, c2001. 216pp.

Alexander, in North Carolina while his father decides whether to remarry and move there, meets the ghost of a Confederate soldier and helps him look for his family.

**Brenaman, Miriam.** *Evvy's Civil War*. Speak, 2004, c2002. 209pp.

In Virginia in 1860, on the verge of the Civil War, fourteen-year-old Evvy chafes at the restrictions that her society places on both women and slaves.

**Crisp, Marty.** *Private Captain: A Story of Gettysburg*. Puffin Books, 2002, c2001. 293pp.

In 1863 Pennsylvania, twelve-year-old Ben and his dog Captain set off in search of Ben's brother, who is missing from the Union Army.

**Elliott, Laura.** *Annie, Between the States*. Katherine Tegen Books, c2004. 488pp.

Instead of spending her teen years at parties and balls, Annie, an idealistic, poetry-loving patriot, finds herself nursing soldiers, hiding valuables, and running the household as the Civil War rages around her family's Virginia home.

**Ernst, Kathleen.** *Ghosts of Vicksburg*. White Mane Kids, c2003. 215pp.

When Jamie Carswell joins the 14th Wisconsin Infantry Regiment fighting in Vicksburg, Mississippi, he finds his cousin Althea living there, trying to make peace with her past and keep her family safe during the Union's siege.

**Hahn, Mary Downing.** *Hear the Wind Blow*. Clarion Books, c2003. 212pp.

With their mother dead and their home burned, a thirteen-year-old boy and his little sister set out across Virginia in search of relatives during the final days of the Civil War.

**Hughes, Pat.** *Guerrilla Season*. Farrar, Straus & Giroux, c2003. 328pp.

Two fifteen-year-old boys in Missouri in 1863 find friendship and family loyalty tested by Quantrell's raiders, a Rebel guerrilla band that roamed under the black flag of "no quarter to be given by Union troops."

**Kay, Alan N.** *No Girls Allowed*. White Mane Kids, c2003. 148pp.

In 1862 two young girls, one a member of an aid society that helps the wounded, and the other disguised as a boy and serving as a soldier in the Union army, find themselves working together at the battle of Antietam.

**Lyons, Mary E.** *Dear Ellen Bee: A Civil War Scrapbook of Two Union Spies*. Atheneum Books for Young Readers, c2000. 161pp.

A scrapbook kept by a young black girl details her experiences and those of the older white woman, "Miss Bet," who had freed her and her family, sent her north from Richmond to get an education, and then worked to bring an end to slavery. Based on the life of Elizabeth Van Lew.

**Matas, Carol.** *The War Within: A Novel of the Civil War*. Simon & Schuster Books for Young Readers, c2001. 151pp.

In 1862, after Union forces expel Hannah's family from Holly Springs, Mississippi, because they are Jews, Hannah reexamines her views regarding slavery and the war.

# Civil War

**McMullan, Margaret.** *How I Found the Strong: A Civil War Story*. Houghton Mifflin, c2004. 136pp.
Frank Russell, known as Shanks, wishes he could have gone with his father and brother to fight for Mississippi and the Confederacy, but his experiences with the war and his changing relationship with the family slave, Buck, change his thinking.

**Myers, Anna.** *Assassin*. Walker (distributed by Holtzbrinck), c2005. 212pp.
In alternating passages, a young White House seamstress named Bella and the actor John Wilkes Booth describe the events that led to the latter's assassination of Abraham Lincoln.

**Peck, Richard.** *The River Between Us*. Dial Books, c2003. 164pp.
During the early days of the Civil War, the Pruitt family takes in two mysterious young ladies who have fled New Orleans to come north to Illinois.

**Reeder, Carolyn.** *Before the Creeks Ran Red*. HarperCollins, c2003. 370pp.
Through the eyes of three different boys, three linked novellas explore the tumultuous times, beginning with the secession of South Carolina and leading up to the first major battle of the Civil War.

**Rinaldi, Ann.** *Numbering All the Bones*. Jump at the Sun/Hyperion Books for Children, c2002. 170pp.
Thirteen-year-old Eulinda, a house slave on a Georgia plantation in 1864, turns to Clara Barton (the real-life founder of the American Red Cross), for help in finding her brother Neddy, who ran away to join the Northern war effort and is rumored to be at Andersonville Prison.

**Rinaldi, Ann.** *Sarah's Ground*. Simon & Schuster Books for Young Readers, c2004. 178pp.
In 1861 eighteen-year-old Sarah Tracy, from New York State, comes to work at Mount Vernon, the historic Virginia home of George Washington, where she tries to protect the safety and neutrality of the site during the Civil War, and where she encounters her future husband, Upton Herbert. Includes historical notes.

**Severance, John B.** *Braving the Fire*. Clarion Books, c2002. 148pp.
Jem joins the Union Army but is not sure of his motives or what he hopes to accomplish, particularly since the Civil War has divided his family and caused much violence and confusion in his life.

**Siegelson, Kim L.** *Trembling Earth*. Philomel Books, c2004. 152pp.
In 1864 two boys, one a slave running toward freedom and one a white boy hoping to collect the reward for capturing him, make their way through Georgia's Okefenokee Swamp, relying on knowledge the white boy's father, disabled by the war, had passed on to him in happier times.

**Taylor, Mildred D.** *The Land*. P. Fogelman, c2001. 375pp.
In the aftermath of the Civil War, Paul-Edward, the son of a part-Indian, part-African slave mother and a White plantation owner father, finds himself caught between the two worlds of his parents as he pursues his dream of owning land.

# Dust Bowl

## Books for Ages 12–15

**Connell, Kate.** *Hoping for Rain: The Dust Bowl Adventures of Patty and Earl Buckler* National Geographic, c2004. 40pp. (NF)
> Sixteen-year-old Earl Buckler, his twelve-year-old sister Patty, and their family endure the droughts, black blizzards, and hardships of the Great Depression and the dust bowl in Oklahoma in 1935 before emigrating to California.

**Coombs, Karen Mueller.** *Children of the Dust Days*. Carolrhoda Books, c2000. 48pp. (NF)
> Focuses on the experiences of children during the Dust Bowl era of the 1930s, when prolonged drought, coupled with ruinous farming techniques, caused massive erosion from Texas to Canada's wheat fields.

**De Angelis, Therese.** *The Dust Bowl*. Chelsea House, c2002. 116pp. (NF)
> Chronicles the plight of farmers living in the dust bowl in the 1930s, discussing the social upheaval that accompanied the loss of their livelihood and the official programs and reforms enacted by the federal government to help them.

**Dearen, Patrick.** *When the Sky Rained Dust*. Eakin Press, c2004. 126pp.
> Fourteen-year-old Josh faces love, a dust storm, and the threat of losing his family's farm during the days of the dust bowl and the Great Depression in 1934.

**Hamilton, John.** *Droughts*. ABDO, c2006. 32pp. (NF)
> Explains how droughts happen, describes the "dust bowl" in 1930s America, presents photos of drought-ravaged places around the world, and discusses what can be done ahead of time to lessen a drought's devastation.

**Heinrichs, Ann.** *The Dust Bowl*. Compass Point Books, c2005. 48pp. (NF)
> Discusses the dust bowl era of the 1930s, when dust storms raged across the heartland of the United States, causing damage that reached from North Dakota to Texas, explains how a combination of bad farming practices and drought caused the deadly conditions, and looks at how people and the government responded to the crisis.

**Henderson, Caroline A.** *Letters from the Dust Bowl*. University of Oklahoma Press, c2001. 278pp. (NF)
> A collection of letters and articles written by Caroline Henderson between 1908 and 1966 provide insight into her life on the Great Plains, featuring both published materials and private correspondence. Includes a biographical profile, chapter introductions, and annotations.

**Hesse, Karen.** *Out of the Dust*. Scholastic Press, c1997. 227pp.
> In a series of poems, fifteen-year-old Billie Jo relates the hardships of living on her family's wheat farm in Oklahoma during the dust bowl years of the Depression.

**Janke, Katelan.** *Survival in the Storm: The Dust Bowl Diary of Grace Edwards*. Scholastic, c2002. 189pp.
> A twelve-year-old girl keeps a journal of her family's and friends' difficult experiences in the Texas panhandle, part of the dust bowl during the Great Depression. Includes a historical note about life in America in 1935.

From Nancy J. Keane, *The Big Book of Teen Reading Lists: 100 Great, Ready-to-Use Book Lists for Educators, Librarians, Parents, and Children*. Westport, CT: Libraries Unlimited, 2006. Copyright © 2006 by Libraries Unlimited.

# Dust Bowl

**Meltzer, Milton.** ***Driven from the Land: The Story of the Dust Bowl***. Benchmark Books, c2000. 111pp. (NF)

> Describes the economic and environmental conditions that led to the Great Depression and the horrific dust storms that drove people west from their homes during the 1930s.

**Moss, Marissa.** ***Rose's Journal: The Story of a Girl in the Great Depression***. Silver Whistle/Harcourt, c2001. 52pp.

> Rose keeps a journal of her family's difficult times on their farm during the days of the dust bowl in 1935.

**Porter, Tracey.** ***Treasures in the Dust***. HarperTrophy, c1999. 148pp.

> Eleven-year-old Annie and her friend Violet tell about the hardships endured by their families when dust storms, drought, and the Great Depression hit rural Oklahoma.

**Stanley, Jerry.** ***Children of the Dust Bowl: The True Story of the School at Weedpatch Camp***. Crown, c1992. 85pp. (NF)

> Describes the plight of the migrant workers who traveled from the dust bowl areas to California during the Great Depression and were forced to live in a federal labor camp; discusses the school that was built for their children.

**Worster, Donald.** ***Dust Bowl: The Southern Plains in the 1930s***. Oxford University Press, c2004. 290pp. (NF)

> Discusses the tragedy that followed the destruction of America's superb Western grasslands and points out useful lessons learned from it.

**Yancey, Diane.** ***Life During the Dust Bowl***. Lucent Books, Thomson/Gale, c2004. 112pp. (NF)

> Discusses the causes and effects of the disastrous dust storms that hit the Great Plains in the 1930s.

## Books for Older Teens

**Slade, Arthur G.** ***Dust***. Wendy Lamb Books, c2003. 183pp.

> Eleven-year-old Robert is the only one who can help when a mysterious stranger arrives, performing tricks and promising to bring rain, and children begin to disappear from a dust bowl farm town in Saskatchewan in the 1930s.

**Steinbeck, John.** ***The Grapes of Wrath***. Penguin, c1992. 619pp.

> The saga of a family in 1939 that struggles through the Great Depression by laboring as dust bowl migrants.

# Ellis Island

## Books for Ages 12–15

**Anderson, Dale.** *Arriving at Ellis Island.* World Almanac Library, c2002. 48pp. (NF)
Discusses immigration to the United States during the nineteenth and early twentieth centuries and describes the small island in New York harbor that served as the point of entry for millions of immigrants from 1892 to 1954.

**Auch, Mary Jane.** *Ashes of Roses.* H. Holt, c2002. 250pp.
Sixteen-year-old Rose Nolan arrives on Ellis Island in 1911 with hopes of starting a new life, but after most of her family is sent back to Ireland, she must find her own way in a new country and fend for herself and her younger sister.

**Houghton, Gillian.** *Ellis Island: A Primary Source History of an Immigrant's Arrival in America.*
Rosen Central Primary Source, c2004. 64pp. (NF)
Primary sources bring to life the immigrant experience through a history of America's most famous point of entry, Ellis Island.

**Lasky, Kathryn.** *Hope in My Heart.* Scholastic, c2003. 106pp.
After her family immigrates to America from Italy in 1903, ten-year-old Sofia is quarantined at the Ellis Island Immigration Station, where she makes a good friend but endures nightmarish conditions. Includes historical notes.

**Marcovitz, Hal.** *Ellis Island.* Mason Crest Publishers, c2003. 48pp. (NF)
Traces the history of Ellis Island, the place where immigrants coming to the United States were once processed, and discusses its significance to the American people.

**Moreno, Barry.** *Encyclopedia of Ellis Island.* Greenwood Press, 2004. 321pp. (NF)
Contains 430 alphabetically arranged articles that provide information about people, places, and events in the history of Ellis Island, including coverage of immigration laws and acts, operations, and organizations.

**Nixon, Joan Lowery.** *Land of Dreams.* G. Stevens, c2001. 153pp.
In 1902 sixteen-year-old Kristin travels with her family from Sweden to a new life in Minnesota, where she finds herself frustrated by the restrictions placed on what girls of her age are expected or allowed to do.

**Nixon, Joan Lowery.** *Land of Hope.* G. Stevens, 2001, c1992. 171pp.
Rebekah, a fifteen-year-old Jewish immigrant arriving in New York City in 1902, almost abandons her dream of getting an education when she is forced to work in a sweatshop.

**Nixon, Joan Lowery.** *Land of Promise.* G. Stevens, 2001, c1993. 169pp.
In 1902 fifteen-year-old Rose travels from Ireland to join family members in Chicago, where she must use all her resources to deal with her father's drinking and her brothers' dangerous involvement in politics.

# Ellis Island

**Raatma, Lucia.** *Ellis Island*. Compass Point Books, c2003. 48pp. (NF)
Traces the history of Ellis Island, focusing on its role as a port for immigrants who came to the United States between 1892 and 1924; provides information about the immigrant experience; and includes discussion of the restoration of Ellis Island as a historic landmark.

**Rebman, Renee C.** *Life on Ellis Island*. Lucent Books, 1999, c2000. 95pp. (NF)
Discusses life on Ellis Island, including detainment and deportation of immigrants, daily activities, the development of the immigration station, its role in the formation of the great melting pot of America, and the later years.

**Sherman, Augustus F.** *Augustus F. Sherman: Ellis Island Portraits, 1905–1920*. Aperture, c2005. 141pp. (NF)
Presents a comprehensive collection of black-and-white photographs of over 200 families, groups, and individuals as they passed through Ellis Island between 1904 and 1920.

# Frontier and Pioneer Life

## Books for Ages 12–15

**Aldrich, Bess Streeter.** *A Lantern in Her Hand.* Puffin Books, c1997. 251pp.
After marrying Will Deal and moving to Nebraska, Abbie endures the difficulties of frontier life and raises her children to pursue the ambitions that were once her own.

**Armstrong, Jennifer.** *Black-eyed Susan*. Knopf, c1997. 120pp.
Ten-year-old Susie and her father love living on the South Dakota prairie with its vast, uninterrupted views of land and sky, but Susie's mother greatly misses their old life in Ohio.

**Brink, Carol Ryrie.** *Caddie Woodlawn.* Aladdin Paperbacks, 1997, c1935. 242pp.
Chronicles the adventures of eleven-year-old Caddie growing up with her six brothers and sisters on the Wisconsin frontier in the mid-nineteenth century.

**Calvert, Patricia.** *Betrayed!* Aladdin Paperbacks, 2004, c2002. 212pp.
In 1867, after his father's death and his mother's remarriage, fourteen-year-old Tyler and his black friend Isaac set out on the Missouri River, headed west to seek their fortunes, encountering an unsavory keel boat captain and a Sioux chief along the way.

**Conrad, Pam.** *My Daniel.* HarperTrophy, 1991, c1989. 137pp.
Ellie and Stevie learn about a family legacy when their grandmother tells them stories of her brother's quest for dinosaur bones on their Nebraska farm.

**Conrad, Pam.** *Prairie Songs*. HarperTrophy, 1987, c1985. 167pp.
Louisa's life in a loving pioneer family on the Nebraska prairie is altered by the arrival of a new doctor and his beautiful, tragically frail wife.

**Couloumbis, Audrey.** *The Misadventures of Maude Marche, Or, Trouble Rides a Fast Horse.* Random House, c2005. 295pp.
After the death of the stern aunt who raised them since they were orphaned, eleven-year-old Sallie and her fifteen-year-old sister escape their self-serving guardians and begin an adventure resembling those in the dime novels Sallie loves to read.

**Cushman, Karen.** *The Ballad of Lucy Whipple*. Clarion Books, c1996. 195pp.
In 1849 twelve-year-old California Morning Whipple, who renames herself Lucy, is distraught when her mother moves the family from Massachusetts to a rough California mining town.

**Durbin, William.** *Blackwater Ben*. Dell Yearling, 2005, c2003. 200pp.
Thirteen-year-old Ben Ward drops out of school and joins his father working as a cook at the Blackwater Logging Camp in Minnesota in the winter of 1898.

**Durbin, William.** *Song of Sampo Lake*. Wendy Lamb, c2002. 217pp.
In 1900, as a family of Finnish immigrants begins farming on the edge of a Minnesota lake, Matti works as a store clerk, teaches English, and works on the homestead, striving to get out of his older brother's shadow and earn their father's respect.

# Frontier and Pioneer Life

**Ellsworth, Loretta.** *The Shrouding Woman.* H. Holt, c2002. 151pp.

When her Aunt Flo comes to help care for eleven-year-old Evie and her younger sister after their mother's death, Evie wants nothing to do with her, and she is especially uncomfortable with her aunt's calling of helping prepare bodies for burial.

**Fleischman, Paul.** *The Borning Room.* HarperTrophy, 1993, c1991. 101pp.

Lying at the end of her life in the room where she was born in 1851, Georgina remembers what it was like to grow up on the Ohio frontier.

**Gregory, Kristiana.** *Across the Wide and Lonesome Prairie: The Oregon Trail Diary of Hattie Campbell.* Scholastic, c1997. 168pp.

In her diary, thirteen-year-old Hattie chronicles her family's arduous journey from Missouri to Oregon in 1847 on the Oregon Trail.

**Gregory, Kristiana.** *Jenny of the Tetons.* Gulliver Books/Harcourt, 2002, c1989. 168pp.

Orphaned by an Indian raid while traveling west with a wagon train, fifteen-year-old Carrie Hill is befriended by the English trapper Beaver Dick and taken to live with his Indian wife, Jenny, and their six children.

**Hahn, Mary Downing.** *The Gentleman Outlaw and Me—Eli: A Story of the Old West.* Clarion Books, c1996. 212pp.

In 1887 twelve-year-old Eliza, disguised as a boy and traveling to Colorado in search of her missing father, falls in with a Gentleman Outlaw and joins him in his illegal schemes.

**Haruf, Kent.** *The Tie That Binds: A Novel.* Vintage Contemporaries, 2000, c1984. 246pp.

Edith Goodnough goes through life without despair or self-pity, denying herself a chance at love and happiness to care for her father and brother until, at the age of eighty, she decides to seek a type of freedom.

**Hite, Sid.** *Stick and Whittle.* Scholastic Signature, 2001, c2000. 202pp.

In 1872, while journeying from Texas to Kansas, a Civil War veteran named Melvin meets a sixteen-year-old orphan, another Melvin, and they give each other nicknames, becoming partners and traveling companions on an exciting adventure.

**Holm, Jennifer L.** *Boston Jane: An Adventure.* HarperCollins, c2001. 273pp. (and sequels)

Schooled in the lessons of etiquette for young ladies in 1854, Miss Jane Peck of Philadelphia finds little use for manners during her long sea voyage to the Pacific Northwest and while living among the American traders and Chinook Indians of Washington Territory.

**Holm, Jennifer L.** *Our Only May Amelia.* HarperCollins, c1999. 253pp.

As the only girl in a Finnish American family of seven brothers, May Amelia Jackson resents being expected to act like a lady while growing up in Washington State in 1899.

**Ingold, Jeanette.** *The Big Burn.* Harcourt, c2002. 295pp.

Three teenagers battle the flames of the Big Burn of 1910, one of the century's largest wildfires.

# Frontier and Pioneer Life

**Ingold, Jeanette.** *Mountain Solo*. Harcourt, c2003. 309pp.

Tess, a violin prodigy who has been playing since age three, throws away all her training and talent to start a new life with her father in Montana, where she realizes having a normal life isn't always so normal.

**Kimmel, Elizabeth Cody.** *In the Eye of the Storm*. HarperCollins, c2003. 132pp.

With the ever-present threat of further violence from pro-slavery border ruffians, nine-year-old Bill must run the farm, even after his father comes home to recuperate from his knife wound, and go to school.

**Kimmel, Elizabeth Cody.** *To the Frontier*. HarperTrophy, 2004, c2002. 182pp.

After the death of his brother, eight-year-old Bill Cody and his family set out from Iowa to make a new home for themselves in the volatile Kansas Territory.

**Koller, Jackie French.** *The Primrose Way*. Harcourt Brace, 1995, c1992. 334pp.

A recent arrival to the New World in 1633, sixteen-year-old Rebekah, a missionary's daughter, befriends a Native American woman and begins to question whether these "savages" need saving after all.

**Lane, Rose Wilder.** *Young Pioneers*. HarperTrophy, c1998. 175pp.

After getting married and settling at Wild Plum Creek, David's and Caroline's lives are turned upside down when disaster strikes and David must go east to find work for the winter.

**Lenski, Lois.** *Indian Captive: The Story of Mary Jemison*. HarperTrophy, 1995, c1941. 298pp.

A fictional retelling of the experiences of twelve-year-old Mary Jemison, who was captured by a Shawnee war party during the French and Indian War, then later rescued and subsequently adopted by two Seneca sisters, with whom she ultimately chose to stay.

**Oswald, Nancy.** *Nothing Here But Stones*. H. Holt, c2004. 215pp.

In 1882 ten-year-old Emma and her family, along with other Russian Jewish immigrants, arrive in Cotopaxi, Colorado, where they face inhospitable conditions as they attempt to start an agricultural colony, and lonely Emma is comforted by the horse whose life she saved.

**Paulsen, Gary.** *Call Me Francis Tucket*. Bantam Doubleday Dell Books for Young Readers, 1996, c1995. 97pp.

Having separated from the one-armed trapper who taught him how to survive in the wilderness of the Old West, fifteen-year-old Francis gets lost and continues to have adventures, involving dangerous men and a friendly mule.

**Paulsen, Gary.** *Tucket's Gold*. Dell Yearling, 2001, c1999. 97pp.

Fifteen-year-old Francis and the two children he has adopted travel across the Old West, evade Comancheros, discover a treasure, and wind up rich beyond their wildest dreams.

**Rudolph, Marian.** *Lovina's Song: A Pioneer Girl's Journey with The Donner Party*. Citron Bay Press, c1999. 187pp.

Presents a fictionalized account of twelve-year-old Lovina Graves's experiences as part of the Donner Party on their ill-fated journey west in 1846–1847.

# Frontier and Pioneer Life

**Spooner, Michael.** *Daniel's Walk*. H. Holt, c2001. 214pp.

With little more than a bedroll, a change of clothes, and a Bible, fourteen-year-old Daniel LeBlanc begins walking the Oregon Trail in search of his father who, according to a mysterious visitor, is in big trouble and needs his son's help.

**Van Leeuwen, Jean.** *Cabin on Trouble Creek*. Dial Books for Young Readers, c2004. 219pp.

In 1803 in Ohio, two young brothers are left to finish the log cabin and guard the land while their father goes back to Pennsylvania to fetch their mother and younger siblings.

**Wilder, Laura Ingalls.** <u>Little House.</u> HarperTrophy, 1994, c1971. 9v.

A collection of nine books that recount the adventures of Laura Ingalls Wilder and her family.

## Books for Older Teens

**Carbone, Elisa Lynn.** *Last Dance on Holladay Street*. Knopf (distributed by Random House), c2005. 196pp.

Thirteen-year-old Eva, left alone in the world after the death of her adoptive parents, goes to Denver, Colorado, in 1878 search of her birth mother in and is shocked to find the address is a house of ill repute, and her mother only too willing to put her to work.

**Cather, Willa.** *My Antonia*. Pocket Books, c2004. 314pp.

A successful lawyer remembers his boyhood in Nebraska and his friendship with an immigrant Bohemian girl. Includes background information, a chronology of the author's life, explanatory notes, critical analyses, and other reference material.

# Holocaust

## Books for Ages 12–15

**Bennett, Cherie.** *Anne Frank and Me*. Putnam, c2001. 291pp.
> After suffering a concussion while on a class trip to a Holocaust exhibit, Nicole finds herself living the life of a Jewish teenager in Paris during the Nazi occupation.

**Denenberg, Barry.** *One Eye Laughing, the Other Weeping: The Diary of Julie Weiss*. Scholastic, c2000. 250pp.
> During the Nazi persecution of the Jews in Austria, twelve-year-old Julie escapes to America to live with her relatives in New York City.

**Drucker, Malka.** *Jacob's Rescue: A Holocaust Story*. Bantam Doubleday Dell Books for Young Readers, 1994, c1993. 117pp.
> In answer to his daughter's questions, a man recalls the terrifying years of his childhood when a brave Polish couple, Alex and Mela Roslan, hid him and other Jewish children from the Nazis. Based on a true story.

**Levitin, Sonia.** *Room in the Heart*. Dutton, c2003. 290pp.
> After German forces occupy Denmark during World War II, fifteen-year-old Julie Weinstein and fifteen-year-old Niels Nelson and their friends and families try to cope with their daily lives, finding various ways to resist the Nazis and, ultimately, to survive.

**Lobel, Anita.** *No Pretty Pictures: A Child of War*. Greenwillow Books, c1998. 193pp. (NF)
> The author, known as an illustrator of children's books, describes her experiences as a Polish Jew during World War II and for years in Sweden afterward.

**Matas, Carol.** *After the War*. Aladdin Paperbacks, 1997, c1996. 133pp.
> After being released from Buchenwald at the end of World War II, fifteen-year-old Ruth risks her life to lead a group of children across Europe to Palestine.

**Matas, Carol.** *Daniel's Story*. Scholastic, c1993. 136pp.
> Daniel, whose family suffers as the Nazis rise to power in Germany, describes his imprisonment in a concentration camp and his eventual liberation.

**Mazer, Norma Fox.** *Good Night, Maman*. Harcourt Brace, c1999. 185pp.
> After spending years fleeing from the Nazis in war-torn Europe, twelve-year-old Karin Levi and her older brother Marc find a new home in a refugee camp in Oswego, New York.

**Orlev, Uri.** *The Lady with the Hat*. Houghton Mifflin, c1995. 183pp.
> In 1947 seventeen-year-old Yulek, the only member of his immediate family to survive the German concentration camps, joins a group of young Jews preparing to live on a kibbutz in Israel, unaware that his aunt, who is living in London, is looking for him.

**Orlev, Uri.** *Run, Boy, Run: A Novel*. Houghton Mifflin, c2003. 186pp.
> Based on the true story of a nine-year-old boy who escapes the Warsaw Ghetto and must survive throughout the war in the Nazi-occupied Polish countryside.

# Holocaust

**Pressler, Mirjam.** *Malka.* Philomel Books, c2003. 280pp.

In the winter of 1943, a Polish physician and her older daughter make a dangerous and arduous trek to Hungary, while seven-year-old Malka, whom they were forced to leave behind when she became ill, fends for herself in a ghetto.

**Spinelli, Jerry.** *Milkweed: A Novel.* Knopf (distributed by Random House), c2003. 208pp.

A street child, known to himself only as Stopthief, finds community when he is taken in by a band of orphans in a Warsaw ghetto, which helps him weather the horrors of the Nazi regime.

**Williams, Laura E.** *Behind the Bedroom Wall.* Milkweed Editions (distributed by Publishers Group West), c1996. 169pp.

Ten-year-old Korinna must decide whether to report her parents to her Hitler youth group when she discovers that they are hiding Jews in a secret space behind Korinna's bedroom wall.

## Books for Older Teens

**Bassani, Giorgio.** *The Garden of the Finzi-Continis.* Knopf (distributed by Random House), c2005. 246pp.

A young middle-class Jew in the Italian city of Ferrara has always been fascinated by the wealthy and aristocratic Jewish family, the Finzi-Continis, and as local Jews begin to gather at the Finzi-Continis estate to escape the racial laws of the Fascists, he falls in love with their wealthy daughter, Micol.

**Goldstein, Jan.** *All That Matters.* Hyperion, c2004. 198pp.

Twenty-three-year-old Jennifer Stempler, her mother dead, her father remarried, and deserted by her lover, makes a failed attempt to kill herself, but her obvious call for help is answered by her beloved grandmother, a Holocaust survivor, who takes Jennifer to her home in New York and tries to give her a reason for living.

**Keizer, Gregg.** *The Longest Night.* Putnam, c2004. 368pp.

Hit man Leonard Weiss is sent to Europe, where he is told to rescue a train of Dutch Jews being sent to one of Hitler's work camps.

**Kertesz, Imre.** *Fatelessness: A Novel.* Vintage International, c2004. 262pp.

Gyorgy Koves, a fourteen-year-old Hungarian Jew who knows neither Yiddish nor Hebrew, attempts to make sense of his experiences in the Auschwitz and Buchenwald concentration camps while being ostracized by the other prisoners.

**Newbery, Linda.** *Sisterland.* David Fickling Books, 2004, c2003. 369pp.

When Hilly's grandmother becomes ill with Alzheimer's disease, her family is turned upside down by revelations about her life during World War II.

**Russell, Mary Doria.** *A Thread of Grace: A Novel.* Random House, c2005. 430pp.

Historical fiction surrounding the family of fourteen-year-old Claudette Blum, Jewish refugees hoping to find safety in Italy in 1943 after the country broke with Germany, but who find that it is anything but peaceful.

# Life on the Home Front During World War II

## Books for Ages 12–15

**Avi.** *Don't You Know There's a War On?* HarperCollins, c2001. 200pp.

In wartime Brooklyn in 1943, eleven-year-old Howie Crispers mounts a campaign to save his favorite teacher from being fired.

**Campbell, Barbara.** *Taking Care of Yoki.* HarperTrophy, 1986, c1982. 167pp.

In St. Louis during the Second World War, Bob makes secret plans to save the life of an old horse that pulls the milk delivery wagon.

**Colman, Penny.** *Rosie the Riveter: Women Working on the Home Front in World War II.* Crown, c1995. 120pp. (NF)

Describes the many roles assumed by women in the United States after the country's entry into World War II.

**Enright, Elizabeth.** *The Four-Story Mistake.* H. Holt, 2002, c1942. 196pp.

During the war, the Melendy family moves to a house in the country, where a secret room, a cupola, a stable, and a brook provide Mona, Rush, Randy, and Oliver with adventures far different from the city life to which they are accustomed.

**Giff, Patricia Reilly.** *Lily's Crossing.* Delacorte Press, c1997. 180pp.

During the summer of 1944, spent at Rockaway Beach, Lily's friendship with a young Hungarian refugee causes her to see the war and her own world differently.

**Giff, Patricia Reilly.** *Willow Run.* Wendy Lamb, c2005. 149pp.

Eleven-year-old Meggie Dillon shares her feelings and experiences on the home front during World War II after her family moves from Rockaway, New York, to Willow Run, Michigan.

**Greene, Bette.** *Summer of My German Soldier.* Dial Books, 2003, c1973. 230pp.

When German prisoners of war are brought to her Arkansas town during World War II, twelve-year-old Patty, a Jewish girl, befriends one of them and must deal with the consequences of that friendship.

**Kochenderfer, Lee.** *The Victory Garden.* Delacorte Press, c2002. 167pp.

Hoping to contribute to the war effort during World War II, eleven-year-old Teresa organizes her friends to care for a sick neighbor's victory garden.

**Krull, Kathleen.** *V Is for Victory: America Remembers World War II.* Knopf (distributed by Random House), c1995. 115pp. (NF)

Chronicles World War II on both the battlefront and the home front, using photographs, letters, and posters to illustrate how the war affected life.

**Lee, Milly.** *Nim and the War Effort.* Farrar, Straus & Giroux, 2002, c1997. 20pp.

In her determination to prove that an American can win a contest for the war effort, Nim does something that leaves her Chinese grandfather both bewildered and proud.

# Life on the Home Front During World War II

**Lisle, Janet Taylor.** *The Art of Keeping Cool.* Atheneum Books for Young Readers, c2000. 207pp.
Robert and his cousin Elliot uncover long-hidden family secrets while staying in their grandparents' Rhode Island town in 1942, where they also become involved with a German artist who is suspected of being a spy.

**Magorian, Michelle.** *Good Night, Mr. Tom.* HarperCollins, 1986, c1981. 318pp.
A battered child learns to embrace life when he is adopted by an old man in the English countryside during World War II.

**Mochizuki, Ken.** *Baseball Saved Us.* Lee & Low, c1993. 32pp.
A Japanese American boy learns to play baseball when he and his family are forced to live in an internment camp during World War II, and his ability to play helps him after the war is over.

**Stein, R. Conrad.** *The Home Front During World War II in American History.* Enslow, c2003. 112pp. (NF)
Describes the experiences of those men and women who remained in the United States during World War II, discussing their emotional ups and downs, financial status, hard work, patriotism, fear, tension, shortages, and loneliness.

**Westall, Robert.** *Kingdom by the Sea.* Farrar, Straus & Giroux, c1991. 175pp.
During World War II twelve-year-old Harry and a stray dog travel through war-torn England in search of safety.

**Weston, Elise.** *The Coastwatcher.* Peachtree, c2005. 132pp.
While eleven-year-old Hugh, his family, and his cousin Tom are spending the summer of 1943 on the South Carolina shore to escape the polio epidemic, Hugh uncovers clues that point to a German plot to sabotage a nearby naval base.

**Whitman, Sylvia.** *V Is for Victory: The American Home Front During World War II.* Lerner, c1993. 80pp. (NF)
Using period photographs, describes life in the United States during World War II, discussing such activities as civil defense, the Japanese relocation, rationing, propaganda, and censorship.

## Books for Older Teens

**Knowles, John.** *A Separate Peace.* Scribner Classics, 1996, c1987. 204pp.
Gene Forrester looks back fifteen years to a year during World War II in which he and his best friend Phineas were roommates in a New Hampshire boarding school. Their friendship is marred by Finny's crippling fall, an event for which Gene is responsible and one that eventually leads to tragedy.

**Reid, Constance.** *Slacks and Calluses: Our Summer in a Bomber Factory.* Smithsonian Institution Press, c1999. 181pp. (NF)
Constance Bowman and Clara Marie Allen describe the summer of 1943, when they—middle-class art and English teachers at San Diego High School—went to work assembling B-24 bombers, known as Liberators, for the war.

# Middle Ages

## Books for Ages 12–15

**Avi.** *Crispin: The Cross of Lead*. Hyperion Books for Children, c2002. 262pp.
Falsely accused of theft and murder, an orphaned peasant boy in fourteenth-century England flees his village and meets a larger-than-life juggler who holds a dangerous secret.

**Branford, Henrietta.** *Fire, Bed & Bone*. Candlewick Press, c1998. 122pp.
In England in 1381, a hunting dog recounts what happens to his beloved master Rufus and his family when they are arrested on suspicion of being part of the peasants' rebellion, led by Wat Tyler and the preacher John Ball.

**Crossley-Holland, Kevin.** *The Seeing Stone*. Arthur A. Levine, c2001. 342pp. (and sequels)
Arthur, a thirteen-year-old boy in late twelfth-century England, tells how Merlin gave him a magical seeing stone, which shows him images of the legendary King Arthur, the events of whose life seem to have many parallels to his own.

**Cushman, Karen.** *Catherine, Called Birdy*. Clarion Books, c1994. 169pp.
The daughter of an English country knight keeps a journal in which she records the events of her life, particularly her longing for adventures beyond the usual role of women and her efforts to avoid being married off.

**Cushman, Karen.** *Matilda Bone*. Clarion, c2000. 167pp.
Fourteen-year-old Matilda, an apprentice bonesetter and practitioner of medicine in a village in medieval England, tries to reconcile the various aspects of her life, both spiritual and practical.

**Cushman, Karen.** *The Midwife's Apprentice*. Clarion Books, c1995. 122pp.
In medieval England, a nameless, homeless girl is taken in by a sharp-tempered midwife. In spite of obstacles and hardship, she eventually gains the three things she most wants: a full belly, a contented heart, and a place in this world.

**Goodman, Joan E.** *Peregrine*. Houghton Mifflin, c2000. 222pp.
In 1144, fifteen-year-old Lady Edith, having lost her husband and child and anxious to avoid marrying a man she detests, sets out from her home in Surrey to go on a pilgrimage to Jerusalem.

**Goodman, Joan E.** *The Winter Hare*. Houghton Mifflin, c1996. 255pp.
In 1140, with England divided between the supporters of King Stephen and those of the Empress Matilda, twelve-year-old Will Belet, small for his age but longing to be a knight, comes to his uncle's castle to be a page and soon finds himself involved in dangerous intrigues and adventures.

**Konigsburg, E. L.** *A Proud Taste for Scarlet and Miniver*. Atheneum, c1973. 201pp.
While waiting in heaven for divine judgment to be passed on her second husband, Eleanor of Aquitaine and three of the people who knew her well recall the events of her life.

**McCaffrey, Anne.** *Black Horses for the King*. Ballantine Books, 1998, c1996. 206pp.
Galwyn, son of a Roman Celt, escapes from his tyrannical uncle and joins Lord Artos, later known as King Arthur, using his talent with languages and way with horses to help secure and care for the Libyan horses that Artos hopes to use in battle against the Saxons.

# Middle Ages

**McKinley, Robin.** *The Outlaws of Sherwood*. Ace, c1989. 278pp.

The author retells the adventures of Robin Hood and his band of outlaws, who live in Sherwood Forest in twelfth-century England.

**Morris, Gerald.** *The Squire, His Knight, & His Lady*. Houghton Mifflin, c1999. 232pp.

After several years at King Arthur's court, Terence, as Sir Gawain's squire and friend, accompanies him on a perilous quest that tests all their skills; its successful completion could mean certain death for Gawain.

**Morris, Gerald.** *The Squire's Tale*. Houghton Mifflin, c1998. 212pp.

In medieval England, fourteen-year-old Terence finds his tranquil existence suddenly changed when he becomes the squire of the young Gawain of Orkney and accompanies him on a long quest, proving Gawain's worth as a knight and revealing an important secret about Terence's own true identity.

**Smith, Sherwood.** *Crown Duel*. Harcourt Brace, c1997. 214pp.

To fulfill their father's dying wish, teenage Countess Meliara and her brother Branaric organize a revolution against a greedy king.

**Temple, Frances.** *The Ramsay Scallop*. HarperTrophy, 1995, c1994. 310pp.

Thirteenth-century couple Elenor and Tom overcome their reluctance to marry after they are sent on a prenuptial journey to Spain and learn more about the world and each other.

**Thomson, Sarah L.** *The Dragon's Son*. Orchard Books, c2001. 181pp.

Based on the Mabinogion, a collection of medieval Welsh tales, as well as later legends; tells about family members and servants important in the life of King Arthur, featuring Nimue, Morgan le Fay, Luned, and Mordred.

**Williams, Laura E.** *The Executioner's Daughter*. H. Holt, c2000. 134pp.

Thirteen-year-old Lily, daughter of the town's executioner in fifteenth-century Europe, decides whether to fight against her destiny or to rise above her fate.

**Yolen, Jane.** *Girl in a Cage*. Philomel Books, c2002. 234pp.

As English armies invade Scotland in 1306, eleven-year-old Princess Marjorie, daughter of the newly crowned Scottish king, Robert the Bruce, is captured by England's King Edward (Longshanks) and held in a cage on public display.

**Yolen, Jane.** *Sword of the Rightful King: A Novel of King Arthur*. Harcourt, c2003. 349pp.

Merlinnus the magician devises a way for King Arthur to prove himself the rightful king of England—pulling a sword from a stone—but trouble arises when someone else removes the sword first.

## Books for Older Teens

**Alder, Elizabeth.** *The King's Shadow*. Bantam Doubleday Dell Books for Young Readers, 1997, c1995. 259pp.

After he is orphaned and has his tongue cut out in a clash with the bullying sons of a Welsh noble, Evyn is sold as a slave and serves many masters, from the gracious Lady Swan Neck to the valiant Harold Godwinson, England's last Saxon king.

From Nancy J. Keane, *The Big Book of Teen Reading Lists: 100 Great, Ready-to-Use Book Lists for Educators, Librarians, Parents, and Children*. Westport, CT: Libraries Unlimited, 2006. Copyright © 2006 by Libraries Unlimited.

# Middle Ages

**Bradley, Marion Zimmer.** *The Mists of Avalon*. Ballantine Books, 2000, c1982. 876pp.

A re-creation of the Arthurian legend following the clash between Christianity and paganism that led to the demise of Camelot.

**Cadnum, Michael.** *The Book of the Lion*. Viking Press, c2000. 204pp.

In twelfth-century England, after his master, a maker of coins for the king, is brutally punished for alleged cheating, seventeen-year-old Edmund finds himself traveling to the Holy Land as squire to a knight crusader on his way to join the forces of Richard Lionheart.

**Jordan, Sherryl.** *The Raging Quiet*. Aladdin Paperbacks, c2000. 266pp.

Suspicious of sixteen-year-old Marnie, a newcomer to their village, the residents accuse her of witchcraft when she discovers that the village madman is not crazy but deaf and she begins to communicate with him through hand gestures.

# South Asia and the South Asian Diaspora

Compiled by Pooja Makhijani (www.poojamakhijani.com), is an essayist, journalist, and writer
of children's literature, editor of *Under Her Skin: How Girls Experience Race in America,*
and author of the picture book *Mama's Saris.*

## Books for Ages 12–15

**Alexander, Lloyd.** *The Iron Ring.* Puffin Books, c1999. 283pp.
Driven by his sense of "dharma," or honor, young King Tamar sets off on a perilous journey, with a significance greater than he can imagine, during which he meets talking animals, villainous and noble kings, demons, and the love of his life.

**Banerjee, Anjali.** *Maya Running.* Wendy Lamb Books, c2005. 209pp.
Maya, a Canadian of East Indian descent, struggles with her ethnic identity, infatuation with a classmate, and the presence of her beautiful Bengali cousin, Pinky, who comes for a visit bearing a powerful statue of the god Ganesh, the Hindu elephant boy.

**Banerjee, Anjali.** *Rani and the Fashion Divas.* (Star Sisterz Sisters no. 4). Mirror Stone, c2005. 137pp.
The fourth title in a new series of adventures that follows a group of friends who receive mysterious messages as they grow in confidence.

**Bosse, Malcolm.** *Tusk and Stone.* Front Street, c2004. 256pp.
After dacoits (thieves) attack his caravan and he loses his identity as a Brahmin, Arjun resigns himself to his new life, becomes an elephant driver, and searches for his kidnapped sister.

**Clarke, Judith.** *Kalpana's Dream.* Front Street, 2005, c2004. 164pp.
Neema's struggle to complete an essay on the topic "Who Am I" for her freshman English class is complicated by the arrival of Kampala, her Indian great-grandmother, who has come to Australia chasing her dream of flying. Although they do not speak the same language, the two find common ground in skateboarder Gull Oliver.

**Desai Hidier, Tanuja.** *Born Confused.* Scholastic Press, c2002. 413pp.
As Dimple Lala turns seventeen, she realizes that life is about to become more complex as her best friend starts pulling away and her parents try to find a suitable boyfriend for Dimple, despite the fact that she is not interested.

**Dhami, Narinder.** *Bindi Babes.* Delacorte Press, 2004, c2003. 184pp.
Three Indian British sisters team up to marry off their traditional, nosy aunt and get her out of the house.

**Dhami, Narinder.** *Bollywood Babes.* Delacorte Press, 2005, c2004. 213pp.
The Indian British Dhillon sisters open their home to a down-on-her-luck former movie star from India and employ her talents to raise money for their school.

**Divakaruni, Chitra Banerjee.** *The Conch Bearer.* Aladdin Paperbacks, 2005, c2003. 265pp.
Twelve-year-old Anand is entrusted with a conch shell that possesses mystical powers and sets out on a journey to return the shell to its rightful home, many hundreds of miles away.

# South Asia and the South Asian Diaspora

**Divakaruni, Chitra Banerjee.** *The Mirror of Fire and Dreaming: A Novel.* Roaring Brook, c2005. 329pp.

As twelve-year-old Anand continues his studies to become a full-fledged member of The Brotherhood of the Conch, he journeys back to Moghul times, where he encounters powerful sorcerers, spoiled princes, noble warriors, and evil jinns.

**Divakaruni, Chitra Banerjee.** *Neela: Victory Song.* Pleasant Co., c2002. 196pp.

In 1939 twelve-year-old Neela meets a young freedom fighter at her sister's wedding and soon after must rely on his help when her father fails to return home from a march in Calcutta against British occupation.

**Fleming, Candace.** *Lowji Discovers America.* Atheneum Books for Young Readers, c2005. 152pp.

A nine-year-old East Indian boy tries to adjust to his new life in suburban America.

**Gilmore, Rachna.** *A Group of One.* H. Holt, c2001. 184pp.

Learning from her grandmother that her family was active in the Quit India movement of 1942—a rebellion against nearly two centuries of British occupation—gives fifteen-year-old Tara new pride in her heritage, but she still objects when her teacher implies that she is not a "regular Canadian."

**Godden, Rumer.** *Premlata and the Festival of Lights.* Greenwillow Books, c1997. 58pp.

In Bengal, India, Premlata's family is too poor to celebrate the Festival of Lights, until fate and an elephant step in.

**Godden, Rumer.** *The Valiant Chatti-Maker.* Viking Press, c1983. 61pp.

When he inadvertently captures the tiger that has been terrorizing the neighborhood, a poor potter not only gains fame and fortune but the unwanted honor of leading the Raja's army against an invading enemy.

**Khan, Rukhsana.** *Dahling, If You LUV Me, Would You Please, Please Smile.* Stoddart Kids, c1999. 206pp.

Zainab, a young North American Muslim, has many difficulties making friends at school. When one of her teachers offers to let her direct the upcoming school play, Zainab's desire to fit in leads her to cast the school's most popular boy, Kevin, despite another student's incredible audition.

**Krishnaswami, Uma.** *Naming Maya.* Farrar, Straus & Giroux, c2004. 178pp.

When Maya accompanies her mother to India to sell her grandfather's house, she uncovers family history relating to her parents' divorce and learns more about herself and her relationship with her mother.

**Lasky, Kathryn.** *Jahanara: Princess of Princesses.* Scholastic, c2002. 186pp.

Beginning in 1627, Princess Jahanara, first daughter of Shah Jahan of India's Mogul Dynasty, writes in her diary about political intrigues, weddings, battles, and other experiences of her life. Includes historical notes on Jahanara's later life and on the Mogul Empire.

**Mukerji, Dhan Gopal.** *Gay-Neck: The Story of a Pigeon.* Dutton, 1968, c1954. 191pp.

The story of the training of a carrier pigeon and its service during the First World War, revealing the bird's courageous and spirited adventures over the housetops of an Indian village, in the Himalayan Mountains, and on the French battlefield.

# South Asia and the South Asian Diaspora

**Nagda, Ann Whitehead.** *Meow Means Mischief.* Holiday House, c2003. 92pp.
A stray kitten turns out to be the perfect way to help Rana make friends in her new school and to feel more comfortable with her grandparents, who are visiting from India while her parents are away.

**Perkins, Mitali.** *Monsoon Summer.* Delacorte Press, c2004. 257pp.
Secretly in love with her best friend and business partner, Steve, fifteen-year-old Jazz must spend the summer away from him when her family goes to India during that country's rainy season to help set up a clinic.

**Perkins, Mitali.** *The Not-So-Star-Spangled Life of Sunita Sen: A Novel.* Little, Brown, c2005. 176pp.
The arrival of her grandparents from India causes thirteen-year-old Sunita to resent her Indian heritage and to be embarrassed by the differences she feels between herself and her friends in California.

**Sheth, Kashmira.** *Blue Jasmine.* Hyperion Books for Children, c2004. 186pp.
When twelve-year-old Seema moves to Iowa City with her parents and younger sister, she leaves friends and family behind in her native India but gradually begins to feel at home in her new country.

**Sreenivasan, Jyotsna.** *Aruna's Journeys.* Smooth Stone Press, c1997. 133pp.
Aruna, an eleven-year-old Indian American girl, reluctantly visits her relatives in India and in the process discovers more about who she is.

**Staples, Suzanne Fisher.** *Shiva's Fire.* Farrar, Straus & Giroux, c2000. 275pp.
In India, a talented dancer sacrifices friends and family for her art.

**Whelan, Gloria.** *Homeless Bird.* HarperCollins, c2000. 216pp.
Thirteen-year-old Koly enters into an ill-fated, arranged marriage and must either suffer a destiny dictated by India's customs or find the courage to oppose tradition.

## Books for Older Teens

**Bosse, Malcolm.** *Ordinary Magic.* Farrar, Straus & Giroux, c1993. 185pp.
Uprooted from his home in India by a tragedy, Ganesh begins a new life in the American Midwest, where his experiences with Hinduism, Yoga, and mantras are considered alien.

**Rana, Indi.** *Roller Birds of Rampur.* H. Holt, c1993. 298pp.
An Indian teenager raised in England returns to India to find her identity.

**Selvadurai, Shyam.** *Swimming in the Monsoon Sea.* Tundra Books, Tundra Books of Northern New York, c2005. 274pp.
In Sri Lanka in 1980, fourteen-year-old Amrith's uneventful summer, filled with typing lessons and hopes of a part in his school's production of *Othello,* is turned upside down when he falls in love with a boy.

**Smith, Rukshana.** *Sumitra's Story.* Coward, McCann, c1983. 168pp.
When her East Indian family is displaced from its home in Uganda by the repressive Idi Amin regime, and resettles in London, the eldest daughter, Sumitra, is torn between two cultures.

# South Asia and the South Asian Diaspora

**Staples, Suzanne Fisher.** *Haveli.* Knopf (distributed by Random House), 1997, c1993. 320pp.
Having reverted to the ways of her people in Pakistan and married the rich older man to whom she was pledged against her will, Shabanu is now the victim of his family's blood feud and the malice of his other wives.

**Staples, Suzanne Fisher.** *Shabanu: Daughter of the Wind.* Dell Laurel-Leaf, 2003, c1989. 240pp.
Eleven-year old Shabanu, the daughter of a nomad in the Cholistan Desert of present-day Pakistan, is pledged in marriage to an older man, whose money will bring prestige to the family, and must either accept the decision, as is the custom, or risk the consequences of defying her father's wishes.

# Vietnamese Conflict

## Books for Ages 12–15

**Antle, Nancy.** *Lost in the War.* Puffin Books, 2000, c1998. 137pp.

Twelve-year-old Lisa Grey struggles to cope with a mother whose traumatic experiences as a nurse in Vietnam during the war are still haunting her.

**Couloumbis, Audrey.** *Summer's End.* Putnam's, c2005. 184pp.

Three teenage cousins worry about their uncle, who is missing in Vietnam, their brothers—one who was drafted and two who are dodging the draft—and the effects of their absence on the four generations gathered at the family farm in the summer of 1965.

**Crist-Evans, Craig.** *Amaryllis.* Candlewick Press, c2003. 184pp.

Jimmy and his older brother Frank share a love of surfing and their problems with a drunken father, until Frank turns eighteen and goes to Vietnam.

**Hobbs, Valerie.** *Sonny's War.* Farrar, Straus & Giroux, c2002. 215pp.

In the late 1960s, fourteen-year-old Cori's life is greatly changed by the sudden death of her father and her brother's tour of duty in Vietnam.

**Paulsen, Gary.** *The Car.* Harcourt Brace, c1994. 180pp.

A teenager left on his own travels west in a kit car he built himself, and along the way picks up two Vietnam veterans, who take him on an eye-opening journey.

**Sherlock, Patti.** *Letters from Wolfie.* Viking Press, c2004. 228pp.

Certain that he is doing the right thing by donating his dog, Wolfie, to the Army's scout program in Vietnam, thirteen-year-old Mark begins to have second thoughts when the Army refuses to say when and if Wolfie will ever return.

**Testa, Maria.** *Almost Forever.* Candlewick Press, c2003. 69pp.

A young girl describes what she, her brother, and their mother do during the year that her doctor father is serving in the Army in Vietnam.

**White, Ellen Emerson.** *The Journal of Patrick Seamus Flaherty, United States Marine Corps.* Scholastic, c2002. 188pp.

An eighteen-year-old Marine records in his journal his experiences in Vietnam during the siege of Khe Sanh, 1967–1968. Includes a history of Vietnam, war timeline, glossary, and related military information.

## Books for Older Teens

**Myers, Walter Dean** *Fallen Angels.* Scholastic, c1988. 309pp.

Seventeen-year-old Richie Perry, just out of his Harlem high school, enlists in the Army in the summer of 1967 and spends a devastating year on active duty in Vietnam.

**Qualey, Marsha.** *Come in from the Cold.* Houghton Mifflin, c1994. 219pp.

In 1969 the Vietnam War protest movement brings together two Minnesota teenagers.

**Qualey, Marsha.** *Too Big a Storm.* Dial Books, c2004. 246pp.

When serious worrier Brady Callahan meets vivacious Sally Cooper, daughter of a wealthy Minnesota family, they develop a close friendship that helps them both grow and survive during the turbulent Vietnam War era.

# Women's Labor Movement

## Books for Ages 12–15

**Auch, Mary Jane.** *Ashes of Roses*. H. Holt, c2002. 250pp.

Sixteen-year-old Rose Nolan arrives on Ellis Island in 1911 hoping to start a new life, but after most of her family is sent back to Ireland, she must find her own way in a new country and fend for herself and her younger sister.

**Bartoletti, Susan Campbell.** *A Coal Miner's Bride: The Diary of Anetka Kaminska*. Scholastic, c2000. 219pp.

A diary account of thirteen-year-old Anetka's life in Poland in 1896, immigration to America, marriage to a coal miner, widowhood, and happiness in finally finding her true love.

**Bartoletti, Susan Campbell.** *Growing Up in Coal Country*. Houghton Mifflin, c1996. 127pp. (NF)

Describes what life was like, especially for children, in coal mines and mining towns in the nineteenth and early twentieth centuries.

**Bartoletti, Susan Campbell.** *Kids on Strike!* Houghton Mifflin, c1999. 208pp. (NF)

Describes the conditions and treatment that drove workers, including many children, to various strikes, from the mill workers' strikes in 1828 and 1836 and the coal strikes at the turn of the century to the work of Mother Jones on behalf of child workers.

**Colman, Penny.** *Rosie the Riveter: Women Working on the Home Front in World War II*. Crown, c1995. 120pp. (NF)

Describes the many roles assumed by women in the United States after the country's entry into World War II.

**Freedman, Russell.** *Kids at Work: Lewis Hine and the Crusade Against Child Labor*. Clarion Books, c1994. 104pp. (NF)

Text and accompanying photographs show the use of children as industrial workers, interwoven with the story of Lewis W. Hine, who took these photographs and whose life work made significant differences in the lives of others.

**Josephson, Judith Pinkerton.** *Mother Jones: Fierce Fighter for Workers' Rights*. Lerner Publications, c1997. 144pp. (NF)

A biography of Mary Harris Jones, the union organizer who worked tirelessly for the rights of workers.

**McCully, Emily Arnold.** *The Bobbin Girl*. Dial Books for Young Readers, c1996. 34pp.

A ten-year-old bobbin girl working in a textile mill in Lowell, Massachusetts, in the 1830s, must make a difficult decision—whether or not she will participate in the first workers' strike in Lowell.

**Paterson, Katherine.** *Lyddie*. Lodestar Books, c1991. 182pp.

Impoverished Vermont farm girl Lyddie Worthen is determined to gain her independence by becoming a factory worker in Lowell, Massachusetts, in the 1840s.

# Women's Labor Movement

**Robinet, Harriette.** *Missing from Haymarket Square*. Atheneum Books for Young Readers, c2001. 143pp.

> Three children in Chicago in 1886 experience the Haymarket Riot in response to exploitative working conditions.

**Ryan, Pam Muñoz.** *Esperanza Rising*. Scholastic, c2000. 262pp.

> Esperanza and her mother are forced to leave their life of wealth and privilege in Mexico to go work in the labor camps of Southern California, where they must adapt to the harsh circumstances facing Mexican farm workers on the eve of the Great Depression.

**Stanley, Jerry.** *Children of the Dust Bowl: The True Story of the School at Weedpatch Camp*. Crown, c1992. 85pp. (NF)

> Describes the plight of the migrant workers who traveled from the dust bowl areas to California during the Great Depression and were forced to live in a federal labor camp; discusses the school that was built for their children.

## Books for Older Teens

**Watson, Bruce.** *Bread and Roses: Mills, Migrants, and the Struggle for the American Dream*. Viking Press, c2005. 337pp. (NF)

> Presents a comprehensive history of the 1912 textile strike in Lawrence, Massachusetts, and describes the struggle of the immigrant and women workers, which included 23,000 strikers from fifty-one different nations.

# World War I

## Books for Ages 12–15

**Bagdasarian, Adam.** *Forgotten Fire*. DK Ink, c2000. 273pp.
The story of how Vahan Kenderian survived the Turkish massacre of the Armenians in 1915.

**Breslin, Theresa.** *Remembrance*. Delacorte Press, c2002. 296pp.
The destinies of two Scottish families, one shopkeepers and one wealthy and powerful, become entwined through their involvement in World War I, social causes, and love.

**Ingold, Jeanette.** *Pictures, 1918*. Harcourt Brace, c1998. 152pp.
Coming of age in a rural Texas community in 1918, fifteen-year-old Asia assists in the local war effort, contemplates romance with a local boy, and expands her horizons through her pursuit of photography.

**Lawrence, Iain.** *Lord of the Nutcracker Men*. Delacorte Press, c2001. 212pp.
An English boy during World War I comes to believe that the battles he enacts with his toy soldiers control the war his father is fighting on the front.

**Levine, Beth Seidel.** *When Christmas Comes Again: The World War I Diary of Simone Spencer.* Scholastic, c2002. 172pp.
Teenage Simone's diaries for 1917 and 1918 reveal her experiences as a carefree member of New York society, then as a "Hello girl," a volunteer switchboard operator for the Army Signal Corps in France.

**Meyer, Carolyn.** *Anastasia, the Last Grand Duchess.* Scholastic, c2000. 220pp.
A novel in diary form in which the youngest daughter of Czar Nicholas II describes the privileged life her family led up until the time of World War I and the tragic events that befell them.

**Morpurgo, Michael.** *Private Peaceful*. Scholastic Press, 2004, c2003. 202pp.
When Thomas Peaceful's older brother is forced to join the British Army, Thomas decides to sign up as well, although he is only fourteen years old, to prove himself to his country, his family, his childhood love, Molly, and himself.

**Rostkowski, Margaret I.** *After the Dancing Days*. HarperTrophy, 1988, c1986. 217pp.
A forbidden friendship with a badly disfigured soldier in the aftermath of World War I forces thirteen-year-old Annie to redefine the word "hero" and to question conventional ideas of patriotism.

## Books for Older Teens

**Follett, Ken.** *The Man from St. Petersburg*. Signet, 1983, c1982. 342pp.
A Russian emissary sent to England to negotiate a Soviet–British alliance is stalked by a deadly anarchist.

**Harris, Ruth Elwin.** *Julia's Story*. Candlewick Press, c2002. 301pp.
Julia Purcell, having grown up in the shadow of her more talented sister, finds a kindred spirit in her guardian's son, and self-worth as a nurse in France during World War

# World War I

**Helprin, Mark.** *A Soldier of the Great War*. Harcourt Brace, c1991. 792pp.
Alessandro Giuliani tells his young companion the story of his life: how he became a solider, a hero, a prisoner, and a deserter during World War I.

**Remarque, Erich Maria.** *All Quiet on the Western Front*. Little Brown, c1958. 291pp.
Depicts the experiences of a group of young German soldiers fighting and suffering during the last days of World War I.

**Spillebeen, Geert.** *Kipling's Choice*. Houghton Mifflin, c2005. 147pp.
In 1915, mortally wounded in Loos, France, eighteen-year-old John Kipling, son of writer Rudyard Kipling, remembers his boyhood and the events leading to what is to be his first and last World War I battle.

**Turtledove, Harry.** *The Great War: Breakthroughs*. Random House, 2001, c2000. 584pp.
Offers an alternative history of World War II that theorizes how the war would have ended if certain events had been different.

**Wilson, John.** *And in the Morning*. Kids Can Press, c2003. 198pp.
Canadian Jim Hay joins the army in World War I and is sent to France, where he meets a tragic end.

# World War II

## Books for Ages 12–15

**Bradley, Kimberly Brubaker.** *For Freedom: The Story of a French Spy.* Delacorte Press, c2003. 181pp.

> A novel based on the experiences of Suzanne David Hall, who, as a teenager in Nazi-occupied France, worked as a spy for the French Resistance while training to be an opera singer.

**Bruchac, Joseph.** *Code Talker: A Novel About the Navajo Marines of World War Two.* Dial Books, c2005. 231pp.

> After being taught in a boarding school run by whites that Navajo is a useless language, Ned Begay and other Navajo men are recruited by the Marines to become Code Talkers, sending messages during World War II in their native tongue.

**Hesse, Karen.** *Aleutian Sparrow.* Margaret K. McElderry Books, c2003. 156pp.

> An Aleutian Islander recounts her suffering during World War II in American internment camps designed to "protect" the population from the invading Japanese.

**Lawrence, Iain.** *B for Buster.* Delacorte Press, c2004. 321pp.

> Sixteen-year-old Kak, desperate to escape his abusive parents, lies about his age in the spring of 1943 to enlist in the Canadian Air Force and soon finds himself based in England as part of a crew flying bombing raids over Germany.

**Maguire, Gregory.** *The Good Liar.* Clarion Books, c1999. 129pp.

> Now an old man living in the United States, Marcel recalls his childhood in German-occupied France, especially the summer that he and his older brother Rene befriended a young German soldier.

**Mah, Adeline Yen.** *Chinese Cinderella and the Secret Dragon Society.* HarperCollins, c2005. 242pp.

> During the Japanese occupation of parts of China, twelve-year-old Ye Xian is thrown out of her father's and stepmother's home, joins a martial arts group, and tries to help her aunt and the Americans in their struggle against the Japanese invaders.

**Matas, Carol.** *After the War.* Aladdin Paperbacks, 1997, c1996. 133pp.

> After being released from Buchenwald at the end of World War II, fifteen-year-old Ruth risks her life to lead a group of children across Europe to Palestine.

**Mazer, Harry.** *A Boy at War: A Novel of Pearl Harbor.* Simon & Schuster Books for Young Readers, c2001. 104pp.

> While fishing with his friends off Honolulu on December 7. 1941, teenage Adam is caught in the midst of the Japanese attack; throughout the chaos of the subsequent days he tries to find his father, a naval officer who was serving on the U.S.S. *Arizona* when the bombs fell.

**Spinelli, Jerry.** *Milkweed: A Novel.* Knopf (distributed by Random House), c2003. 208pp.

> A street child, known to himself only as Stopthief, finds community when he is taken in by a band of orphans in a Warsaw ghetto, which helps him weather the horrors of the Nazi regime.

**Vande Velde, Vivian.** *A Coming Evil.* Houghton Mifflin, c1998. 213pp. -

> In 1940, during the German occupation of France, thirteen-year-old Lisette meets a ghost while living with her aunt, who harbors Jewish and Gypsy children in the French countryside.

From Nancy J. Keane, *The Big Book of Teen Reading Lists: 100 Great, Ready-to-Use Book Lists for Educators, Librarians, Parents, and Children.* Westport, CT: Libraries Unlimited, 2006. Copyright © 2006 by Libraries Unlimited.

# World War II

**Wilson, John.** *Flames of the Tiger*. Kids Can Press, c2003. 176pp.

Dieter grows to be a young man in Germany believing in the pronouncements and policies of Hitler and the Nazis, but as World War II intensifies and he is called upon to fight for his country, Dieter begins to question everything he once believed.

**Winter, Kathryn.** *Katarina: A Novel*. Scholastic Signature, 1999, c1998. 257pp.

During World War II in Slovakia, a young Jewish girl in hiding becomes a devout Catholic and is sustained by her belief that she will return home to her family as soon as the war ends.

**Wulffson, Don L.** *Soldier X*. Viking Press, c2001. 226pp.

In 1943, sixteen-year-old Erik experiences the horrors of war when he is drafted into the German army and sent to fight on the Russian front.

## Books for Older Teens

**Chambers, Aidan.** *Postcards from No Man's Land*. Dutton Books, c2002. 312pp.

Alternates between two stories: In the present day, seventeen-year-old Jacob visits a daunting Amsterdam at the request of his English grandmother ,and in the past, nineteen-year-old Geertrui relates her experience of British soldiers' attempts to liberate Holland from German occupation.

**Disher, Garry.** *The Divine Wind*. Scholastic, 2004, c1998. 153pp.

On the eve of World War II, Hart, an Australian boy, and Mitsy, a Japanese Australian girl, fall in love but are driven apart.

**Newbery, Linda.** *Sisterland*. David Fickling Books, 2004, c2003. 369pp.

When Hilly's grandmother becomes ill with Alzheimer's disease, her family is turned upside down by revelations about her life during World War II.

**Salisbury, Graham.** *Eyes of the Emperor*. Wendy Lamb Books, c2005. 229pp.

Following orders from the U.S. Army, several young Japanese American men train K-9 units to hunt Asians during World War II.

# Part 5

## Subjects

# Almost Famous

Researched and compiled by Melissa Rabey, Teen Librarian, Pt. Pleasant Boro Library, Pt. Pleasant, New Jersey.

## Books for Ages 12–15

**Brian, Kate.** *The Princess & the Pauper.* Simon & Schuster Books for Young Readers, c2003. 266pp.
Julia has never been like the other students at her elite high school: instead of worrying about her looks, she is worrying about finding a way to keep a roof over her family's head, and when a princess who happens to look exactly like Julia offers her $10,000 to switch places for one day, Julia thinks she has finally found a way to help her family.

**Cabot, Meg.** *All-American Girl.* HarperCollins, c2002. 247pp.
Sophomore Samantha Madison stops a presidential assassination attempt, is appointed teen ambassador to the United Nations, and catches the eye of the very cute First Son.

**Cabot, Meg.** *The Princess Diaries.* HarperCollins, c2000. 238pp.
Fourteen-year-old Mia, who is trying to lead a normal life as a teenage girl in New York City, is shocked to learn that her father is the Prince of Genovia, a small European principality, and that she is a princess and the heir to the throne.

**Sheldon, Dyan.** *Confessions of a Teenage Drama Queen.* Candlewick Press, 2004, c1990. 335pp.
In her first year at a suburban New Jersey high school, Mary Elizabeth Cep, who now calls herself "Lola," sets her sights on the lead in the annual drama production, and finds herself in conflict with the most popular girl in school.

**Tashjian, Janet.** *The Gospel According to Larry.* H. Holt, c2001. 227pp.
Seventeen-year-old Josh, a loner-philosopher who wants to make a difference in the world, tries to maintain his secret identity as the author of a Web site that is receiving national attention.

**Wilkens, Rose.** *So Super Starry.* Dial Books, c2004. 230pp.
Fifteen-year-old Octavia Clairbrook-Cleeve, the daughter of a famous television actress and a respected film and theater director, feels out of place amid the glamour, wealth, and high society that surround her, and when she begins dating a rich and handsome older boy, her doubts about this lifestyle become impossible to ignore.

## Books for Older Teens

**Cohn, Rachel.** *Pop Princess.* Simon & Schuster Books for Young Readers, c2004. 311pp.
Yearning to escape the small Massachusetts town where her family retreated after her sister's death, Wonder Blake gets her chance when her sister's manager offers Wonder a record contract on her sixteenth birthday.

**Dean, Zoey.** *The A-list.* Little, Brown, c2003. 243pp.
Seventeen-year-old blueblood Anna Percy leaves Manhattan to spend the second half of her senior year with her father in Los Angeles, where she quickly becomes involved in the lives of the rich and famous at Beverly Hills High School.

# Almost Famous

**Jemas, Bill.** *Ultimate Spider-Man. Vol. 1.* Marvel Comics, c2002. 184pp.
Contains issues 1–13 of the comic *Ultimate Spider-Man* and number 15 of *Amazing Fantasy,* which chronicle the early adventures of Peter Parker, a timid student transformed into a superhero by a radioactive spider; also includes correspondence between editor Bill Jemas and writer Brian Michael Bendis, as well as character sketches.

**Manning, Sarra.** *Guitar Girl.* Dutton Children's Books, 2004, c2003. 217pp.
Seventeen-year-old Molly Montgomery learns the cost of fame when her band, The Hormones, a group started with her friends just for fun, suddenly becomes all the rage.

**Nolan, Han.** *Born Blue.* Harcourt, c2001. 277pp.
Janie was four years old when she nearly drowned due to her mother's neglect. Throughout an unhappy foster home experience and years of feeling that she is unwanted, she keeps alive her dream of someday being a famous singer.

**Obana, Miho.** *Kodocha. Vol. 1. Sana's Stage.* Tokyopop, c2002. 193pp.
Child star Sana Kurata faces off with the bane of her existence, Akito Hayama, when his bullying and blackmailing—of both students and teachers—goes too far.

**Shaw, Tucker.** *Confessions of a Backup Dancer.* Simon Pulse, c2004. 265pp.
Kelly Kimbal lands a job as a backup dancer for pop diva, Darcy Barnes, but is soon fired by Darcy's overbearing mother. Then Darcy develops the courage to tell her mother off and bring Kelly back into the show.

**Triana, Gaby.** *Backstage Pass.* HarperCollins, c2004. 218pp.
After moving to Miami, Florida, sixteen-year-old Desert McGraw, whose life as the daughter of a rock star has been anything but normal, determines to make a permanent home for herself and her family—even if it means breaking up the band.

**Von Ziegesar, Cecily.** *Gossip Girl.* Warner Books, 2003, c2002. 265pp.
Gossip Girl, an unknown narrator, shares the inside scoop on her friends and foes in a privileged private school in New York City, focusing on the return of the beautiful Serena van der Woodson, who is rumored to have been kicked out of boarding school.

# Big Brother Is Watching

## Books for Ages 12–15

**Farmer, Nancy** *The House of the Scorpion.* Atheneum Books for Young Readers, c2002. 380pp.
In a future where humans despise clones, Matt enjoys special status as the young clone of El Patron, the 142-year-old leader of a corrupt drug empire nestled between Mexico and the United States.

**Lowry, Lois.** *Gathering Blue.* Houghton Mifflin, c2000. 215pp.
Lame and suddenly orphaned, Kira is mysteriously removed from her squalid village to live in the palatial Council Edifice, where she is expected to use her gifts as a weaver to do the bidding of the all-powerful Guardians.

**Lowry, Lois.** *The Giver.* Dell Laurel-Leaf, 2002, c1993. 179pp.
Given his lifetime assignment at the Ceremony of Twelve, Jonas becomes the receiver of memories shared by only one other. He then learns the terrible truth about the Community.

**Lowry, Lois.** *Messenger.* Houghton Mifflin, c2004. 169pp.
In this novel that unites characters from *The Giver* and *Gathering Blue,* Matty, a young member of a utopian community that values honesty, conceals an emerging healing power that he cannot explain or understand.

**Stahler, David.** *Truesight.* Eos, c2004. 168pp.
In a distant frontier world, thirteen-year-old Jacob is uncertain of his future in a community that considers blindness a virtue and "Seers" aberrations.

**Weyn, Suzanne.** *The Bar Code Tattoo.* Scholastic, c2004. 252pp.
Kayla is ostracized at school because she refused to get the required tattooed bar code, and now she and her family must run to avoid the threats against them.

## Books for Older Teens

**Anderson, M. T.** *Feed*. Candlewick Press, c2002. 237pp.
In a future where most people have computer implants in their heads to control their environment, a boy meets an unusual girl who is in serious trouble.

**Atwood, Margaret Eleanor.** *The Handmaid's Tale.* Anchor Books, 1998, c1986. 311pp.
In the near future, America has become a puritanical theocracy, and Offred tells her story of living as a Handmaid under the new social order.

**Bradbury, Ray.** *Fahrenheit 451.* Simon & Schuster, 2003, c1953. 190pp.
After learning that books are a vital part of a culture he never knew, a book-burning official in a future fascist state clandestinely pursues reading, until he is betrayed. Includes an introduction written by the author in 2003.

**Orwell, George.** *1984: A Novel.* Signet Classic, 1977, c1949. 268pp.
Depicts life in a totalitarian regime of the future.

# Community Service

## Books for Ages 12–15

**Fleischman, Paul.** *Seedfolks.* HarperCollins, c1997. 69pp.

One by one, a number of people of varying ages and backgrounds transform a trash-filled inner-city lot into a productive and beautiful garden; in doing so, the gardeners are themselves transformed.

**Gauthier, Gail.** *Saving the Planet & Stuff.* Putnam, c2003. 232pp.

After losing his summer job with his uncle, sixteen-year-old Michael agrees to go to work for an environmentalist magazine in Vermont run by friends of his grandparents.

**Mills, Claudia.** *Makeovers by Marcia.* Farrar, Straus & Giroux, c2005. 149pp.

At the beginning of eighth grade, all Marcia can think about is what nail polish to use, how to lose weight, and whether Alex will ask her to the dance, but after giving makeovers in a nursing home for a school project, she begins to appreciate the value of inner beauty.

**Sorenson, Margo.** *Funny Man Gets Rolling.* Perfection Learning, c2004. 103pp.

Derrick must put his joking manner aside to complete a community volunteer requirement that could prevent him from graduating.

**Wittlinger, Ellen.** *Gracie's Girl.* Simon & Schuster Books for Young Readers, c2000. 186pp.

As she starts middle school, Bess volunteers to work on the school musical in hopes of fitting in, but when she and a friend get to know an elderly homeless woman, Bess changes her mind about what is really important.

## Books for Older Teens

**McCafferty, Megan.** *Sloppy Firsts: A Novel.* Three Rivers Press, c2001. 298pp.

Sixteen-year-old Jessica Darling is devastated when her best friend moves away and leaves Jessica to face the trials of high school on her own.

# Community Service as Punishment

## Books for Ages 12–15

**Christopher, Matt. *Baseball Turnaround*.** Little, Brown, c1997. 120pp.
Sandy is drawn unknowingly into a shoplifting incident; his community service sentence involves his beloved baseball, and he meets people who help him finally put the past behind him.

**Cooney, Caroline B. *Burning Up: A Novel*.** Dell Laurel-Leaf, 2001, c1999. 230pp.
When a girl she had met at an inner-city church is murdered, fifteen-year-old Macey channels her grief into a school project that leads her to uncover prejudice she had not imagined in her grandparents and their wealthy Connecticut community.

**Kehret, Peg. *Cages*.** Puffin Books, 2001, c1991. 150pp.
Kit gains a new perspective on her life and future after she is sentenced to twenty hours of volunteer work at the humane society for shoplifting a bracelet.

**Rottman, S. L. *Hero*.** Peachtree Publishers, c1997. 134pp.
After years of abuse from his mother and neglect from his father, ninth-grader Sean Parker is headed for trouble when he is sent to do community service at a farm owned by an old man, who teaches Sean that he can take control of his own life.

**Shusterman, Neal. *The Schwa Was Here*.** Dutton Children's Books, c2004. 228pp.
A Brooklyn eighth-grader nicknamed Antsy befriends the Schwa, an "invisible-ish" boy who is tired of blending into his surroundings and going unnoticed by nearly everyone.

**Siebold, Jan. *Doing Time Online*.** Whitman, c2002. 88pp.
After he is involved in a prank that led to an elderly woman's injury, twelve-year-old Mitchell must make amends by participating in a police program in which he chats online with a nursing home resident.

## Books for Older Teens

**Coleman, Michael. *On the Run*.** Dutton Children's Books, c2004. 199pp.
When a persistent youth offender is caught yet again, he is sentenced to community service as the partner to a blind runner.

**Matheson, Shirlee Smith. *Fastback Beach*.** Orca Book, c2003. 97pp.
When Miles is put on probation for stealing a car, he learns about hot rods and rebuilding cars. When the project is stolen, Miles has to face up to his friends.

**Nixon, Joan Lowery. *Nobody's There*.** Dell Laurel-Leaf, 2001, c2000. 200pp.,
Following an act of vandalism against her father's girlfriend, a seventeen-year-old girl is paired by the court with an eccentric senior citizen whose hobby as a sleuth turns deadly.

**Thomas, Rob. *Doing Time*.** Simon & Schuster, c1997. 184pp.
Each of these ten short stories focuses on a high school student's mandatory 200 hours of community service and each youth's response to the required project.

# Criminally Minded

Compiled by Patti Cook, Wired for Youth Librarian, Austin Public Library, Texas.

## Books for Ages 12–15

**Ewing, Lynne.** *Drive-by*. HarperTrophy, 1998, c1996. 85pp.

Twelve-year-old Tito, while helping to care for his little sister, struggles to find his way during the aftermath of his brother's death in a gang-related shooting.

**Hinton, S. E.** *That Was Then, This Is Now*. Viking Press, c1971. 159pp.

Sixteen-year-old Mark and Bryon have been like brothers since childhood, but now, as their involvement with girls, gangs, and drugs increases, their relationship seems to gradually disintegrate.

**Lipsyte, Robert.** *The Contender*. HarperTrophy, c1967. 167pp.

After a successful start in a boxing career, a Harlem high school dropout decides that competing in the ring isn't enough of life and resolves to aim for different goals.

**McDonald, Janet.** *Brother Hood*. Farrar, Straus & Giroux, c2004. 165pp.

Sixteen-year-old Nate, an academically gifted student who attends an exclusive private boarding school, straddles two cultures as he returns home for occasional visits to see his family and "gangsta crew" in Harlem, New York.

**Myers, Walter Dean.** *Scorpions*. HarperCollins, c1988. 216pp.

After reluctantly taking on the leadership of the Harlem gang, the Scorpions, Jamal finds that his enemies treat him with respect when he acquires a gun—until a tragedy occurs.

**Soto, Gary.** *The Afterlife*. Harcourt, c2003. 161pp.

A senior at East Fresno High School lives on as a ghost after his brutal murder in the restroom of a club where he had gone to dance.

**Walter, Virginia.** *Making Up Megaboy*. DK Publishing, c1998. 62pp.

When thirteen-year-old Robbie shoots an old man in a liquor store, everyone who knows the quiet, withdrawn youth struggles to understand this act of seemingly random violence.

**Wittlinger, Ellen.** *The Long Night of Leo and Bree*. Simon & Schuster Books for Young Readers, c2002. 111pp.

On the anniversary of his sister's murder Leo, tormented by his mother's insane accusations and his own waking nightmares, kidnaps a wealthy girl, intending to kill her, but instead their long night together helps them both face their futures.

## Books for Older Teens

**Brooks, Kevin.** *Kissing the Rain*. Scholastic, c2004. 320pp.

Fifteen-year-old Moo Nelson, shy, overweight, and bullied by his classmates, finds his life spinning out of control after he witnesses a car chase and a fight that results in a murder.

**Burgess, Melvin.** *Smack*. H. Holt, c1998. 327pp.

After running away from their troubled homes, two English teenagers move in with a group of squatters in the port city of Bristol and try to find ways to support their growing addiction to heroin.

# Criminally Minded

**Ewing, Lynne.** *Party Girl.* Knopf (distributed by Random House), 1999, c1998. 110pp.

The death of her best friend, Ana, in a drive-by shooting causes fifteen-year-old Kata to question her position in Los Angeles gang life.

**Gantos, Jack.** *Hole in My Life.* Farrar, Straus & Giroux, c2002. 199pp.

The author relates how, as a young adult, he became a drug user and smuggler, was arrested, did time in prison, and eventually got out and went to college, all the while hoping to become a writer.

**Halliday, John.** *Shooting Monarchs.* Margaret K. McElderry Books, c2003. 135pp.

Macy and Danny, two teenage boys who have both grown up under difficult circumstances, turn out very differently—one becomes a hero, the other a murderer.

**McCall, Nathan.** *Makes Me Wanna Holler: A Young Black Man in America.* Vintage, 1995, c1994. 416pp. (NF)

*Washington Post* reporter Nathan McCall recounts the story of his journey from troubled youth to professional journalist, providing insight into what it's like to be a young African American male in this country.

# Dating Abuse

## Books for Ages 12–15

**Anderson, Laurie Halse.** *Speak*. Farrar, Straus & Giroux, c1999. 197pp.
A traumatic event near the end of the summer has a devastating effect on Melinda's freshman year in high school.

**Dessen, Sarah.** *Dreamland: A Novel.* Viking Press, c2000. 250pp.
After her older sister runs away, sixteen-year-old Caitlin decides that she needs to make a major change in her own life and begins an abusive relationship with a boy who is mysterious, brilliant, and dangerous.

**Flake, Sharon.** *Who Am I Without Him?: Short Stories About Girls and the Boys in Their Lives.* Jump at the Sun/Hyperion Books for Children, c2004. 168pp.
Presents ten short stories about teenage girls struggling with issues of self-worth.

## Books for Older Teens

**Andrews, Sarah.** *Fault Line.* St. Martin's Minotaur, c2002. 307pp.
Forensic geologist Emily Hansen finds herself called to Salt Lake City, Utah, when a small earthquake rocks the city on the eve of hosting the Olympics, and although the first quake is minor, Emily must convince the city officials that there is a good chance a more severe quake will hit the city in the very near future.

**Flinn, Alexandra.** *Breathing Underwater.* HarperCollins, c2001. 263pp.
Sent to counseling for hitting his girlfriend, Caitlin, and ordered to keep a journal, sixteen-year-old Nick recounts his relationship with Caitlin, examines his controlling behavior and anger, and describes living with his abusive father.

**Giles, Gail.** *Playing in Traffic.* Roaring Brook Press, c2004. 176pp.
Shy and unremarkable, seventeen-year-old Matt Lathrop is surprised and flattered to find himself singled out for the sexual attentions of the alluring Skye Colby, until he discovers the evil purpose behind her actions.

**Jones, Patrick.** *Things Change.* Walker, c2004. 216pp.
Sixteen-year-old Johanna, one of the best students in her class, develops a passionate attachment for troubled seventeen-year-old Paul and finds her plans for the future changing in unexpected ways.

**Lynch, Chris.** *Inexcusable*. Atheneum Books for Young Readers, c2005. 165pp.
High school senior and football player Keir sets out to enjoy himself on graduation night, but when he attempts to comfort a friend whose date has left her stranded, things go terribly wrong.

**Schraff, Anne E.** *Someone to Love Me.* Townsend Press, c2002. 162pp.
Cindy Gibson, an African American teenager struggling with her mother's neglect and her mother's boyfriend's emotional abuse, must find strength she did not know she had when the boy she thought would be her savior begins beating her.

**Stratton, Allan.** *Leslie's Journal: A Novel.* Annick Press, (distributed in the United States by Firefly Books (U.S.)), c2000. 196pp.
Leslie's life seems to settle from chaos to wonderful when Jason, the new guy in school, asks her out. Things quickly change, however, and spin out of control as she finds out that Jason is not as nice as she thought and she must find a way to break out of the relationship.

# Ecowarriors

## Books for Ages 12–15

**Bang, Molly.** *Nobody Particular: One Woman's Fight to Save the Bays.* H. Holt, c2000. 46pp. (NF)
Describes a female shrimper's attempt to stop a large chemical company from polluting a bay in East Texas.

**Cooper, Susan.** *Green Boy.* Margaret K. McElderry Books, c2002. 195pp.
Twelve-year-old Trey and his seven-year-old brother Lou, who does not speak, cross the barrier between two worlds, that of their island in the Bahamas, and a land called Pangaia, and play a mysterious role in restoring the natural environment in both places.

**DeFelice, Cynthia C.** *Lostman's River.* Avon Books, c1995. 156pp.
In the early 1900s, thirteen-year-old Tyler encounters vicious hunters whose actions threaten to destroy the Everglades ecosystem; as a result, he joins the battle to protect that fragile environment.

**George, Jean Craighead.** *Who Really Killed Cock Robin?: An Eco Mystery.* HarperTrophy, 1992, c1971. 191pp.
Eighth-grader Tony Isidoro follows a trail of environmental clues to try to figure out what ecological imbalances might have caused the death of the town's best-known robin.

**Hiaasen, Carl.** *Hoot.* Knopf (distributed by Random House), c2002. 292pp.
Roy, who is new to his small Florida community, becomes involved in another boy's attempt to save a colony of burrowing owls from a proposed construction site.

**Hobbs, Valerie.** *Stefan's Story.* Farrar, Straus & Giroux, c2003. 165pp.
Thirteen-year-old, wheelchair-bound Stefan renews his friendship with Carolina as they work together to save an old-growth forest from destruction by loggers.

**Hobbs, Will.** *The Maze.* Morrow Junior Books, c1998. 197pp.
Rick, a fourteen-year-old foster child, escapes from a juvenile detention facility near Las Vegas and travels to Canyonlands National Park in Utah, where he meets a bird biologist working on a project to reintroduce condors to the wild.

**Hoose, Phillip M.** *The Race to Save the Lord God Bird.* Farrar, Straus & Giroux, c2004. 196pp. (NF)
Tells the story of the ivory-billed woodpecker's extinction in the United States, describing the encounters between this species and humans, and discussing what these encounters have taught us about preserving endangered creatures.

**Klass, David.** *California Blue.* Scholastic, c1994. 199pp.
When seventeen-year-old John Rodgers discovers a new subspecies of butterfly that may necessitate closing the mill where his dying father works, he and his father find themselves on opposite sides of an environmental conflict.

**Spinelli, Jerry.** *Crash.* Knopf (distributed by Random House), c1996. 162pp.
Seventh-grader John "Crash" Coogan has always been comfortable with his tough, aggressive behavior, until his relationship with an unusual Quaker boy and his grandfather's stroke make him consider the meaning of friendship and the importance of family.

# Ecowarriors

**Taylor, Theodore.** *The Weirdo.* Harcourt Brace Jovanovich, c1991. 289pp.
Seventeen-year-old Chip Clewt fights to save the black bears in the Powhaten National Wildlife Refuge.

**Van Draanen, Wendelin.** *Flipped.* Knopf (distributed by Random House), c2001. 212pp.
In alternating chapters, two teenagers describe how their feelings about themselves, each other, and their families have changed over the years.

## Books for Older Teens

**Abbey, Edward.** *The Monkey Wrench Gang.* Perennial Classics, 2000, c 1975. 421pp.
A burnt-out veteran, a mad doctor, a sexy revolutionary, and a polygamist outdoorsman team up in a concerted effort to halt what they see as a big government/big business conspiracy to destroy the environment of the American West.

**Harr, Jonathan.** *A Civil Action.* Vintage Books, 1996, c1995. 502pp. (NF)
Follows a lawsuit brought against W.R. Grace & Co. for contaminating the drinking water in Woburn, Massachusetts.

**Hill, Julia Butterfly.** *The Legacy of Luna: The Story of a Tree, a Woman, and the Struggle to Save the Redwoods.* HarperSanFrancisco, 2001, c2000. 256pp. (NF)
Presents information on Julia Butterfly Hill's two-year "tree-sit," which she hoped would stop the Pacific Lumber company from clear-cutting the ancient redwood forest in California, and discusses how she inaugurated a new era in environmental movements around the world.

**Kingsolver, Barbara.** *Prodigal Summer: A Novel.* HarperCollins, c2000. 444pp.
The coming of summer to Appalachia's Zebulon Mountain brings a blossoming in nature as well as in the lives of reclusive wildlife biologist Deanna Wolfe, young hunter Eddie Bondo, transplanted city-girl Lusa Landowski, and a pair of elderly, feuding neighbors.

# Extreme Sports

## Books for Ages 12–15

**Bass, Scott.** *Surf!: Your Guide to Longboarding, Shortboarding, Tubing, Aerials, Hanging Ten, and More.* National Geographic, c2003. 64pp. (NF)
> Presents guidance and tips on several different kinds of surfing and includes facts on the sport's history.

**Deady, Kathleen W.** *Extreme Mountain Biking Moves.* Capstone High-Interest Books, c2003. 32pp. (NF)
> Discusses the sport of mountain biking, describing some of the racing and trick moves as well as safety concerns.

**Doeden, Matt.** *BMX Freestyle.* Capstone Press, c2005. 32pp. (NF)
> Describes the sport of BMX freestyle, including tricks and safety information.

**Doeden, Matt.** *Motocross Freestyle.* Capstone Press, c2005. 32pp. (NF)
> Presents an introduction to freestyle motocross, telling how the sport began and discussing the special features of the bikes, different freestyle tricks, and safety gear and practices.

**Doeden, Matt.** *Snowboarding.* Capstone Press, c2005. 32pp. (NF)
> Describes the sport of snowboarding, including tricks and safety information.

**Firestone, Mary.** *Extreme Downhill BMX Moves.* Capstone High-Interest Books, c2004. 32pp. (NF)
> Discusses the sport of extreme downhill Bicycle Motocross racing, describing some of the jumping and passing techniques as well as safety concerns.

**Firestone, Mary.** *Extreme Halfpipe Snowboarding Moves.* Capstone High-Interest Books, c2004. 32pp. (NF)
> Discusses the elements of the sport of snowboarding that take it to the extreme in snowy halfpipes.

**Firestone, Mary.** *Extreme Waterskiing Moves.* Capstone High-Interest Books, c2004. 32pp. (NF)
> Discusses the sport of extreme waterskiing, describing some of the trick steps and aerials as well as safety concerns.

**Freimuth, Jeri.** *Extreme Skateboarding Moves.* Capstone High-Interest Books, c2001. 32pp. (NF)
> Discusses the sport of extreme skateboarding, including the moves involved in the sport.

**Glaser, Jason.** *Bungee Jumping.* Capstone High/Low Books, c1999. 48pp. (NF)
> Discusses the history, stunts, competitions, equipment, and safety measures of bungee jumping.

**Gutman, Bill.** *Catching Air: The Excitement and Daring of Individual Action Sports—Snowboarding, Skateboarding, BMX Biking, In-Line Skating.* Citadel Press/Kensington Pub, Corp, c2004. 170pp. (NF)
> Provides a comprehensive overview of the equipment, techniques, and skills of various individual extreme sports, including snowboarding, skateboarding, BMX biking, and in-line skating.

**Hayhurst, Chris.** *Bicycle Stunt Riding!: Catch Air.* Rosen Central, c2000. 64pp. (NF)
> Describes the sport of bicycle stunt riding, plus how to purchase equipment, practice stunts, ride safely, and enter competitions.

# Extreme Sports

**Horton, Ron.** *Awesome Athletes.* Lucent Books, Thomson/Gale, c2004. 112pp. (NF)
Profiles five athletes who participate in the extreme sports of skateboarding, snowboarding, surfing, rock climbing, and mountain bike racing.

**Maurer, Tracy.** *ATV Riding.* Rourke, c2003. 48pp. (NF)
Provides information about all-terrain vehicles, describing their different components, discussing riding techniques and safety, and looking at the competition circuit.

**Maxwell, E. J.** *Xtreme Sports: Cutting Edge.* Scholastic, c2003. 95pp. (NF)
Presents photographs, facts, and profiles of Tori Allen, Apolo Anton Ohno, Shaun White, and other stars of extreme sports such as surfing, rock climbing, and snowboarding.

**McKenna, A. T.** *Big-Air Snowboarding.* Capstone High/Low Books, c1999. 48pp. (NF)
Describes the history, equipment, techniques, and safety measures of big air snowboarding.

**Oleksy, Walter G.** *Barefoot Waterskiing.* Capstone Books, c2000. 48pp. (NF)
Describes the history, techniques, practice, and competition related to the sport of barefoot waterskiing.

**Parr, Danny.** *Extreme Bicycle Stunt Riding Moves.* Capstone High-Interest Books, c2001. 32pp. (NF)
Discusses the sport of extreme bicycle stunt riding, including the moves involved in the sport.

**Perry, Phyllis Jean.** *Boardsailing*. Capstone Books, c2000. 48pp. (NF)
Describes the history, equipment, techniques, competition, and safety concerns related to the sport of boardsailing or windsurfing.

**Peterson, Christine.** *Extreme Surfing.* Capstone Press, c2005. 32pp. (NF)
Describes surfing and surfboards, and provides illustrated definitions of surfing terms.

**Peterson, Christine.** *Wakeboarding*. Capstone, c2005. 32pp. (NF)
Using text and photos, describes the sport of wakeboarding, including tricks and safety information.

**Peterson, Monique.** *Bike!: Your Guide to Mountain Biking, BMX, Road and Fast-Track Racing, C-X Racing and More.* National Geographic, c2002. 64pp. (NF)
Explores various aspects of biking, including mountain biking, BMX biking, road racing, and fast-track racing.

**Schaefer, A. R.** *Extreme Wakeboarding Moves.* Capstone High-Interest Books, c2003. 32pp. (NF)
Discusses the sport of extreme wakeboarding, including the moves involved in the sports.

**Shafran, Michael.** *Skate!: Your Guide to Inline, Aggressive, Vert, Street, Roller Hockey, Speed Skating, Dance, Fitness Training, and More.* National Geographic, c2003. 64pp. (NF)
Provides instruction in everything from standing on skates for the first time to dancing or exercising on them.

**Takeda, Pete.** *Climb!: Your Guide to Bouldering, Sport Climbing, Trad Climbing, Ice Climbing, Alpinism, and More.* National Geographic, c2002. 64pp. (NF)
An introduction and guide to climbing, including bouldering, sport climbing, trad climbing, ice climbing, and alpinism.

# Extreme Sports

## Books for Older Teens

**Covert, Kim.** *Extreme Diving.* Capstone Press, c2005. 32pp. (NF)
Presents several different types of extreme diving, including free diving (diving without breathing gear), cave diving, and ice diving. Also provides information on equipment and diving competitions.

**Covert, Kim.** *Skeleton: High-Speed Ice Sliding.* Capstone Press, c2005. 32pp. (NF)
Introduces the sport of skeleton, including its history, equipment, and famous skeleton athletes.

**Murdico, Suzanne J.** *Skateboarding in the X Games.* Rosen Central, c2003. 47pp. (NF)
This book describes five skateboarding events in the X Games competition and tells about the athletes who have earned metals in this premier event.

**Murdico, Suzanne J.** *Street Luge and Dirtboarding.* Rosen Central, c2003. 47pp. (NF)
An introduction to two new extreme sports that combine aspects of skateboarding with another sport, street luge and dirtboarding.

**Preszler, Eric.** *Kiteboarding.* Capstone Press, c2005. 32pp. (NF)
Introduces the sport of kiteboarding, including necessary gear, tricks, and famous kiteboarders.

**Roberts, Jeremy.** *Rock & Ice Climbing: Top the Tower.* Rosen Central, c2000. 63pp. (NF)
Introduces the sports of rock and ice climbing, describing the history, equipment, safety tips, and outstanding performers.

**Tomlinson, Joe.** *Extreme Sports: In Search of the Ultimate Thrill.* Firefly Books (U.S.), c2004. 192pp. (NF)
Contains photographs and descriptions of a variety of extreme sports, including bungee jumping, mountain biking, snowboarding, and others, and provides information on clothing and equipment, safety, tricks and techniques, and venues.

**Weil, Ann.** *Aggressive In-Line Skating.* Capstone Press, c2005. 32pp. (NF)
Presents an introduction to aggressive in-line skating, looks at different skating styles, discusses skates and safety gear, describes various tricks and extreme moves, and profiles some of the stars of the sport and its competitions, the X Games and the Gravity Games.

**Weil, Ann.** *BMX Racing.* Capstone Press, c2005. 32pp. (NF)
Presents the history of BMX racing, the racetracks, and the superstars, including Samantha Cools, Kyle Bennett, Alice Jung, Christophe Leveque, and Randy Stumpfhauser.

# Faeries and Faraway Realms

Prepared by Joanna Nigrelli, Wired for Youth Librarian, Austin Public Library, Texas.

## Books for Ages 12–15

**Bell, Hilari.** *The Goblin Wood*. EOS, c2003. 294pp.
A young Hedgewitch, an idealistic knight, and an army of clever goblins fight against the ruling hierarchy, which is trying to rid the land of all magical creatures.

**Brennan, Herbie.** *Faerie Wars*. Bloomsbury (distributed by Holtzbrinck), c2003. 367pp.
Troubled by family problems, Henry finds his life taking a whole new dimension when he and his friend, old Mr. Fogarty, become involved with Prince Pyrgus Malvae, who has been sent from the faerie world to escape the treacherous Faeries of the Night.

**Colfer, Eoin.** *Artemis Fowl*. Hyperion Books for Children, c2001. 277pp. (and sequels)
When a twelve-year-old evil genius tries to restore his family fortune by capturing a fairy and demanding a ransom in gold, the fairies fight back with magic, technology, and a particularly nasty troll.

**DiTerlizzi, Tony.** <u>The Spiderwick Chronicles.</u> Simon & Schuster Books for Young Readers, c2003–2004. 5v.
Chronicles the adventures of the Grace children after they go to stay at their Great-Aunt Lucinda's worn Victorian house and discover a field guide to fairies and other magical creatures.

**Dunkle, Clare B.** *The Hollow Kingdom.* H. Holt, c2003. 356pp.
In nineteenth-century England, Marak, a powerful sorcerer and king of the Goblins, chooses Kate, the elder of two orphan girls who recently arrived at their ancestral home, Hallow Hill, to be his bride and queen.

**McGraw, Eloise Jarvis.** *The Moorchild.* Margaret K. McElderry Books, c1996. 241pp.
Feeling that she is neither fully human nor "Folk," a changeling learns her true identity and attempts to find the human child whose place she had been given.

**Pattou, Edith.** *East*. Harcourt, c2003. 498pp.
A young woman journeys to a distant castle on the back of a great white bear who is the victim of a cruel enchantment.

**Pratchett, Terry.** *The Wee Free Men*. HarperCollins, c2003. 263pp.
Tiffany, a young witch-to-be in the land of Discworld, teams up with the Wee Free Men, a clan of six-inch-high blue toughs, to rescue her baby brother and ward off a sinister invasion from Fairyland.

**Stroud, Jonathan.** *The Amulet of Samarkand*. Miramax Books/Hyperion Books for Children, c2003. 462pp.
Nathaniel, a young magician's apprentice, becomes caught in a web of magical espionage, murder, and rebellion, after he summons the djinni Bartimaeus and instructs him to steal the Amulet of Samarkand from the powerful magician Simon Loveland.

# Faeries and Faraway Realms

## Books for Older Teens

**Black, Holly.** *Tithe: A Modern Faerie Tale.* Simon & Schuster, c2002. 310pp.
Sixteen-year-old Kaye, who has been visited by faeries since childhood, discovers that she herself is a magical faerie creature with a special destiny.

**Block, Francesca Lia.** *I Was a Teenage Fairy.* Joanna Cotler, 2000, c 1998. 186pp.
A feisty, sexy fairy helps a young woman heal traumas from her past.

**Springer, Nancy.** *I Am Morgan Le Fay: A Tale from Camelot.* Firebird, 2002, c2001. 227pp.
In war-torn England where her half-brother Arthur will eventually become king, the young Morgan le Fay comes to realize that she has magic powers and links to the faerie world.

# Genocide

## Books for Ages 12–15

**Denenberg, Barry.** *One Eye Laughing, the Other Weeping: The Diary of Julie Weiss.* Scholastic, c2000. 250pp.
> During the Nazi persecution of the Jews in Austria, twelve-year-old Julie escapes to America to live with her relatives in New York City.

**Isaacs, Anne.** *Torn Thread.* Scholastic Press, c2000. 188pp.
> In an attempt to save his daughter's life, Eva's father sends her from Poland to a labor camp in Czechoslovakia, where she and her sister survive the war.

**Kherdian, David.** *The Road from Home: The Story of an Armenian Girl.* Greenwillow Books, c1979. 238pp. (NF)
> A biography of the author's mother, concentrating on her childhood in Turkey before the Turkish government deported its Armenian population.

**Matas, Carol.** *After the War.* Aladdin Paperbacks, 1997, c1996. 133pp.
> After being released from Buchenwald at the end of World War II, fifteen-year-old Ruth risks her life to lead a group of children across Europe to Palestine.

**Orlev, Uri.** *Run, Boy, Run: A Novel.* Houghton Mifflin, c2003. 186pp.
> Based on the true story of a nine-year-old boy who escapes the Warsaw Ghetto and must survive the war in the Nazi-occupied Polish countryside.

**Radin, Ruth Y.** *Escape to the Forest: Based on a True Story of the Holocaust.* HarperCollins, c2000. 90pp.
> A young Jewish girl living with her family in the town of Lida at the beginning of World War II recalls the horrors of life under first, the Russians, then the Nazis, before fleeing to join Tuvia Bielski, a partisan who tried to save as many Jews as possible. Based on a true story.

**Strasser, Todd.** *Thief of Dreams.* Putnam, c2003. 160pp.
> Thirteen-year-old Martin's parents are always too busy making money to pay much attention to him, so he enjoys the attention he gets from his Uncle Lawrence, until he discovers that his uncle has a secret life.

*We Are Witnesses: Five Diaries of Teenagers Who Died in the Holocaust.* H. Holt, c1995. 196pp. (NF)
> Excerpts from five diaries written by Jewish teenagers about their families' experiences during World War II.

**Yolen, Jane.** *The Devil's Arithmetic.* Viking Kestrel, c1988. 170pp.
> Hannah resents stories about her Jewish heritage and the past until, when opening the door during a Passover Seder, she finds herself in Poland during World War II, where she experiences the horrors of a concentration camp, and learns why she—and we—must remember the past.

# Materialism

## Books for Ages 12–15

**Keizer, Garret.** *God of Beer.* HarperTempest, 2003, c2002. 242pp.
To complete a class assignment at his high school in rural Vermont, Kyle and his friends, Quake and Diana, do a social protest project involving alcohol.

**Koja, Kathe.** *Buddha Boy.* Farrar, Straus & Giroux, c2003. 117pp.
Justin spends time with Jinsen, the unusual and artistic new student whom the school bullies torment and call Buddha Boy, and ends up making choices that affect Jinsen, himself, and the entire school.

**Myers, Bill.** *My Life as a Walrus Whoopee Cushion.* Tommy Nelson, c1999. 116pp.
When Wally, Opera, and Wall Street win the Gazillion Dollar Lotto, they confront the dangers of greed and materialism through a series of incidents involving bungling bad guys, a break-in at the zoo, and a SWAT team.

**Nye, Naomi Shihab.** *Going Going.* Greenwillow Books, c2005. 232pp.
Florrie, a sixteen-year-old living in San Antonio, Texas, leads her friends and a new boyfriend in a campaign that supports small businesses and protests the effects of chain stores.

**Tashjian, Janet.** *The Gospel According to Larry.* H. Holt, c2001. 227pp.
Seventeen-year-old Josh, a loner-philosopher who wants to make a difference in the world, tries to maintain his secret identity as the author of a Web site that is receiving national attention.

**Westerfeld, Scott.** *So Yesterday: A Novel.* Razorbill, c2004. 225pp.
Hunter Braque, a New York City teenager who is paid by corporations to spot what is "cool," combines his analytical skills with girlfriend Jen's creative talents to find a missing person and thwart a conspiracy directed at the heart of consumer culture.

**Woolf, Alex.** *Chrysalis Education* (distributed in the United States by Smart Apple Media), c2004. 61pp. (NF)
Examines some of the fundamental questions surrounding the issues of consumerism and discusses how it affects underdeveloped countries, why some people are opposed to it, and what drives people to consume.

## Books for Older Teens

**Anderson, M. T.** *Feed.* Candlewick Press, c2002. 237pp.
In a future where most people have computer implants in their heads to control their environment, a boy meets an unusual girl who is in serious trouble.

**Menzel, Peter.** *Material World: A Global Family Portrait.* Sierra Club Books, c1995. 255pp. (NF)
A photo-journey through the homes and lives of thirty families, revealing culture and economic levels around the world.

# Medical Thrillers

## Books for Ages 12–15

**Anderson, Laurie Halse.** *Fever, 1793.* Simon & Schuster Books for Young Readers, c2000. 251pp.
Sixteen-year-old Matilda Cook, separated from her sick mother, learns about perseverance and self-reliance when she is forced to cope with the horrors of the yellow fever epidemic in Philadelphia in 1793.

**Cooney, Caroline B.** *Code Orange.* Delacorte Press, c2005. 200pp.
While conducting research for a school paper on smallpox, Mitty finds an envelope containing 100-year-old smallpox scabs and fears that he has infected himself and all of New York City.

**DeFelice, Cynthia C.** *The Apprenticeship of Lucas Whitaker.* Farrar, Straus & Giroux, c1996. 151pp.
After his family dies of consumption in 1849, twelve-year-old Lucas becomes a doctor's apprentice.

**Farmer, Nancy.** *The House of the Scorpion.* Atheneum Books for Young Readers, c2002. 380pp.
In a future where humans despise clones, Matt enjoys special status as the young clone of El Patron, the 142-year-old leader of a corrupt drug empire nestled between Mexico and the United States.

**Haddix, Margaret Peterson.** *Running Out of Time.* Simon & Schuster Books for Young Readers, c1995. 184pp.
When a diphtheria epidemic hits her village in 1840, thirteen-year-old Jessie discovers it is actually a 1995 tourist site under observation by heartless scientists, and it's up to Jessie to escape the village and save the lives of the dying children.

**Philbrick, W. R.** *The Last Book in the Universe.* Blue Sky Press, c2000. 223pp.
After an earthquake has destroyed much of the planet, an epileptic teenager nicknamed Spaz begins the heroic fight to bring human intelligence back to Earth of a distant future.

## Books for Older Teens

**Bear, Greg.** *Blood Music.* Simon & Schuster, c2002. 344pp.
While experimenting with advanced biochips, researcher Vergil Ulam creates a microscopic intelligence that threatens to bring about the end of the world as it mutates.

**Bear, Greg.** *Darwin's Children.* Del Rey/Ballantine, 2004, c2003. 493pp.
Scientists Kaye Lang and Mitch Rafelson, parents of Stella, a genetically enhanced child born as a result of mutations in the human genome caused by the SHEVA virus, lose the struggle to keep their daughter safe from a repressive government that wants to control the virus children by isolating them from the general population.

**Bear, Greg.** *Darwin's Radio.* Ballantine Books, c1999. 430pp.
Molecular biologist Kay Lang, a specialist in retroviruses, teams up with virus hunter Christopher Dicken and anthropologist Mitch Rafelson in an attempt to trace the ancient source of a flu-like disease that is killing expectant mothers and their offspring and threatening the future of the human race.

# Medical Thrillers

**Crichton, Michael.** *The Andromeda Strain.* Avon Books, 2003, c1969. 331pp.

For five days, American scientists struggle to identify and control a deadly new form of life.

**Crichton, Michael.** *The Terminal Man.* Avon Books, 2002, c1972. 266pp.

Harry Benson, a man who suffers from violent seizures, is implanted with electrodes that are designed to send soothing pulses to the pleasure centers of his brain, but something goes wrong with the operation, and Benson sets out to get revenge on the doctors he believes are trying to turn him into a machine.

**Picoult, Jodi.** *My Sister's Keeper: A Novel.* Atria Books, c2004. 423pp. (adult)

Thirteen-year-old Anna, conceived specifically to provide blood and bone marrow for her sister Kate, who was diagnosed with a rare form of leukemia at the age of two, decides to sue her parents for control of her body when her mother wants her to donate a kidney to Kate.

**Preston, Richard.** *The Hot Zone.* Anchor Books, c1995. 422pp.

Tells the dramatic story of U.S. Army scientists and soldiers who worked to stop the outbreak of a deadly and extremely contagious virus in 1989.

**Werlin, Nancy.** *Double Helix.* Dial Books, c2004. 252pp.

Eighteen-year-old Eli discovers a shocking secret about his life and his family while working for a Nobel Prize–winning scientist whose specialty is genetic engineering.

# Peace

## Picture Books for Everyone

**Bunting, Eve.** *Gleam and Glow*. Harcourt, c2001. 32pp.
After his home is destroyed by war, eight-year-old Viktor finds hope in the survival of two very special fish.

**Bunting, Eve.** *The Wall*. Clarion Books, c1990. 32pp.
A boy and his father come from far away to visit the Vietnam War Memorial in Washington and find the name of the boy's grandfather, who was killed in the conflict.

**Cronin, Doreen.** *Click, Clack, Moo: Cows That Type*. Simon & Schuster Books for Young Readers, c2000. 32pp.
When Farmer Brown's cows find a typewriter in the barn, they start making demands, then go on strike when the farmer refuses to give them what they want.

**Cutler, Jane.** *The Cello of Mr. O*. Dutton Children's Books, c1999. 32pp.
When a concert cellist plays in the square for his neighbors in a war-besieged city, his priceless instrument is destroyed by a mortar shell, but he finds the courage to return the next day.

**DiSalvo-Ryan, DyAnne.** *Grandpa's Corner Store*. HarperCollins, c2000. 36pp.
Grandfather's corner grocery business is threatened by a new supermarket, but his granddaughter, Lucy, organizes the neighbors to convince him to stay.

**English, Karen.** *Hot Day on Abbott Avenue*. Clarion Books, c2004. 32pp.
After having a fight, two friends spend the day ignoring each other, until the lure of a game of jump rope helps them to forget about being mad.

**Fox, Mem.** *Whoever You Are*. Harcourt Brace, c1997. 32pp.
Despite the differences between people around the world, there are similarities that join us together, such as pain, joy, and love.

**Kellogg, Steven.** *The Island of the Skog*. Dial Books for Young Readers, c1973. 32pp.
To escape the dangers of urban life, Jenny and her friends sail away to an island, only to be faced with a new problem—its single inhabitant—the Skog.

**Kuskin, Karla.** *The Upstairs Cat*. Clarion Books, c1997. 32pp.
The fights between a mean, old cat and a lean, young cat always end in a draw and result in a waste of energy that proves the futility of war.

**Leaf, Munro.** *The Story of Ferdinand*. Viking Press, c1964. 70pp.
Ferdinand likes to sit quietly and smell the flowers, but one day he gets stung by a bee, and his snorting and stomping convince everyone that he is the fiercest of bulls.

**Lionni, Leo.** *The Alphabet Tree*. Knopf (distributed by Random House), 2004, c1968. 33pp.
After a storm blows some of them away, the letters on the alphabet tree learn from a strange bug to be stronger by forming words, then a caterpillar comes along and tells them that words are not enough; they must say something important.

# Peace

**Lobel, Anita.** *Potatoes, Potatoes.* Greenwillow Books, c2004. 40pp.
Recounts how a mother's love and potatoes ended a war.

**McPhail, David M.** *Mole Music.* H. Holt, c1999. 32pp.
Feeling that something is missing in his simple life, Mole acquires a violin and learns to make beautiful, joyful music.

**Muth, Jon J.** *Zen Shorts.* Scholastic Press, c2005. 40pp.
When Stillwater the bear moves into the neighborhood, the stories he tells to three siblings teach them to look at the world in new ways.

**Say, Allen.** *Home of the Brave.* Houghton Mifflin, c2002. 32pp.
Following a kayaking accident, a man experiences the feelings of children interned during World War II and children on Indian reservations.

**Seuss, Dr.** *The Butter Battle Book.* Random House, c1984. 48pp.
Engaged in a long-running battle, the Yooks and the Zooks develop more and more sophisticated weaponry as they attempt to outdo each other.

**Shigekawa, Marlene.** *Blue Jay in the Desert.* Polychrome, c1993. 40pp.
While living in a relocation camp during World War II, a young Japanese American boy receives a message of hope from his grandfather.

**Trivizas, Eugenios.** *The Three Little Wolves and the Big Bad Pig.* Margaret K. McElderry Books, c1993. 32pp.
An altered retelling of the traditional tale about the conflict between pig and wolf—with a surprise ending.

## Books for Ages 12–15

**Deedy, Carmen Agra.** *The Yellow Star: The Legend of King Christian X of Denmark.* Peachtree, c2000. 32pp.
Retells the story of King Christian X and the Danish resistance to the Nazis during World War II.

**Demi.** *Gandhi.* Margaret K. McElderry Books, c2001. 36pp. (NF)
Color illustrations fill this chronicle of legendary pacifist social activist Mohandas Gandhi, whose work to change India's caste system and free India from British rule inspired both Martin Luther King Jr. and Nelson Mandela.

**Gilley, Jeremy.** *Peace One Day.* Putnam, c2005. 44pp. (NF)
Jeremy Gilley describes his efforts to gather support for the creation of World Peace Day, a plan adopted by the United Nations to set aside September 21 as an annual plea for a global ceasefire and day of nonviolence.

**Innocenti, Roberto.** *Rose Blanche.* Creative Paperbacks, 1995, c1985. 32pp.
During World War II, a young German girl's curiosity leads her to discover something far more terrible than the day-to-day hardships and privations that she and her neighbors have experienced.

# Peace

**Ishii, Takayuki.** *One Thousand Paper Cranes: The Story of Sadako and the Children's Peace Statue.* Laurel-Leaf Books, 2001, c1997. 97pp. (NF)

> Hospitalized with the dreaded atom bomb disease, leukemia, a child in Hiroshima by the name of Sadako races against time to fold 1,000 paper cranes to verify the legend that by doing so a sick person will become healthy. After her death, Sadako's classmates campaign to build the Children's Peace Statue in memory of Sadako and the other children who were victims of the atomic bombing of Hiroshima.

**Lalli, Judy.** *Make Someone Smile: And 40 More Ways to Be a Peaceful Person.* Free Spirit, c1996. 71pp. (NF)

> A collection of photographs of children modeling the skills of peacemaking and conflict resolution.

**Marsden, John.** *Prayer for the Twenty-First Century.* Lothian Books (distributed by Star Bright Books), c1997. 32pp.

> A poem, illustrated by photographs, illustrations, collages, and paintings, in which the author expresses his hopes for a future of freedom, peace, and understanding.

**Maruki, Toshi.** *Hiroshima No Pika.* Lothrop, Lee & Shepard, c1980. 48pp. (NF)

> A retelling of a mother's account of what happened to her family during the "Flash" that destroyed Hiroshima in 1945.

**Mochizuki, Ken.** *Baseball Saved Us.* Lee & Low, c1993. 32pp.

> A Japanese American boy learns to play baseball when he and his family are forced to live in an internment camp during World War II, and his ability to play helps him after the war is over.

**Nye, Naomi Shihab.** *19 Varieties of Gazelle: Poems of the Middle East.* Greenwillow Books, c2002. 142pp.

> A collection of sixty poems in which the Arab American author examines life in the Middle East.

**Rappaport, Doreen.** *Martin's Big Words: The Life of Dr. Martin Luther King, Jr.* Jump at the Sun/Hyperion Books for Children, c2001. 34pp. (NF)

> Looks at the life of Dr. Martin Luther King, explaining his work to bring about a peaceful end to segregation.

**Rose, Naomi C.** *Tibetan Tales for Little Buddhas.* Clear Light, c2004. 63pp.

> Three traditional tales about mystical beings, yaks, an enormous sow, and yeti introduce Tibetan culture and wisdom. Includes a foreword from the Dalai Lama, map of Tibet, glossary of Tibetan terms, and description of a Tibetan chant.

**Smith, David J.** *If the World Were a Village: A Book About the World's People.* Kids Can Press, c2002. 32pp. (NF)

> Breaks down the population of the world into a collection of 100 representative people and describes what one would find in this global village, covering languages, ages, religions, food, air and water, schooling, and possessions, accompanied by vivid color illustrations.

**Zeman, Ludmila.** *Gilgamesh the King* Tundra Books, c1992. 24pp.

> Retells the ancient Sumerian legend of Gilgamesh, the king who was part god and part man.

# Peace

## Books for Older Teens

**Chambers, Aidan.** *Postcards from No Man's Land.* Dutton Books, c2002. 312pp.

Alternates between two stories in the present,, seventeen-year-old Jacob visits a daunting Amsterdam at the request of his English grandmother, while in the past, nineteen-year-old Geertrui relates her experience of British soldier's attempts to liberate Holland from its German occupation.

**Koplewicz, Harold S.** *Turbulent Times, Prophetic Dreams: Art from Israeli and Palestinian Children.* Devora Publishing, c2000. 87pp. (NF)

Presents more than thirty drawings by Palestinian and Israeli children about the way they see the violence between their peoples and what they would like the future to be like.

**Meltzer, Milton.** *Ain't Gonna Study War No More: The Story of America's Peace Seekers.* Random House, 2002. 290pp. (NF)

Presents a history of pacifism and those who have protested against war, concentrating on war resistance in the United States from colonial days to the present and concerns about nuclear arms and terrorism.

**Rall, Ted.** *To Afghanistan and Back: A Graphic Travelogue.* Nantier, Beall, Minoustchine, c2002. 112pp. (NF)

New York cartoonist and columnist Ted Rall discusses his firsthand experiences in Afghanistan and other countries in the region before and after September 11. 2001, criticizing U.S. military actions there, and presenting a graphic novel about the war.

**Sacco, Joe.** *Safe Area Gorazde.* Fantagraphics Books, c2001. 227pp. (NF)

A graphic novel based on the author's 1995–1996 visits to Gorazde, one of the UN-created "safe areas" in Eastern Bosnia, showing the brutality and humanity that coexisted there during the Bosnian War of 1992–1995.

# Picture Books About War

## Books for All Ages

**Abells, Chana Byers.** *The Children We Remember.* Greenwillow Books, c1986. 50pp. (NF)
Text and photographs briefly describe the fate of Jewish children in World War II Europe after the Nazis began to control their lives.

**Balgassi, Haemi.** *Peacebound Trains.* Clarion Books, c1996. 47pp.
Sumi's grandmother tells the story of her family's escape from Seoul during the Korean War, while they watch the trains that will eventually bring Sumi's mother back from army service.

**Benchley, Nathaniel.** *Sam, the Minuteman.* HarperCollins, c1969. 62pp.
An easy-to-read account of Sam and his father fighting as Minutemen against the British in the Battle of Lexington.

**Borden, Louise.** *The Little Ships: The Heroic Rescue at Dunkirk in World War II.* Aladdin, 2003, c1997. 32pp.
A young English girl and her father take their sturdy fishing boat and join the scores of other civilian vessels crossing the English Channel in a daring attempt to rescue Allied and British troops trapped by Nazi soldiers at Dunkirk.

**Borden, Louise.** *Sleds on Boston Common: A Story from the American Revolution.* Margaret K. McElderry Books, c2000. 40pp.
Henry complains to the royal governor, General Gage, after his plan to sled down the steep hill at Boston Common is thwarted by the masses of British troops camped there.

**Bunting, Eve.** *The Wall.* Clarion Books, c1990. 32pp.
A boy and his father come from far away to visit the Vietnam War Memorial in Washington to find the name of the boy's grandfather, who was killed in the conflict.

**Cutler, Jane.** *The Cello of Mr. O.* Dutton Children's Books, c1999. 32pp.
When a concert cellist plays in the square for his neighbors in a war-besieged city, his priceless instrument is destroyed by a mortar shell, but he finds the courage to return the next day.

**Dabba Smith, Frank.** *My Secret Camera: Life in the Lodz Ghetto.* Harcourt, c2000. 42pp. (NF)
Photographs taken secretly by a young Jewish man document the fear, hardship, generosity, and humanity woven through the daily life of the Jews forced to live in the Lodz ghetto during the Holocaust.

**Fleming, Candace.** *Boxes for Katje.* Farrar, Straus & Giroux, c2003. 34pp.
After a young Dutch girl writes to her new American friend with thanks for the care package sent after World War II, she begins to receive increasingly larger boxes.

**Fox, Mem.** *Feathers and Fools.* Harcourt Brace, c1996. 34pp.
A modern fable about some peacocks and swans who allow the fear of their differences to become so great that they end up destroying each other.

From Nancy J. Keane, *The Big Book of Teen Reading Lists: 100 Great, Ready-to-Use Book Lists for Educators, Librarians, Parents, and Children.* Westport, CT: Libraries Unlimited, 2006. Copyright © 2006 by Libraries Unlimited.

# Picture Books About War

**Granfield, Linda.** *In Flanders Fields: The Story of the Poem by John Mccrae.* Stoddart Kids, c1996, c1995. 32pp.

    Presents the context for the writing of the famous poem by the Canadian medical officer who attended injured soldiers in Flanders during the First World War.

**Heide, Florence Parry.** *Sami and the Time of the Troubles.* Clarion, c1992. 33pp.

    A ten-year-old Lebanese boy goes to school, helps his mother with chores, plays with his friends, and lives with his family in a basement shelter when bombings occur and fighting begins on his street.

**Kirkpatrick, Katherine.** *Redcoats and Petticoats.* Holiday House, c1999. 32pp.

    Members of a family in the village of Setauket on Long Island are displaced by the Redcoats and serve as spies for the Revolutionary Army of George Washington.

**Lee, Milly.** *Nim and the War Effort.* Farrar, Straus & Giroux, c1997. 40pp.

    In her determination to prove that an American can win the contest for the war effort, Nim does something that leaves her Chinese grandfather both bewildered and proud.

**Maruki, Toshi.** *Hiroshima No Pika.* Lothrop, Lee & Shepard, c1980. 48pp. (NF)

    A retelling of a mother's account of what happened to her family during the "Flash" that destroyed Hiroshima in 1945.

**Mochizuki, Ken.** *Baseball Saved Us.* Lee & Low, c1993. 32pp.

    A Japanese American boy learns to play baseball when he and his family are forced to live in an internment camp during World War II, and his ability to play helps him after the war is over.

**Oppenheim, Shulamith Levey.** *The Lily Cupboard.* HarperCollins, c1992. 29pp.

    During the German occupation of Holland, Miriam, a young Jewish girl, is forced to leave her parents and hide with strangers in the country.

**Polacco, Patricia.** *The Butterfly.* Philomel Books, c2000. 50pp.

    During the Nazi occupation of France, Monique's mother hides a Jewish family in her basement and tries to help them escape to freedom.

**Rubin, Susan Goldman.** *Fireflies in the Dark: The Story of Friedl Dicker-Brandeis and the Children of Terezin.* Holiday House, c2000. 47pp. (NF)

    Covers the years during which Friedl Dicker, a Jewish woman from Czechoslovakia, taught art to children at the Terezin Concentration Camp. Includes art created by teacher and students, excerpts from diaries, and interviews with camp survivors.

**Say, Allen.** *Grandfather's Journey.* Houghton Mifflin, c1993. 32pp.

    A Japanese American man recounts his grandfather's journey to America, which he later also undertakes, and the feeling of being torn by love for two different countries.

**Seuss, Dr.** *The Butter Battle Book.* Random House, c1984. 48pp.

    Engaged in a long-running battle, the Yooks and the Zooks develop more and more sophisticated weaponry as they attempt to outdo each other.

# Picture Books About War

**Turner, Ann Warren.** *The Drummer Boy: Marching to the Civil War.* HarperCollins, c1998. 32pp.
> A thirteen-year-old soldier, coming of age during the American Civil War, beats his drum to raise tunes and spirits and muffle the sounds of the dying.

**Turner, Ann Warren.** *Katie's Trunk.* Aladdin Paperbacks, 1997, c1992. 32pp.
> Katie, whose family is not sympathetic to the rebel soldiers during the American Revolution, hides under the clothes in her mother's wedding trunk when they invade her home.

**Uchida, Yoshiko.** *The Bracelet.* Philomel Books, c1993. 32pp.
> Emi, a Japanese American in the second grade, is sent with her family to an internment camp during World War II, but the loss of the bracelet her best friend has given her proves that she does not need a physical reminder of that friendship.

# Pirates

## Books for Ages 12–15

**Fleischman, Sid.** *The Giant Rat of Sumatra, or, Pirates Galore.* Greenwillow Books, c2005. 194pp.
A cabin boy on a pirate ship finds himself in San Diego in 1846 as war breaks out between the United States and Mexico.

**Jacques, Brian.** *The Angel's Command: A Tale from the Castaways of the Flying Dutchman.* Philomel Books, c2003. 374pp.
Ben and Ned, a boy and dog gifted with eternal youth and the ability to communicate with one another nonverbally, encounter pirates on the high seas and rescue a kidnapped prince from a band of gypsy thieves.

**Lawrence, Iain.** *The Buccaneers.* Delacorte Press, c2001. 244pp.
In the eighteenth century, sixteen-year-old John Spencer sails from England in his schooner, the *Dragon,* to the Caribbean, where he and the crew encounter pirates, fierce storms, fever, and a strange man who some fear may be cursed.

**Meyer, L. A.** *Bloody Jack: Being An Account of the Curious Adventures of Mary "Jacky" Faber, Ship's Boy.* Harcourt, c2002. 278pp. (and sequels)
Reduced to begging and thievery in the streets of London, a thirteen-year-old orphan disguises herself as a boy and connives her way onto a British warship setting out for high sea adventure in search of pirates.

**Montgomery, Hugh.** *The Voyage of the Arctic Tern.* Candlewick Press, c2002. 212pp.
A simple fisherman betrays his village for a handful of jewels, a group of courageous Englishmen foil a treacherous Spanish pirate, and a lost soul seeks to redress an ancient wrong by finding a treasure chest.

**Moore, Robin.** *The Man with the Silver Oar.* HarperCollins, c2002. 183pp.
In 1718, fifteen-year-old Daniel leaves his guardian uncle's Quaker household to stow away on a ship in pursuit of a pirate captain bent on raiding the coast of North America before returning to port in Hispaniola.

**Platt, Richard.** *Pirate Diary: The Journal of Jake Carpenter.* Candlewick Press, c2001. 64pp.
The fictional diary of a ten-year-old boy, who in 1716 sets off from North Carolina to become a sailor, but ends up a pirate instead.

## Books for Older Teens

**Bunch, Chris.** *Corsair.* Warner Books, c2001. 406pp.
Captain Gareth Radnor leads a war of revenge against the Linyati, who enslaved and murdered his family—but his battle against them takes on a new dimension when he discovers that the Linyati are not human.

# Pirates

**Dumas, Alexandre.** *The Count of Monte Cristo.* Penguin Books, c2003. 1276pp.

After escaping from the island fortress where he has been imprisoned for treason, young sailor Edmund Dantes sets out to discover the treasure of Monte Cristo and seek revenge against the people who falsely accused him.

**Lee, Tanith.** *Piratica: Being a Daring Tale of a Singular Girl's Adventure Upon the High Seas.* Dutton Children's Books, 2004, c2003. 288pp.

Artemesia finally escapes the prim and proper world of finishing schools and sets out to win her mother's title as pirate queen of the seas, until she meets her match in Goldie Girl, the treacherous captain of the pirate ship *Enemy.*

**Llywelyn, Morgan.** *Grania: She-King of the Irish Seas.* Forge, c2003. 412pp.

Brings to life the spirited story of Grace O'Malley, an Irish chieftain-pirate who struggled to survive the attacks of England's Elizabeth I in the sixteenth century.

**Rees, Celia.** *Pirates!: The True and Remarkable Adventures of Minerva Sharpe and Nancy Kington, Female Pirates.* Bloomsbury (distributed to the trade by Holtzbrinck), c2003. 379pp.

At the dawn of the eighteenth century, Nancy Kington and Minerva Sharpe set sail from Jamaica on a pirate vessel, hoping to escape from an arranged marriage and slavery.

# Questionable Medical Ethics

## Books for Ages 12–15

**Farmer, Nancy.** *The House of the Scorpion.* Atheneum Books for Young Readers, c2002. 380pp.
In a future where humans despise clones, Matt enjoys special status as the young clone of El Patron, the 142-year-old leader of a corrupt drug empire nestled between Mexico and the United States.

**Haddix, Margaret Peterson.** *Among the Hidden.* Simon & Schuster Books for Young Readers, c1998. 153pp. (and sequels)
In a future where the Population Police enforce the law limiting a family to only two children, Luke has lived all his twelve years in isolation and fear on his family's farm, until another "third" convinces him that the government is wrong.

**Haddix, Margaret Peterson.** *Double Identity.* Simon & Schuster Books for Young Readers, c2005. 218pp.
Thirteen-year-old Bethany's parents have always been overprotective, so when they suddenly drop out of sight with no explanation, leaving her with an aunt she never knew existed, Bethany uncovers shocking secrets that make her question everything she thought she knew about herself and her family.

**Haddix, Margaret Peterson.** *Running out of Time.* Simon & Schuster Books for Young Readers, c1995. 184pp.
When a diphtheria epidemic hits her village in 1840, thirteen-year-old Jessie discovers that it is actually a 1995 tourist site under observation by heartless scientists, and it's up to Jessie to escape the village and save the lives of the dying children.

**Haddix, Margaret Peterson.** *Turnabout*. Simon & Schuster Books for Young Readers, c2000. 223pp.
Melly and Anny Beth agree to participate in Project Turnabout, a scientific experiment in which they are given a shot that will make them grow younger, until they receive a second injection that will stop the aging process. But when other participants die after receiving the second shot, Melly and Anny Beth refuse to have the shot and set out to find someone to care for them when they become too young to do it themselves.

**Halam, Ann.** *Dr. Franklin's Island.* Dell Laurel-Leaf, 2003, c2002. 245pp.
When their plane crashes over the Pacific Ocean, three science students are left stranded on a tropical island and then imprisoned by a doctor who is performing horrifying experiments on humans involving the transfer of animal genes.

**Halam, Ann.** *Taylor Five.* Wendy Lamb Books, c2004. 197pp.
Fourteen-year-old Taylor is still dealing with the fact that she is a clone produced by the same company that funds the Orangutan Reserve that is her home on the island of Borneo, when the Reserve is attacked and she flees with her younger brother and her uncle, the Reserve's mascot.

**Lowry, Lois.** *The Giver.* Houghton Mifflin, c1993. 180pp.
Given his lifetime assignment at the Ceremony of Twelve, Jonas becomes the receiver of memories shared by only one other in his community and discovers the terrible truth about the society in which he lives.

# Questionable Medical Ethics

## Books for Older Teens

**Cook, Robin.** *Coma*. Center Point, Bolinda, 2003, c1977. 415pp. (adult)
   The deaths of several patients who were admitted to the hospital for routine surgeries and ended up with destroyed brains prompts a medical student to investigate what is really going on.

**Crichton, Michael.** *Jurassic Park*. Ballantine Books, c1991. 400pp. (adult)
   An account of the attempt, through a hair-raising twenty-four hours on a remote jungle island, to avert a global emergency—a crisis triggered by today's rush to commercialize genetic engineering.

**Dickinson, Peter.** *Eva*. Bantam Doubleday Dell Books for Young Readers, 1990, c 1988. 219pp.
   After a terrible accident, a young girl wakes up to discover that she has been given the body of a chimpanzee.

**Keyes, Daniel.** *Flowers for Algernon*. Harcourt Brace, c1966. 286pp.
   After being mentally retarded for all of his thirty-two years, Charlie Gordon undergoes an operation designed to change his life.

**Layne, Steven L.** *This Side of Paradise.* Pelican Books, c2001. 215pp.
   After his father begins working for the mysterious Eden Corporation, Jack uncovers a sinister plot that threatens the existence of his entire family.

**Trueman, Terry.** *Stuck in Neutral*. HarperCollins, c2000. 114pp.
   Fourteen-year-old Shawn McDaniel, who suffers from severe cerebral palsy and cannot function, relates his perceptions of his life, his family, and his condition, especially as he believes his father is planning to kill him.

# Tattooing and Body Art

## Books for Ages 12–15

**Almond, David.** *The Fire-Eaters.* Yearling, c2005. 218pp.
Despite observing his father's illness and the suffering of the fire-eating Mr. McNulty, as well as enduring abuse at school and the stress of the Cuban Missile Crisis, Bobby Burns and his family and friends, living in England in 1962, still find reasons to rejoice in their lives and to have hope for the future.

**Bass, L. G.** *Sign of the Qin.* Hyperion Books for Children, c2004. 383pp.
In long-ago China, Prince Zong, the mortal young Starlord chosen to save humankind from destruction, joins the twin outlaws, White Streak and Black Whirlwind, to fight the Lord of the Dead and his demon hordes.

**Brin, Susannah.** *The Rabbit Tattoo.* Artesian Press, c2001. 67pp.
A teenager named Bags is intrigued by his new neighbor, Alexander, a young man with a sharp tongue, a talent for magic, and a mysterious rabbit tattoo on his neck.

**Dahl, Roald.** *Skin and Other Stories.* Viking Press, c2000. 212pp.
Introduces teenagers to the adult short stories of Roald Dahl.

**Desai Hidier, Tanuja.** *Born Confused.* Scholastic Press, c2002. 413pp.
As Dimple Lala turns seventeen, she realizes that life is about to become more complex as her best friend starts pulling away and her parents try to find a suitable boyfriend for Dimple, despite the fact that she is not interested.

**Hoffman, Alice.** *Green Angel.* Scholastic Press, c2003. 116pp.
Haunted by grief and her past after losing her family in a fire, fifteen-year-old Green retreats into her ruined garden as she struggles to survive emotionally and physically on her own.

**Meyer, L. A.** *Bloody Jack: Being an Account of the Curious Adventures of Mary "Jacky" Faber, Ship's Boy.* Harcourt, c2002. 278pp.
Reduced to begging and thievery in the streets of London, a thirteen-year-old orphan disguises herself as a boy and connives her way onto a British warship setting out for high sea adventure in search of pirates.

**Meyer, L. A.** *Curse of the Blue Tattoo: Being an Account of the Misadventures of Jacky Faber, Midshipman and Fine Lady.* Harcourt, c2004. 488pp.
In 1803, after being exposed as a girl and forced to leave her ship, Jacky Faber finds herself attending school in Boston, where, instead of learning to be a lady, she battles her snobbish classmates, roams the city in search of adventure, and learns to ride a horse.

**Weyn, Suzanne.** *The Bar Code Tattoo.* Scholastic, c2004. 252pp.
Kayla is ostracized at school because she refused to get the required tattooed bar code, and now she and her family must run to avoid the threats against them.

**Wilson, Jacqueline.** *The Illustrated Mum.* Delacorte Press, 2005, c1999. 282pp.
Ten-year-old Dolphin is determined to stay with her family, no matter what, but when her sister goes to live with her newly discovered father, sending their mother further into manic depression, Dolphin's life takes a turn for the better.

# Vampires

## Books for Ages 12–15

**Hautman, Pete.** *Sweetblood*. Simon & Schuster Books for Young Readers, c2003. 180pp.

After a lifetime of being a model student, sixteen-year-old Lucy Szabo is suddenly in trouble at school, at home, with the so-called vampires she has met online and in person, and most of all with her uncontrolled diabetes.

**Klause, Annette Curtis.** *The Silver Kiss*. Dell, 1992, c1990. 198pp.

A mysterious teenage boy harboring a dark secret helps Zoe come to terms with her mother's terminal illness.

**Rees, Douglas.** *Vampire High*. Delacorte Press, c2003. 226pp.

When his family moves from California to New Sodom, Massachusetts, and Cody enters Vlad Dracul Magnet School, many things seem strange, from the dark-haired, pale-skinned, supernaturally strong students to Charon, the wolf who guides him around campus on the first day.

**Schreiber, Ellen.** *Vampire Kisses*. HarperCollins, c2003. 197pp.

Sixteen-year-old Raven, an outcast who always wears black and hopes to become a vampire some day, falls in love with the mysterious new boy in town, eager to find out if he can make her dreams come true.

**Vande Velde, Vivian.** *Companions of the Night*. Harcourt Brace, c1995. 212pp.

When sixteen-year-old Kerry Nowicki helps a young man escape from a group of men who claim he is a vampire, she finds herself faced with some bizarre and dangerous choices.

## Books for Older Teens

**Anderson, M. T.** *Thirsty*. Candlewick Press, 2003, c1997. 249pp.

From the moment he knows that he is destined to be a vampire, Chris thirsts for the blood of people around him while also struggling to remain human.

**Atwater-Rhodes, Amelia.** *Demon in My View.* Delacorte Press, c2000. 176pp.

Seventeen-year-old Jessica Allodola discovers that the vampire world of her fiction is real when she develops relationships with an alluring vampire named Aubrey and the teenage witch who is trying to save Jessica from his clutches.

**Atwater-Rhodes, Amelia.** *In the Forests of the Night.* Dell Laurel-Leaf, 2000, c 1999. 147pp.

Risika, a teenage vampire, wanders back in time to the year 1684 when, as a human, she died and was transformed against her will.

**Atwater-Rhodes, Amelia.** *Midnight Predator.* Dell Laurel-Leaf, 2003, c2002. 248pp.

Vampire hunter Turquoise Draka goes undercover as a human slave to enter the fabled vampire realm of Midnight and assassinate Jeshikah, one of the cruelest vampires in history. But her disguise brings up old memories of her past enslavement, and she finds herself comforted by her benign master, Jaguar.

From Nancy J. Keane, *The Big Book of Teen Reading Lists: 100 Great, Ready-to-Use Book Lists for Educators, Librarians, Parents, and Children.* Westport, CT: Libraries Unlimited, 2006. Copyright © 2006 by Libraries Unlimited.

# Vampires

**Atwater-Rhodes, Amelia.** *Shattered Mirror.* Delacorte Press, c2001. 227pp.
As seventeen-year-old Sarah, daughter of a powerful line of vampire-hunting witches, continues to pursue the ancient bloodsucker Nikolas, she finds herself in a dangerous friendship with two vampire siblings in her high school.

**Bennett, Nigel.** *His Father's Son.* Baen, (distributed by Simon & Schuster), c2001. 337pp.
Richard Dun—a vampire for more than a thousand years who has had many identities in that time, including Sir Lancelot of Arthur's court—tries to cull wisdom from the centuries-old advice of his former lover, the high priestess Sabra, in order to protect his current love, Stephanie, from danger and accept the fact that, due to his life as a vampire, he cannot be her partner.

**King, Stephen.** *'Salem's Lot.* Doubleday, c1975. 451pp. (adult)
A stranger with an evil secret harms the lives of many inhabitants of a small New England town.

**McKinley, Robin.** *Sunshine.* Berkley Books, c2003. 389pp.
Sunshine is abducted by a vampire, and as she waits throughout the night, fearing the worst, she forms an unlikely bond with her captor.

**Meyer, Stephenie.** *Twilight.* Little, Brown, c2005. 498pp.
When seventeen-year-old Bella leaves Phoenix to live with her father in Forks, Washington, she meets an exquisitely handsome boy at school, for whom she feels an overwhelming attraction, and who she comes to realize is not wholly human.

**Rice, Anne.** *Interview with the Vampire.* Knopf, c1976. 371pp.
Contains the e hypnotic, shocking, and erotic confessions of a vampire.

**Stine, R. L.** *Dangerous Girls: A Novel.* HarperCollins, c2003. 247pp.
After sixteen-year-old Destiny and her twin sister Livvy are turned into partial vampires at a summer camp, they try to find the "Restorer," who can return them to normal.

# Violence

## Books for Ages 12–15

**Adoff, Jaime.** *Names Will Never Hurt Me.* Dutton Children's Books, c2004. 185pp.
Several high school students relate their feelings about school, themselves, and events as they unfold on the fateful one-year anniversary of the killing of a fellow student.

**Flake, Sharon.** *The Skin I'm In.* Jump at the Sun/Hyperion Books for Children, c1998. 171pp.
Thirteen-year-old Maleeka, uncomfortable because her skin is extremely dark, meets a new teacher with a birthmark on her face and makes some discoveries about how to love who she is and what she looks like.

**Flinn, Alex.** *Fade to Black.* HarperTempest, c2005. 184pp.
An HIV-positive high school student hospitalized after being attacked; the bigot accused of the crime; and the only witness, a classmate with Down Syndrome, reveal how the assault has changed their lives as they tell about its aftermath.

**Howe, James.** *The Misfits.* Atheneum Books for Young Readers, c2001. 274pp.
Four students who do not fit in at their small-town middle school decide to create a third party for the student council elections to represent all students who have ever been called names.

**Huser, Glen.** *Stitches.* Groundwood Books (distributed by Publishers Group West), c2003. 198pp.
Travis, a middle school student who wants to become a professional puppeteer, has endured years of torment from a trio of bullies, but he finds himself fighting for his life when the harassment turns to violence just after the ninth-grade dance.

**Koertge, Ronald.** *Margaux with an X.* Candlewick Press, c2004. 165pp.
Margaux, known as a "tough chick" at her Los Angeles high school, makes a connection with Danny, who, like her, struggles with the emotional impact of family violence and abuse.

**Koja, Kathe.** *Buddha Boy.* Farrar, Straus & Giroux, c2003. 117pp.
Justin spends time with Jinsen, the unusual and artistic new student whom the school bullies torment and call Buddha Boy, and ends up making choices that affect Jinsen, himself, and the entire school.

**Koss, Amy Goldman.** *The Girls.* Dial Books for Young Readers, c2000. 121pp.
Each of the girls in a middle school clique reveals the strong, manipulative hold that one of the group exerts on the others, causing hurt and self-doubt among the girls.

**Lynch, Chris.** *Who the Man.* HarperCollins, c2002. 186pp.
Thirteen-year-old Earl Pryor is much too big for his age, and much too powerful for the anger that rages within him when classmates tease him, the girl he likes disappoints him, or his parents' problems get too real.

**Plum-Ucci, Carol.** *The Body of Christopher Creed.* Harcourt, c2000. 248pp.
Torey Adams, a high school junior with a seemingly perfect life, struggles with doubts and questions surrounding the mysterious disappearance of the class outcast.

# Violence

**Plum-Ucci, Carol.** *What Happened to Lani Garver.* Harcourt, c2002. 307pp.

Sixteen-year-old Claire is unable to face her fears about a recurrence of her leukemia, her eating disorder, her need to fit in with the popular crowd on Hackett Island, and her mother's alcoholism, until the enigmatic Lani Garver helps her get control of her life at the risk of his own.

**Strasser, Todd.** *Give a Boy a Gun.* Simon Pulse, 2002, c2000. 208pp.

Events leading up to a night of terror at a high school dance are told from the point of view of various people involved.

## Books for Older Teens

**Atkins, Catherine.** *Alt Ed.* Putnam, c2003. 198pp.

Participating in a special after-school counseling class with other troubled students, including a sensitive gay classmate, helps Susan, an overweight tenth grader, develop a better sense of herself.

**Brugman, Alyssa.** *Walking Naked.* Delacorte Press, 2004, c2002. 185pp.

After being in detention with a girl called "The Freak," Megan finds herself torn between the developing friendship the two share and her involvement with a popular clique.

**Carbone, Elisa Lynn.** *The Pack.* Viking Press, c2003. 153pp.

Akhil Vyas, a new boy in school, reluctantly decides that to prevent a violent crime, he must tell Omar and Becky his secret.

**Crutcher, Chris.** *Whale Talk.* Greenwillow Books, c2001. 220pp.

Intellectually and athletically gifted, TJ, a multiracial, adopted teenager, shuns organized sports and the gung-ho athletes at his high school, until he agrees to form a swimming team and recruits some of the school's less popular students.

**Flinn, Alex.** *Breaking Point.* HarperTempest, 2003, c2002. 240pp.

Fifteen-year-old Paul enters an exclusive private school and falls under the spell of a charismatic boy who may be using him.

**Flinn, Alex.** *Breathing Underwater.* HarperTempest, 2002, c2001. 263pp.

Sent to counseling for hitting his girlfriend, Caitlin, and ordered to keep a journal, sixteen-year-old Nick recounts his relationship with Caitlin, examines his controlling behavior and anger, and describes living with his abusive father.

**Giles, Gail.** *Shattering Glass.* Roaring Brook Press, c2002. 215pp.

Rob, the charismatic leader of the senior class, provokes unexpected violence when he turns the school nerd into Prince Charming.

**Mac, Carrie.** *The Beckoners.* Orca Book, c2004. 217pp.

Zoe, unhappy to be moving once again, falls in with the Beckoners, a group of bullies at her new school, but she soon finds herself trying to get free from the gang, whose actions against their favorite target, a girl they call Dog, are escalating to violence.

**Myers, Walter Dean.** *Autobiography of My Dead Brother.* HarperTempest, c2005. 212pp.

Jesse pours his heart and soul into his sketchbook to make sense of life in his troubled Harlem neighborhood and of the loss of a close friend.

# Violence

**Myers, Walter Dean.** *Monster*. HarperCollins, c1999. 281pp.

While on trial as an accomplice to a murder, sixteen-year-old Steve Harmon records his experiences in prison and in the courtroom, in the form of a film script, as he tries to come to terms with the course his life has taken.

**Myers, Walter Dean.** *Shooter*. HarperTempest, 2005, c2004. 223pp.

Written in the form of interviews, reports, and journal entries, the story of three troubled teenagers ends in a tragic school shooting.

# What's Real? Books That Question Our Reality

Compiled by Patti Cook, Wired for Youth Librarian, Austin Public Library, Texas.

## Books for Ages 12–15

**Almond, David.** *Skellig*. Delacorte Press, 1999, c1998. 182pp.
Unhappy about his baby sister's illness and the chaos of moving into a dilapidated old house, Michael retreats to the garage, where he finds a mysterious stranger who is something like a bird and something like an angel.

**Clements, Andrew.** *Things Not Seen*. Philomel Books, c2002. 251pp.
When fifteen-year-old Bobby wakes up and finds himself invisible, he and his parents and his new blind friend, Alicia, try to find out what caused his condition and how to reverse it.

**Hoffman, Alice.** *Green Angel*. Scholastic Press, c2003. 116pp.
Haunted by grief and her past after losing her family in a fire, fifteen-year-old Green retreats into her ruined garden as she struggles to survive emotionally and physically on her own.

**L'Engle, Madeleine.** *A Wrinkle in Time*. Farrar, Straus & Giroux, 1999, c1962. 203pp.
Three extraterrestrial beings take Meg and her friends to another world.

**Lowry, Lois.** *The Giver*. Houghton Mifflin, c1993. 180pp.
Given his lifetime assignment at the Ceremony of Twelve, Jonas becomes the receiver of memories shared by only one other in his community and discovers the terrible truth about the society in which he lives.

**Rylant, Cynthia.** *God Went to Beauty School*. HarperTempest, c2003. 56pp.
A novel in poems that reveal God's discovery of the wonders and pains in the world he has created.

**Walter, Virginia.** *Making up Megaboy*. Dorling Kindersley, c1998. 64pp.
When thirteen-year-old Robbie shoots an old man in a liquor store, everyone who knows the quiet, withdrawn youth struggles to understand this act of seemingly random violence.

## Books for Older Teens

**Block, Francesca Lia.** *I Was a Teenage Fairy*. Joanna Cotler, 2000, c1998. 186pp.
A feisty, sexy fairy helps a young woman heal traumas from her past.

**Burgess, Melvin.** *Lady: My Life as a Bitch*. H. Holt, c2002. 235pp.
Seventeen-year-old Sandra Francy is having way too much fun, and even though everyone wants her to calm down and be sensible, she refuses, until she is accidentally turned into a dog and finds that life as a canine has its own appeal.

**Sebold, Alice.** *The Lovely Bones*. Little, Brown, c2002. 328pp. (adult)
Fourteen-year-old Susie Salmon, the victim of a sexual assault and murder, looks on from the afterlife as her family deals with their grief, and waits for her killer to be brought to some type of justice.

# Winter

## Books for Ages 12–15

**Colfer, Eoin.** *Artemis Fowl: The Arctic Incident.* Hyperion Paperbacks for Children, c2002. 277pp.
Thirteen-year-old criminal mastermind Artemis Fowl must join forces with his nemesis, Captain Holly Short of the LEPrecon fairy police, to save his father—one of the few people in the world Artemis loves—who has been kidnapped by the Russian Mafiya.

**Cooper, Susan.** *The Dark Is Rising* Aladdin Paperbacks, 1986, c1973. 244pp.
On his eleventh birthday Will Stanton discovers that he is the last of the Old Ones, destined to seek the six magical Signs that will enable the Old Ones to triumph over the evil forces of the Dark.

**Crutcher, Chris.** *Stotan!* Greenwillow Books, c1986. 183pp.
A high school coach invites members of his swimming team to a memorable week of rigorous training that tests their moral fiber as well as their physical stamina.

**Gray, Dianne E.** *Together Apart.* Houghton Mifflin, c2002. 193pp.
In 1888, a few months after barely surviving a deadly blizzard that has killed two of her brothers, fifteen-year-old Hannah goes to work at the home of a wealthy widow whose progressive social ideas scandalize the town of Prairie Hill, Nebraska.

**Hobbs, Will.** *Far North.* Morrow Junior Books, c1996. 226pp.
After the destruction of their float plane, sixteen-year-old Gabe and his Dene friend, Raymond, struggle to survive a winter in the wilderness of the Northwest Territories of Canada.

**Horowitz, Anthony.** *Stormbreaker*. Philomel Books, 2001, c2000. 192pp.
After the death of the uncle who had been his guardian, fourteen-year-old Alex Rider is coerced into continuing his uncle's dangerous work for Britain's intelligence agency, MI6.

**Houston, James A.** *Frozen Fire: A Tale of Courage.* Margaret K. McElderry, 1986, c1977. 149pp.
Determined to find his father, who has been lost in a storm, a young boy and his Eskimo friend brave windstorms, starvation, wild animals, and wild men during their search in the Canadian Arctic.

**Lester, Alison.** *The Snow Pony.* Houghton Mifflin, c2003. 194pp.
Prolonged drought has strained Dusty's ranching family to the breaking point, but she finds consolation with her wild and beautiful horse.

**Lewis, C. S.** *The Lion, the Witch, and the Wardrobe.* HarperCollins, 2000, c 1978. 50pp.
An illustrated, abridged version of C. S. Lewis's classic, in which four English schoolchildren find their way through the back of a wardrobe into the magic land of Narnia and assist its ruler, the golden lion Aslan, to triumph over the White Witch, who has cursed the land with eternal winter.

**London, Jack.** *The Call of the Wild.* Atheneum Books for Young Readers, c1999. 112pp.
Buck, who is half St. Bernard and half Scotch shepher, is abducted and taken to the Klondike, where he reverts to the wild and becomes the leader of a pack of wolves.

**Mack, Tracy.** *Birdland*. Scholastic Press, c2003. 198pp.
Thirteen-year-old Jed spends Christmas break working on a school project filming a documentary about his East Village, New York City, neighborhood, where he is continually reminded of his older brother, Zeke, a promising poet who died the summer before.

# Winter

**Naylor, Phyllis Reynolds.** *Blizzard's Wake.* Atheneum Books for Young Readers, c2002. 212pp.

In March 1941, when a severe blizzard suddenly hits Bismarck, North Dakota, a girl trying to save her stranded father and brother inadvertently helps the man who killed her mother four years before.

**Pattou, Edith.** *East.* Harcourt, c2003. 498pp.

A young woman journeys to a distant castle on the back of a great white bear who is the victim of a cruel enchantment.

**Paulsen, Gary.** *Brian's Winter.* Delacorte Press, c1996. 133pp.

Instead of being rescued from a plane crash, as in the author's other book, *Hatchet,* this story portrays what would have happened to Brian had he been forced to survive a winter in the wilderness with only his survival pack and hatchet.

**Paulsen, Gary.** *Dogsong.* Atheneum Books for Young Readers, c1985. 177pp.

A fourteen-year-old Eskimo boy who feels assailed by the modernity of his life takes a 1,400-mile journey by dog sled across ice, tundra, and mountains, seeking his own "song" of himself.

**Paulsen, Gary.** *The Winter Room.* Orchard Books, c1989. 103pp.

A young boy growing up on a northern Minnesota farm describes the scenes around him and recounts his old Norwegian uncle's tales of an almost mythological logging past.

**Peyton, K. M.** *Snowfall.* Houghton Mifflin, c1998. 343pp.

Desperate to see the world beyond her grandfather's vicarage, sixteen-year-old Charlotte convinces her older brother to take her along on a mountain-climbing trip to Switzerland, where her life becomes intertwined with an assortment of people in Victorian society.

**Plummer, Louise.** *The Unlikely Romance of Kate Bjorkman.* Dell Laurel-Leaf, c1995. 183pp.

Seventeen-year-old Kate hopes for romance when her older brother's friend Richard comes to stay at their house during Christmas vacation.

**Rottman, S. L.** *Slalom.* Viking Press, c2004. 246pp.

Sandro Birch has a good chance of making the ski team and having a real family with his girlfriend, but first he must deal with his anger against his father, especially when the man returns after a seventeen-year absence.

**Woodson, Jacqueline.** *If You Come Softly.* Putnam, c1998. 181pp.

After meeting at their private school in New York, fifteen-year-old Jeremiah, who is black and whose parents are separated, and Ellie, who is white and whose mother has twice abandoned her, fall in love and then try to cope with people's reactions.

## Books for Older Teens

**Davis, Claire.** *Winter Range.* Picador USA, c2000. 262pp.

Sheriff Ike Parsons tries to help a local rancher who is down on his luck, but his good intentions are rejected, and the rancher is so insulted that he plots to kill Ike's wife.

# Winter

**Frazier, Charles.** *Cold Mountain.* Atlantic Monthly Press, c1997. 356pp.
Inman, a wounded Confederate soldier, leaves the hospital where he is being treated and determines to walk home to his sweetheart, Ada, only to find the land and the girl he remembers as changed by the war as he is.

**Guterson, David.** *Snow Falling on Cedars.* Harcourt Brace, c1994. 345pp.
When a newspaper journalist covers the trial of a Japanese American accused of murder, he must come to terms with his own past.

**Judson, William.** *Cold River: A Novel.* Signet, 1976, c1974. 182pp.
In the frozen Adirondacks in 1921, fourteen-year-old Lizzy and her younger brother Tim battle for survival after losing their father in one of the worst snowstorms of the century.

**Lawrence, Michael.** *A Crack in the Line.* Greenwillow Books, 2004, c2003. 323pp.
Sixteen-year-old Alaric discovers how to travel to an alternate reality, where his mother is alive and his place in the family is held by a girl named Naia.

**Martin, Nora.** *A Perfect Snow.* Bloomsbury Children's Books (distributed by St. Martin's Press), c2002. 144pp.
Seventeen-year-old Ben, living in a trailer park with his unemployed father and younger brother David, becomes involved in a violent white supremacy hate group operating in their small Montana town, but with the help of new girlfriend Eden, and a growing friendship with a local "rich kid," Ben begins to see the error in his thinking and tries to save his brother before it is too late.

**McDaniel, Lurlene.** *Starry, Starry Night: Three Holiday Stories.* Bantam Books, 2000, c1998. 255pp.
A collection of three stories in which teenagers face life-altering situations.

**Shreve, Anita.** *Light on Snow: A Novel.* Little, Brown, c2004. 305pp.
Twelve-year-old Nicky Dillon, still dealing with the loss of her mother and baby sister two years earlier and her grieving father's sudden decision to move to an isolated New England farmhouse, takes further steps into the adult world when she and her dad find an abandoned newborn clinging to life in the woods near their home, and later come to know the young mother and learn her story.

**Spinelli, Jerry.** *Milkweed: A Novel.* Knopf (distributed by Random House), c2003. 208pp.
A street child, known to himself only as Stopthief, finds community when he is taken in by a band of orphans in the Warsaw ghetto, which helps him weather the horrors of the Nazi regime.

**Werlin, Nancy.** *Black Mirror: A Novel.* Dial Books, c2001. 249pp.
Convinced her brother's death was murder rather than suicide, sixteen-year-old Frances begins her own investigation into suspicious student activities at her boarding school.

From Nancy J. Keane, *The Big Book of Teen Reading Lists: 100 Great, Ready-to-Use Book Lists for Educators, Librarians, Parents, and Children.* Westport, CT: Libraries Unlimited, 2006. Copyright © 2006 by Libraries Unlimited.

# Winter

## Nonfiction

### Books for Ages 12–15

**Paulsen, Gary.** *How Angel Peterson Got His Name: And Other Outrageous Tales About Extreme Sports.* Wendy Lamb Books, c2003. 111pp. (NF)
> Author Gary Paulsen relates tales from his youth in a small town in northwestern Minnesota in the late 1940s and early 1950s, such as skiing behind a souped-up car and imitating daredevil Evel Knievel.

**Pfetzer, Mark.** *Within Reach: My Everest Story.* Puffin Books, 2000, c 1998. 224pp. (NF)
> The author describes how he spent his teenage years climbing mountains in the United States, South America, Africa, and Asia, with an emphasis on his two expeditions up Mount Everest.

### Books for Older Teens

**Krakauer, Jon.** *Into Thin Air: A Personal Account of the Mount Everest Disaster*. Villard, c1997. 293pp. (adult) (NF)
> The author relates his experiences climbing Mount Everest during its deadliest season and examines what it is about the mountain that makes people willingly subject themselves to such risk, hardship, and expense.

**Paulsen, Gary.** *Winterdance: The Fine Madness of Running the Iditarod.* Harcourt Brace, c1994. 256pp. (NF)
> The author's account of his most ambitious quest: to know a world beyond his knowing, to train for and run the Iditarod.

**Read, Piers Paul.** *Alive: The Story of the Andes Survivors.* Avon Books, 2002, c1974. 398pp. (NF)
> Discusses the ordeal of the survivors of an airplane crash in 1972 in the Andes wilderness.

# World Literature; Global Fiction for Teens

Compiled by Beth Gallaway Youth Services Consultant/Trainer,
Metrowest MA Regional Library System, Massachusetts.

## Books for Ages 12–15

**Abelove, Joan.** *Go and Come Back*. Puffin Books, c2000. 176pp.
Anthropologists study a group of Peruvian natives in the late seventies.

**Alverez, Julia.** *Before We Were Free*. Knopf, c2002. 167pp.
Fictional account of growing up under the dictatorship of the Trujillo regime in the Dominican Republic.

**Belpre, Pura.** *Firefly Summer*. Pinata Books, c1996. 205pp.
At a plantation in rural Puerto Rico around the turn of the nineteenth century, the foreman pursues the mystery surrounding his family.

**Carmi, Danielle.** *Samir and Yonatan*. Arthur A. Levine Books, c2000. 183pp.
Samir, a young Palestinian boy, dreads going to an Israeli hospital for an operation, but once there, he bonds with an Israeli boy named Yonatan.

**Choi, Sook Nyul.** *The Year of Impossible Goodbyes*. Houghton Mifflin, c1991. 171pp.
A young Korean girl survives the oppressive Japanese and Russian occupation of North Korea during the 1940s, to later escape to freedom in South Korea.

**Ellis, Deborah.** *The Breadwinner*. Douglas & McIntyre, c2002. 170pp.
The Taliban hauls away Parvana's father, leaving her to become the "breadwinner" and disguise herself as a boy to support her mother, two sisters, and baby brother in war-ravaged Afghanistan.

**Hidier, Desai.** *Born Confused*. Scholastic, c2002. 413pp.
Seventeen-year-old Dimple, whose family is from India, discovers that she is not Indian enough for the Indians and not American enough for the Americans, as she sees her hypnotically beautiful, manipulative best friend taking possession of both her heritage and the boy she likes

**Ho, Minfong.** *The Clay Marble*. Farrar, Straus & Giroux, c1993. 163pp.
In the late 1970s, twelve-year-old Dara joins a refugee camp in war-torn Cambodia and becomes separated from her family.

**Na, An.** *A Step from Heaven*. Front Street, c2001. 156pp.
A young Korean girl and her family find it difficult to learn English and adjust to life in America.

**Napoli, Donna Jo.** *Beast*. Atheneum Books for Young Readers, c2000. 260pp.
Retelling of the legend of Beauty and the Beast, set in Persia

**Ryan, Pam Muñoz.** *Esperanza Rising*. Scholastic, c2000. 262pp.
Esperanza and her mother are forced to leave their life of wealth and privilege in Mexico to work in the labor camps of Southern California, where they must adapt to the harsh circumstances facing Mexican farm workers on the eve of the Great Depression.

From Nancy J. Keane, *The Big Book of Teen Reading Lists: 100 Great, Ready-to-Use Book Lists for Educators, Librarians, Parents, and Children*. Westport, CT: Libraries Unlimited, 2006. Copyright © 2006 by Libraries Unlimited.

# World Literature; Global Fiction for Teens

**Watkins, Yoko Kawashima.** *So Far from the Bamboo Grove*. Beech Tree Books, 1994, c1986. 183pp.
When World War II comes to an end, Japanese on the Korean peninsula near China's border are forced to move.

**Whelan, Gloria.** *Homeless Bird*. HarperCollins, c2000. 216pp.
When thirteen-year-old Koly enters into an ill-fated arranged marriage, she must either suffer a destiny dictated by India's tradition or find the courage to oppose it.

## Books for Older Teens

**Bagdasarian, Adam.** *Forgotten Fire*. DK Ink, c2000. 273pp.
Vahan survives the Turkish slaughter of Armenians between 1915 and 1923.

**Cisneros, Sandra.** *The House on Mango Street*. Knopf, c1998. 134pp.
Esperanza doesn't want to belong to the run-down Chicago suburan neighborhood she lives in, so she struggles to find a way to reinvent herself.

**Dalkey, Karen.** *Little Sister*. Harcourt, c1996. 200pp.
Thirteen-year-old Fujiwara no Mitsuko, daughter of a noble family in the imperial court of twelfth-century Japan, enlists the help of a shape-shifter and other figures from Japanese mythology in her efforts to save her older sister's life.

**Esquival, Laura.** *Like Water for Chocolate*. Doubleday, c1992. 245pp. (adult)
Romantic fantasy set in the early twentieth century about a young couple blocked from marrying by the demands of her cold and selfish mother. To be near his love the young man marries her sister, and she expresses her passion for him through her cooking.

**Hamilton, Morse.** *Yellow Blue Bus Means I Love You*. Greenwillow Books, c1994. 180pp.
Boarding school experience from the point of view of a Russian immigrant

**Kim, Helen.** *A Long Season of Rain*. H. Holt, c1996. 275pp.
When an orphan boy comes to live with her family, eleven-year-old Junehee begins to realize that the demands placed on Korean women can destroy their lives.

**Paton, Alan.** *Cry, the Beloved Country*. Scribner Classics, c2003, c1948. 316pp.
A deeply moving story of Zulu pastor Stephen Kumalo and his son Absalom, set against the backdrop of a land and people driven by racial inequality and injustice, remains the most famous and important novel in South Africa's history

**Vijayaraghavan, Vineeta.** *The Motherland*. Soho, c2001. 231pp.
Concerned that fifteen-year-old Maya may have fallen under the bad influence of her New York friends, her parents send her to their extended family in Kerala, India, for the summer, where she discovers family secrets and her heritage.

# Part 6

## Audience

# Books That Changed the World

## Books for Ages 12–15

**Nelson, Peter.** *Left for Dead: A Young Man's Search for Justice for the USS* **Indianapolis**. Delacorte Press, c2002. 201pp. (NF)
> Recalls the sinking of the U.S.S. *Indianapolis* at the end of World War II, the Navy cover-up and unfair court martial of the ship's captain, and how a young boy helped the survivors set the record straight fifty-five years later.

**Rowling, J. K.** *Harry Potter and the Sorcerer's Stone*. A. A. Levine Books, c1998. 309pp.
> Rescued from the outrageous neglect of his aunt and uncle, a young boy with a great destiny proves his worth while attending Hogwarts School of Witchcraft and Wizardry.

## Books for Older Teens

**Caro, Robert A.** *The Power Broker: Robert Moses and the Fall of New York*. Knopf, 1994. 1,246pp. (NF)
> Biography of Robert Moses, a public administrator who created and carried out public works projects in New York City costing $27 billion over the course of forty-four years, looking at his powerful influence with some of the city's most important politicians and financiers.

**Darwin, Charles.** *The Origin of Species*. Oxford University Press, c1998. 439pp. (NF)
> Darwin's 1859 text, in which he defines his theory of evolution, arguing that species change over time, evolving or dying out entirely, through the process of natural selection.

*The Federalist Papers.* Signet Classic, c2003. 648pp. (NF)
> An annotated edition of *The Federalist Papers,* in which James Madison, Alexander Hamilton, and John Jay set forth the principles of American government, leading to the ratification of the U.S. Constitution. Includes an introduction by Isaac Kramnick and the text of the Constitution.

**Friedan, Betty.** *The Feminine Mystique*. W. W. Norton, 2001, c1963. 430pp. (NF)
> A reissue of the 1963 text that sparked the feminist movement through its analysis of the changing role and status of women, and includes an introduction by author Anna Quindlen in which she discusses the influence of the book on her personal history and society as a whole.

**Haley, Alex.** *Roots*. Dell, c1976. 729pp. (NF)
> Magnificent saga tracing the heritage of an American family from eighteenth-century Africa to the present.

**Harr, Jonathan.** *A Civil Action*. Vintage, 1996, c1995. 502pp. (NF)
> Follows a lawsuit brought against W.R. Grace & Co. for contaminating the drinking water in Woburn, Massachusetts.

**Lewis, Anthony.** *Gideon's Trumpet*. Vintage, 1989, c1964. 277pp. (NF)
> Account of Clarence Earl Gideon, who in 1962 was tried at the Supreme Court without a lawyer because he could not afford one, and how his case has changed the law of the United States.

# Books That Changed the World

**Locke, John.** *Two Treatises of Government.* Cambridge University Press, c1988. 464pp. (NF)
Locke's seventeenth-century classic work on political and social theory; includes a history of the text, as well as notes and a bibliography.

**Sinclair, Upton.** *The Jungle.* Amereon House, c1999. 341pp.
Describes the conditions of the Chicago stockyards through the eyes of a young immigrant struggling to get by in America.

**Tey, Josephine.** *The Daughter of Time.* Scribner Paperback Fiction, 1995, c1979. 206pp.
Follows Alan Grant, an injured policeman currently hospitalized and bored, as he searches for the truth behind the belief that Richard III murdered the little princes in the tower.

# Father-Son Book Club

## Books for Ages 12–15

**Bauer, Joan.** *Stand Tall.* Putnam, c2002. 182pp.
Tree, a six-foot-three-inch twelve-year-old, copes with his parents' recent divorce and his failure as an athlete by helping his grandfather, a Vietnam vet and recent amputee, and Sophie, a new girl at school.

**Colfer, Eoin.** *Artemis Fowl.* Hyperion Books for Children, c2001. 277pp. (and sequels)
When a twelve-year-old evil genius tries to restore his family fortune by capturing a fairy and demanding a ransom in gold, the fairies fight back with magic, technology, and a nasty troll.

**Farmer, Nancy.** *The Ear, the Eye, and the Arm.* Orchard Books, 2004, c1994. 311pp.
In 2194 in Zimbabwe, General Matsika's three children are kidnapped and put to work in a plastic mine, while three mutant detectives use their special powers to search for them.

**Hiaasen, Carl.** *Flush.* Knopf (distributed by Random House), c2005. 263pp.
With their father jailed for sinking a river boat, Noah Underwood and his younger sister, Abbey, must gather evidence that the owner of the floating casino is emptying his bilge tanks into the protected waters around their Florida Keys home.

**Hiaasen, Carl.** *Hoot.* Knopf (distributed by Random House), c2002. 292pp.
Roy, who is new to his small Florida community, becomes involved in another boy's attempt to save a colony of burrowing owls from a proposed construction site.

**Hoobler, Dorothy.** *The Demon in the Teahouse.* Philomel Books, c2001. 181pp.
In eighteenth-century Japan, fourteen-year-old Seikei, a merchant's son in training to be a samurai, helps his patron investigate a series of murders and arson in the capital city of Edo, each of which is associated in some way with a popular geisha.

**Hoobler, Dorothy.** *The Ghost in the Tokaido Inn.* Philomel Books, c1999. 214pp.
In eighteenth-century Japan, while attempting to solve the mystery of a stolen jewel, Seikei, a merchant's son who longs to be a samurai, joins a group of kabuki actors.

**Horowitz, Anthony.** *Stormbreaker.* Philomel Books, 2001, c2000. 192pp.
After the death of the uncle who had been his guardian, fourteen-year-old Alex Rider is coerced into continuing his uncle's dangerous work for Britain's intelligence agency, MI6.

**Karr, Kathleen.** *Playing with Fire.* Farrar, Straus & Giroux, c2001. 185pp.
Greer spends the summer of 1924 at a Long Island seashore mansion, where she helps her psychic mother and a sinister magician conduct séances, and finds new direction for her life.

**Mikaelsen, Ben.** *Red Midnight.* HarperCollins/Rayo, c2002. 212pp.
After soldiers kill his family, twelve-year-old Santiago and his four-year-old sister flee Guatemala in a kayak and try to reach the United States.

**Oppel, Kenneth.** *Silverwing.* Aladdin Paperbacks, 1999, c1997. 216pp.
When a newborn bat named Shade but sometimes called "Runt" becomes separated from his colony during migration, he grows in ways that prepare him for even greater journeys.

# Father-Son Book Club

**Paulsen, Gary.** *Guts: The True Stories Behind Hatchet and the Brian Books.* Delacorte Press, c2001. 148pp.

> The author relates incidents in his life and how they inspired parts of his books about the character Brian Robeson.

**Plum-Ucci, Carol.** *The Body of Christopher Creed,* Harcourt, c2000. 248pp.

> Torey Adams, a high school junior with a seemingly perfect life, struggles with doubts and questions surrounding the mysterious disappearance of the class outcast.

**Sachar, Louis.** *Holes*. Farrar, Straus & Giroux, c1998. 233pp.

> As further evidence of his family's bad fortune, which they attribute to a curse on a distant relative, Stanley Yelnats is sent to a hellish correctional camp in the Texas desert, where he finds his first real friend, a treasure, and a new sense of himself.

**Salisbury, Graham.** *Eyes of the Emperor.* Wendy Lamb Books, c2005. 229pp.

> Following orders from the U.S. Army, several young Japanese American men train K-9 units to hunt Asians during World War II.

**Salisbury, Graham.** *Lord of the Deep*. Delacorte Press, c2001. 182pp.

> Working for his stepfather on a charter fishing boat in Hawaii teaches thirteen-year-old Mikey not just about fishing, but also about taking risks, making sacrifices, and facing some of life's difficult choices.

**Spinelli, Jerry.** *Maniac Magee: A Novel*. Little, Brown, c1990. 184pp.

> After his parents die, Jeffrey Lionel Magee's life becomes legendary, as he accomplishes athletic and other feats that awe his contemporaries.

**Trueman, Terry.** *Stuck in Neutral*. HarperCollins, c2000. 114pp.

> Fourteen-year-old Shawn McDaniel, who suffers from severe cerebral palsy and cannot function, relates his perceptions of his life, his family, and his condition, especially as he believes his father is planning to kill him.

**Wynne-Jones, Tim.** *The Boy in the Burning House*. Farrar, Straus & Giroux, 2001, c2000. 213pp.

> Trying to solve the mystery of his father's disappearance from their rural Canadian community, fourteen-year-old Jim gets help from the disturbed Ruth Rose, who suspects her stepfather, a local pastor.

**Yolen, Jane.** *Dragon's Blood.* Magic Carpet Books/Harcourt, 1996, c1982. 303pp.

> Jakkin, a bond boy who works as a Keeper in a dragon nursery on the planet Austar IV, secretly trains a fighting pit dragon of his own in hopes of winning his freedom.

**Yolen, Jane.** *Mightier Than the Sword: World Folktales for Strong Boys*. Harcourt, c2003. 112pp.

> A collection of folktales from around the world that demonstrate the triumph of brains over brawn.

**Yolen, Jane.** *Not One Damsel in Distress: World Folktales for Strong Girls*. Silver Whistle/Harcourt, c2000. 116pp.

> A collection of thirteen traditional tales from various parts of the world, each of whose main character is a fearless, strong, heroic, and resourceful woman.

# Father-Son Book Club

**Yolen, Jane.** *Odysseus in the Serpent Maze.* HarperCollins, c2001. 248pp.
Thirteen-year-old Odysseus, who longs to be a hero, has many opportunities to prove himself during an adventure that involves pirates and satyrs, a trip to Crete's Labyrinth, and more.

## Books for Older Teens

**Lubar, David.** *Hidden Talents.* Starscape, 2003, c1999. 213pp.
Thirteen-year-old Martin, a new student at an alternative school for misfits and problem students, falls in with a group of boys with psychic powers and discovers something surprising about himself.

# (Books That Appeal to) Goths

## Books for Ages 12–15

**Augarde, Steve.** *The Various*. David Fickling Books, c2004. 447pp.

While staying on her uncle's rundown farm in the Somerset countryside, twelve-year-old Midge discovers that she has a special connection to the Various, a tribe of "strange, wild—and sometimes deadly" fairies struggling to maintain their existence in the nearby woods.

**Barker, Clive.** *Abarat*. Joanna Cotler Books, c2002. 388pp. (and sequels)

Candy Quackenbush of Chickentown, Minnesota, journeys to the Abarat, an archipelago filled with strange wonders, and has a curious revelation: she has been here before, and it is her responsibility to save this mysterious place from the evil forces that threaten it.

**Cary, Kate.** *Bloodline: A Novel*. Razorbill, c2005. 324pp.

Nineteen-year-old John Shaw returns from World War I and is haunted by nightmares of not only the battles but the horrifying discovery that his regimental commander is descended from Count Dracula.

**Clarke, Judith.** *Kalpana's Dream*. Front Street, 2005, c2004. 164pp.

Neema's struggle to complete an essay on the topic "Who Am I" for her freshman English class is complicated by the arrival of Kampala, her Indian great-grandmother, who has come to Australia chasing her dream of flying. Although they do not speak the same language, the two find common ground in skateboarder Gull Oliver.

**Golden, Christopher.** *Prowlers*. Pocket Pulse, c2001. 290pp.

Nineteen-year-old Jack Dwyer searches for the killer of his best friend and discovers a band of beasts called the Prowlers, who disguise themselves as humans and feed on them as well.

**Gruber, Michael.** *The Witch's Boy*. HarperTempest, c2005. 377pp.

A grotesque foundling turns against the witch who sacrificed almost everything to raise him when he becomes consumed by the desire for money and revenge against those who have hurt him, but he eventually finds his true heart's desire.

**Halam, Ann.** *Dr. Franklin's Island*. Dell Laurel-Leaf, 2003, c2002. 245pp.

When their plane crashes into the Pacific Ocean, three science students are left stranded on a tropical island and then imprisoned by a doctor who is performing horrifying experiments on humans involving the transfer of animal genes.

**Hautman, Pete.** *Sweetblood*. Simon & Schuster Books for Young Readers, c2003. 180pp.

After a lifetime of being a model student, sixteen-year-old Lucy Szabo is suddenly in trouble at school, at home, with the so-called vampires she has met online and in person, and most of all with her uncontrolled diabetes.

**Hoffman, Alice.** *Green Angel*. Scholastic Press, c2003. 116pp.

Haunted by grief and her past after losing her family in a fire, fifteen-year-old Green retreats into her ruined garden as she struggles to survive emotionally and physically on her own.

From Nancy J. Keane, *The Big Book of Teen Reading Lists: 100 Great, Ready-to-Use Book Lists for Educators, Librarians, Parents, and Children*. Westport, CT: Libraries Unlimited, 2006. Copyright © 2006 by Libraries Unlimited.

# (Books That Appeal to) Goths

**Hoffman, Nina Kiriki.** *A Stir of Bones.* Viking Press, c2003. 211pp.
> After discovering the secrets that lie in an abandoned house, fourteen-year-old Susan Backstrom, with the help of some new friends, has the ability to make a safe, new life for herself.

**Klause, Annette Curtis.** *The Silver Kiss.* Dell, 1992, c1990. 198pp.
> A mysterious teenage boy harboring a dark secret helps Zoe come to terms with her mother's terminal illness.

**Naylor, Phyllis Reynolds.** *Jade Green: A Ghost Story.* Atheneum, c1999. 168pp.
> While living with her uncle in a house haunted by the ghost of a young woman, recently orphaned Judith Sparrow wonders if her one small transgression has caused mysterious happenings.

**Sedgwick, Marcus.** *The Book of Dead Days.* Wendy Lamb Books, c2004. 273pp.
> After making a pact with the devil years before, a magician named Valerian has only the days between Christmas and New Year's day to save his own life. He seeks the help of a servant boy and an orphan girl named Willow.

**Shan, Darren.** *Cirque du Freak.* Little, Brown, c2001. 266pp.
> Two boys who are best friends visit an illegal freak show, where an encounter with a vampire and a deadly spider forces them to make life-changing choices.

**Shusterman, Neal.** *Full Tilt: A Novel.* Simon & Schuster Books for Young Readers, c2003. 201pp.
> When sixteen-year-old Blake goes to a mysterious, by-invitation-only carnival, he somehow knows that it could save his comatose brother, but soon learns that much more is at stake if he fails to meet the challenge presented there by the beautiful Cassandra.

**Snyder, Midori.** *Hannah's Garden.* Viking Press, c2002. 247pp.
> Seventeen-year-old Cassie Brittman, looking forward to her violin recital and the prom, finds her life taking a very different direction when she and her mother are called to attend her dying grandfather. They arrive to discover his farm nearly destroyed—apparently by two feuding supernatural clans.

**Zevin, Gabrielle.** *Elsewhere.* Farrar, Straus & Giroux, c2005. 275pp.
> After fifteen-year-old Liz Hall is hit by a taxi and killed, she finds herself in a place that is both like and unlike Earth, where she must adjust to her new status and figure out how to "live."

## Books for Older Teens

**Aikawa, Yu.** *Dark Edge. 1*. ComicsOne, c2004. 194pp.
> Kurou Takagi is summoned to Yotsuji Private High School after his mother's death, where he finds his father—whom he believed was dead—is the proprietor, but he soon learns something strange is going on when he and some other students break the rule against being on campus after sundown and are attacked by zombies.

**Anderson, M. T.** *Thirsty*. Candlewick Press, 2005, c1997. 237pp.
> From the moment he knows that he is destined to be a vampire, Chris thirsts for the blood of people around him while also struggling to remain human.

# (Books That Appeal to) Goths

**Atwater-Rhodes, Amelia.** *Shattered Mirror*. Delacorte Press, c2001. 227pp.

As seventeen-year-old Sarah, daughter of a powerful line of vampire-hunting witches, continues to pursue the ancient bloodsucker Nikolas, she finds herself in a dangerous friendship with two vampire siblings in her high school.

**Banks, L. A.** *The Awakening: A Vampire Huntress Legend*. St. Martin's Griffin, c2003. 264pp.

When different factions in the vampire world set out to claim her for their own purposes, powerful vampire huntress Danali must place her trust in an ex-lover turned vampire in an effort to survive..

**Brooks, Bruce.** *All That Remains*. Atheneum Books for Young Readers, c2001. 168pp.

Contains three stories about young people who are doing their best to handle the loss of a loved one.

**Klause, Annette Curtis.** *Blood and Chocolate*. Bantam Doubleday Dell Books for Young Readers, 1999, c1997. 264pp.

Having fallen for a human boy, a beautiful teenage werewolf must battle both her packmates and the fear of the townspeople to decide where she belongs and with whom.

**Koontz, Dean R.** *Watchers*. Berkley Books, 2003, c1987. 487pp.

Relates the adventures of two creatures that have escaped from a secret, sinister government laboratory where experiments in genetic engineering are conducted.

**Kostova, Elizabeth.** *The Historian: A Novel*. Little, Brown, c2005. 642pp.

A young woman discovers an ancient book and a cache of old letters in her father's library, and thus begins her adventurous quest for the truth about Vlad the Impaler, a search that will span continents and generations and will involve a confrontation with the darkest powers of evil.

**Martinez, A. Lee.** *Gil's All Fright Diner*. Tor, c2005. 268pp.

Earl and Duke stop in at a roadside diner in Rockwood County, and Loretta, the cafe's owner, asks them to help solve the zombie problem that is troubling the town.

**Meyer, Stephenie.** *Twilight*. Little, Brown, c2005. 498pp.

When seventeen-year-old Bella leaves Phoenix to live with her father in Forks, Washington, she meets an exquisitely handsome boy at school, for whom she feels an overwhelming attraction and who she comes to realize is not wholly human.

**Rees, Douglas.** *Vampire High*. Delacorte Press, c2003. 226pp.

When his family moves from California to New Sodom, Massachusetts, and Cody enters Vlad Dracul Magnet School, many things seem strange, from the dark-haired, pale-skinned, supernaturally strong students to Charon, the wolf who guides him around campus on the first day.

**Westerfeld, Scott.** *Peeps: A Novel*. Razorbill, c2005. 312pp.

Cal Thompson is a carrier of a parasite that causes vampirism, and he must hunt down all of the girlfriends he has unknowingly infected.

**Young, Karen Romano.** *Cobwebs*. Greenwillow Books, c2004. 388pp.

Sixteen-year-old Nancy enjoys the colorful ethnic mix of her heritage in several different Brooklyn households, not suspecting how very strange that heritage is.

# Nonfiction for Reluctant Readers

## Books for Ages 12–15

**Adams, Simon.** *Code Breakers: From Hieroglyphs to Hackers.* DK, c2002. 96pp. (NF)
Describes the use of codes and code breaking, from ancient times to the present.

**Armstrong, Jennifer.** *Shipwreck at the Bottom of the World: The Extraordinary True Story of Shackleton and the* **Endurance.** Crown, 2000, c1998. 134pp. (NF)
Describes the events of the 1914 Shackleton Antarctic expedition during which, after being trapped in a frozen sea for nine months, their ship, *Endurance,* was finally crushed, forcing Shackleton and his men to make a very long and perilous journey to reach inhabited land.

**Bartoletti, Susan Campbell.** *Black Potatoes: The Story of the Great Irish Famine, 1845–1850.* Houghton Mifflin, c2001. 184pp. (NF)
Draws from letters, diaries, and other documents to chronicle the Irish potato famine of 1845–1850, describing the political and personal impact it had on Ireland and its people, and presenting illustrations from contemporary newspapers.

**Campbell, Andrea.** *Forensic Science: Evidence, Clues, and Investigation.* Chelsea House, 1999, c2000. 135pp. (NF)
Examines forensic science and how it can be used to apprehend criminals by finding clues in rug fibers, the way a bone is broken, DNA "fingerprints," and more.

**Fleischman, John.** *Phineas Gage: A Gruesome But True Story About Brain Science.* Houghton Mifflin, c2002. 86pp. (NF)
The true story of Phineas Gage, whose brain was pierced by an iron rod in 1848but who survived and became a case study in how the brain functions.

**Freedman, Russell.** *The Life and Death of Crazy Horse.* Holiday House, c1996. 166pp. (NF)
A biography of the Oglala leader who relentlessly resisted the white man's attempts to take over Indian lands.

**Glover, Savion.** *Savion!: My Life in Tap.* Morrow, c2000. 79pp. (NF)
Examines the life and career of the young tap dancer who speaks with his feet and who choreographed the Tony Award–winning Broadway show *Bring in da Noise, Bring in da Funk.*

**Hawk, Tony.** *Hawk: Occupation: Skateboarder.* Regan Books, 2001, c2000. 307pp. (NF)
Internationally known American skateboarding champ Tony Hawk chronicles his life and his very eventful involvement with the sport.

**Jackson, Livia Bitton.** *I Have Lived a Thousand Years: Growing Up in the Holocaust.* Aladdin Paperbacks, 1999, c1997. 234pp. (NF)
A memoir by Elli Friedmann, in which she tells about her experiences at Auschwitz concentration camp, where she was taken at the age of thirteen in 1944 when the Nazis invaded her native Hungary.

# Nonfiction for Reluctant Readers

**Jiang, Ji-li.** *Red Scarf Girl: A Memoir of the Cultural Revolution.* HarperCollins, c1997. 285pp. (NF)
The author tells about the happy life she led in China until she was twelve years old, when her family became a target of the Cultural Revolution, and discusses the choice she had to make between denouncing her father and breaking with her family, or refusing to speak against him and losing her future in the Communist Party.

**Kallner, Donna Jackson.** *The Bone Detectives: How Forensic Anthropologists Solve Crimes and Uncover Mysteries of the Dead.* Little, Brown, c1996. 48pp. (NF)
Explores the world of forensic anthropology and its applications in solving crimes.

**Kallner, Donna Jackson.** *Twin Tales: The Magic and Mystery of Multiple Birth.* Little, Brown, c2001. 48pp. (NF)
Explores aspects of the topic of twins, including why and how they are born, twin telepathy, identical and fraternal twins, separation of twins, and more.

**Krull, Kathleen.** *Lives of Extraordinary Women: Rulers, Rebels (and What the Neighbors Thought).* Harcourt, c2000. 95pp. (NF)
Profiles twenty historically significant women, highlighting their great accomplishments and unique quirks; also includes color caricatures.

**Lewin, Ted.** *I Was a Teenage Professional Wrestler.* Orchard Books, c1993. 128pp. (NF)
Text and accompanying photographs describe the author's early days supporting himself as a professional wrestler.

**Murphy, Jim.** *An American Plague: The True and Terrifying Story of the Yellow Fever Epidemic of 1793.* Clarion Books, c2003. 165pp. (NF)
Provides an account of the yellow fever epidemic that swept through Philadelphia in 1793, discussing the chaos that erupted when people began evacuating in droves, leaving the city without government, goods, or services, and examining efforts by physicians, the Free African Society, and others to cure and care for the sick.

**Murphy, Jim.** *Blizzard!: The Storm That Changed America.* Scholastic, c2000. 136pp. (NF)
Presents a history, based on personal accounts and newspaper articles, of the massive snowstorm that hit the Northeast in 1888, focusing on the events in New York City.

**Murphy, Jim.** *The Great Fire.* Scholastic, c1995. 144pp. (NF)
Photographs and text, along with personal accounts of actual survivors, tell the story of the great fire of 1871 in Chicago.

**Murphy, Jim.** *Pick & Shovel Poet: The Journeys of Pascal D'Angelo.* Clarion Books, c2000. 162pp. (NF)
A biography of an Italian peasant who immigrated to America in the early twentieth century and endured poverty and the difficult life of an unskilled laborer, determined to become a published poet.

**Myers, Walter Dean.** *The Greatest: Muhammad Ali.* Scholastic, c2001. 172pp. (NF)
An illustrated biography of boxing great Muhammad Ali that addresses his politics, his fight against Parkinson's disease, and boxing's dangers.

# Nonfiction for Reluctant Readers

**Nelson, Peter.** *Left for Dead: A Young Man's Search for Justice for the USS* **Indianapolis.** Delacorte Press, c2002. 201pp. (NF)

>   Recalls the sinking of the U.S.S. *Indianapolis* at the end of World War II, the Navy cover-up and unfair court martial of the ship's captain, and how a young boy helped the survivors set the record straight fifty-five years later.

**Opdyke, Irene Gut.** *In My Hands: Memories of a Holocaust Rescuer.* Knopf (distributed by Random House), c1999. 276pp. (NF)

>   Recounts the experiences of the author who, as a young Polish girl, hid and saved Jews during the Holocaust.

**Paulsen, Gary.** *My Life in Dog Years.* Delacorte Press, c1998. 137pp. (NF)

>   The author describes how dogs have affected his life from childhood through the present day, recounting the stories of his first dog, Snowball, in the Philippines; Dirk, who protected him from bullies; and Cookie, who saved his life.

**Pfetzer, Mark.** *Within Reach: My Everest Story.* Puffin Books, 2000, c1998. 224pp. (NF)

>   The author describes how he spent his teenage years climbing mountains in the United States, South America, Africa, and Asia, with an emphasis on his two expeditions up Mount Everest.

**Philbrick, Nat.** *Revenge of the Whale: The True Story of the Whaleship* **Essex.** Putnam, c2002. 164pp. (NF)

>   Recounts the sinking in 1820 of the whaleship *Essex* by an enraged sperm whale and how the crew of young men survived against impossible odds. Based on the author's adult book *In the Heart of the Sea.*

**Spinelli, Jerry.** *Knots in My Yo-Yo String: The Autobiography of a Kid.* Knopf (distributed by Random House), c1998. 148pp. (NF)

>   This Italian American Newbery Medalist presents a humorous account of his childhood and youth in Norristown, Pennsylvania.

**Sullivan, George.** *Don't Step on the Foul Line: Sports Superstitions.* Millbrook Press, c2000. 64pp. (NF)

>   Describes a variety of superstitions observed by athletes in such sports as baseball, hockey, tennis, and football.

**Wormser, Richard.** *American Islam: Growing Up Muslim in America.* Walker, 2002, c1994. 130pp. (NF)

>   Young Muslims tell how they keep their identity and adapt their traditions to fit into American society.

## Books for Older Teens

**Arden, John Boghosian.** *America's Meltdown: The Lowest-Common-Denominator Society.* Praeger, c2003. 234pp. (NF)

>   Examines contemporary American consciousness, focusing on the factors that have driven society toward gossip and sensationalism at the cost of substance and depth.

# Nonfiction for Reluctant Readers

**Duey, Kathleen.** *More Freaky Facts About Natural Disasters.* Aladdin Paperbacks, c2001. 217pp. (NF)
Provides strange and interesting facts about a wide range of natural disasters.

**Gantos, Jack.** *Hole in My Life.* Farrar, Straus & Giroux, c2002. 199pp. (NF)
The author relates how, as a young adult, he became a drug user and smuggler, was arrested, did time in prison, and eventually got out and went to college, all the while hoping to become a writer.

**Greene, Meg.** *Buttons, Bones, and the Organ-Grinder's Monkey: Tales of Historical Archaeology.* Linnet Books, c2001. 122pp. (NF)
Describes five archaeological excavations, examining the mysteries uncovered by historical archaeologists. Includes La Salle's ship *Belle,* the Jamestown settlement, the battlefield of the Little Bighorn, Monticello's slave quarters, and the nineteenth-century New York City neighborhood Five Points.

**Hickam, Homer H.** *October Sky: A Memoir.* Dell, 2000, c1998. 428pp. (NF)
Homer Hickam, the introspective son of a mine superintendent and a mother determined to get him out of Coalwood, West Virginia, forever, nurtures a dream to send rockets into outer space—an ambition that changes his life and the lives of everyone living in Coalwood in 1957.

**Krakauer, Jon.** *Into Thin Air: A Personal Account of the Mount Everest Disaster.* Villard, c1997. 293pp. (adult) (NF)
The author relates his experience climbing Mount Everest during its deadliest season and examines what it is about the mountain that makes people willingly subject themselves to such risk, hardship, and expense.

**Owen, David.** *Hidden Evidence: 40 True Crimes and How Forensic Science Helped Solve Them.* Firefly Books, 2000. 240pp. (NF)
Profiles forty true crime cases and explains how their investigations were aided by the use of forensic science.

**Pelzer, David J.** *A Child Called "It": One Child's Courage to Survive.* Health Communications, c1995. 184pp. (NF)
David Pelzer, victim of one of the worst child abuse cases in the history of California, tells the story of how he survived his mother's brutality and triumphed over his past.

**Shakur, Tupac.** *The Rose That Grew from Concrete.* Pocket Books/MTV Books, c1999. 149pp. (NF)
A collection of poems written by rap artist and actor Tupac Shakur at the age of nineteen.

**Spiegelman, Art.** *Maus: A Survivor's Tale.* Pantheon Books, c1997. 295pp. (NF)
Memoir about Vladek Spiegleman, a Jewish survivor of Hitler's Europe, and about his son, a cartoonist who tries to come to terms with his father, his story, and history itself. Cartoon format portrays Jews as mice and Nazis as cats.

**Zindel, Paul.** *The Pigman & Me.* HarperCollins, c1992. 168pp. (NF)
An account of Paul Zindel's teenage years on Staten Island, when his life was enriched by finding his own personal pigman, or mentor.

# Read-Alouds for High School Students

## Books for Ages 12–15

**Avi.** *The True Confessions of Charlotte Doyle.* Orchard Books, 2003, c1990. 215pp.
> Thirteen-year-old Charlotte Doyle, the only passenger aboard a seedy ship on a transatlantic voyage from England to America in 1832, becomes caught up in a feud between the murderous captain and his mutinous crew.

**Bauer, Joan.** *Rules of the Road.* Putman, c1998. 201pp.
> Sixteen-year-old Jenna gets a job driving the elderly owner of a chain of successful shoe stores from Chicago to Texas to confront the son who is trying to force the woman to retire. Along the way Jenna hones her talents as a saleswoman and finds the strength to face her alcoholic father.

**Curtis, Christopher Paul.** *The Watsons Go to Birmingham—1963: A Novel.* Delacorte Press, c1995. 210pp.
> The ordinary interactions and everyday routines of the Watsons, an African American family living in Flint, Michigan, are drastically changed after they visit Grandma in Alabama in the summer of 1963.

**Lowry, Lois.** *The Giver.* Houghton Mifflin, c1993. 180pp.
> Given his lifetime assignment at the Ceremony of Twelve, Jonas becomes the receiver of memories shared by only one other in his community and discovers the terrible truth about the society in which he lives.

**Mikaelsen, Ben.** *Petey.* Hyperion Books for Children, c1998. 280pp.
> In 1922 Petey, who has cerebral palsy, is misdiagnosed as an idiot and institutionalized. Sixty years later, still in the institution, he befriends a boy and shares with him the joy of life.

**Peck, Robert Newton.** *A Day No Pigs Would Die.* Knopf (distributed by Random House), c1999. 150pp.
> To a thirteen-year-old Vermont farm boy whose father slaughters pigs for a living, maturity comes early as he learns "doing what's got to be done," especially regarding his pet pig, who cannot produce a litter.

**Philbrick, W. R.** *The Last Book in the Universe.* Blue Sky Press, c2000. 223pp.
> After an earthquake has destroyed much of the planet, an epileptic teenager nicknamed Spaz begins the heroic fight to bring human intelligence back to Earth of a distant future.

## Books for Older Teens

**Albom, Mitch.** *Tuesdays with Morrie.* Wheeler, c1998. 171pp. (adult) (NF)
> The author, an alumnus of Brandeis University, tells about his meetings with a former professor suffering from Lou Gehrig's disease and the lessons he learned about life and death from this college mentor.

**Boulle, Pierre.** *Planet of the Apes: A Novel.* Ballantine Books, 2001, c1963. 268pp.
> Explorers in space find a planet that is identical to Earth, with the exception that on the planet Betelgeuse the roles of ape and human are reversed.

# Read-Alouds for High School Students

**Bradbury, Ray.** *The Martian Chronicles.* Avon Books, c1997. 268pp.

The first Earth people to attempt the colonization of Mars try to build their new world in the image of the civilization they left behind.

**Coupland, Douglas.** *All Families Are Psychotic: A Novel.* Bloomsbury (distributed by St. Martin's Press), c2001. 279pp.

The Drummond family has reunited after years apart to watch their daughter Sarah rocket into space, but they seem to encounter danger at every turn, and soon Sarah's mission, and life, is threatened.

**Goldman, William.** *The Princess Bride: S. Morgenstern's Classic Tale of True Love and High Adventure: The "Good Parts" Version.* Ballantine Books, c1998. 399pp.

Westley, a farm boy, goes off to seek his fortune shortly after declaring his love for Buttercup, the most beautiful woman in the world, but their relationship is put to the test when his ship is captured by pirates and she is summoned to become the bride of the prince.

**King, Stephen.** *The Girl Who Loved Tom Gordon.* Scribner, c1999. 224pp. (adult)

Nine-year-old Trisha McFarland, lost in the woods after she wanders off to escape the bickering between her mom and her brother, boosts her courage by imagining that her hero, Boston Red Sox relief pitcher Tom Gordon, is with her, helping her survive an unknown enemy.

**Marsden, John.** *So Much to Tell You.* Fawcett Books, c1990. 119pp.

Sent to a boarding school by her mother, Marina, a disfigured Australian girl who refuses to speak, reveals her thoughts and feelings in a diary.

**Tarbox, Katherine.** *A Girl's Life Online.* Plume, 2004, c2000. 196pp. (NF)

The author recalls her harrowing experiences as a thirteen-year-old who struck up an online relationship with twenty-three-year-old Mark, and offers advice and insight on online sexual predators.

**Werlin, Nancy.** *The Killer's Cousin.* Dell Laurel-Leaf, 2000, c1998. 229pp.

After being acquitted of murder, seventeen-year-old David goes to stay with relatives in Cambridge, Massachusetts, where he finds himself forced to face his past as he learns more about his strange young cousin, Lily.

**White, Robb.** *Deathwatch.* Bantam Doubleday Dell Books for Young Readers, 1973, c1972. 220pp.

Needing money for school, a college student accepts a job as a guide on a desert hunting trip and nearly loses his life.

From Nancy J. Keane, *The Big Book of Teen Reading Lists: 100 Great, Ready-to-Use Book Lists for Educators, Librarians, Parents, and Children.* Westport, CT: Libraries Unlimited, 2006. Copyright © 2006 by Libraries Unlimited.

# Read-Alouds for Middle School Students

## Books for Ages 12–15

**Bloor, Edward.** *Tangerine*. Harcourt Brace, c1997. 294pp.
> Twelve-year-old Paul, who lives in the shadow of his football hero brother Erik, fights for the right to play soccer despite his near blindness and slowly begins to remember the incident that damaged his eyesight.

**Curtis, Christopher Paul.** *The Watsons Go to Birmingham—1963: A Novel.* Delacorte Press, c1995. 210pp.
> The ordinary interactions and everyday routines of the Watsons, an African American family living in Flint, Michigan, are drastically changed after they visit Grandma in Alabama in the summer of 1963.

**Davidson, Diane Mott.** *Tough Cookie.* Bantam Books, 2001, c2000. 319pp.
> Caterer Goldy Schulz, temporarily shut down while her kitchen is remodeled, must cook up a quick crime-solving recipe when she makes arrangements to sell an item from her husband's collection of war memorabilia, only to have her buyer turn up suspiciously dead on the ski slopes.

**DiCamillo, Kate.** *Because of Winn-Dixie*. Candlewick Press, c2000. 182pp.
> Ten-year-old India Opal Buloni describes her first summer in Naomi, Florida, and all the good things that happen to her because of her big ugly dog, Winn-Dixie.

**DiCamillo, Kate.** *The Tale of Despereaux: Being the Story of a Mouse, a Princess, Some Soup, and a Spool of Thread.* Candlewick Press, c2003. 267pp.
> The adventures of Despereaux Tilling, a small mouse of unusual talents, the princess whom he loves, the servant girl who longs to be a princess, and a devious rat determined to bring them all to ruin.

**Gantos, Jack.** *Joey Pigza Swallowed the Key.* Farrar, Straus & Giroux, c1998. 153pp. (and sequels)
> To the constant disappointment of his mother and his teachers, Joey has trouble paying attention or controlling his mood swings when his prescription meds wear off, and he starts getting worked up and acting wired.

**Haddix, Margaret Peterson.** *Among the Hidden*. Simon & Schuster Books for Young Readers, c1998. 153pp. (and sequels)
> In a future where the Population Police enforce the law limiting a family to only two children, Luke has lived all his twelve years in isolation and fear on his family's farm, until another "third" convinces him that the government is wrong.

**Jacques, Brian.** *Redwall*. Philomel Books, c1986. 351pp. (and sequels)
> When the peaceful life of ancient Redwall Abbey is shattered by the arrival of the evil rat Cluny and his villainous hordes, Matthias, a young mouse, determines to find the legendary sword of Martin the Warrior, which, he is convinced, will help Redwall's inhabitants destroy the enemy.

**Kehret, Peg.** *Small Steps: The Year I Got Polio.* Whitman, c1996. 179pp. (NF)
> The author describes her battle against polio when she was thirteen and her efforts to overcome its debilitating effects.

# Read-Alouds for Middle School Students

**Korman, Gordon.** *No More Dead Dogs.* Hyperion Books for Children, c2000. 180pp.
Eighth-grade football hero Wallace Wallace is sentenced to detention attending rehearsals of the school play.Despite himself, he becomes wrapped up in the production and begins to suggest changes that improve not only the play but his life as well.

**Lawrence, Iain.** *The Wreckers.* Bantam Doubleday Dell Books for Young Readers, 1999, c1998. 196pp.
Shipwrecked after a vicious storm, fourteen-year-old John Spencer attempts to save his father and himself while also dealing with an evil secret about the Cornish coastal town where they are stranded.

**Mikaelsen, Ben.** *Touching Spirit Bear.* HarperCollins, c2001. 241pp.
After his anger erupts into violence, fifteen year-old Cole, to avoid going to prison, agrees to participate in a sentencing alternative based on the Native American Circle Justice. He is sent to a remote Alaskan Island, where an encounter with a huge Spirit Bear changes his life.

**Paulsen, Gary.** *Harris and Me: A Summer Remembered.* Harcourt Brace, c1993. 157pp.
Sent to live with relatives on their farm because of his unhappy home life, an eleven-year-old city boy meets his distant cousin, Harris, and is given an introduction to a whole new world.

**Paulsen, Gary.** *Nightjohn.* Delacorte Press, c1993. 92pp.
Twelve-year-old Sarny's brutal life as a slave becomes even more dangerous when a newly arrived slave offers to teach her how to read.

**Peck, Richard.** *A Long Way from Chicago: A Novel in Stories.* Dial Books for Young Readers, c1998. 148pp.
A boy recounts his annual summer trips to rural Illinois with his sister during the Great Depression to visit their larger-than-life grandmother.

**Peck, Robert Newton.** *A Day No Pigs Would Die.* Knopf (distributed by Random House), c1999. 150pp.
To a thirteen-year-old Vermont farm boy whose father slaughters pigs for a living, maturity comes early as he learns "doing what's got to be done," especially regarding his pet pig, who cannot produce a litter.

**Philbrick, W. R.** *Freak the Mighty.* Scholastic, c1993. 169pp.
At the beginning of eighth grade, learning disabled Max and his new friend, Freak, whose birth defect has affected his body but not his brilliant mind, find that when they combine forces they make a powerful team.

**Robinson, Barbara.** *The Best Christmas Pageant Ever.* HarperTrophy, 1988, c1972. 80pp.
The six mean Herdman kids lie, steal, smoke cigars (even the girls), and then become involved in the community Christmas pageant.

**Ruckman, Ivy.** *Night of the Twisters.* HarperCollins, c1984. 153pp.
A fictional account of the night freakish and devastating tornadoes hit Grand Island, Nebraska, as experienced by a twelve-year-old, his family, and friends.

# Read-Alouds for Middle School Students

**Sachar, Louis.** *Holes.* Farrar, Straus & Giroux, c1998. 233pp.

As further evidence of his family's bad fortune, which they attribute to a curse on a distant relative, Stanley Yelnats is sent to a hellish correctional camp in the Texas desert, where he finds his first real friend, a treasure, and a new sense of himself.

**Spinelli, Jerry.** *Maniac Magee: A Novel.* Little, Brown, c1990. 184pp.

After his parents die, Jeffrey Lionel Magee's life becomes legendary, as he accomplishes athletic and other feats that awe his contemporaries.

**Spinelli, Jerry.** *Space Station Seventh Grade.* Little, Brown, c1982. 232pp.

Seventh-grader Jason narrates the events of his year, from school, hair, and pimples, to mothers, little brothers, and a girl.

**Zindel, Paul.** *The Pigman: A Novel.* HarperCollins, c1968. 182pp.

A teenage boy and a girl, high school sophomores from unhappy homes, tell about their bizarre relationship with an old man.

# Reluctant Boy Readers

## Books for Ages 12–15

**Avi.** *The True Confessions of Charlotte Doyle.* Orchard Books, 2003, c1990. 215pp.
Thirteen-year-old Charlotte Doyle, the only passenger aboard a seedy ship on a transatlantic voyage from England to America in 1832, becomes caught up in a feud between the murderous captain and his mutinous crew.

**Bunting, Eve.** *Someone Is Hiding on Alcatraz Island.* Berkley Books, 1994, c1984. 136pp.
When he offends the toughest gang in his San Francisco school, Danny tries to elude them by going to Alcatraz, only to find himself and a Park Service employee trapped by the gang in an old prison cell block.

**Butcher, A. J.** *Spy High: Mission One.* Little, Brown, 2004, c2003. 214pp.
As students at a special high school that trains them to be secret agents, six teenagers struggle to complete the training exercises as a team before being sent out into the field to sink or swim.

**Colfer, Eoin.** *Artemis Fowl.* Hyperion Books for Children, c2001. 277pp.
When a twelve-year-old evil genius tries to restore his family fortune by capturing a fairy and demanding a ransom in gold, the fairies fight back with magic, technology, and a particularly nasty troll.

**Curtis, Christopher Paul.** *Bucking the Sarge.* Wendy Lamb Books, c2004. 259pp.
Deeply involved in his cold and manipulative mother's shady business dealings in Flint, Michigan, fourteen-year-old Luther keeps a sense of humor while running the Happy Neighbor Group Home for Men, all the while dreaming of going to college and becoming a philosopher.

**Curtis, Christopher Paul.** *Bud, Not Buddy.* Delacorte Press, c1999. 245pp.
Ten-year-old Bud, a motherless boy living in Flint, Michigan, during the Great Depression, escapes a bad foster home and sets out in search of the man he believes to be his father—the renowned bandleader, H. E. Calloway of Grand Rapids.

**Curtis, Christopher Paul.** *The Watsons Go to Birmingham—1963: A Novel.* Delacorte Press, c1995. 210pp.
The ordinary interactions and everyday routines of the Watsons, an African American family living in Flint, Michigan, are drastically changed after they visit Grandma in Alabama in the summer of 1963.

**Hinton, S. E.** *The Outsiders.* Puffin Books, 1997, c1967. 180pp.
The struggle of three brothers to stay together after their parent's death and their quest for identity among the conflicting values of their adolescent society.

**Horowitz, Anthony.** *Stormbreaker.* Philomel Books, 2001, c2000. 192pp.
After the death of the uncle who had been his guardian, fourteen-year-old Alex Rider is coerced to continue his uncle's dangerous work for Britain's intelligence agency, MI6.

**Koja, Kathe.** *Buddha Boy.* Farrar, Straus & Giroux, c2003. 117pp.
Justin spends time with Jinsen, the unusual and artistic new student whom the school bullies torment and call Buddha Boy, and ends up making choices that affect Jinsen, himself, and the entire school.

# Reluctant Boy Readers

**Korman, Gordon.** *Son of the Mob*. Hyperion, c2002. 262pp.

Seventeen-year-old Vince's life is constantly complicated by the fact that he is the son of a powerful Mafia boss, a relationship that threatens to destroy his romance with the daughter of an FBI agent.

**Mikaelsen, Ben.** *Touching Spirit Bear*. HarperCollins, c2001. 241pp.

After his anger erupts into violence, fifteen year-old Cole, to avoid going to prison, agrees to participate in a sentencing alternative based on the Native American Circle Justice. He is sent to a remote Alaskan Island, where an encounter with a huge Spirit Bear changes his life.

**Paulsen, Gary.** *Harris and Me: A Summer Remembered.* Harcourt Brace, c1993. 157pp.

Sent to live with relatives on their farm because of his unhappy home life, an eleven-year-old city boy meets his distant cousin, Harris, and is given an introduction to a whole new world.

**Paulsen, Gary.** *How Angel Peterson Got His Name: And Other Outrageous Tales About Extreme Sports.* Wendy Lamb Books, c2003. 111pp. (NF)

Author Gary Paulsen relates tales from his youth in a small town in northwestern Minnesota in the late 1940s and early 1950s, such as skiing behind a souped-up car and imitating daredevil Evel Knievel.

**Philbrick, W. R.** *Freak the Mighty*. Scholastic, c1993. 169pp.

At the beginning of eighth grade, learning disabled Max and his new friend, Freak, whose birth defect has affected his body but not his brilliant mind, find that when they combine forces they make a powerful team.

**Trueman, Terry.** *Inside Out.* HarperTempest, c2003. 117pp.

A sixteen-year-old with schizophrenia is caught up in the events surrounding an attempted robbery by two other teens, who eventually hold him hostage.

**Trueman, Terry.** *Stuck in Neutral*. HarperCollins, c2000. 114pp.

Fourteen-year-old Shawn McDaniel, who suffers from severe cerebral palsy and cannot function, relates his perceptions of his life, his family, and his condition, especially as he believes his father is planning to kill him.

## Books for Older Teens

**Choyce, Lesley.** *Thunderbowl*. Orca Book, c2004. 102pp.

Sixteen-year-old Jeremy, caught up in the excitement of playing guitar for the hot band Thunderbowl, begins to lose control of the rest of his life.

**Cormier, Robert.** *The Rag and Bone Shop: A Novel.* Delacorte Press, c2001. 154pp.

Trent, an ace interrogator from Vermont, works to procure a confession from an introverted twelve-year-old accused of murdering his seven-year-old friend in Monument, Massachusetts.

**Forsyth, Christine.** *Adrenaline High.* James Lorimer (distributed in the United States by Orca Book), c2003. 126pp.

Sixteen-year-old D'Arcy, always on the lookout for drama, finds herself in over her head when she attempts to help her classmate, Zania, whose mother is being held hostage by a drug-dealing boyfriend.

# Reluctant Boy Readers

**Halvorson, Marilyn.** *Bull Rider.* Orca Book, c2003. 92pp.

Sixteen-year-old Layne faces a dangerous challenge when he defies his mother and enters himself in a bull riding contest—the same rodeo event in which his father was killed.

**Heneghan, James.** *Hit Squad.* Orca Book, c2003. 106pp.

Students in an upscale high school decide to take on the bullies and take back their school, with decidedly mixed consequences.

**Lubar, David.** *Hidden Talents.* Starscape, c2003, c1999. 213pp.

Thirteen-year-old Martin, a new student at an alternative school for misfits and problem students, falls in with a group of boys with psychic powers and discovers something surprising about himself.

**Matheson, Shirlee Smith.** *Fastback Beach.* Orca Book, c2003. 97pp.

When Miles is put on probation for stealing a car, he learns about hot rods and rebuilding cars. When the project is stolen, Miles has to face up to his friends.

**McNamee, Graham.** *Acceleration.* Wendy Lamb Books, c2003. 210pp.

Stuck working in the lost and found department of the Toronto Transit Authority for the summer, seventeen-year-old Duncan finds the diary of a serial killer and sets out to stop him.

**Myers, Walter Dean.** *Monster*. HarperCollins, c1999. 281pp.

While on trial as an accomplice to a murder, sixteen-year-old Steve Harmon records his experiences in prison and in the courtroom, in the form of a film script, as he tries to come to terms with the course his life has taken.

**Thomas, Rob.** *Rats Saw God.* Aladdin Paperbacks, c1996. 202pp.

In hopes of graduating, Steve York agrees to complete a hundred-page writing assignment, which helps him to sort out his relationship with his famous astronaut father and the events that changed him from a promising student into a troubled teen.

**Volponi, Paul.** *Black and White.* Viking Press, c2005. 185pp.

After committing a crime together and getting caught, two star high school basketball players, one black and one white, experience the justice system differently.

**Walters, Eric.** *Grind*. Orca Book, c2004. 100pp.

When he begins videotaping himself and posting the movies on a Web site to make money, Philip, obsessed with skateboarding, finds himself pushed to perform more and more dangerous stunts.

**Walters, Eric.** *Overdrive.* Orca Book, c2004. 102pp.

When Jake is involved in a street-racing accident, he struggles to do the right thing.

# Reluctant Girl Readers

## Books for Ages 12–15

**Anderson, Laurie Halse.** *Speak*. Farrar, Straus & Giroux, c1999. 197pp.
A traumatic event near the end of the summer has a devastating effect on Melinda's freshman year in high school.

**Bechard, Margaret.** *Hanging on to Max*. Roaring Brook Press, c2002. 142pp.
When his girlfriend decides to give their baby away, seventeen-year-old Sam is determined to keep him and raise him alone.

**Dessen, Sarah.** *Dreamland*. Speak, 2004, c2000. 250pp.
After her older sister runs away, Caitlin decides that she needs to make a major change in her own life and begins an abusive relationship with a boy who is mysterious, and dangerous.

**Ferris, Jean.** *Bad*. Aerial Fiction/Farrar, Straus & Giroux, 2001, c1998. 181pp.
In an attempt to please her boyfriend, sixteen-year-old Dallas goes along with a plan to rob a convenience store. When her father refuses the judge's offer to let her come home on probation, she is sentenced to six months in the Girls' Rehabilitation Center.

**Johnson, Angela.** *The First Part Last*. Simon & Schuster Books for Young Readers, c2003. 131pp.
Bobby's carefree teenage life changes forever when he becomes a father and must care for his adored baby daughter.

**Koja, Kathe.** *Buddha Boy*. Farrar, Straus & Giroux, c2003. 117pp.
Justin spends time with Jinsen, the unusual and artistic new student whom the school bullies torment and call Buddha Boy, and ends up making choices that affect Jinsen, himself, and the entire school.

**Koja, Kathe.** *Straydog*. Farrar, Straus & Giroux, c2002. 105pp.
Rachel, a teenager with a healthy dose of both aptitude and attitude, begins to feel at home volunteering at an animal shelter, until the arrival of a feral dog with whom she senses a special kinship.

**Myracle, Lauren.** *Ttyl*. Amulet Books, c2004. 209pp.
Chronicles, in "instant message" format, the day-to-day experiences, feelings, and plans of three friends, Zoe, Maddie, and Angela, as they begin tenth grade.

**Spinelli, Jerry.** *Stargirl*. Knopf (distributed by Random House), c2000. 186pp.
Stargirl, a teen who animates quiet Mica High with her colorful personality, suddenly finds herself shunned for her refusal to conform.

**Tashjian, Janet.** *The Gospel According to Larry*. H. Holt, c2001. 227pp.
Seventeen-year-old Josh, a loner-philosopher who wants to make a difference in the world, tries to maintain his secret identity as the author of a Web site that is receiving national attention.

**Woodson, Jacqueline.** *Hush*. Putnam, c2002. 181pp.
Twelve-year-old Toswiah finds her life changed when her family enters the witness protection program.

# Reluctant Girl Readers

## Books for Older Teens

**Brooks, Kevin.** *Candy*. The Chicken House/Scholastic, c2005. 364pp.
Joe, an English boy from the right side of the tracks, is poised to get everything he has ever wanted, but he risks it all when he falls for Candy and is drawn into her seedy, dangerous world.

**Castellucci, Cecil.** *Boy Proof*. Candlewick Press, c2005. 203pp.
Feeling alienated from everyone around her, high school senior and cinephile Victoria Denton hides behind the identity of a favorite movie character, until an interesting new boy arrives at school and helps her realize that there is more to life than just the movies.

**Frank, E. R.** *Life Is Funny: A Novel*. DK Ink, c2000. 263pp.
The lives of a number of young people of different races, economic backgrounds, and family situations living in Brooklyn, New York, become intertwined over a seven-year period.

**Frost, Helen.** *Keesha's House*. Farrar, Straus & Giroux, c2003. 116pp.
Seven runaway teens facing such problems as pregnancy, closeted homosexuality, and abuse each describe in poetic forms what caused them to leave home and where they found home again.

**Giles, Gail.** *Dead Girls Don't Write Letters*. Roaring Brook Press, c2003. 136pp.
Fourteen-year-old Sunny is stunned when a total stranger shows up at her house posing as her older sister Jazz, who supposedly died in a fire months earlier.

**Giles, Gail.** *Playing in Traffic*. Roaring Brook Press, c2004. 176pp.
Shy and unremarkable, seventeen-year-old Matt Lathrop is surprised and flattered to find himself singled out for the sexual attentions of the alluring Skye Colby, until he discovers the evil purpose behind her actions.

**Going, Kelly.** *Fat Kid Rules the World*. Putnam, c2003. 187pp.
Seventeen-year-old Troy, depressed, suicidal, and weighing nearly 300 pounds, gets a new perspective on life when Curt, a semi-homeless teen who is a genius on guitar, asks Troy to be the drummer in a rock band.

**Hopkins, Ellen.** *Crank*. Simon Pulse, c2004. 537pp.
Kristina Georgia Snow's life is turned upside down when she visits her absentee father, gets turned on to the drug "crank," becomes addicted, and is led down a desperate path that threatens her mind, soul, and life.

**Koja, Kathe.** *The Blue Mirror*. Farrar, Straus & Giroux, c2004. 119pp.
Seventeen-year-old loner Maggy Klass, who frequently seeks refuge from her alcoholic mother's apartment by sitting and drawing in a local cafe, becomes involved in a destructive relationship with a charismatic homeless youth named Cole.

**Rosoff, Meg.** *How I Live Now*. Wendy Lamb Books, c2004. 194pp.
To get away from her pregnant stepmother in New York City, fifteen-year-old Daisy goes to England to stay with her aunt and cousins, with whom she instantly bonds, but soon war breaks out and rips apart the family while devastating the land.

# Reluctant Girl Readers

**Sones, Sonya.** *What My Mother Doesn't Know.* Simon & Schuster Books for Young Readers, c2001. 259pp.

Sophie describes her relationships with a series of boys as she searches for Mr. Right.

**Trueman, Terry.** *Stuck in Neutral.* HarperCollins, c2000. 114pp.

Fourteen-year-old Shawn McDaniel, who suffers from severe cerebral palsy and cannot function, relates his perceptions of his life, his family, and his condition, especially as he believes his father is planning to kill him.

# Romance for Boy Readers

## Books for Ages 12–15

**Bagdasarian, Adam.** *First French Kiss and Other Traumas.* Farrar, Straus & Giroux, c2002. 134pp.
The author recounts humorous, sad, traumatic, romantic, and confusing episodes from his childhood.

**Crutcher, Chris.** *Running Loose.* Greenwillow Books, c1983. 190pp.
Louie, a high school senior in a small Idaho town, learns about sportsmanship, love, and death as he matures into manhood.

**Korman, Gordon.** *Son of the Mob.* Hyperion, c2002. 262pp.
Seventeen-year-old Vince's life is constantly complicated by the fact that he is the son of a powerful Mafia boss, a relationship that threatens to destroy his romance with the daughter of an FBI agent.

**Petersen, P. J.** *Rob&sara.com.* Delacorte Press, c2004. 210pp.
Rob, who lives at a school for troubled teenagers, and Sara, the sixteen-year-old daughter of an army colonel, meet in a poetry chat room and develop a close relationship via e-mail.

**Powell, Randy.** *Is Kissing a Girl Who Smokes Like Licking an Ashtray?* Farrar, Straus & Giroux, 2003, c1992. 199pp.
An eighteen-year-old pinball addict and a smart-mouthed girl who don't quite fit in with anyone else develop a special relationship.

**Young, Karen Romano.** *The Beetle and Me: A Love Story.* HarperTrophy, 2001, c1999. 207pp.
Surrounded by her busy extended family and their many cars, fifteen-year-old Daisy pursues her goal of single-handedly restoring the car of her dreams, the old purple Volkswagen Beetle from her childhood.

## Books for Older Teens

**Black, Jonah.** *The Black Book. Vol. 1.Girls, Girls, Girls :Diary of a Teenage Stud.* Avon Books, c2001. 233pp.
Jonah Black, whose thoughts are filled with fantasies about a Pennsylvania girl named Sophie, chronicles in his journal his first six weeks back in Florida after being expelled from a Pennsylvania prep school, during which time he is forced to watch his old friend and new crush, Posie, get friendly with a womanizer.

**Bradley, Alex.** *24 Girls in 7 Days.* Dutton Books, c2005. 265pp.
Unlucky in love, teenager Jack Grammar cannot get a date for the prom, until his friends play a practical joke and place a personal ad in the school online newspaper on his behalf. Now Jack has twenty-four dates, and it is just seven days until the prom.

**Green, John.** *Looking for Alaska.* Dutton Books, c2005. 221pp.
Sixteen-year-old Miles's first year at Culver Creek Preparatory School in Alabama includes good friends and great pranks but is defined by the search for answers about life and death after a fatal car crash.

# Romance for Boy Readers

**Koertge, Ronald.** *Stoner & Spaz.* Candlewick Press, c2002. 169pp.

A troubled youth with cerebral palsy struggles toward self-acceptance with the help of a drug-addicted young woman.

**Koertge, Ronald.** *Where the Kissing Never Stops.* Candlewick Press, c2005. 250pp.

While trying to cope with his father's death, his mother's new job as a stripper, and his own libido, high school junior Walker meets a new girl, who makes life seem pretty wonderful after all.

**Nelson, Blake.** *Rock Star, Superstar.* Viking Press, c2004. 229pp.

When Pete, a talented bass player, moves from playing in the high school jazz band to playing in a popular rock group, he finds the experience exhilarating, even as his new fame jeopardizes his relationship with his girlfriend, Margaret.

**Ripslinger, Jon.** *How I Fell in Love & Learned to Shoot Free Throws.* Roaring Brook Press, c2003. 170pp.

Seventeen-year-old Danny Henderson, an indifferent basketball player, has his eye on Angel McPherson, star of the girls' team in their Iowa high school.

**Shaw, Tucker.** *Flavor of the Week.* Hyperion, c2003. 220pp.

Cyril, an overweight boy who is good friends with Rose but wishes he could be more, helps his best friend Nick woo her with culinary masterpieces, which Cyril himself secretly creates. Includes recipes from the story.

**Strasser, Todd.** *Cut Back.* Simon Pulse, c2004. 305pp.

Kai tries to help his surfing partner, Spazzy, win a competition against Lucas, the local star.

**Wooding, Chris.** *Crashing.* Push/Scholastic, c2003, c1998. 142pp.

While his parents are out of town, decides to throw a start-of-summer party to cement his relationship with friends who will be going to different schools next term, and hopefully begin a relationship with Jo, a girl he has had a crush on for years, but things start to go wrong when misunderstandings and gate crashers intrude.

## If you liked *Give a Boy a Gun* by Todd Strasser, try:

- Adoff, Jaime. *Names Will Never Hurt Me.* Dutton Children's Books, c2004.

- Bernall, M. *She Said Yes: The Unlikely Martyrdom of Cassie Bernall.* Pocket Books, c2000.

- McDonald, Joyce. *Swallowing Stones.* Bantam Doubleday Dell Books for Young Readers, 1999.

- Mikaelsen, Ben. *Touching Spirit Bear.* HarperCollins, c2001.

- Myers, Walter Dean. *Shooter.* HarperTempest, 2005, c2004

- Prose, Francine. *After.* Joanna Cotler Books, c2003.

## If you liked *Give a Boy a Gun* by Todd Strasser, try:

- Adoff, Jaime. *Names Will Never Hurt Me.* Dutton Children's Books, c2004.

- Bernall, M. *She Said Yes: The Unlikely Martyrdom of Cassie Bernall.* Pocket Books, c2000.

- McDonald, Joyce. *Swallowing Stones.* Bantam Doubleday Dell Books for Young Readers, 1999.

- Mikaelsen, Ben. *Touching Spirit Bear.* HarperCollins, c2001.

- Myers, Walter Dean. *Shooter.* HarperTempest, 2005, c2004

- Prose, Francine. *After.* Joanna Cotler Books, c2003.

From Nancy J. Keane, *The Big Book of Teen Reading Lists: 100 Great, Ready-to-Use Book Lists for Educators, Librarians, Parents, and Children.* Westport, CT: Libraries Unlimited, 2006. Copyright © 2006 by Libraries Unlimited.

# If you liked *The Misfits* by James Howe, try:

- Bloor, Edward *Tangerine*. Harcourt Brace, c1997.

- Crutcher, Chris. *Staying Fat for Sarah Byrnes*. Greenwillow Books, c1993.

- Hiaasen, Carl. *Hoot*. Knopf, c2002.

- Howe, James. *Totally Joe*. Atheneum Books for Young Readers, c2005.

- Koja, Kathe. *Buddha Boy*. Farrar, Straus & Giroux, 2003.

- Koss, Amy Goldman. *The Girls*. Dial Books for Young Readers, c2000.

- Langan, Paul. *The Gun*. Townsend Press, c2002.

- McKay, Hilary. *Indigo's Star*. Margaret K. McElderry Books, 2004, c2003.

- *Odd Girl Speaks Out: Girls Write About Bullies, Cliques, Popularity, and Jealousy*. Harcourt, c2004.

- Peters, Julie Anne. *Define "Normal": A Novel*. Little, Brown, c2000.

- Sanchez, Alex. *Rainbow Boys*. Simon & Schuster, c2001.

- Sanchez, Alex. *So Hard to Say*. Simon & Schuster Books for Young Readers, c2004.

- Spinelli, Jerry. *Loser*. Joanna Cotler Books, c2002.

- Spinelli, Jerry. *Stargirl*. Knopf (distributed by Random House), c2000.

- Wilhelm, Doug. *The Revealers*. Farrar, Straus & Giroux, 2003.

# If you liked *The Misfits* by James Howe, try:

- Bloor, Edward *Tangerine*. Harcourt Brace, c1997.

- Crutcher, Chris. *Staying Fat for Sarah Byrnes*. Greenwillow Books, c1993.

- Hiaasen, Carl. *Hoot*. Knopf, c2002.

- Howe, James. *Totally Joe*. Atheneum Books for Young Readers, c2005.

- Koja, Kathe. *Buddha Boy*. Farrar, Straus & Giroux, 2003.

- Koss, Amy Goldman. *The Girls*. Dial Books for Young Readers, c2000.

- Langan, Paul. *The Gun*. Townsend Press, c2002.

- McKay, Hilary. *Indigo's Star*. Margaret K. McElderry Books, 2004, c2003.

- *Odd Girl Speaks Out: Girls Write About Bullies, Cliques, Popularity, and Jealousy*. Harcourt, c2004.

- Peters, Julie Anne. *Define "Normal": A Novel*. Little, Brown, c2000.

- Sanchez, Alex. *Rainbow Boys*. Simon & Schuster, c2001.

- Sanchez, Alex. *So Hard to Say*. Simon & Schuster Books for Young Readers, c2004.

- Spinelli, Jerry. *Loser*. Joanna Cotler Books, c2002.

- Spinelli, Jerry. *Stargirl*. Knopf (distributed by Random House), c2000.

- Wilhelm, Doug. *The Revealers*. Farrar, Straus & Giroux, 2003.

From Nancy J. Keane, *The Big Book of Teen Reading Lists: 100 Great, Ready-to-Use Book Lists for Educators, Librarians, Parents, and Children*. Westport, CT: Libraries Unlimited, 2006. Copyright © 2006 by Libraries Unlimited.

## If you liked *A Child Called It* by Dave Peltzer, try (for older teens):

- Atkins, Catherine. *When Jeff Comes Home.* Putnam, c1999.

- Burch, Jennings Michael. *They Cage the Animals at Night.* Signet, c1984.

- Fitch, Janet. *White Oleander: A Novel.* Little, Brown, c1999.

- Flinn, Alexandra. *Breathing Underwater.* HarperCollins, c2001.

- Frank, E. R. *America: A Novel.* Atheneum Books for Young Readers, c2002.

- Goobie, Beth. *Who Owns Kelly Paddik?* Orca Book, 2003.

- Hayden, Torey L. *Ghost Girl: The True Story of a Child in Peril and the Teacher Who Saved Her.* Avon Books, 1992, c1991.

- Hayden, Torey L. *Murphy's Boy.* Avon Books, c1983.

- Hunt, Irene. *The Lottery Rose.* Berkley Books, 1996, c1976.

- Nolan, Han. *Born Blue.* Harcourt, c2001.

From Nancy J. Keane, *The Big Book of Teen Reading Lists: 100 Great, Ready-to-Use Book Lists for Educators, Librarians, Parents, and Children.* Westport, CT: Libraries Unlimited, 2006. Copyright © 2006 by Libraries Unlimited.

## If you liked *A Child Called It* by Dave Peltzer, try (for older teens):

- Atkins, Catherine. *When Jeff Comes Home.* Putnam, c1999.

- Burch, Jennings Michael. *They Cage the Animals at Night.* Signet, c1984.

- Fitch, Janet. *White Oleander: A Novel.* Little, Brown, c1999.

- Flinn, Alexandra. *Breathing Underwater.* HarperCollins, c2001.

- Frank, E. R. *America: A Novel.* Atheneum Books for Young Readers, c2002.

- Goobie, Beth. *Who Owns Kelly Paddik?* Orca Book, 2003.

- Hayden, Torey L. *Ghost Girl: The True Story of a Child in Peril and the Teacher Who Saved Her.* Avon Books, 1992, c1991.

- Hayden, Torey L. *Murphy's Boy.* Avon Books, c1983.

- Hunt, Irene. *The Lottery Rose.* Berkley Books, 1996, c1976.

- Nolan, Han. *Born Blue.* Harcourt, c2001.

From Nancy J. Keane, *The Big Book of Teen Reading Lists: 100 Great, Ready-to-Use Book Lists for Educators, Librarians, Parents, and Children.* Westport, CT: Libraries Unlimited, 2006. Copyright © 2006 by Libraries Unlimited.

## If you liked *A Child Called It* by Dave Pelzer, try (for ages 12 and up):

- Coman, Carolyn. *What Jamie Saw.* Puffin Books, 1997, c1995.
- Deans, Sis Boulos. *Racing the Past.* H. Holt, 2001.
- Deem, James M. *3NBs of Julian Drew.* Graphia, c1994.
- Draper, Sharon M. *Forged by Fire.* Atheneum Books for Young Readers, c1997.
- Gibbons, Kaye. *Ellen Foster.* Vintage, 1990, c1987.
- Klass, David. *You Don't Know Me: A Novel.* Farrar, Straus & Giroux, 2001.
- Konigsburg, E. L. *Silent to the Bone.* Atheneum Books for Young Readers, c2000.
- McCord, Patricia. *Pictures in the Dark.* Bloomsbury, c2004.
- Mikaelsen, Ben. *Petey.* Hyperion Books for Children, c1998.
- Rottman, S. L. *Hero.* Peachtree, c1997.
- Shaw, Susan. *The Boy from the Basement.* Dutton Children's Books, c2004.
- Vance, Susanna. *Sights.* Delacorte Press, 2001.
- Vries, Anke de. *Bruises.* Front Street/Lumniscaat , 1995.
- Woodson, Jacqueline. *I Hadn't Meant to Tell You This.* Bantam Doubleday Dell Books for Young Readers, 1995, c1994.

## If you liked *A Child Called It* by Dave Pelzer, try (for ages 12 and up):

- Coman, Carolyn. *What Jamie Saw.* Puffin Books, 1997, c1995.
- Deans, Sis Boulos. *Racing the Past.* H. Holt, 2001.
- Deem, James M. *3NBs of Julian Drew.* Graphia, c1994.
- Draper, Sharon M. *Forged by Fire.* Atheneum Books for Young Readers, c1997.
- Gibbons, Kaye. *Ellen Foster.* Vintage, 1990, c1987.
- Klass, David. *You Don't Know Me: A Novel.* Farrar, Straus & Giroux, 2001.
- Konigsburg, E. L. *Silent to the Bone.* Atheneum Books for Young Readers, c2000.
- McCord, Patricia. *Pictures in the Dark.* Bloomsbury, c2004.
- Mikaelsen, Ben. *Petey.* Hyperion Books for Children, c1998.
- Rottman, S. L. *Hero.* Peachtree, c1997.
- Shaw, Susan. *The Boy from the Basement.* Dutton Children's Books, c2004.
- Vance, Susanna. *Sights.* Delacorte Press, 2001.
- Vries, Anke de. *Bruises.* Front Street/Lumniscaat , 1995.
- Woodson, Jacqueline. *I Hadn't Meant to Tell You This.* Bantam Doubleday Dell Books for Young Readers, 1995, c1994.

From Nancy J. Keane, *The Big Book of Teen Reading Lists: 100 Great, Ready-to-Use Book Lists for Educators, Librarians, Parents, and Children.* Westport, CT: Libraries Unlimited, 2006. Copyright © 2006 by Libraries Unlimited.

## If you liked *Cirque du Freak* by Darren Shan, try (for older teens):

- Anderson, M. T. *Thirsty*. Candlewick Press, 2005, c1997.
- Atwater-Rhodes, Amelia. *Midnight Predator*. Delacorte Press, c2002.
- Hahn, Mary Downing. *Look for Me by Moonlight*. Clarion Books, c1995.
- Hoffman, Nina Kiriki. *A Stir of Bones*. Viking Press, 2003.
- Huntington, Geoffrey. *Demon Witch*. ReganBooks, c2003.
- Huntington, Geoffrey. *Sorcerers of the Nightwing*. ReganBooks, c2002.
- Klause, Annette Curtis. *Blood and Chocolate*. Bantam Doubleday Dell Books for Young Readers, 1999, c1997.
- Meyer, Stephenie. *Twilight*. Little, Brown, 2005.
- Pierce, Meredith Ann. *The Darkangel*. Magic Carpet Books/Harcourt Brace, 1998.
- Rees, Douglas. *Vampire High*. Delacorte Press, c2003.
- Rice, Anne. *Interview with the Vampire*. Knopf, 1976.
- Soto, Gary. *The Afterlife*. Harcourt, c2003.
- Stine, R. L. *Dangerous Girls: A Novel*. HarperCollins, c2003.
- Vande Velde, Vivian. *Companions of the Night*. Harcourt Brace, c1995.
- Zindel, Paul. *Reef of Death*. Hyperion Paperbacks for Children, 1999.

## If you liked *Cirque du Freak* by Darren Shan, try (for older teens):

- Anderson, M. T. *Thirsty*. Candlewick Press, 2005, c1997.
- Atwater-Rhodes, Amelia. *Midnight Predator*. Delacorte Press, c2002.
- Hahn, Mary Downing. *Look for Me by Moonlight*. Clarion Books, c1995.
- Hoffman, Nina Kiriki. *A Stir of Bones*. Viking Press, 2003.
- Huntington, Geoffrey. *Demon Witch*. ReganBooks, c2003.
- Huntington, Geoffrey. *Sorcerers of the Nightwing*. ReganBooks, c2002.
- Klause, Annette Curtis. *Blood and Chocolate*. Bantam Doubleday Dell Books for Young Readers, 1999, c1997.
- Meyer, Stephenie. *Twilight*. Little, Brown, 2005.
- Pierce, Meredith Ann. *The Darkangel*. Magic Carpet Books/Harcourt Brace, 1998.
- Rees, Douglas. *Vampire High*. Delacorte Press, c2003.
- Rice, Anne. *Interview with the Vampire*. Knopf, 1976.
- Soto, Gary. *The Afterlife*. Harcourt, c2003.
- Stine, R. L. *Dangerous Girls: A Novel*. HarperCollins, c2003.
- Vande Velde, Vivian. *Companions of the Night*. Harcourt Brace, c1995.
- Zindel, Paul. *Reef of Death*. Hyperion Paperbacks for Children, 1999.

From Nancy J. Keane, *The Big Book of Teen Reading Lists: 100 Great, Ready-to-Use Book Lists for Educators, Librarians, Parents, and Children.* Westport, CT: Libraries Unlimited, 2006. Copyright © 2006 by Libraries Unlimited.

# If you liked *Cirque du Freak* by Darren Shan, try (for ages 12 and up):

- Hautman, Pete. *Sweetblood*. Simon & Schuster Books for Young Readers, c2003.

- Klause, Annette Curtis. *The Silver Kiss*. Dell, 1992, c1990.

- Plum-Ucci, Carol. *The She*. Harcourt, c2003.

- Rees, Douglas. *Vampire High*. Delacorte Press, c2003.

- Schreiber, Ellen. *Vampire Kisses*. HarperCollins, c2003.

- Shusterman, Neal. *Full Tilt: A Novel*. Simon & Schuster Books for Young Readers, c2003.

- Sleator, William. *The Boy Who Couldn't Die*. Amulet, 2004.

- Vande Velde, Vivian. *Companions of the Night*. Harcourt Brace, c1995.

# If you liked *Cirque du Freak* by Darren Shan, try (for ages 12 and up):

- Hautman, Pete. *Sweetblood*. Simon & Schuster Books for Young Readers, c2003.

- Klause, Annette Curtis. *The Silver Kiss*. Dell, 1992, c1990.

- Plum-Ucci, Carol. *The She*. Harcourt, c2003.

- Rees, Douglas. *Vampire High*. Delacorte Press, c2003.

- Schreiber, Ellen. *Vampire Kisses*. HarperCollins, c2003.

- Shusterman, Neal. *Full Tilt: A Novel*. Simon & Schuster Books for Young Readers, c2003.

- Sleator, William. *The Boy Who Couldn't Die*. Amulet, 2004.

- Vande Velde, Vivian. *Companions of the Night*. Harcourt Brace, c1995.

From Nancy J. Keane, *The Big Book of Teen Reading Lists: 100 Great, Ready-to-Use Book Lists for Educators, Librarians, Parents, and Children.* Westport, CT: Libraries Unlimited, 2006. Copyright © 2006 by Libraries Unlimited.

## If you liked *Gossip Girl* by Cecily von Ziegesar, try:

- Abbott, Hailey. *Summer Boys.* Scholastic, c2004.

- Brashares, Ann. *The Sisterhood of the Traveling Pants.* Delacorte, c2001.

- Burgess, Melvin. *Doing It.* Henry Holt, 2004, c2003.

- De la Cruz, Melissa. *The Au Pairs: A Novel.* Simon & Schuster Books for Young Readers, c2004.

- Dean, Zoey. *The A-list.* Little, Brown, c2003.

- Dent, Grace. *LBD: It's a Girl Thing.* Putnam's, 2003.

- Harrison, Lisi. *The Clique: A Novel.* Little, Brown, c2004.

- Krulik, Nancy E. *Ripped at the Seams.* Simon Pulse, 2004.

- Mayer, Melody. *The Nannies.* Delacorte Press, c2005.

- McCafferty, Megan. *Sloppy Firsts: A Novel.* Three Rivers Press, c2001.

- Minter, J. *The Insiders.* Bloomsbury Children's Books, 2004.

## If you liked *Gossip Girl* by Cecily von Ziegesar, try:

- Abbott, Hailey. *Summer Boys.* Scholastic, c2004.

- Brashares, Ann. *The Sisterhood of the Traveling Pants.* Delacorte, c2001.

- Burgess, Melvin. *Doing It.* Henry Holt, 2004, c2003.

- De la Cruz, Melissa. *The Au Pairs: A Novel.* Simon & Schuster Books for Young Readers, c2004.

- Dean, Zoey. *The A-list.* Little, Brown, c2003.

- Dent, Grace. *LBD: It's a Girl Thing.* Putnam's, 2003.

- Harrison, Lisi. *The Clique: A Novel.* Little, Brown, c2004.

- Krulik, Nancy E. *Ripped at the Seams.* Simon Pulse, 2004.

- Mayer, Melody. *The Nannies.* Delacorte Press, c2005.

- McCafferty, Megan. *Sloppy Firsts: A Novel.* Three Rivers Press, c2001.

- Minter, J. *The Insiders.* Bloomsbury Children's Books, 2004.

From Nancy J. Keane, *The Big Book of Teen Reading Lists: 100 Great, Ready-to-Use Book Lists for Educators, Librarians, Parents, and Children.* Westport, CT: Libraries Unlimited, 2006. Copyright © 2006 by Libraries Unlimited.

## If you liked *Series of Unfortunate Events* by Lemony Snicket, try:

- Abbott, Tony. *The Hidden Stairs and the Magic Carpet.* Scholastic, c1999.

- Aiken, Joan. *The Wolves of Willoughby Chase.* Dell Yearling, 2001, c1962.

- Ardagh, Philip. *The Fall of Fergal, Or, Not So Dingly in the Dell.* H. Holt, c2004.

- Ardagh, Philip. *A House Called Awful End.* H. Holt, c2002.

- Dahl, Roald. *Matilda.* Viking Press, c1988.

- Dahl, Roald. *The Witches.* Farrar, Straus & Giroux, c1983.

- DiTerlizzi, Tony. <u>The Spiderwick Chronicles.</u> Simon & Schuster Books for Young Readers, c2003–2004.

- Ibbotson, Eva. *Dial-a-ghost.* Puffin Books, 2003, c1996.

- Stewart, Paul. *Beyond the Deepwoods.* David Fickling Books, 2004, c1998.

## If you liked *Series of Unfortunate Events* by Lemony Snicket, try:

- Abbott, Tony. *The Hidden Stairs and the Magic Carpet.* Scholastic, c1999.

- Aiken, Joan. *The Wolves of Willoughby Chase.* Dell Yearling, 2001, c1962.

- Ardagh, Philip. *The Fall of Fergal, Or, Not So Dingly in the Dell.* H. Holt, c2004.

- Ardagh, Philip. *A House Called Awful End.* H. Holt, c2002.

- Dahl, Roald. *Matilda.* Viking Press, c1988.

- Dahl, Roald. *The Witches.* Farrar, Straus & Giroux, c1983.

- DiTerlizzi, Tony. <u>The Spiderwick Chronicles.</u> Simon & Schuster Books for Young Readers, c2003–2004.

- Ibbotson, Eva. *Dial-a-ghost.* Puffin Books, 2003, c1996.

- Stewart, Paul. *Beyond the Deepwoods.* David Fickling Books, 2004, c1998.

From Nancy J. Keane, *The Big Book of Teen Reading Lists: 100 Great, Ready-to-Use Book Lists for Educators, Librarians, Parents, and Children.* Westport, CT: Libraries Unlimited, 2006. Copyright © 2006 by Libraries Unlimited.

# If you liked *Rats Saw God* by Rob Thomas, try:

Compiled by Cathy Belben, Senior Levels Chair, Washington Library Media Association. Librarian, Burlington-Edison High School, Burlington, Washington.

- Amis, Martin. *The Rachel Papers*. Vintage, c1992.
- Anderson, Laurie Halse. *Speak*. Farrar, Straus & Giroux, c1999.
- Black, Jonah. *The Black Book (Diary of a Teenage Stud) Volume I: Girls, Girls, Girls*. (and sequels). Avon Books, c2001.
- Boylan, James. *Getting In*. Warner Books, c1998.
- Brizzi, Enrico. *Jack Frusciante Has Left the Band: A Love Story—With Rock 'N' Roll*. Grove Press, c1997.
- Canty, Kevin. *Into the Great Wide Open*. Vintage, c1997.
- Chbosky, Stephen. *The Perks of Being a Wallflower*. MTV Books/Pocket Books, c1999.
- Clark, Catherine. *Truth or Dairy*. HarperTempest, c2000.
- Coupland, Douglas. *Shampoo Planet*. Simon & Schuster, c1992.
- Crutcher, Chris. *Staying Fat for Sarah Byrnes*. Greenwillow Books, c1993.
- Dann, Patty. *Mermaids*. St. Martin's Press, 2004, c1986.
- Davis, Terry. *If Rock and Roll Were a Machine*. Delacorte Press, c1992.
- Davis, Terry. *Vision Quest*. Delacorte Press, 2005, c1979.
- Duncan, David James. *The Brothers K*. Bantam Books, 1996, c1992.
- Fuhrman, Chris. *The Dangerous Lives of Alter Boys*. University of Georgia Press, c2001.
- Gallagher, Hugh. *Teeth*. Pocket Books, c1998.
- Hedges, Peter. *An Ocean in Iowa*. Scribner Paperback Fiction, c1999.
- Hedges, Peter. *What's Eating Gilbert Grape?* Washington Square Press, 1999, c1991.
- Hornburg, Michael. *Downers Grove*. Grove Press, 2001, c1999.
- Hornby, Nick. *High Fidelity*. Riverhead Books, 2000, c1995.
- Howe, Norma. *The Adventures of Blue Avenger*. H. Holt, 1999.
- Irving, John. *A Prayer for Owen Meany*. Ballantine Books, 1990, c1989.
- Irving, John. *The World According to Garp*. Ballantine Books, 1998, c1976.
- Mccants, William. *Anything Can Happen in High School*. Browndeer Press, Harcourt Brace, c1993.
- Payne, C.D. *Youth in Revolt*. Doubleday, c1996.
- Perrotta, Tom. *Bad Haircut*. Berkley Books, 1997, c1994.
- Perrotta, Tom. *Election*. Berkley Books, c1998.
- Powell, Randy. *Tribute to Another Dead Rock Star*. Farrar, Straus & Giroux, c1999.
- Powell, Randy. *The Whistling Toilets*. Farrar, Straus & Giroux, 2001, c1996.
- Rennison, Louise. *Angus, Thongs, and Full-Frontal Snogging*. HarperCollins, c2000.
- Salzman, Mark. *Lost in Place*. Vintage, c2005.
- Sedaris, David. *Me Talk Pretty One Day*. Little, Brown, c2000.
- Sedaris, David. *Naked*. Little, Brown, 1998, c1997.
- Sheldon, Dyan. *Confessions of a Teenage Drama Queen*. Candlewick Press, c1999.
- Townsend, Sue. *The Adrian Mole Diaries*. Avon Books, c1997.
- Vizzini, Ned. *Teen Angst? Naaah*. Free Spirit, c2000.
- Weisberg, Joe. *10th Grade*. Random House, 2003, c2002.
- Wittlinger, Ellen. *Hard Love*. Aladdin Paperbacks, 2001, c1999.
- Wittlinger, Ellen. *What's in a Name?* Simon & Schuster Books for Young Readers, c2000.

From Nancy J. Keane, *The Big Book of Teen Reading Lists: 100 Great, Ready-to-Use Book Lists for Educators, Librarians, Parents, and Children*. Westport, CT: Libraries Unlimited, 2006. Copyright © 2006 by Libraries Unlimited.

From Nancy J. Keane, *The Big Book of Teen Reading Lists: 100 Great, Ready-to-Use Book Lists for Educators, Librarians, Parents, and Children*. Westport, CT: Libraries Unlimited, 2006. Copyright © 2006 by Libraries Unlimited.

## If you liked *The Princess Diaries* by Meg Cabot, try:

- Brian, Kate. *The Princess & the Pauper.* Simon & Schuster Books for Young Readers, c2003.

- Dessen, Sarah. *Keeping the Moon.* Viking Press, 1999.

- Hopkins, Cathy. *Mates, Dates, and Inflatable Bras.* Simon Pulse, 2003, c2001. (and sequels)

- Mackler, Carolyn. *The Earth, My Butt, and Other Big Round Things.* Candlewick Press, 2003.

- Maxwell, Katie. *The Year My Life Went Down the Loo.* Dorchester, c2003.

- Moriarty, Jaclyn. *Feeling Sorry for Celia.* St. Martin's Griffin, c2000.

- O'Connell, Tyne. *Pulling Princes.* Bloomsbury, 2004.Sheldon, Dyan. *Confessions of a Teenage Drama Queen.* Candlewick Press, 2004, c1999.

- Whytock, Cherry. *My Cup Runneth Over: The Life of Angelica Cookson Potts.* Simon & Schuster Books for Young Readers, 2003.

- Wilson, Jacqueline. *Girls in Love.* Dell Laurel-Leaf, 2002, c1997.

- Wyatt, Melissa. *Raising the Griffin.* Wendy Lamb Books, c2004.

## If you liked *The Princess Diaries* by Meg Cabot, try:

- Brian, Kate. *The Princess & the Pauper.* Simon & Schuster Books for Young Readers, c2003.

- Dessen, Sarah. *Keeping the Moon.* Viking Press, 1999.

- Hopkins, Cathy. *Mates, Dates, and Inflatable Bras.* Simon Pulse, 2003, c2001. (and sequels)

- Mackler, Carolyn. *The Earth, My Butt, and Other Big Round Things.* Candlewick Press, 2003.

- Maxwell, Katie. *The Year My Life Went Down the Loo.* Dorchester, c2003.

- Moriarty, Jaclyn. *Feeling Sorry for Celia.* St. Martin's Griffin, c2000.

- O'Connell, Tyne. *Pulling Princes.* Bloomsbury, 2004.Sheldon, Dyan. *Confessions of a Teenage Drama Queen.* Candlewick Press, 2004, c1999.

- Whytock, Cherry. *My Cup Runneth Over: The Life of Angelica Cookson Potts.* Simon & Schuster Books for Young Readers, 2003.

- Wilson, Jacqueline. *Girls in Love.* Dell Laurel-Leaf, 2002, c1997.

- Wyatt, Melissa. *Raising the Griffin.* Wendy Lamb Books, c2004.

From Nancy J. Keane, *The Big Book of Teen Reading Lists: 100 Great, Ready-to-Use Book Lists for Educators, Librarians, Parents, and Children.* Westport, CT: Libraries Unlimited, 2006. Copyright © 2006 by Libraries Unlimited.

## If you liked
## *Romeo and Juliet*, try:

- Atwater-Rhodes, Amelia. *Hawksong.* Delacorte Press, c2003.

- Avi. *Romeo and Juliet—Together (And Alive!) at Last.* Avon Books, 1988, c1987.

- Dai, Fan. *Butterfly Lovers: a Tale of the Chinese Romeo and Juliet.* Homa & Sekey Books, c2000.

- Draper, Sharon M. *Romiette and Julio.* Atheneum Books for Young Readers, c1999.

- Jones, Diana Wynne. *The Magicians of Caprona.* Greenwillow Books, 2001, c1980.

- Korman, Gordon. *Son of the Mob.* Hyperion, c2002.

- Pearson, Mary *Scribbler of Dreams.* Harcourt, c2001.

- Randle, Kristen D. *Breaking Rank.* HarperTempest, 2002, c1999.

- Ray, Jeanne. *Julie and Romeo: A Novel.* Harmony Books, c2000.

- Sutherland, Tui. *This Must Be Love.* HarperCollins, c2004.

- Woodson, Jacqueline. *If You Come Softly.* Putnam, 1998.

## If you liked
## *Romeo and Juliet*, try:

- Atwater-Rhodes, Amelia. *Hawksong.* Delacorte Press, c2003.

- Avi. *Romeo and Juliet—Together (And Alive!) at Last.* Avon Books, 1988, c1987.

- Dai, Fan. *Butterfly Lovers: a Tale of the Chinese Romeo and Juliet.* Homa & Sekey Books, c2000.

- Draper, Sharon M. *Romiette and Julio.* Atheneum Books for Young Readers, c1999.

- Jones, Diana Wynne. *The Magicians of Caprona.* Greenwillow Books, 2001, c1980.

- Korman, Gordon. *Son of the Mob.* Hyperion, c2002.

- Pearson, Mary *Scribbler of Dreams.* Harcourt, c2001.

- Randle, Kristen D. *Breaking Rank.* HarperTempest, 2002, c1999.

- Ray, Jeanne. *Julie and Romeo: A Novel.* Harmony Books, c2000.

- Sutherland, Tui. *This Must Be Love.* HarperCollins, c2004.

- Woodson, Jacqueline. *If You Come Softly.* Putnam, 1998.

From Nancy J. Keane, *The Big Book of Teen Reading Lists: 100 Great, Ready-to-Use Book Lists for Educators, Librarians, Parents, and Children.* Westport, CT: Libraries Unlimited, 2006. Copyright © 2006 by Libraries Unlimited.

## If you liked *Sisterhood of the Traveling Pants* by Ann Brashares, try:

- Cabot, Meg. *The Princess Diaries.* HarperCollins, 2000 (and sequels)

- Chbosky, Stephen. *The Perks of Being a Wallflower.* MTV Books/Pocket Books, c1999.

- Clark, Catherine. *Truth or Dairy.* Harper Tempest, 2000.

- Hopkins, Cathy. *Mates, Dates, and Inflatable Bras.* Simon Pulse, 2003.

- Oates, Joyce Carol.*Big Mouth & Ugly Girl.* HarperTempest, 2002.

- O'Connell, Tyne. *Pulling Princes.* Bloomsbury Pub. (distributed by Holtzbrinck), 2004 (and sequels).

- Rennison, Louise *Angus, Thongs and Full-Frontal Snogging: Confessions of Georgia Nicolson.* HarperCollins, 2000 (and sequels).

- Sheldon, Dyan. *Confessions of a Teenage Drama Queen.* Candlewick, 2002.

- Whytock, Cherry. *My Cup Runneth Over: The Life of Angelica Cookson Potts.* Simon & Schuster Books for Young Readers, 2003 (and sequels).

- Wilson, Jacqueline. *Girls in Love.* Dell Laurel-Leaf, 2002, c1997 (and sequels).

## If you liked *Sisterhood of the Traveling Pants* by Ann Brashares, try:

- Cabot, Meg. *The Princess Diaries.* HarperCollins, 2000 (and sequels)

- Chbosky, Stephen. *The Perks of Being a Wallflower.* MTV Books/Pocket Books, c1999.

- Clark, Catherine. *Truth or Dairy.* Harper Tempest, 2000.

- Hopkins, Cathy. *Mates, Dates, and Inflatable Bras.* Simon Pulse, 2003.

- Oates, Joyce Carol.*Big Mouth & Ugly Girl.* HarperTempest, 2002.

- O'Connell, Tyne. *Pulling Princes.* Bloomsbury Pub. (distributed by Holtzbrinck), 2004 (and sequels).

- Rennison, Louise *Angus, Thongs and Full-Frontal Snogging: Confessions of Georgia Nicolson.* HarperCollins, 2000 (and sequels).

- Sheldon, Dyan. *Confessions of a Teenage Drama Queen.* Candlewick, 2002.

- Whytock, Cherry. *My Cup Runneth Over: The Life of Angelica Cookson Potts.* Simon & Schuster Books for Young Readers, 2003 (and sequels).

- Wilson, Jacqueline. *Girls in Love.* Dell Laurel-Leaf, 2002, c1997 (and sequels).

From Nancy J. Keane, *The Big Book of Teen Reading Lists: 100 Great, Ready-to-Use Book Lists for Educators, Librarians, Parents, and Children.* Westport, CT: Libraries Unlimited, 2006. Copyright © 2006 by Libraries Unlimited.

## If you liked *Weetzie Bat* by Francesca Lia Block, try:

- Allende, Isabel. *The Stories of Eva Luna.* Scribner Classics, 1999, c1989.

- Barker, Clive. *Abarat.* Joanna Cotler Books, c2002.

- Black, Holly. *Tithe: A Modern Faerie Tale.* Simon & Schuster, c2002.

- Cohn, Rachel. *Gingerbread.* Simon & Schuster Books for Young Readers, c2002.

- Corrigan, Eireann. *You Remind Me of You: A Poetry Memoir.* Push/Scholastic, c2002.

- Donoghue, Emma. *Kissing the Witch: Old Tales in New Skins.* HarperCollins, 1999, c1997.

- Esquivel, Laura. *Like Water for Chocolate: A Novel in Monthly Installments, with Recipes, Romances, and Home Remedies.* Doubleday, c1992.

- Eugenides, Jeffrey. *The Virgin Suicides.* Farrar, Straus & Giroux, 1993.

- Gaiman, Neil. *Neverwhere.* Avon Books, c1997.

- García Márquez, Gabriel. *Chronicle of a Death Foretold.* Knopf, 1995.

- High, Linda Oatman. *Sister Slam and the Poetic Motormouth Roadtrip.* Bloomsbury (distributed to the trade by Holtzbrinck), c2004.

- Hoffman, Alice. *Aquamarine.* Scholastic Press, 2001.

- Hoffman, Alice. *Green Angel.* Scholastic Press, 2003.

- Hoffman, Alice. *The Probable Future.* Doubleday, c2003.

- Johnson, Angela. *Looking for Red.* Simon & Schuster Books for Young Readers, c2002.

- Koja, Kathe. *The Blue Mirror.* Farrar, Straus & Giroux, 2004.

- McNamee, Graham. *Hate You.* Dell, 2000, c1999.

- Moon, Russell. *Witch Boy.* HarperTempest, 2002.

- Rosenberg, Liz. *17: A Novel in Prose Poems.* Cricket Books, 2002.

- Trope, Zoe. *Please Don't Kill the Freshman: A Memoir.* HarperTempest, c2003.Wittlinger, Ellen. *Hard Love.* Simon & Schuster Books for Young Readers, c1999.

- Wolff, Virginia Euwer. *Make Lemonade.* H. Holt, c1993.

# Index

# About the Author

**NANCY J. KEANE** is Library Media Specialist, Rundlett Middle School, Concord, New Hampshire. She is author of *Booktalking across the Curriculum: The Middle Years* (Libraries Unlimited, 2002) and several other titles; and she is recipient of the 2004 Association for Library Service to Children (ALSC)/Sagebrush Education Resources Literature Program Award. For more than a decade, she has hosted a popular booktalk Web site (www.nancykeane.com). Nancy is also author of *The Big Book of Children's Reading Lists* (Libraries Unlimited, 2006).